COLLINS FIELD GUIDE

SPIDERS

OF BRITAIN & NORTHERN EUROPE

COLLINS FIELD GUIDE

SPIDERS

OF BRITAIN AND NORTHERN EUROPE

MICHAEL J. ROBERTS

Illustrated by the author

Collins

HarperCollins Publishers Ltd
1 London Bridge Street
London SE1 9GF

WilliamCollinsBooks.com

Collins is a registered trademark of
HarperCollins Publishers

First published 1996

15 14

11

A catalogue record for this book is available from the British Library.

ISBN: 978 0 00 219981 0

Edited and designed by D & N Publishing, Berkshire
Printed and bound by Printing Express, Hong Kong

Contents

Preface

In common with most forms of life, spiders are thoroughly fascinating creatures. Although there has always been a small group of people actively studying them, and an increasing number are becoming interested, they have not, so far, attracted a large popular audience. The number of species in Britain and northern Europe is neither overwhelmingly large, nor too small to invite study and there is great diversity in appearance and biology even within this region. The secondary sex organs are easily visible externally, so that no dissection is required, and identification is rather less difficult than with many other groups. Many organizations directly concerned with nature conservation have tended to focus on more popular groups. It seems strange that spiders and other invertebrates are largely ignored since these are often better indicators of habitat diversity and pollution.

It is surely no coincidence that the most popular subjects with amateur naturalists – birds, flowers, butterflies – have all been profusely illustrated and there are many field guides available. This guide, for the first time, allows colour illustrations, and illustrations of epigynes and male palpal organs, to be taken out and used in the field. When used in conjunction with a small field microscope and a 'spi-pot' (see pp. 33–4), spiders become as accessible in the field as any other group of plants or animals. Naturally, some species will require more detailed examination than others. Some people will be content to flick through the colour plates, identifying distinctive species and getting others to the right genus. For those who wish to take identification further, the facility is there and may be used in the field or at home.

In previous work, I have illustrated epigynes and male palps to the same scale. For the smaller format of this work they are all illustrated to the same size; scale lines are excluded as they would constitute too much clutter.

For the illustration of the colour plates, epigynes and male palps, I have received enormous help with specimens from a number of people. Some have provided a single specimen, unobtainable elsewhere; others have sent many. Very many thanks to: S.I. Baldwin, E. Bauchhenss, E.L. Bee, T. Blick, R. Bosmans, J. Crocker, M.B. Davidson, C. Felton, M. Grasshoff, C. Hambler, P. Harvey, H. Hiebsch, J. Heurtault, R.D. Jones, M. Linfield, P. Merrett, F.M. Murphy, J. Murphy, R. Platen, C. Rollard, R. Ruffell, H.-B. Schikora, C.J. Smith, R. Snazell, J.A. Stewart, K. Thaler, C.J. Topping, A. Wolf, and J. Wunderlich. Thanks also to Hampshire Micro for the loan of a field microscope for evaluation in field trials. I am extremely grateful to David Price-Goodfellow and staff at D & N Publishing, and to Myles Archibald, Harper Collins, for the great care they have taken in the production of this book.

My wife, Deborah, has been of tremendous help and support, in addition to putting up with being a 'spider widow' for the last couple of years. When asked what daddy is doing, Daniel no longer says 'piedahs' but has moved on to 'tap, tap, tap', which is a relief for us all.

Michael J. Roberts
Burns, Cornhill, Banff 1995

How to Use this Book

The **text** provides a general introduction to spiders, their structure and biology, and this is followed, on pp. 24–8, by details of how to find and collect them for identification. Practical information on techniques for identifying spiders is given on pp. 30–4 and includes details of a very simple device which allows spiders to be restrained, measured and examined easily in the field.

There are very few common names for spiders, but any fears over this should be allayed by the brief explanation of the scientific names, and their pronunciation, on pp. 35–7. This is followed by the Key to the Families, on pp. 38–56, which begins with details of how to determine the sex and maturity of specimens. Descriptions and illustrations of the distinctive characters of each family may be usefully referred back to when the possible identity of a specimen has been reached simply by the colour plates.

Details of egg sacs are given on pp. 57–60 and webs on pp. 61–75, the latter often being of help in identifying the family, and sometimes the genus.

Each family is then described, beginning, where necessary, with an illustrated key to the separate genera. The species within each genus are then described and illustrations of the female epigyne and male palpal organs allow final identification.

Some spiders can be identified simply from the **colour plates**, but take careful note of the size range given on the **caption pages** opposite since the spiders are all illustrated at roughly the same size irrespective of their actual size (explained on the page preceding the colour plates). Select the illustration most like the one you want to identify and turn to the page indicated, where you may find several similar species described. It may also be useful to refer back to the illustrated details of each family and genus in order to learn more about the structure, as well as to check the identity in case of doubt.

The symbol △ for a family, genus or species indicates that it does not normally occur in the British Isles.

The symbol ⚇ in the keys is followed by guidance mainly for those just using a ×10 lens. However, the information may also be of use if using a ×20 lens or a field microscope.

Throughout this book, jargon is kept to a minimum. All the terms used are explained in the introductory chapters, or as they appear, but a glossary is provided on pp. 371–3.

Finally, the list of Associations, Societies and suppliers, together with the selected Bibliography, should all help with further studies.

The area covered by this guide includes northern France, Belgium, Holland, Germany, Denmark, Norway, Sweden and Finland. To the south and east of this area, the number of species increases.

Over 450 species are fully described and illustrated here, the biggest problem being what to include in the space available. I felt it reasonable, in a Field Guide, to exclude the small, black 'money spiders' from detailed treatment; experience shows that most people ignore these to begin with anyway. This allows far more comprehensive coverage of the other species and gives the reader a clearer idea of what is missing. A few more endemic species from the far north are excluded as are some which occur only rarely in the south. One or two species are excluded because they were unobtainable from the numerous individuals and museums approached – a reasonable indication of rarity. However, many of the species described also occur far to the south and east of the region covered by this guide.

Introduction

Spiders are regarded by different people in widely differing ways and may invoke fear, hatred, admiration or wonderment; sometimes they are treated with complete indifference. The diversity and strength of some of these emotions might seem even more surprising when one considers that they are based on almost total ignorance. It is, of course, the ignorance itself which allows and fosters this range of views. This book should help, whether you wish to study spiders in depth, or just get a broad idea of the range and activities of our native species. I often feel that the Introduction might be better placed at the end of a book; by that time the reader is in more of a position to understand it. However, it is necessary to convey the basic make-up of these animals and to place them in context with other creatures. I hope the reader will find the following text a useful short cut to the understanding of spiders and not just an assemblage of uninspiring facts.

Spiders are predatory, carnivorous arthropods. The prey of spiders very largely consists of insects, but other arthropods (including other spiders) are often consumed. Some species in the region will occasionally capture tadpoles and small fish; some large, tropical species will also tackle small frogs and birds. The vast group of arthropods contains over three-quarters of all known species of animals. In formal classification they used to be considered as a separate phylum, the Arthropoda, but they are now generally regarded as an informal group of a larger Sub-Kingdom, the Metazoa.

A literal translation of the word arthropod is 'jointed foot', but it is taken to mean 'jointed leg'. All of these animals have an external skeleton (exoskeleton) and the implications of this are an important key to understanding the whole group. You might reasonably point out that we all have jointed legs; however, our joints (and bones) are internal whereas those of arthropods are external and obvious. The exoskeleton of arthropods is made of chitin and is hardened like a suit of armour.

Spiders have two parts to the body. Whilst the abdomen (the hind part) is soft, the cephalothorax (the front part) has an upper shell of armour called the carapace and, underneath, a shell called the sternum. The two halves of this 'sandwich' are held together by membranes and muscles, and the fluid, organs and other muscles are contained within. Eight hollow legs come out from the sides of the cephalothorax. Although large parts of the exoskeleton are rigid, the various joints and articular membranes ensure that there is no sacrifice of mobility. We ourselves have muscles working on both sides of each joint which are used to bring about both flexion and extension of various parts of the limbs. The rigid, tubular legs of spiders contain fluid and also muscles, which bring about flexion at all joints but extension at only some. In fact two of the largest joints have no extensor muscles at all; extension here is brought about by an increase in hydraulic pressure. The hydraulic pressure in the legs is increased by contraction of the muscles joining the carapace and sternum, which forces the fluid contents of this 'sandwich' out into the legs. Compressing the carapace of a freshly killed spider will cause the legs to extend; but not if their tips are cut off. A more practical aspect of this mechanism occurs when spiders are collected in pitfall traps and the soft internal tissues swell. This not only causes the legs to extend but may also completely expand the male palpal organs.

The exoskeleton not only provides support for the animal and its muscles and contents, but also acts as a protection against water loss. Furthermore, parts of it may be modified to form jaws and teeth, complex structures for mating, ridges and files for stridulation, and lenses for eyes. One very significant implication of the exoskeleton relates to growth; the arthropod is obliged, periodically, to undergo a process of moulting (ecdysis) when it becomes too large for its suit of armour.

In current classification, the arthropods are regarded as comprising three groups: the Unirama (insects, centipedes, millipedes), the Crustacea (crabs, shrimps, waterfleas, woodlice) and the Chelicerata (spiders and their allies).

The vast majority of arthropod species are insects (class Insecta); in fact the insects, with well over a million species, constitute over half of all known animals. Their three pairs of legs, three body divisions and (usually) wings clearly separates them from other arthropods, including spiders. However, you may sometimes need to look closely since some insects mimic spiders and some spiders mimic insects. For example, the nymphal stages of the Dark Bush Cricket (*Pholidoptera griseoaptera*) mimic the wolf spider *Pardosa lugubris* and many spiders, such as *Myrmarachne formicaria,* mimic ants in both appearance and movement. The other members of the Unirama, centipedes (Chilopoda) and millipedes (Diplopoda), have many pairs of legs and are so well known that confusion with spiders is impossible.

The Crustacea mainly comprises aquatic animals but also includes woodlice (Isopoda) which, although land-dwelling, still prefer damp habitats.

The Chelicerata includes a small marine group, the king- or horseshoe-crabs (Merostomata) and the large class Arachnida to which spiders and their near relatives belong.

Spiders and their Near Relatives

The class Arachnida comprises animals with four pairs of legs, although some mites may have fewer. They have no wings and no antennae, although the palps may sometimes appear like antennae. There are only two body regions and these are fused together in some groups. Of the eleven orders that make up the Arachnida, only five occur in the region and these are illustrated opposite. Scorpions are easily recognizable, well-known animals which typically inhabit hot, dry parts of the world. One Mediterranean species, *Euscorpius flavicaudis* (DeGeer) is sometimes found further north and colonies have existed in Sheerness, Kent, for over a century. Pseudoscorpions are also easily recognizable but, being only about 2–4mm long, are easily overlooked; they inhabit moss, leaf-litter and soil and some species live in association with man. The only spider to have the superficial appearance of a large pseudoscorpion is *Marpissa nivoyi* (Plate 12). Both scorpions and pseudoscorpions are carnivorous, vigorously hunting and catching their prey with their pincer-like pedipalps; scorpions additionally have a sting which may be used with larger prey.

The harvestmen (order Opiliones) and the mites and ticks (order Acari) are the groups most likely to be confused with spiders. This confusion is perhaps mainly the result of certain common names affecting public perception – harvestmen are sometimes called 'harvest spiders' or 'shepherd spiders'; some mites are commonly called 'spider mites'.

In harvestmen, the two parts of the body are broadly joined together so that it appears to be in just one piece. Spiders have the body clearly divided into two pieces which are joined by a narrow stalk, the pedicel. Harvestmen have only two eyes which are usually placed centrally on a tubercle and directed sideways. This ocular tubercle, or ocularium, is often furnished with two rows of teeth or spines. Spiders usually have six or eight eyes (very rarely two) which are arranged in a wide variety of ways. The males of some money spiders may have one or two pairs of these

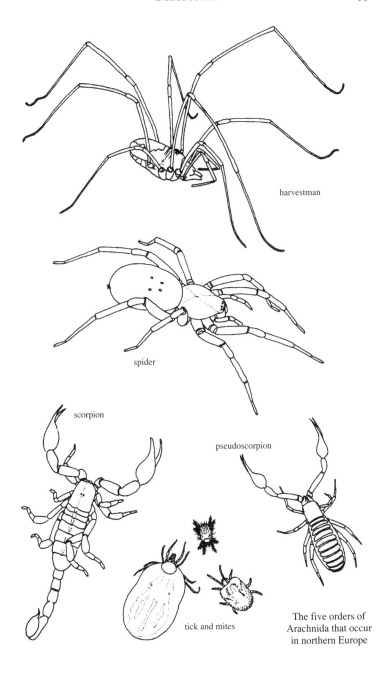

harvestman

spider

scorpion

pseudoscorpion

tick and mites

The five orders of
Arachnida that occur
in northern Europe

eyes set on lobes or turrets (p. 348). Most harvestmen feed on a wide variety of other arthropods and invertebrates including other harvestmen, other arachnids, insects, woodlice, small snails and earthworms; dead and faecal material may also be eaten.

Mites and ticks also have the two parts of the body fused into one piece. Although adults of most species have four pairs of legs, some have fewer, and the larval stages of many species have only three pairs. They far outstrip all other arachnids in terms of numbers and many live in highly specialized habitats (e.g. bee tracheae). Whilst many damage crops and produce, or are parasites and spread disease to both plants and animals, others are of great economic importance in breaking down leaf-litter to produce humus.

Finally, spiders are unique in having spinners, situated near the hind end of the abdomen, which produce silk. Harvestmen have no silk glands or spinners; some mites produce copious amounts of silk, but this is produced by glands in the palp and there are no spinners.

The Biology of Spiders

The little we already know of spider biology would fill many books; what follows here is the briefest of accounts and much more may be gained from reading some of the books given in the Bibliography (p. 375). There is tremendous scope for research into spider biology and some of this will require specialist equipment and statistical analysis only available in large institutions. However, the amateur may discover a great deal by simple, patient observation.

The Structure of Spiders

Some basic implications of the arthropod exoskeleton are given in the Introduction (pp. 9–10). The body of a spider is divided into two parts which are joined by a narrow stalk called the pedicel. The front part, called the cephalothorax (or prosoma), is enclosed within a relatively hard and unyielding chitinous shell. The hind part, called the abdomen (or opisthosoma) is soft and capable of expansion, as happens with feeding or egg development. The length of spiders is measured from the front of the cephalothorax to the hind end of the abdomen.

The cephalothorax has its dorsal (upper) surface protected by the carapace and its ventral (under) surface protected by the sternum. Issuing from between these two parts of the shell are the legs, palps, chelicerae and mouthparts. The carapace can usually be seen to comprise two areas – head and thorax – delineated by markings or a shallow groove, the cephalo-thoracic junction. The head (cephalic) region of the carapace carries the eyes – usually eight, but sometimes six. The size and arrangement of the eyes varies greatly and is of considerable value in identification, as will be seen from the various keys in this book. The eyes of spiders are described as 'simple'. This is not a pejorative term but is used to contrast with the 'compound' eyes of insects, which are made up of large numbers of facets or ommatidia, and in this sense, our own eyes are 'simple'. The eyes of salticid (jumping) spiders have a greater range of movement than our own, elaborate focusing, binocular vision and are probably sensitive to colour and polarized light, which adds up to the greatest visual acuity of all arthropods. For descriptive purposes, the eyes are always considered as forming two rows – an anterior row (with anterior median and anterior

External features of a female spider

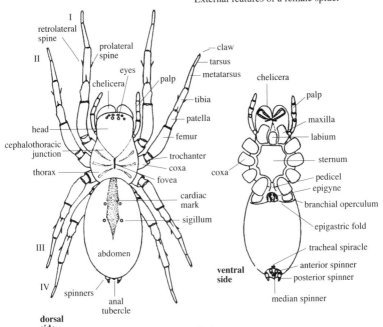

dorsal side

ventral side

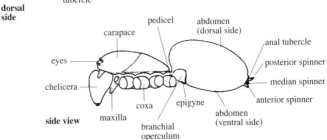

side view

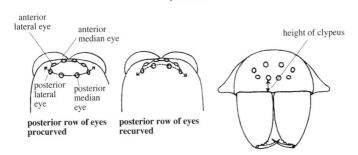

posterior row of eyes procurved

posterior row of eyes recurved

height of clypeus

lateral eyes) and a posterior row (with posterior median and posterior lateral eyes). This nomenclature is maintained even when the posterior lateral eyes are separated so far back as to form a third row. When there are only six eyes (Dysderidae, Segestriidae, Oonopidae) it is the anterior median eyes which are missing. Each row of eyes may be in a straight transverse row, or they may be curved to varying degrees and this is made use of in the identification keys. If a row of eyes, *when viewed from above*, is curved so that the lateral eyes are further forward than the median eyes then that row is said to be procurved (curved forwards). If the lateral eyes are further back than the medians, then the row is said to be recurved (curved backwards; see illustration on p. 13). These terms obviously do not apply when the eyes are viewed from in front (although you may see them used); in this situation the terms should be curved dorsally (upwards) or curved ventrally (downwards). When viewed from in front, the part of the carapace between the anterior eyes and the front edge of the carapace is called the clypeus. The height of the clypeus is the distance between the anterior eyes and the front edge of the carapace and is used in the identification keys (see illustration on p. 13). Frequently the eyes may be surrounded by a broad ring of black pigment; estimates or measurements of the size of an eye relate to the lens margin, not to the dimensions of the surrounding pigment. Some spiders have eyes set on small tubercles; the males of many small, black linyphiid species (money spiders) have the head region raised to form lobes or turrets which also carry some of the eyes.

The thoracic part of the carapace often has a short, dark midline mark called the fovea. At this point, the exoskeleton projects inwards and provides attachment for the dorsal muscles of the powerful sucking stomach. In some theridiid species, the thoracic region has a series of fine ridges near the rear margin which are opposed by small teeth or a sclerotized ridge under the front of the abdomen. These teeth and ridges are used in stridulation.

The sternum, on the underside of the cephalothorax, is a heart-shaped or oval plate indented opposite the coxa of each leg. Usually it is a more or less flat or slightly convex plate which may be marked with paired, impressed spots (sigilla) in a few species. Males of *Theridion bimaculatum* have a small tubercle in the centre of the sternum. In a number of species, the sternum has markings which may be of limited use in identification.

Attached to the front margin of the sternum is the labium; occasionally it is fused to the sternum, but in most species it has a membranous attachment and is capable of hinged movement. The shape of the labium is sometimes of use in identification. On each side of the labium are the maxillae, which are modifications of the base of each palp. They have rows of denticles and long hairs along their front margins which are used in crushing and filtering food. The mouth opening is just in front of the labium.

Arising from under the front margin of the carapace are the chelicerae which are used to bite the prey, to inject venom and to crush the victim. Each chelicera has a large basal portion and a fang. The fang folds into a groove on the basal portion and there may be a number of teeth on the front and rear edges of this groove, referred to as the anterior and posterior cheliceral teeth, respectively. Each fang has a small opening near its tip and fine ducts lead from there to the poison glands within the head region. The spitting spider *Scytodes* has additional glands which produce a gluey substance. This is squirted out in an oscillating stream over a distance of 10mm or so, sticking the prey down; the spider then advances and bites. Spiders of the family

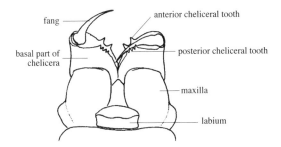

Structure of the mouthparts

Uloboridae have no poison glands and rely on secure and elaborate wrapping with silk for the restraint of prey. The chelicerae vary greatly in size and appearance in different species and are useful in identification.

The first pair of appendages, arising from the maxillae, just behind the chelicerae, are the palps (the word 'palp' is shortened from 'pedipalp' and is in general usage). Each palp consists of six segments: coxa (also modified to form the maxilla), trochanter, femur, patella, tibia and tarsus. The tarsus of the female palp often has a small claw at its tip. **In adult male spiders, the palps are greatly modified as secondary sexual organs; they are the single most important structures for identifying male spiders to species level and are dealt with later**.

Behind the palps, arising from between the sides of the carapace and the sternum, are the four pairs of walking legs; they are referred to as legs I, II, III and IV in the descriptions, being numbered from the front. Each leg consists of seven segments: coxa, trochanter, femur, patella, tibia, metatarsus and tarsus. The tip of each tarsus has claws which vary in size and number. Web-spinners have three claws – paired upper claws and a smaller median claw – and sometimes have additional hairs which are modified to form auxiliary claws. Hunting and wandering spiders have only two foot claws which are often partly obscured by tufts of hairs. These claw tufts are sometimes augmented by a brush of hairs, or scopula, along the whole length of the under surface of the tarsus and, sometimes, the metatarsus. The individual hairs in the scopula may have 'split-ends' or 'feet' which, when combined with the capillary effect of the fine film of water covering most surfaces, allow adhesion.

Segment of leg showing hairs and spines

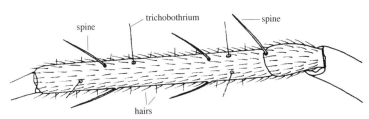

The legs and palps (and the body) are furnished with a wide variety of hairs and spines which are frequently of use in identification. Many hairs are apparently simple structures, but in some species, particularly on the body, they may be club-shaped, scale-like, serrated or feathery. They may also be white, pigmented or iridescent and may form patterns which can obscure or reinforce those on the underlying surface. Spines also vary greatly in length and thickness. In the keys and descriptions, the position of leg spines is referred to as if the limb were stuck straight out to the side. Thus, dorsal and ventral spines originate from the upper or lower surface respectively; prolateral and retrolateral from the side pointing forwards or the side pointing backwards respectively. Some of the apparently simple hairs, particularly the more erect ones towards the ends of the legs, are chemosensitive, allowing 'taste' by touching. Other long, fine hairs, called trichobothria, arise from tiny sockets and are highly sensitive to air vibration and currents. Of the other 'simple' hairs, almost all have a nerve supply and are sensitive to touch.

The abdomen shows great variation in shape, markings and size across the range of species. Even within a single species it may vary enormously in size depending on feeding and whether eggs are developing. Males usually have a smaller abdomen and any pattern tends to be more concentrated. The dorsal (upper) surface of the abdomen frequently has a narrow pointed mark in the front part of the midline. This is called the cardiac mark and a close examination of this area in the living spider will reveal a beating heart below the surface. Abdominal markings and patterns are very variable and absent in some species; when present they can assist identification to genus or even species level by naked eye alone. Parts of the dorsal pattern sometimes have the appearance of a leaf and this is then referred to as the folium. Patterns and markings may be made up of pigment cells within the abdomen, pigments on the surface of the cuticle, and variously coloured or iridescent hairs. These different types of marking may exist separately or in combination. The appearance of hairy specimens preserved in alcohol is usually very different from that of the living animal; colours and markings fade to a varying degree on preservation. There is usually a series of paired, reddish, depressed spots called sigilla (singular: sigillum) on the dorsal surface and these mark points of internal muscle attachments. A few species have a hard, often shiny, sclerotized plate called a scutum on the dorsal surface; sometimes there is another ventrally. The ventral (under) side of the abdomen is marked near the front end by a curved transverse line – the epigastric fold. In the midline, just in front of this fold, are the genital openings. This area is inconspicuous in most adult males and in immature females, but in adult females of the majority of species it is modified into a variably shaped, more or less sclerotized structure called the epigyne. **The epigyne of the adult female is the single most important structure for identifying female spiders to species level and is dealt with later**. On each side of the epigyne, just in front of the epigastric fold, are light or orange, hairless plates called the branchial opercula. These overlie the book lungs, the opening to which is a slit at the hind margin. The term book lungs refers to the arrangement of blood-filled leaves of tissue stacked with air spaces between. Most species have only one pair of book lungs; *Atypus* has two pairs. In addition to book lungs most spiders also have a second respiratory system in the form of paired tracheae; *Atypus* has none. The external opening to the tracheae – the tracheal spiracle – is usually just in front of the spinners and difficult to see. In some families (Anyphaenidae, Argyronetidae, Hahniidae) it is much further forward and easily visible. In the Dysderidae and Segestriidae, the paired spiracles are just behind the lungs.

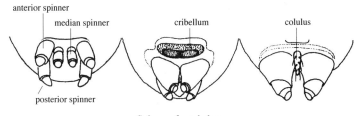

anterior spinner
median spinner
cribellum
colulus
posterior spinner

Spinners from below

At or near the hind end of the abdomen are the three pairs of spinners, described as posterior, anterior and median. Silk, produced in glands within the abdomen, is extruded through tiny spigots on the spinners and plays a varied and vital part in the life history of spiders. In addition, some groups of spiders have a sieve-like plate, the cribellum, just in front of the spinners. This structure, which may be divided into two halves, has the surface covered in a large number of tiny spigots which produce incredibly fine silk. Spiders possessing this organ are conveniently grouped together as the cribellate spiders, but their true relationships are unknown. However, all cribellate spiders also have a comb, or calamistrum, on the metatarsus of the fourth leg which is used to pull and comb the silk produced by the cribellum into flocculent bands. This cribellate silk has a bluish appearance when fresh and acts like Velcro when combined with the spines on insects. Another structure, sometimes present in front of the spinners, is a variably sized tubercle called the colulus; it is probably functionless and derived from spinners present ancestrally. The size and shape of the spinners and related structures can assist in identification to family and sometimes genus level. The anal opening is just above (dorsal) to the spinners and is sometimes situated on a small anal tubercle.

The palps of adult male spiders are modified to function as secondary sex organs; these develop within the swollen tarsus of immatures and only become fully apparent after the final moult. They do not actually produce the semen. The latter (spermatozoa in fluid) is produced by the testes, a pair of convoluted tubes within the abdomen, and is issued through the inconspicuous genital opening. The semen is deposited on a small web and then drawn into the palp, probably by capillary action aided, in many species, by gravity. The palp is then later used to transfer the semen to the female, via the epigyne, for storage prior to fertilization. A glance through the pages of this book will show the enormous variation in structure and complexity both of the palpal organs and other segments of the palp. In the simplest forms (e.g. *Oonops, Scytodes, Segestria*) the palpal tarsus is largely unmodified and the palpal organs take the form of a simple, tapering bulb. A coiled, tapering duct leads from the semen reservoir in the bulb and opens at the end of a fine tip, the embolus. However, in the majority of cases, the palpal tarsus is swollen and hollowed out to form a cymbium (L. = a small drinking vessel) which partially contains and protects the palpal organs. Sometimes the cymbium is further modified or split to form a second projection, or a free structure, the paracymbium. Other segments of the palp may be furnished with various projections, or apophyses, (referred to as tibial, patellar, or femoral apophyses – singular: apophysis). In their most complex form, the palpal organs consist of three groups of discrete, hardened structures (sclerites) separated from each other and the cymbium by three elastic balloons (haematodochae). A proximal haematodocha attaches to the cymbium and to a sclerite called the subtegulum; the latter connects via a middle haematodocha with sclerites called the tegulum and median apophysis and these are finally connected to the terminal sclerites, conductor and embolus, by a distal haematodocha. In the normal, resting state the haematodochae are collapsed and largely hidden, with the sclerites nestling together. During mating, the haematodochae are distended hydraulically, pushing out and rotating the sclerites. This can be demonstrated in the preserved palp by immersing it in hot lactic acid; it also frequently happens to specimens caught in pitfall traps.

Throughout this book the unexpanded left palp is illustrated, usually from the outside. Sometimes it is illustrated from below where this gives a better or alternative view. It is obviously important to get the palp into just the right position for comparison with the illustrations; this may be difficult with live specimens, and even with preserved material one may occasionally have to detach the palp or an obscuring leg. Inevitably, there is always slight variation between the palps of individual specimens of the same species. Many of the complex palpal structures are clearly functional, either for direct connection with the female epigyne or for providing stable interlocking of sclerites when the palp is expanded. Other structures and apophyses on the palp, including the tibia, patella and femur, often appear to have little or no part to play in the mechanics of insemination. Some of these structures are quite large, irregular and cumbersome to carry around; they must surely increase the risk of fatal complications during the final moult. It therefore seems quite conceivable that some aspects of palpal complexity relate to ensuring that only the fittest survive.

Adult females of most species have the genital opening modified to form a more or less sclerotized structure called the epigyne. Some vague structure is frequently seen in subadults, but experience will soon enable you to recognize the difference. In a few families (Atypidae, Oonopidae, Dysderidae, Segestriidae, and Scytodidae) the female genital opening is simple, there is no epigyne, and species identification is based on other structures. Epigynes vary greatly in complexity and structure; those of the Tetragnathidae are simple, others more complex and sclerotized, sometimes with a tongue-like process (or scape) in the midline. Openings in the epigyne lead, through semen ducts, to paired sacs internally (spermathecae) which store semen introduced by the male. The semen is then later passed through separate paired fertilization ducts as the eggs are laid. The spermathecae and ducts are frequently visible through the integument of the epigyne. It is interesting to note that all of these structures are part of the exoskeleton and are shed during moulting. Females of long-lived spiders, which continue periodic moulting in adulthood, require fresh insemination after each moult. Only the ovaries, which produce the eggs, are strictly speaking *inside* the body. When examining specimens, the epigyne should be viewed from directly above with the specimen on its back; if protruding to an unusual degree, it may need to be viewed from slightly in front. Epigynes do vary slightly amongst individuals of the same species.

Finally little has been mentioned of the internal anatomy of spiders; dissection is not necessary for identification as it is with some groups, such as snails. Suffice it to say that the cephalothorax contains the central nervous system, arteries, poison glands, sucking stomach, endosternite and muscles; the abdomen contains heart, arteries, lungs, tracheae, gut, excretory apparatus, spinning glands and ovaries (or testes). Reference to other works, listed in the Bibliography (p. 375), is recommended.

Senses and Communication

Spiders are active creatures, with a well-developed nervous system, and are equipped with a wide array of receptor organs which enable them to discern the world and other creatures around them. Many of the senses have been mentioned above but a brief review may be helpful. Light is sensed by the eyes; in some families this amounts to little more than the perception of the degree, direction and polarization of light, the latter helping in orientation; at the other extreme, jumping spiders (Salticidae) have the greatest visual acuity known amongst arthropods. A keen sense of touch is afforded by the many hairs covering the spider, each of which is supplied by a nerve. Tiny membrane-filled openings (slit, or lyriform, organs) near joints measure mechanical deformation stresses in the surrounding exoskeleton and small pits on the tarsi detect pheromones and humidity changes. Within the joints are receptors which relay information on the position of the joint (proprioception). Some hairs on the legs are capable of 'tasting' food or noxious substances and there may also be taste receptors in the mouth region. Ultra-fine, erect hairs arising from a socket (trichobothria) are incredibly sensitive to air currents and vibration; sometimes they occur in rows of different lengths, each length being naturally attuned to a different range of frequencies. Apart from the polarized light, we humans almost measure up to this range of sensitivities.

These various senses enable spiders to communicate with one another in a wide variety of ways. Vision plays an important part in families such as the Salticidae and Lycosidae, where courtship rituals involve display and movement of palps and legs which are variously coloured and modified in distinctive ways. Spiders with less visual acuity rely more on acoustic/vibratory mechanisms for physical communication. This may take the form of percussive tapping on the substrate (leaf surface, web, or on the surface of water) or the plucking of silk threads. Males of some species (and also some females and juveniles) have stridulatory apparatus with opposing files and scrapers located on the palps, chelicerae, abdomen and carapace. In close contact, touch can be important and considerable stroking may be employed. Spiders also use chemical communication by the production and detection of pheromones; the latter may be airborne or laid down on silk draglines.

Life History

Spiders exploit virtually all environments, including the air, and exhibit great diversity in form and behaviour. What follows is a brief and general account, and it is convenient to start and finish with the egg.

The egg, fertilized, laid and usually protected by some form of silken sac or larger cell, may start developing within a few hours, or it may lie dormant over the winter. Within the sac, the developing egg may have but a single companion, but in most species there will be dozens, scores, hundreds or even a couple of thousand in the same batch. Gradually, the embryo, nourished by the yolk, takes on a vague shape; grooves, formed by the developing legs, become visible on the surface of the egg. During this period the female may have been within the cell, guarding loosely wrapped eggs or a number of sacs. Or she may have been periodically rolling the whole egg sac around, perhaps to ensure even development. She may have carried it around with her, periodically fussing over it, or simply guarded it, at least for a time; or it may have been abandoned altogether (see Egg Sacs, p. 57). The embryo develops into a prelarva, a largely immobile, incompletely developed spiderling which must moult before it can grow any more. At this or the next stage it will also break free from the surrounding egg membranes by tearing through them with the aid of small teeth on the palps. Once moulted it enters the larval stage; a little more mobile, with more structures differentiated, but still within the egg sac and dependent on the yolk for food and water. At this stage (in some wolf spiders (Lycosidae) and possibly other families) the egg sac may be opened periodically by the female who will supply extra fluid from her mouth and then reseal the sac with silk. The larva grows and must soon moult again; there may be a separate moulting chamber within the sac. This time it emerges as a nymph – a fully mobile spiderling, increasingly dependent on prey for food, and, apart from the sexual organs, fully differentiated as a spider. Being still within the egg sac, its first available prey will be the weaker spiderlings in the brood; some cannibalism occurs, especially when there are large numbers, but many spiderlings will have enough food from their yolk supply to last for about a week. In some species, the spiderlings make their own way out of the sac by cutting or tearing a hole; others are unable to do this (wolf spiders, Lycosidae) and the female opens the sac for them.

The spiderlings may initially remain with the female. Female wolf spiders (Lycosidae) carry the young brood on their back for the first week; some species in the family Theridiidae regurgitate liquefied food and feed their young mouth-to-mouth. Others catch prey too large for the spiderlings to overpower and leave it for them to devour. Feeding by regurgitation and prey-sharing may continue until the spiderlings are quite large, and sometimes until the female dies, when she herself becomes food. This has long been known to happen in the genus *Coelotes* (Agelenidae) and I have frequently observed it in *Amaurobius* (Amaurobiidae) and once in *Segestria* (Segestriidae) and it probably occurs with a number of other species. In many species the female may have abandoned the egg sac, or died long before the spiderlings emerge. In the orb-weaving *Araneus* species (Araneidae), where there may be hundreds of eggs, the newly emerged spiderlings remain clustered together for a short time forming a furry ball on a fine, communal web. The slightest disturbance causes the ball to disappear as the spiderlings run in all directions. Growing spiderlings soon become aggressive to one another and must disperse. Although there are 20 or so species worldwide which live socially or communally, none occur in the region.

Dispersal of many spiderlings involves simply wandering off, or finding the nearest unoccupied space which will support a web. However, for moving quickly to a completely new area, spiderlings go by air. This aerial dispersal (commonly called 'ballooning') is most effectively carried out when warm days follow a cold spell and air currents are rising. A variety of techniques are used, but basically the spider moves to a relatively high point, stands on 'tiptoe' pointing the abdomen skywards, and lets out strands of silk from the spinners. There may be one, or several threads, and pieces of fluffy white silk may be incorporated, increasing air drag like a kite. These strands may fall to the ground or become entangled, but success comes when they are carried upwards. The spiderling is very light and, when the pull of air current on silk is established, it lets go with the foot claws and sails aloft. Spiderlings of many large species can do this, as can adults and spiderlings of small species. However, the most notable mass dispersals are made by the small black-bodied linyphiids which we call 'money spiders' (p. 345). Sometimes, the vast numbers involved cover the whole area in a huge blanket of silk and result in a mass of fine threads (gossamer) floating through the air. Aerial dispersal, whilst undoubtedly very effective, does have its down side. Aeronauts may be eaten by swallows, caught in the webs of other spiders, frozen several thousand metres up, drowned in the sea or lakes or may land in other unfavourable environments. They are occasionally a useful incoming food source for animals living on permanent snow fields.

Feeding continues to be a preoccupation wherever the spiderling moves to and methods of catching and dealing with prey are very diverse. Broadly speaking, some species actively hunt for prey, some lie in wait and others spin webs which are used as snares. Of these three groups, some are diurnal and others nocturnal. Some are narrow specialists in one type of prey, whilst others have a very varied diet. Growth of the spiderling allows larger prey to be captured and this may necessitate moving to a different habitat or using different strategies. The various webs used to catch prey are outlined separately (p. 61); the various other methods of prey capture would involve a long summary and are dealt with as each family is described in the main text. However, the actual process of feeding is similar in all spiders. Once the prey has been injected with venom and/or securely wrapped in silk, the spider regurgitates a digestive fluid. Spiders with large cheliceral teeth mash up the body of the victim whilst alternately pouring on digestive juices and sucking back liquefied prey; this continues for some time and the end result is a tiny mashed pellet of indigestible remains. Spiders with no cheliceral teeth make a small hole in the victim through which they alternately blow in juices and suck out prey; the end result here is a lightweight husk which is still presentable as an entomological specimen. Feeding and growth continue to be interrupted by the obligatory process of moulting.

Moulting, or ecdysis, is necessary every time the young spider becomes too large for the hard external cuticle. The soft abdomen is often quite distended before a moult and the spider stops feeding. If possible, the spider will find a safe retreat, since the moulting process renders it temporarily rather vulnerable. Most European spiders seem to moult hanging upside down on silk threads. The carapace separates at the front end and gradually falls away, and this is followed by a split along each side of the abdomen. Finally, the legs and appendages are withdrawn. It takes a little time and involves considerable hydraulic manoeuvrings by the spider. The newly moulted spider is pale and it takes a while longer for the newly exposed cuticle and spines to harden and darken. During this hardening the limbs are repeatedly flexed and extended – a 'running in' period for the joints which may otherwise stiffen. Moulting is most easily observed if spiderlings are fed in captivity. Spiders frequently die during moulting, either through failure to extract limbs or from predation at this vulnerable stage. Spiders which have previously lost limbs may regenerate them and the new, rather shorter limb appears at the next moult. After moulting, the spider will have a larger cephalothorax and legs, but a smaller abdomen. The cast-off parts of the cuticle (exuvia) are very commonly seen and most people mistake them for dead spider remains. The period between successive moults increases as the spider grows. Most European species moult five to ten times (depending on size) before they reach adulthood and then no more; after this they reproduce and die. Females of long-lived species may continue to moult from time to time; males never. Eventually the young spider will moult into an adult. The female will then have a fully differentiated epigyne. The immature or subadult male will, over the last few moults, have had a gradually increased swelling of the palpal tarsi and, prior to the final moult, these may appear like a pair of smooth boxing gloves. After this moult, the palpal organs are revealed in all their complexity. The adult male spider, which just prior to the moult appeared as large as the female, now has a small, slim abdomen and often a broader carapace and rather longer legs. The colour plates show many examples of differences in appearance between the sexes. The spiders are now able to reproduce.

Reproduction is also a complex process involving a wide range of mating tactics. (Parthenogenesis is vanishingly rare in spiders but there have been instances reported in species of *Dysdera*, none in the region. There are a few species, mostly tiny spiders, where males have never been found.) The structure and function of male palps and female epigynes has been discussed earlier. The male generally moults into maturity just before the female and may then seek out a mate by sensing her pheromones, which may be airborne or on draglines of her silk. Before he can mate, he has to transfer spermatozoa, produced within the abdomen by the testes, to the reservoir in his palpal organs, since it is these structures which are actually used for insemination. For this purpose he spins a tiny horizontal web, triangular or rectangular in shape, suspended by two or three long threads; occasionally a single thread is used, with no web. A droplet of seminal fluid is then exuded from the genital opening, on the underside of the abdomen, on to the upper surface of the web. Moving to the under surface of the web, he then moistens the palps with his mouthparts and alternately dips them into the drop of semen. He may do this *through* the web, or by curling the palps round to reach a droplet near the edge. The uptake of semen into the palp is probably achieved by a combination of capillary and gravitational forces. The female, often freshly moulted into adulthood, can then be inseminated; in this state, her cuticle, spines and chelicerae are relatively soft, and she presents a slightly less formidable challenge. It is possible that in some species the epigyne needs to be in a pliable state in order to receive the palp; in others it may need to have hardened before the mechanics of insemination are possible and stable.

In approaching the female, the correct, prescribed ritual must be observed; blundering in simply will not do and could prove fatal. All of the various senses are employed, to varying degrees, in the courtship ritual – visual display, pheromones, vibration and touch – and the strategies used vary in different species and are widely diverse in different families. The various positions adopted in the physical act of union also differ widely; these, and the courtship rituals, are mentioned as each family is discussed in the main text. Having followed the correct ritual and adopted the correct position for mating, the male's palp is then coupled with the female's epigyne. Those spiders with a simple bulb insert most of this; those with a complex palp insert only the embolus, which in some species is very long (for structure of male palps and female epigynes see p. 17–18). The elastic haematodochae are then distended hydraulically, pushing out and rotating the sclerites of the palpal organs, some of which lock it in position. The seminal fluid, containing spermatozoa, is then transferred to the female's spermathecae where it is stored until required to fertilise the eggs. In order to assure their paternity, the males of some species then seal the epigyne. This post-coital 'chastity belt' takes a variety of forms. The males of some *Theridion* species seal the epigyne with a secretion (I think produced by the mouthparts and plastered with the palps) which dries to form a smooth, hard plug. Males of *Araneus* species have a cap on the tip of the embolus which breaks off and seals the epigyne; in *Argiope* the tip of the embolus itself breaks off. *Hypsosinga* males have a flat, transparent scale along the length of the embolus which lodges in, and completely obscures, the epigyne. The epigyne of some orb-weavers has a scape, or tongue, which is pulled on by the palpal organs during mating; in some species it is pulled completely off, making further coupling impossible. In other species, the epigyne seems not to be sealed (although this may have gone unnoticed if internal), but the male continues to live harmoniously with the female and to repel new suitors. In other cases, the female may be capable of multiple matings, with previous inseminations being partly displaced. After mating, the male and female of some species remain together; others part, sometimes never to meet again. Sometimes repeated matings occur between the same individuals. It is rare for a fit male to be eaten by the female, but the female of *Argiope* wraps her diminutive mate in silk and may start eating him during mating. Most males have a very short life as adults, during which they wander around mating with different females. Eventually, as they become less vigorous and agile, they may fall prey to a female of their own species. From the species' point of view, this is much better than simply dying or being eaten by a bird. After mating, the female carries on feeding and developing the still unfertilized eggs within her ovaries.

The eggs pass from the ovaries, down the oviducts and out through the genital opening. They are fertilized in transit as they pass the fertilization ducts, which pour on the spermatozoa stored in the spermathecae. They may be laid in numerous small batches, or fewer large batches and this may take place for a considerable time after the initial mating. Since eggs are tasty morsels for a wide range of other creatures, and may also be parasitized, some protective covering of silk is required. A few species spin but a few light strands (*Pholcus, Scytodes*) but the egg sac is always carried around by the female. The rest spin a special sac for the eggs which they may abandon, guard or carry around (see Egg Sacs, p. 57). The basic method of egg sac production involves spinning a circular disc of silk and then building up a cylindrical wall. The egg mass is then laid within this cavity and a covering of silk applied; a separate moulting chamber may also be provided. The whole sac may be covered in coloured or thick woolly silk, covered with loops of wiry silk, made smooth and tough using spit and polish, disguised with mud or bits of prey, and hung by threads or placed on a stalk. Which takes us back to the beginning.

The time scale and seasons of the year over which all of this takes place varies between species. Adults of some species, living in stable environments such as in caves or indoors, may be found at most times of the year; others may have a much shorter period of maturity and some males may be here and gone within a few days. The likely season of maturity is indicated as each species is described, but this will be influenced by weather and latitude. A particularly cold or warm spring or summer may delay or accelerate development by its effect on both the spider and its potential prey. A species maturing within a year in the south of the region may spread its life cycle over two years in the north.

Throughout the whole of their development, spiders may fall victim to other predators. From the egg stage to adulthood they may be eaten by insects, other arachnids (including spiders), birds, mammals, reptiles, amphibians and fish. Perhaps the only thing worse than being eaten alive is being eaten alive *slowly*. Some parasitic wasps (Hymenoptera) lay their eggs in spiders' egg sacs or on the spiders themselves. The larvae hatch and either eat the eggs, or feed on the living spider as it moves around. You may frequently find spiders with a parasitic larva attached to the front of the abdomen and it is interesting to keep such specimens, feeding and watering sparingly (to avoid mould), to see what finally pupates and emerges. Parasitic worms (phylum Nematomorpha) also affect spiders, usually developing in the abdomen. These worms are pale, unsegmented, very thin and thread-like, and very long. Affected spiders will be seen to have a 'lumpy' abdomen and the worm eventually emerges, either by snaking out or by bursting free in a seemingly inextricable, tangled knot. Occasionally, spiders are parasitized by mites and it is not unusual to see tiny, often bright red specimens attached to various parts of the body.

Spider Bites

If a particular breed of dog badly savages a child, it is generally reported in the press. Hundreds of other people are bitten and scratched by dogs and cats every day, but this is never newsworthy. Millions of midge bites and thousands of bee and wasp stings similarly go unreported and even if the sting causes death from anaphylactic shock it may only get a couple of column inches. But a spider giving someone a totally insignificant bite is rather different – media hype and popular misconceptions combine to produce a flurry of journalistic activity and some sizeable articles. This interesting phenomenon is of course partly due to the fact that, in our part of the world, spiders very rarely bite man. All spiders bite, and virtually all inject venom into their prey, but the vast majority of species are physically incapable of penetrating human skin and very few will bite man, even if severely provoked. A few of our native spiders can bite and penetrate human skin, but, of the dozen or so species implicated, the vast majority have been provoked in some way and the effects of the bite are totally insignificant. The water spider (*Argyroneta aquatica*) can give a fairly painful bite, but this is not as severe as the bites and stings of many insects. Some European species of *Cheiracanthium* can cause generalized illness and unpleasant wounds which are slow to heal. In warm parts of the world there certainly are species which are dangerous to man. They are mostly well known: the black widows or redback spiders (*Latrodectus*) and Sydney funnel-web spiders (*Atrax*), are both dangerous and have caused a small number of fatalities; the Brazilian wandering spider, *Phoneutria fera*, is aggressive and gives an extremely painful bite. Of the 35,000 species of spider known worldwide, about 500 are known to cause painful bites in man and about a dozen can cause really serious symptoms from the venom injected. There is, however, absolutely nothing to fear from the native spiders of this region and only *Argyroneta aquatica*, *Steatoda nobilis*, and the larger species of *Cheiracanthium* require slight caution when handling.

Collecting and Preserving Spiders

Hunting

Spiders may be found almost everywhere and at all times of the year. Whilst adults of some species may be found all year round, other species will only be found in a mature state for a few weeks of the year and adult males, in particular, may have a very short season. Obviously some sites, with a wide diversity of habitats and lack of disturbance, will provide a large range of species from different families.

Unimproved grassland, rich meadows, areas of ancient woodland, mosses, bogs and the margins of streams, ponds and lakes will all support a good range of spiders. Hunting on the sea-shore, mountain tops and caves will yield fewer spiders but some of these will be species that do not occur elsewhere. If you have never looked for spiders before, a good place to start is in and around your own home and garden. The presence of many species may be detected by the webs they have made. Sometimes the spider will be seen sitting in the web or perhaps catching prey. Alternatively the spider may be hidden away in a retreat or tube and may need to be enticed out by introducing a live fly or touching the web with a vibrating tuning fork. On a damp morning you may have passed a bush or hedge covered in webs, and returned later to find that they have all gone; spraying with a plant mister will give instant recall! Other species spin no webs and may be found running on the ground or on walls, or hiding beneath stones and logs. Night-time hunting with a torch can also be very productive; many nocturnal species will be found wandering on walls or occupying a web which seemed empty during daylight hours. But before you actually set out hunting you will need to make a pooter to catch your spiders with, so that you may examine them more closely.

The pooter is the single most important piece of apparatus for the arachnologist and deserves detailed description. It enables you to suck up spiders quickly and efficiently without damaging them and then blow them into a container for examination or preservation. I have made hundreds of them, for myself and others, and my earlier models were made from glass and rubber tubing. They worked extremely well, but people kept breaking them. It was also difficult to obtain exactly the right size of glass and rubber tube to obtain a good push-fit, one into the other. I have had far fewer requests for the new model, partly because they don't break and partly because people can readily obtain materials to make their own. A visit to your home-brewing shop will enable you to buy clear plastic tubing of about 8mm internal diameter used for syphoning beer and wine. You will also be able to get plastic tubing of 8mm outside diameter (for an entirely plastic pooter) or similar sized glass tubing (for a plastic and glass pooter). Check that the glass or small plastic tubing is a good push-fit into the larger tubing. You will also need a piece of nylon gauze or stocking from one of the stronger areas in a pair of tights. If making a glass and plastic model (like the one

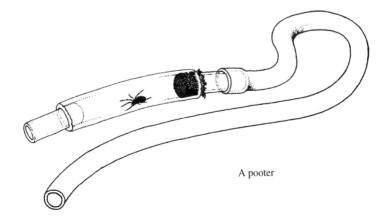

A pooter

illustrated), you will first need to cut two pieces of glass tubing about 35mm long. This is easily achieved by filing a groove with a metal file, taking the tube firmly with a thumb and first finger each side of the groove, and snapping. The sharp, cut edges of the tube should then be held, with forceps, in a gas flame until the glass at the end glows orange, and allowed to cool. Then cut a 90mm length of the large plastic tubing and a piece of gauze about 20mm diameter or square. Fold the gauze *loosely* over the end of one piece of glass tube and push into the plastic tube. If the gauze is stretched too tightly over the glass tube before pushing it in, the latter action stretches it more and breaks the fibres. The other piece of glass tube is placed in the opposite end, but not too tightly since you will want to remove it for catching larger specimens. All that remains is to attach a suitable length of tubing (about 500mm) for you to suck through. You can use the large plastic tube but I prefer rubber since it is more flexible, particularly in cold weather. The all-plastic pooter is even easier to make: cut a 90mm length of large tubing, then one 35mm length and one 500mm length of small tubing. The nylon gauze is then placed over the end of the 500mm long tube and pushed in. A trickle of PVA glue around the join, *after* it has been pushed in, is advisable. The 35mm length is placed in the opposite end. The thinner plastic tubing used for suction in this model is reasonably flexible. The only disadvantage of the plastic pooter is that examination of specimens within it is not as easy as it is through glass. However, once you have made a spi-pot (p. 33) this ceases to be a problem.

In addition to the pooter you will also need a number of containers. If you are killing and preserving the spiders (see **Preservation**, below) you can place many specimens in the same container of alcohol. If you are temporarily keeping them alive then you should place only one specimen in each container, since they may otherwise eat one another. Once you have thoroughly searched for webs and free-running spiders, grubbed about and generally left no stone unturned, you may wish to try other methods of hunting:

1. **Sweeping with a Net** Spiders on grassland and low herbage can be swept up with a strong short-handled net; a butterfly net is not suitable. Such a net can easily be made by bending a length of metal rod roughly into a circle and then bending 12cm or so of each end out to form a handle. These ends can be taped together and covered with thicker material to form a handle. A strong cotton or canvas sheet is then sewn into a bag shape which is sewn around the frame of the net. If your metal rod is not too thick, a length of large plastic tubing (above), cut lengthwise, can be pushed over the rim of the net to protect the material from abrasion. The net is swept briskly through the vegetation and any spiders gathered are sucked out with the pooter. Finally, the water spider, *Argyroneta aquatica*, lives an almost entirely submerged existence and should be sought by sweeping underwater vegetation with a pond net.

2. **Beating** Spiders in bushes and on the lower branches of trees can be dislodged by beating the branches sharply with a stick. You need something for the spiders to fall on to and this can be a square of material stretched over a collapsible frame, or a plastic tray, or a plastic sheet placed on the ground.

3. **Sieving** Many spiders living within moss, leaf-litter and other detritus are most easily extracted using a sieve. Plastic sieves with a mesh of about 10mm are obtainable from garden centres and these are both durable and light to carry around. The moss or litter is placed in the sieve, teased apart if necessary, and then shaken over a sheet. Spiders landing on the sheet (with both sieving and beating) often play dead for a short time (catalepsy) and you should watch carefully until they resume movement. For the sheet, I use a piece of thick plastic pond liner coloured blue on one side

and beige on the other. White sheets are painful to use in bright sunshine; cotton sheets get dirty very quickly; flimsy sheets blow away easily and get torn. A strong plastic sheet is easily cleaned (even in a nearby stream), is useful for sitting on to eat lunch and can also provide shelter from a heavy downpour of rain.

4. **Bark-brushing** A number of spiders live on the bark of trees and can be difficult to spot *in situ*. They can be dislodged with a hand brush and collected in an upturned umbrella pushed up against the bark. If making your own sweep net, you could incorporate a slightly concave curve, on the opposite side to the handle, specifically for this purpose.

Trapping

A number of methods can be used to trap spiders which may otherwise be elusive. Such traps are left in place for days or weeks and are thus equivalent to many hours of hand collecting. Obviously, traps are indiscriminate and, in addition to spiders, will collect many other creatures. Wherever possible you should arrange to pass on any dead material to other naturalists working on these groups.

1. **Pitfall Traps** For these, plastic cups such as cream or yoghurt cartons are buried flush with the ground surface. In most situations this is easily achieved using a bulb-planting tool which removes a plug of earth of the same size as the cup. (Glass jam jars are hazardous, for a variety of reasons, and are difficult to carry to the site because they are heavy and do not stack.) Wandering spiders and other invertebrates fall in and are unable to escape. The trap can be left dry, but in this case it will need inspecting two or three times a day since the trapped animals will eat one another. It is more practical to fill the bottom 2–3cm of the trap with a killing/preserving liquid. The most useful agent here is ethylene glycol (antifreeze) and the addition of a drop of detergent will reduce the surface tension and ensure that the animals sink. The trap should be provided with a raised cover to stop small vertebrates (shrews, mice, frogs) from falling in and to keep rainwater out. For this, a square of plywood, with dowelling or nails at each corner, is lightly pushed into the ground over the trap. When setting out a series of traps, try to do it in an orderly way and note their position carefully using significant landmarks. Traps set out in March may be obscured by a forest of herbage in summer. The traps should be visited weekly and emptied; the catch should be taken away for sorting since it is not normally practical to do this in the field. The easiest way to empty a series of traps is to take several squares of open-weave material (cheesecloth, muslin, nappy liner) each in a polythene bag numbered to correspond with the traps. The contents of each trap are poured through the material and the preservative collected in a fresh cup which is then replaced in the hole. The material plus contents is then rolled up and placed in the polythene bag for examination later. One problem with pitfall trap material is that the palps of male spiders may be partly or completely expanded; this alters the relative position of the structures and can make identification difficult for the beginner. The reason for this expansion is given in the Introduction (p. 9).

2. **Litter Traps** In certain situations there may be little or no leaf litter, or what there is may be spread very thinly. Artificial piles of litter may be created by scraping together the naturally occurring vegetation, or by using straw or wood shavings. If these piles are placed on plastic sheets, the whole lot can be uplifted after two or three weeks and taken away for sorting. The litter is then returned for further colonisation. Smaller parcels of litter, wrapped in chicken-wire, may be placed up in trees and will attract species which occur in high canopy and birds' nests.

3. **Artificial Retreats** Spiders frequently take refuge under stones, bark and other larger pieces of debris; many species moult or lay their eggs in such situations. Some open areas with very short vegetation may have very little natural cover, or crevices within large boulders may be totally inaccessible. Artificial retreats may be created using a wide variety of materials. Small sheets of corrugated iron work very well but are difficult to carry! I have used small polystyrene boxes (as used for seedlings) and egg boxes, which are pegged down with wire.

4. **Bark Traps** These are invaluable for sampling the fauna of tree bark and originally were made of corrugated cardboard; however, polythene bubblewrap is better and more durable. Cut two lengths of bubbled polythene (20–30mm diameter bubbles) and a similar length of black polythene (to exclude light). Place one length of bubblewrap on top of the other (bubbles together) and cover with the black polythene. Tack these three layers loosely together with durable twine along their length, top and bottom, leaving good lengths of twine at each end for tying around the tree. The trap need not completely encircle the tree so the length is optional; a width of around 30cm is generally manageable. After a few weeks the trap is removed; normally one can see through the polythene whether the trap has been well colonised. The whole trap may be placed quickly into a plastic bag and taken away. Alternatively the spiders can be removed on the spot and the trap replaced. To do this, the trap is placed on a large sheet, the twine pulled loose at each tacking point, and the three layers gently separated and shaken. What follows is usually a great test of dexterity with the pooter as the spiders rush to the edge of the sheet in a bid to escape.

Codes of Conduct and Safety

These can be considered under four headings and apply generally to all naturalists engaged in field work:

1. **Safety and Prudence** The countryside is wonderful but some areas, often of outstanding natural beauty, can be dangerous. For example, you should make sure that you are well equipped and have a weather forecast if collecting in mountainous areas; if leading a party you should make sure that everyone else is well equipped. The sunshine in the visitors' car park can make it incredibly difficult to convey the likely conditions a little higher up. Apart from these general considerations, some aspects of your collecting can have an impact on others: when looking under stones on slopes or clifftops, be careful not to dislodge any boulders on to people below; do not place pitfall traps near footpaths or where small children have access (they might drink the contents, not fall in!) and avoid using glass jars. Although the spiders are completely harmless, there are slight dangers or discomforts which may arise from other creatures as you invade their space: adders are seldom a problem, even where there are large populations, since they move out of the way as you approach. Particularly concentrated buzzing sounds are best not ignored since wasps easily take offence when their nest is beaten or sieved. In certain areas there may be large populations of ticks which spend intermittent parts of their life cycle on the local deer; they may opt to spend some time on you and can transmit Lyme disease. Do a tick check if you have collected in such areas and seek advice if you develop a rash, joint pains and unexplained fever. Infection can be diagnosed easily with a blood test and treated easily with antibiotics in the early stages. If untreated, later problems can prove more refractory. Ticks hang on with their mouthparts and drop off once

engorged. Advice abounds on how to remove them complete with mouthparts; I simply hold them with forceps and unscrew them anticlockwise. Finally, the cause of greatest misery is the midges (*Culicoides*); have a good insect repellent with you.

2. **Legal** In some parts of Europe it is illegal to collect any plant or animal unless you belong to a scientific institution or have obtained a special permit. In Britain, two endangered spider species are protected by inclusion in Schedule 5 of the Wildlife and Countryside Act 1981 and their collection is prohibited without a licence; they are *Eresus cinnaberinus* (=*E. niger*) and *Dolomedes plantarius*. Permission is always required for collecting on nature reserves and on other sites of conservation interest; adhere to any stipulations and provide a species list. Permission to collect must be obtained from the Forestry Commission and from the Ministry of Defence if you wish to collect on their land; you may have to sign a document freeing them of any responsibility should you have an accident. Permission should also always be sought from private landowners or tenants, most of whom are extremely helpful; many are keen naturalists and appreciate a species list. Some have shooting parties at various times of the year and this is not compatible with collecting spiders.

3. **The Environment** Try to damage the environment as little as possible; avoid undue trampling and make yourself aware of any particularly rare or sensitive plants and animals which might be growing or breeding in the area. Replace moss and similar vegetation after it has been examined for spiders; replace stones and logs after you have looked under them, and replace bark from dead timber. Do not remove bark from living trees. Use restraint when beating trees and bushes. Make sure that pitfall traps exclude shrews, mice, frogs etc. Remove the traps (and fill the hole) once the survey is finished; pass on non-arachnid material to other naturalists.

4. **The Spiders** Some people are totally averse to killing spiders or any other animals. It is possible to identify many spiders to species level in the field using a field microscope (sometimes just a hand lens) and a spi-pot (p. 33). They can then be returned to their habitat. Other species can be reliably identified only by killing them and carefully examining the preserved specimen under a more powerful microscope. This has little to do with the size or rarity of the species; *Eresus cinnaberinus* is large and rare, *Crustulina guttata* small and common but both are identifiable using the naked eye. *Tegenaria duellica* and *Tegenaria saeva* are both large, common spiders but are sometimes difficult to separate even with a microscope. The male of *Pholcomma gibbum* (1.25–1.5mm) is identifiable with a hand lens. Some people will be quite content if they can place a spider in the correct genus and get some to species level; this is in any case a good way to start. However, if your interest grows, as I hope it will, you may find the need to identify more species and perhaps to participate in the spider recording scheme. For this you will need to kill and preserve at least some species and, in this way, a collection will grow. If you were to spend a whole day collecting and killing spiders, this would be but a tiny fraction of the number killed by birds and other predators and you would have inadvertently run over or trampled many others on your way to the site. Killing spiders should not be undertaken lightly but it can, if done in a true spirit of enquiry, eventually benefit the spiders by increasing our understanding, and identifying sites where spiders are threatened. Bearing all this in mind, you should release readily identifiable species where captured, try to avoid taking too many specimens of the same species, avoid visiting the same site year after year, and avoid collecting in sites which are already well worked and contain known rarities. Finally, do not collect and kill spiders at all unless you are prepared to spend time identifying the preserved material.

Preservation

1. **Preservatives** Spiders cannot be preserved in a dry state like butterflies on a pin since they are soft-bodied and simply shrivel and go mouldy. They can be freeze-dried, but this is really a museum display technique. The best and most reliable medium for killing and preserving spiders is 70–75 per cent alcohol. This is purchased as Industrial Methylated Spirit B.P. 66 OP. and normally comes in 2-litre bottles. It consists of 95 per cent ethyl alcohol and 5 per cent methyl alcohol and should be diluted to 70–75 per cent with distilled water. Any pharmacy should be able to obtain it for you but in Britain you will first need to obtain a licence from HM Customs and Excise. There is no charge for the licence and you should apply to your local office. An acceptable alternative to ethyl alcohol is iso-propyl alcohol which can be diluted to 50–60 per cent and requires no licence. I have no personal experience of the long-term effectiveness of this medium.

2. **Containers** Most people use glass containers in the form of slender tubes with polythene closures or (for larger species and whole collections from one site) diminutive, dumpy bottles with snap-on polythene lids. The size and number of containers will depend upon how you intend to organize and store your collection. The most important consideration is that alcohol is volatile and evaporates rapidly, therefore the containers must have secure polythene closures. Corks and rubber stoppers are quite unsatisfactory.

3. **Storage** The colour of preserved spiders fades in time; reds and greens fade particularly quickly. This process is hastened by exposure to light and specimens left in direct sunlight for a few months may be bleached almost white. Specimens stored in cabinets retain their colours for much longer and most patterns and markings will remain almost indefinitely. Tubes may be stored upright in a cabinet with trays which are about 50mm in depth. Partitions for the rows of tubes may be made either by drilling rows of holes in a hardboard insert or by using fine chicken wire or squared plastic panels used in light diffusers. The organization of a collection depends largely on personal preference, but many people split it into a reference collection, which contains a few specimens of each species, and a general collection, where each tube contains all the specimens collected from a single locality on one day. You will need a system of numbering for the tubes, labels within each tube giving details of species, grid reference, date etc., and a system of cross-referencing to field notebooks.

4. **Labelling** This is a vital aspect of any form of preservation and specimens without labels are of little scientific value. Each tube should contain a label, written in indian ink, on good quality paper. The data should include species name and sex, locality, grid reference, habitat, date, collector's name and the serial number of your system of indexing. Write small and use both sides!

Identifying and Recording Spiders

The identification of any group of plants or animals requires books (and other literature) and equipment. This book will enable you to identify the majority of British and northern European spiders to species level with the exception of the small grey or black-bodied members of the Linyphiidae known as 'money spiders'. For species outside the scope of this book you will need to consult the literature given in the Bibliography (p. 375). Some of the equipment for identification can be made; most will need to be purchased, but may prove useful in other fields.

Identifying Preserved Spiders

You should try, whenever possible, to identify spiders you have collected in alcohol later on the same day; I always insist on this when running field courses even if we have to work into the small hours. Firstly, this avoids an ever-increasing backlog and the accumulation of material which, in the end, may never be identified. Secondly, if a particularly rare species is found, you can revisit the site the following day to investigate further; or, in the case of subadults, revisit the next week to collect adults. Thirdly, the colours of some species fade fairly rapidly in alcohol (and in your memory) and this aid to identification may be lost. Obviously it is not always possible to examine the material quickly, for instance when examining collections made by someone else or from pitfall traps. Spiders preserved in alcohol are examined in alcohol and for this you will need a microscope, lighting and various other bits and pieces.

1. **The Microscope** For spider identification the stereoscopic binocular microscope is by far the best and gives an upright, three-dimensional view of the specimen. A large range of models is available. A magnification of ×20 to ×30 is necessary for low-power work, as when sorting through specimens or examining large spiders. Further magnification of ×80 or ×90 is required for examining smaller species in detail. In some models the magnification is changed by sliding different power objective lenses into place, or by swivelling a turret. Other models have a zoom facility which enables smooth movement between magnifications. Some microscopes have a light source built into them; do not buy one of these – the lighting is invariably inadequate for working on spiders. Generally it is advisable to purchase the best model you can afford; this is cheaper in the long run than having to upgrade your equipment later on. Remember too that a microscope has countless other uses. Attending a field course will allow you to see a wide range of microscopes in use and this will help you choose a suitable model. A perfectly adequate microscope can be purchased new for less than the cost of a one-year road fund licence for a motor car.

2. **Lighting** Good high-intensity lighting is as important as the microscope, if not more so, and there are many models to choose from. In terms of cost, and performance, and the cost and life of the bulbs, by far the best model currently available is the Flexispot (see Suppliers, p. 375) and it costs rather less than a television licence. I used a total of six bulbs in preparing the illustrations for the whole of this book. It is unnecessary to buy the model with a rheostat since the brightest illumination is nearly always required and any dimming can be achieved by moving the light source further away.

3. **Techniques** The illustration overleaf shows the microscope, light and specimen set up for identification. The specimen is examined in a small dish containing alcohol. It is important to get the light source close to the subject; the amount of illumination varies inversely with the distance squared and as the light source is moved away the illumination drops off rapidly. It will be necessary to manipulate specimens into different positions; a pair of fine forceps and a mounted needle will suffice and a small artist's paintbrush may be useful for transferring specimens between tubes and dish. In order to hold the specimen in any desired position, a layer of sand or fine glass beads is placed in the bottom of the dish; the spider is simply pushed into this layer in the required position. Sand costs little or nothing but needs thorough washing. glass beads, which have the appearance of caster sugar, cost rather more. Your pharmacy should be able to order them from the supplier (BDH Chemicals); ask for glass beads, approx. 80 mesh, for gas chromatography; 500g will last for years. There may be other outlets, since glass beads are also used in some sterilizers and

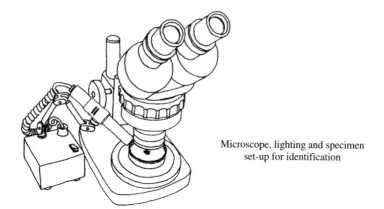

Microscope, lighting and specimen
set-up for identification

for reflective road markings. The position required for examining various structures will be obvious from the illustrations in this book. You may need to move legs out of the way if they are obscuring other structures and this is easily done with forceps and needle. Since the male palps and female epigynes of spiders are external structures, there is no need for dissection. Occasionally, it may be difficult to get a male palp into exactly the right position, particularly if it has to be viewed from below. If all else fails, just pull it off by holding the base of the palpal femur with forceps and pushing the spider away from it with the needle.

Identifying Spiders in the Field

Although a number of spiders can be identified in the field by their naked-eye appearance (sometimes supplemented by the type of web), most species will require some form of magnification. Some method of restraining the spider will also be required, particularly at higher magnifications.

1. **Hand Lens** A hand lens is an essential part of equipment. Get a good-quality achromatic glass lens; a magnification of ×10 is most commonly used for examining specimens confined within a glass tube, and combination lenses are also available with magnifications of ×8 and ×15. Lenses with a magnification of ×20 are unsuitable for this purpose, but may be used with a spi-pot (below), where the spider is confined to a narrow focal plane. The lens should be worn around the neck with a strong cord. Many people use a lens incorrectly; it should be held as close as possible to the eye and the specimen brought up to it until in focus – a distance of about 20mm with a ×10 lens.

2. **Field Microscope** This piece of equipment is a combined short-focus telescope and low-power microscope. One I have recently tested is the 'Specwell' CF-82; this is the model I have illustrated in use (see Suppliers, p. 375). Apart from its use as a conventional telescope, it focuses down to a distance of 250mm giving a ×8 view of spiders *in situ* (attempting to use a ×8 lens close up to the spider would disturb it). Add on the micro lens with detachable transparent stand and it becomes a ×25 microscope. It costs the same as a one-year television licence but will give many years of viewing. An even cheaper microscope, tested recently, is the Geoscope from the

Natural History Museum catalogue. Essentially, it is an educational toy but, with coated glass lenses, the optics are quite good. It gives a magnification of ×30 and, although the image is reversed, this is soon got used to. Structures such as the tarsal claws, cribellum, calamistrum and colulus are easily seen. The built-in light source does enable identification in total darkness – e.g. when collecting in caves or at night. With this degree of magnification it is necessary to restrain the spider, both to stop it running about and to keep it within a narrow depth of focus.

3. **The Spi-pot** Various methods of restraining live spiders for microscopical examination have been tried over the years. One method involves cutting down a plastic hypodermic syringe and gluing a glass coverslip over the end leaving a hole for air to escape. The spider is placed inside the barrel and the plunger advanced until the spider is trapped against the coverslip. It works quite well, but many people have found that syringes are not easily available. Additionally, the inside of the glass coverslip can be difficult to clean and the plastic of some syringes deteriorates rapidly and becomes brittle. With this and other methods there is also the risk of squashing the spider. All of these problems are overcome with a simply made device (arrived at whilst preparing this book) which I call a 'spi-pot'. It should also be of considerable use to entomologists. To make one you will require two clear plastic pots, a small piece of polystyrene sheet and a piece of clingfilm. I use pots with a 50mm diameter base, 67mm high, which originally contained glacé cherries or mixed peel. When stacked together there is a gap of 8mm between the bases. The polystyrene sheet, 8mm thick, comes from packing or tiles. The base of one pot is cut out leaving a rim of 5mm for rigidity (pot A in the illustration). Place the second pot on the polystyrene sheet, draw around the base of the pot and cut out the circle of polystyrene with a sharp knife. Stick the polystyrene to the base with PVA glue (pot B in the illustration). Inclusion of a mm. scale on the polystyrene is very useful for measuring the length of specimens in the field. This can be done with indian ink and a rapidograph pen, ruling a scale line or a grid of mm. squares, or a piece of mm. square graph paper can be stuck on. Finally, take a piece of clingfilm (about 25cm square) and stretch this tightly and evenly over the cut base of pot A, wrapping the surplus loosely around the sides. The captured spider is placed in pot A and trapped between the clingfilm and polystyrene when pot B is pushed in. Don't worry if the edge of the polystyrene is a bit ragged; parts of this will help grip, and parts will allow the passage of air when the cups are separated again.

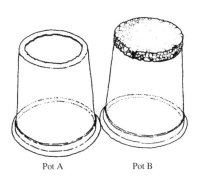

Pot A   Pot B   Spi-pot assembled and
                              holding spider

Spi-pot

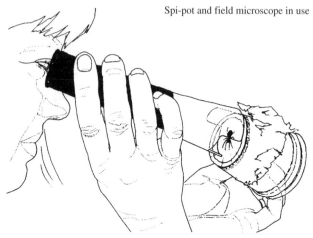

Spi-pot and field microscope in use

The thickness of polystyrene is not too critical, but it must reach up to the base of pot A. If you wish to examine the upper surface of the spider, hold the pot base up and trap the spider as it walks on the polystyrene. For a view of the under surface, hold the pot the other way up whilst manoeuvring. For a side view, fiddle around a bit and catch it unawares. Try to trap the spider in the centre of the pot. When examining male palps from the side, slightly compress the specimen once the palp is in clear view. When examining the underside of the palp, wait until the spider extends the palp before slightly compressing it, and then view slightly from behind. The clingfilm is very durable and very good optically when stretched tightly and evenly. When it becomes dirty, simply unravel and move on to another section. It is useful to place a third pot over the cling film to keep it clean when carrying around. The method of holding spi-pot and field microscope is illustrated. The base of the microscope rests on the edge of the spi-pot, the wrists/lower forearms are pressed together for stability and fine focusing is achieved by rocking one side of the base up and down slightly. Obviously you need to stand with the sun coming from behind and to one side. I have also used the spi-pot with a lightweight binocular microscope, hand held, poking it through the hole in the base. It can also be used with the usual identification set-up indoors, but some microscopes will require a slightly shorter version. It makes examination of spiders much easier even with a lens, and allows the use of models with ×20 magnification.

The Spider Recording Scheme

The British Spider Recording Scheme was established in 1987 by the British Arachnological Society in association with the Biological Records Centre. The eventual aim is to produce an up-to-date distribution atlas of British spiders based on records from each 10km square in the country. Large numbers of recorders submit their observations, on specially designed recording cards, to around forty area organisers spread throughout the country. Additional recorders are always required but a reasonable proficiency in identification is important. Before you reach this stage, additional identification literature will be required, particularly for the Linyphiidae, and you may also have attended a field course. Many records will require checking for correct identification so that it will be necessary to collect and preserve the spiders. The address for details and recording cards appears on p. 374. Although there is much work to be done on the recording of British spiders, work has hardly begun in many parts of Europe, and there is tremendous scope for discovery.

The Names and Classification of Spiders

Names

Some years ago I had a fairly lengthy telephone conversation with the late G.H. Locket concerning the comparative structure of the male palpal organ in various related genera and families of spider. A visitor, on overhearing this conversation, became visibly intrigued and waited with increasing impatience to ask his question: 'what language were you speaking just then?' This is, of course, entirely normal; virtually every form of human interest and activity has its own jargon which may be partially or totally unintelligible to the outsider. Whilst some jargon is unnecessarily or deliberately obscure, most evolves alongside the pursuit and speeds communication between participants. It removes the need to explain each circumstance or object in detail every time it comes up. Listening to banter at the fish market or to a group of golfers, computer experts or lawyers would all require knowledge of at least some specialist terms. In natural history, there are many concepts, structures and creatures which have no 'common' names. The most important thing for the would-be naturalist is not to be afraid or embarrassed to use the scientific terms; they are simply words which are as easily learned as any others.

Many of our conspicuous plants and animals have common or colloquial names. These names are thoroughly part of our living language and have evolved their usage over millennia. The corresponding scientific names for these organisms are a relatively new imposition and are less frequently used, even by students of the subject. You are, for example, unlikely to hear anyone say 'look at that *Troglodytes troglodytes*' because the wren might have departed before the understanding arrived. However, you would need to use the word 'roitelet' in France, 'Zaunkönig' in Germany and different words for all the other countries where the bird is resident. Within each country you might also find a considerable number of very local names for the same creature. The scientific names attempt to avoid confusion by ensuring that there is but one universally accepted name for each of the millions of plants and animals, most of which have no common names.

Very few spiders have common names; even the names 'house spider' and 'garden spider' could refer to several different species. The name 'water spider' is one example of a common name which clearly relates to one species – *Argyroneta aquatica*. There are a few common names which relate to families; thus 'jumping spiders' and 'wolf spiders' are the Salticidae and Lycosidae respectively. Although it would be possible to produce a whole series of English names for spiders (perhaps using translations of the scientific name) these would still be invented names and not genuinely common or colloquial.

Scientific naming, or nomenclature, does not simply occur on a willy-nilly basis, but is inextricably linked to the classification of organisms. Such classification, or arrangement into groups, should ideally reflect relationships; the study and practice of such classification is known as taxonomy. The application of scientific names is governed by the Code of the International Commission on Zoological Nomenclature. The starting point of zoological nomenclature was fixed at 1 January 1758, but some of Clerck's 1757 names are admitted. The rules are designed to provide maximum stability in nomenclature whilst allowing freedom of taxonomic thought and action. Taxonomy takes the form of a branching hierarchy: kingdom divides into various phyla which each divide into classes, orders, suborders, families, genera and, finally, species. Spiders belong to the Animal kingdom, subkingdom Metazoa, phylum Chelicerata, class Arachnida, order Araneae. Other members of the class Arachnida include the orders Acari, Opiliones, Scorpions and Pseudoscorpions (p. 10) Whilst the practice of nomenclature is subject to a well-defined code, the criteria used in classification and taxonomy are much more open to personal interpretation and this will be discussed later.

The spiders described in this book are placed within different families. Within each family there are one or more genera and it is the the name of the genus (always starting with a capital letter) which forms the first part of the scientific name. Within each genus there are one or more species, and the name of the species forms the second part of the scientific name; the species name never starts with a capital letter. The two parts of this binomial scientific name are always in Latin (or latinized versions of other languages) and printed in italics. Finally the name of the person who described and named the species (the authority) is added, together with the date. An example of a full scientific name of a common spider is:

Linyphia minuta Blackwall 1833

A literal translation of this name means 'small (*minuta*) weaver of linen'; this conveys the nature of the spider fairly well and also indicates that it is a relatively small member of the genus *Linyphia*. Some 60 years after Blackwall's first description, it was realised that the species known as *Linyphia minuta* actually belonged in the genus *Lepthyphantes*. When a species is transferred to another genus, the specific name remains the same but may change gender to match that of the new genus (in this case from feminine to masculine). The name of the authority and the date remain unchanged but are placed in brackets. The species is now known as:

Lepthyphantes minutus (Blackwall 1833)

An unfortunate consequence of this (entirely justified) manoeuvring is that the scientific name has now become rather incongruous. The genus *Lepthyphantes* presents no problem – this translates as 'thin weaver' and the new recruit certainly has thin legs and a rather pointed abdomen. But *minutus* is a pretty difficult name to square with what is now one of the largest species of *Lepthyphantes*!

It sometimes happens (through poor communication or inadequate description) that several workers have independently given different names to the same species. In this case the name published first is the only valid one. This name is eventually used by everyone, although it may take some considerable time for all the synonyms to be discovered and relegated.

Although every scientific name must be unique, it is permissible for species in separate genera to have the same specific name – e.g. *Lepthyphantes minutus* (Blackwall 1833)(a fairly large linyphiid spider) and *Maro minutus* O.P.-Cambridge 1906 (a very small linyphiid spider). Normally this presents no problems, but you might ask what would happen if *Maro minutus* were transferred to the genus *Lepthyphantes*. Each of these would become secondary homonyms. The senior of these homonyms would be the one first established, i.e. by Blackwall in 1833, and *Lepthyphantes minutus* would continue to have the same name. Although the spider *Maro minutus* was described by O.P.-Cambridge in 1906, the same animal was described as *Maro humicola* by Falconer in 1919 and as *Gongylidiellum minutissimum* by Schenkel in 1929. The next available name, and that adopted by the new recruit, would be *Lepthyphantes humicola* (Falconer 1919).

It was suggested earlier that the criteria used and weighed in classification and taxonomy were rather subjective and permitted a fairly wide personal interpretation of relationships. Taxonomy is simply a filing system for organisms; it should allow both easy retrieval of the information stored and easy filing of new information. A comparison might be made with a store which stocked many different types of screw. The manager might allot separate areas for brass screws, steel screws and for those made of other metals. Within each of these areas there might be further division into slotted and cross-headed screws, which could in turn be separated into round-headed, flat-headed, countersunk etc. There would need to be provision for different pitches of thread and whether the screw was for wood, metal or self-tapping, and there might be specialist or decorative screws which did not fit any other category. Each of these groups would then be separated into different lengths of screw. Obviously there are many ways in which such stock could be organized and no particular way could be considered 'right'. The most important consideration is that the system is stable and that staff can locate items efficiently. Occasionally there may be good practical reasons for changing things; for example, some of the 'brass' screws may be brass-plated and better placed in a different category, reflecting the underlying metal and greater strength. Much more disruptive is the new manager who feels it necessary to change the system, perhaps in order to make his mark. Even though the new system may be perfectly logical, the staff are temporarily in a state of chaos; and they may know, from past experience, that the next new manager might revert to the old system! This situation also occurs with organisms, the 'staff' being all those who collect, identify and record plants and animals. Whilst we know precisely what any screw is made of and where it came from, we can only form opinions on the lines of origin (phylogeny) of plants and animals; and these opinions are often hotly disputed. In view of all this, it is not surprising that the names of species occasionally change, and that species may be moved to different or entirely new genera and families.

The names of species, genera and families used in this book are largely uncontroversial and follow those used in other works. I have indicated any recent name changes which have been generally adopted, together with others which have yet to gain acceptance. I have not rushed headlong into adopting changes which I suspect may be reversed in the future.

Pronunciation

In addition to learning how to spell scientific names, the newcomer also needs to know how they are pronounced. Lack of confidence or embarrassment in this area may be the most important factor behind the fear which some people have of scientific names. Basically, the vowels should be pronounced: 'a' as in 'at', 'e' as in 'egg', 'i' as in 'it', 'o' as in 'on' and 'u' as in 'club'. The letters 'c' and 'g' are pronounced as soft when they occur before 'e' and 'i' ('cell', 'cider', 'gem', 'gin') and hard when they occur before 'a', 'o' and 'u' ('call', 'cold', 'cup', 'gall', 'gold', 'gun'). 'Ch' is always pronounced hard, as 'k' and 'ph' as 'f'. In practice, the pronunciation of scientific names, as with normal speech, varies quite widely, both in Britain and abroad. The main thing is not to worry too much about it, after all, many people pronounce 'bath' as though it had an 'r' in it.

Key to the Families of Northern European Spiders

The complete newcomer to spiders may initially just compare the specimen with the colour plates and sometimes come up with the correct identification; the experienced arachnologist will seldom use the keys at all. Between these two extremes, the key should enable a specimen to be tracked down to the correct family in an ordered sequence. There is nothing particularly clever or 'scientific' in slavishly using a key and if you can find a quicker, alternative route to the family, genus, genitalia and final identification, then use it! However, in addition to being an aid to identification, the key presents concise details of the characters of each family and it can be a useful exercise to work through it, even though the specimen has been identified by general appearance alone. As far as possible, the key utilises easily visible structures, and is designed to work whether using a stereomicroscope on preserved specimens indoors, or a field microscope/lens in the field (see p. 32). Where characters are not fairly easily seen with the lens in the field, the symbol ⚠ is followed by alternative guidelines, including any web structure. The latter is dealt with in more detail under Webs (p. 61) and reference to this will in any case be of use in the field. Some spiders are identifiable to species level using the naked eye or a hand lens. Others will require the use of a low-power field microscope or higher-power stereomicroscope for full identification, although it will still be possible to place them in the correct family or genus. When using the key, it is important to start at the beginning and work through systematically. The key is partly dichotomous, but sometimes several alternatives are given, one after the other, partly to avoid confusion and partly to avoid undue repetition of 'spider not like this'. Any terms used which you do not understand will be found in The Structure of Spiders (p. 12) or in the Glossary (p. 371), but the accompanying illustrations should largely avoid any confusion. The size of a spider is measured from the front of the carapace to the hind tip of the abdomen and the ranges given relate to adults only. Identification to species level usually requires examination of the secondary sexual organs, which are visible externally. The female epigyne is on the underside of the abdomen; the *left* male palp is illustrated for each species – usually from the outside, sometimes from below. Before starting the key proper, it is necessary to determine the sex and maturity of the specimen, since problems may arise with immatures. Remember, some large specimens may be immatures of large species; some tiny specimens may be adult.

Preliminary Examination – Sex and Maturity

1.	Tarsus of palp not swollen or modified in any way	2
	Tarsus of palp swollen or modified into complex structures	3
2.	Underside of abdomen with epigyne (a sclerotized structure or projecting tongue) in the midline, just in front of epigastric fold.	ADULT FEMALE
	No such epigyne structure visible	4
3.	Swollen tarsus of palp smooth, with no projections	IMMATURE MALE
	Tarsus with various projecting structures	ADULT MALE

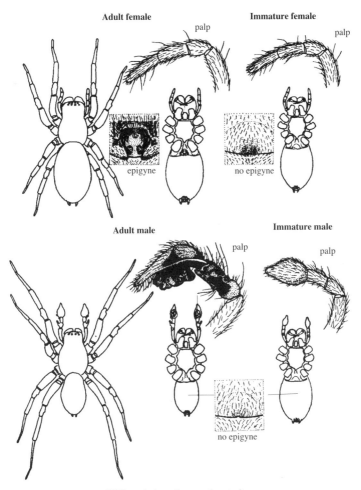

Differentiation of sex and maturity

4a. Spider with only six eyes, grouped closely   FOLLOW MAIN KEY FROM 7

4b. Spider with chelicerae as long as carapace   FOLLOW MAIN KEY FROM 1

4c. Spider not like this and not like the colour illustrations of
        Pachygnatha and *Tetragnatha* (Plate 26)   IMMATURE FEMALE

If your specimen is immature, it may still be possible to identify it to family or genus level, but any measurements given in the key will not apply. A small △ in the key indicates that the family has not been recorded in Britain.

The Family Key

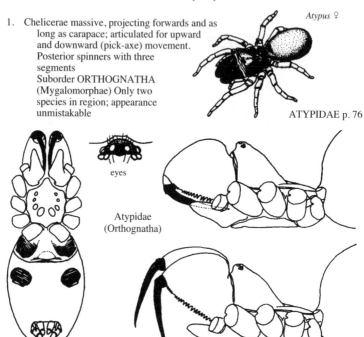

1. Chelicerae massive, projecting forwards and as long as carapace; articulated for upward and downward (pick-axe) movement. Posterior spinners with three segments
    Suborder ORTHOGNATHA (Mygalomorphae) Only two species in region; appearance unmistakable   ATYPIDAE p. 76

Atypus ♀

eyes

Atypidae (Orthognatha)

Chelicerae large, small or projecting, but articulated for inward and outward (pincer) movement. Posterior spinners never with more than two segments
                    Suborder LABIDOGNATHA (Araneomorphae) 2

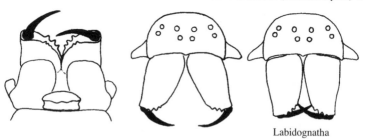

Labidognatha

2. Cribellum present anterior to spinners (reduced in male). Female with calamistrum on metatarsus IV   Cribellate spiders 3

¶ These structures visible only in larger species; all cribellate species appear on Plates 1 and 2; webs of commonest species composed of woolly cribellate silk which appears bluish when fresh (Webs, p. 62–4).

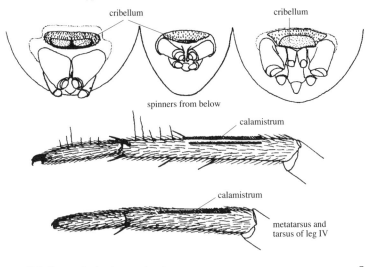

Cribellum and calamistrum absent   7

3. Head region large, bulbous: characteristic eye arrangement. Female velvety black; male abdomen scarlet with black spots   ERESIDAE p. 78

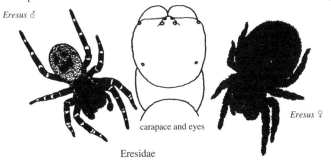

Not as above   4

4. Eyes grouped closely together; posterior medians irregular in shape. Anal tubercle with fringe of long curved hairs. Pale yellowish spider with black markings. Adults 2–2.5mm in length (illustration next page)   OECOBIIDAE p. 89

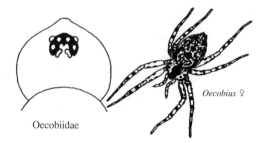

Oecobiidae

Oecobius ♀

Not as above   5

5. Anterior and posterior lateral eyes widely separated; meta-
    tarsus IV and calamistrum curved when viewed from side

                                                          ULOBORIDAE p. 90

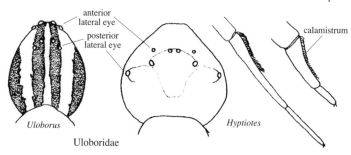

anterior lateral eye
posterior lateral eye
calamistrum

Uloborus   *Hyptiotes*

Uloboridae

Anterior and posterior lateral eyes close together   6

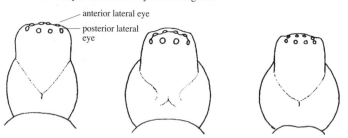

anterior lateral eye
posterior lateral eye

6a. Fairly large spider, 5–15mm. Abdominal pattern broadly
     similar in all species. Calamistrum with double row of
     bristles (illustration next page)   AMAUROBIIDAE p. 78

6b. Abdomen either unicolorous brown-grey with no markings
whatsoever, or clearly marked with two pairs of light
blotches △ TITANOECIDAE p. 81

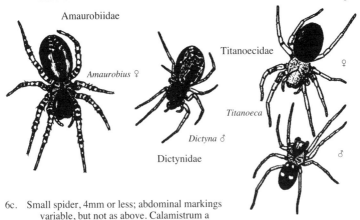

Amaurobiidae

Amaurobius ♀

Titanoecidae

♀

Titanoeca

Dictyna ♂

Dictynidae

♂

6c. Small spider, 4mm or less; abdominal markings
variable, but not as above. Calamistrum a
single row of bristles DICTYNIDAE p. 82

7. Spider with only six eyes, easily seen from above, in a fairly
compact group. Male palpal organs relatively simple;
no epigyne in adult female. Haplogyne spiders 8

Spider with eight eyes, sometimes in rows together (laterals
may be touching), sometimes widely separated (with some
not easily seen at first). Male palpal organs relatively
more complex; adult female with epigyne Entelegyne spiders 9

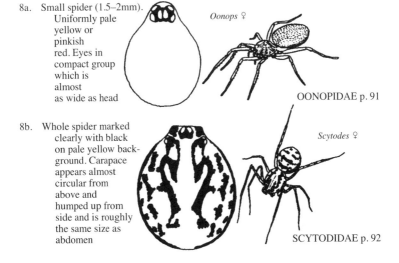

8a. Small spider (1.5–2mm).
Uniformly pale
yellow or
pinkish
red. Eyes in
compact group
which is
almost
as wide as head

Oonops ♀

OONOPIDAE p. 91

8b. Whole spider marked
clearly with black
on pale yellow back-
ground. Carapace
appears almost
circular from
above and
humped up from
side and is roughly
the same size as
abdomen

Scytodes ♀

SCYTODIDAE p. 92

8c.   Eyes clustered almost
        to form a
        circle. No
        abdominal
        pattern

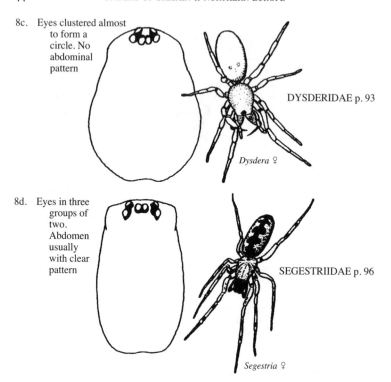

DYSDERIDAE p. 93

Dysdera ♀

8d.   Eyes in three
        groups of
        two.
        Abdomen
        usually
        with clear
        pattern

SEGESTRIIDAE p. 96

Segestria ♀

9a.   Carapace almost circular; as wide as long. Anterior median
        eyes much smaller than the rest, which are arranged closely
        in two groups of three. Legs extremely long; tarsi with
        flexible false segments

PHOLCIDAE p. 98

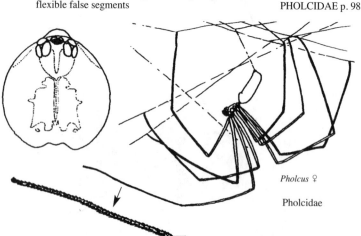

Pholcus ♀

Pholcidae

9b.   Carapace square-fronted; four large eyes on the front, a
        smaller pair one each side further back, and a scarcely
        visible pair one each side between front and rear eyes   SALTICIDAE p. 179

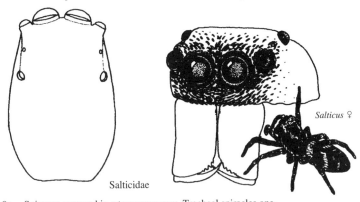

Salticus ♀

Salticidae

9c.   Spinners arranged in a transverse row. Tracheal spiracles one-
        third to half-way from spinners to epigastric fold. Small
        spider   HAHNIIDAE p. 253

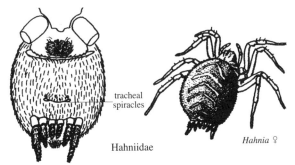

tracheal
spiracles

Hahniidae

Hahnia ♀

9d.   Eyes arranged in hexagonal pattern; small anterior medians
        may not be visible from directly above. Very long leg
        spines   OXYOPIDAE p. 206

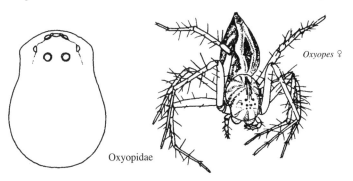

Oxyopes ♀

Oxyopidae

9e. Anterior spinners much larger than the rest and arising from
      a large, pale, cylindrical projection. Anterior median eyes
      larger than the rest; posterior medians small and irregular.
      Upper surface of abdomen dark; under surface pale   ZODARIIDAE p. 100

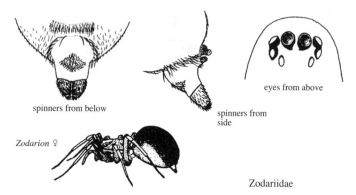

spinners from below

spinners from side

eyes from above

Zodarion ♀

Zodariidae

9f. Front face of carapace with a row of four small, equal-sized
      anterior eyes, not easily seen from above; above and
      behind these a larger pair of posterior median eyes and
      further back a pair of posterior lateral eyes of the same
      size. From in front, they sometimes appear as three
      separate rows. From above, a line through the median
      and lateral eyes of the posterior row crosses the midline
      ahead of the carapace   LYCOSIDAE p. 209

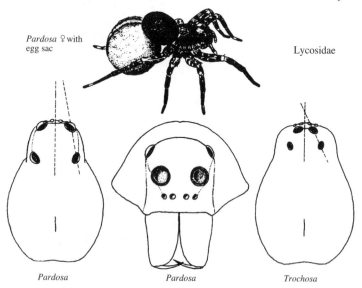

Pardosa ♀ with
egg sac

Lycosidae

Pardosa   *Pardosa*   *Trochosa*

9g. Front face of carapace with a row of four small, equal-sized
anterior eyes, easily seen from above; above and behind
these a slightly larger pair of posterior median eyes, and
further back a pair of posterior lateral eyes of the same
size. From in front they appear as two rows. From above,
a line through the median and lateral eyes of the posterior
row crosses the midline on or behind the front of the
carapace   PISAURIDAE p. 236
Note: *Textrix* (Agelenidae) has recurved posterior eyes
unequal in size and conspicuous long spinners.

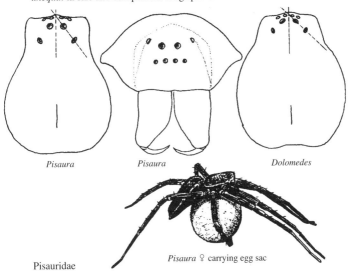

Pisaura   *Pisaura*   *Dolomedes*

Pisauridae   *Pisaura* ♀ carrying egg sac

9h. Front slope of carapace with a row of four eyes which are
roughly the same size as those in the strongly recurved
posterior row. Eyes closely grouped; separated by
scarcely more than their diameters. Carapace pale
yellowish with a pair of brown bands running
longitudinally   ZORIDAE p. 144

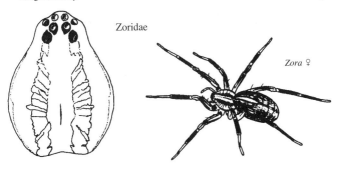

Zoridae

Zora ♀

9i. Legs III and IV furnished thickly with long, fine hairs,
       contrasting markedly with legs I and II which have sparse,
       very short hairs. Tracheal spiracles just behind epigastric
       fold. The only known species has an almost entirely
       submerged, aquatic existence   ARGYRONETIDAE p. 238

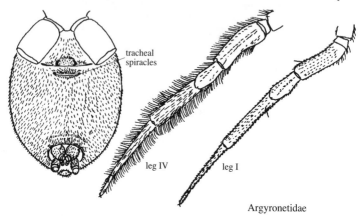

tracheal
spiracles

leg IV   leg I

Argyronetidae

9j. Tracheal spiracles easily visible half-way between spinners
       and epigastric fold. Dorsal surface of abdomen marked
       with distinctive dark patches   ANYPHAENIDAE p. 146

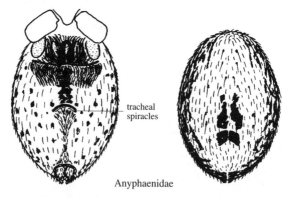

tracheal
spiracles

Anyphaenidae

9k. Legs I and II, viewed from above, with a series of prominent
       curved spines on the inner surface, pointing forwards. Set
       between these are smaller curved spines. Viewed from the
       side, the metatarsi appear curved. One to three pairs of
       small tubercles are present on the abdomen but may be
       difficult to see (see illustrations at top of next page)   MIMETIDAE p. 257

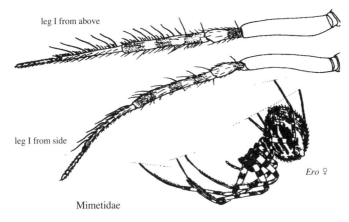

leg I from above

leg I from side

Ero ♀

Mimetidae

91.   Posterior spinners longer than anteriors and of two segments. Median
      spinners easily visible. A series of trichobothria, of increasing
      length, present on each tarsus, which also has 3 claws.
      ❈ In females of *Cryphoeca* these features are difficult
      to see, but the single, small species has a highly
      distinctive appearance in both sexes (Plate 20).   AGELENIDAE p. 240

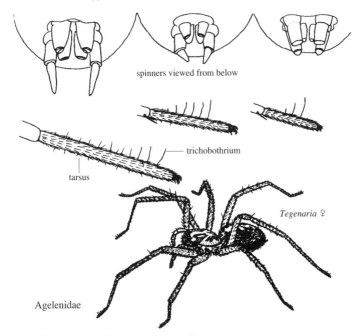

spinners viewed from below

trichobothrium

tarsus

Tegenaria ♀

Agelenidae

Spider not fitting descriptions in 9a to 9l   10

10. Eyes black and beady when each viewed from
        directly above (occasionally dark blue-grey)
        and usually surrounded by a paler area

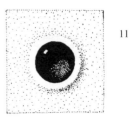

11

Eyes pale or pearly when each viewed from above
    (**apart from anterior medians, which may be
    darker**) and often surrounded by a ring of
    black pigment

12

11. Posterior row of eyes, viewed from above, recurved (curved
        backwards); sometimes almost straight, but never
        procurved (curved forwards). Many species crab-like,
        with legs I and II longer and stouter than the rest; others
        not at all crab-like   THOMISIDAE p. 147

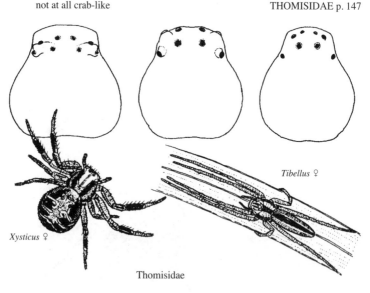

Tibellus ♀

Xysticus ♀

Thomisidae

Posterior row of eyes, viewed from above, slightly
    procurved. All eyes ringed with white. Female
    spider entirely green; male with red abdominal stripes
    along midline and sides   HETEROPODIDAE p. 147

⚠ Look carefully at the eyes; the extremely hairy male of the European species *Heriaeus hirtus* (Thomisidae) is sometimes hastily misidentified as that of *Micrommata virescens* (Heteropodidae).

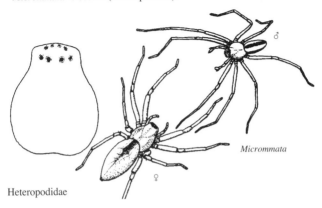

Micrommata

Heteropodidae

12. Tarsi with three claws, an upper pair and a single median claw, easily visible and not obscured by tufts of hair; sometimes also with auxiliary foot claws   15

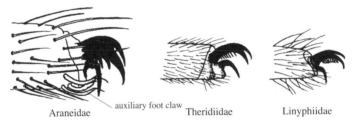

Araneidae   auxiliary foot claw   Theridiidae   Linyphiidae

Tarsi with only two claws which may be partly obscured by tufts of hair   13

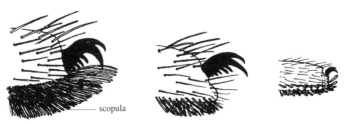

scopula

⚠ The claws may be visible with a lens in larger species but impossible to see in others. If the spider has been found in a web used for catching prey, it will definitely have three claws. If free-running, or found under stones, or in a silken cell with no snare, *and* if it has a cylindrical body with mousy hairs or iridescence, then it will almost certainly have only two claws. The families in the rest of the key with only two claws are on Plates 2–6 (Gnaphosidae, Clubionidae, Liocranidae) and a quick glance at these should enable you to proceed. If the specimen looks like none of these, it may be a web spinner on the loose (especially males), or could be a three-clawed species which has abandoned web-spinning altogether.

13.   Anterior spinners cylindrical, slightly longer than posteriors, and separated so that median spinners are easily visible between them (from below). Posterior median eyes usually oval or irregular in shape (circular in *Scotophaeus* and some *Zelotes*)   GNAPHOSIDAE p. 101

carapaces from above; spinners from below

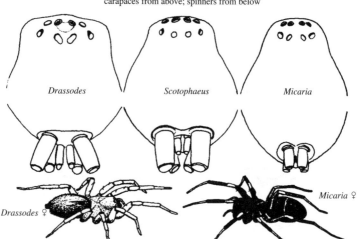

Drassodes   *Scotophaeus*   *Micaria*

Micaria ♀

Drassodes ♀

Gnaphosidae

❧ Spinners easily seen with a lens in most species, but not in *Micaria* where the characteristic eyes are also too small to see properly. These iridescent, rather ant-like spiders (illustration here and on Plate 5) are easily recognisable in the field but you should also check the specimen with illustrations of *Phrurolithus* (Plate 6) and *Steatoda phalerata* (Plate 23).

Anterior spinners cylindrical or conical, and close together, obscuring the median spinners. Posterior spinners often slightly longer and occasionally of two segments. Posterior median eyes circular (see illustrations at top of following page)   14

14.   Total width of eye group at least half the width of carapace at its widest point. Labium appreciably longer than broad (see illustrations on following page)   CLUBIONIDAE p. 124

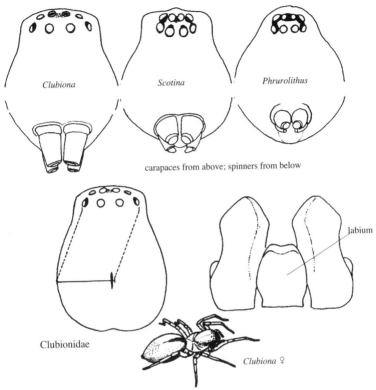

carapaces from above; spinners from below

labium

Clubionidae

Clubiona ♀

Total width of eye group less than half the width of carapace
at its widest point. Labium as broad as long   LIOCRANIDAE p. 136

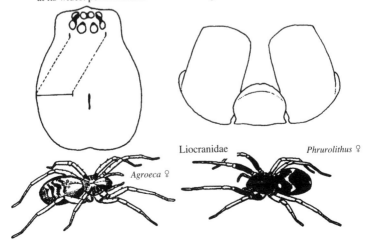

Liocranidae

Agroeca ♀

Phrurolithus ♀

15.   Tarsus IV with a comb of serrated bristles on the under
        (ventral) surface (See note, ♦, below). Legs with very few
        spines; one or two on each patella, two on each
        tibia and none at all on any of the
        femora. Most species
        with an

abdominal pattern or at
least some light markings,
but a *very* few are
unicolorous grey-black   16

    Tarsus IV with no comb of serrated bristles. Legs, in well-
        patterned species, generally with many spines and with at
        least one, prolaterally, on femur I, but many species with a
        unicolorous grey-black abdomen have very few spines (see below)   17

   ♦ The comb of serrated bristles can be very difficult to see even at high
magnification in small species and in males, so the following will help whether
using a lens or microscope. If the specimen has been found on an orb web or a
sheet web (perhaps supported by criss-cross threads), follow the key from 17.
If from a three-dimensional web mainly composed of haphazard criss-cross
threads (and no well-developed sheet) then just follow 16 in the key. If the
specimen has one or more spines on femur I, then it has no tarsal comb and you
should follow the key from 17. If there are no spines on femur I and the
specimen has an abdominal pattern then check the illustrations of *Pachygnatha*
(Plate 26), *Cyclosa conica* (Plate 29) and *Frontinellina* (Plate 32), all of which
have no tarsal comb; go straight to the main text if the specimen matches one
of these. The rare *Neriene radiata* (p. 368) lacks femoral spines but has an
unmistakable web (p. 74). If it is none of these then follow the key from 16. If
the spider is grey or black-bodied with no trace of pattern or light markings, it
may have a tarsal comb but only if it belongs to the genera *Dipoena* (Plate 21,
p. 268), *Robertus* (Plate 25, p. 293), *Pholcomma* (p. 295), *Theonoe* (p. 295) or
the species *Enoplognatha thoracica* (p. 290); continue in the main text if the
specimen matches. If it is none of these, it is a 'money spider' (part of the
family Linyphiidae) so go straight to p. 345. Although the above is a diversion
from the key, it is worth pursuing since it will acquaint you with two very
common pitfalls at the outset.

16.   Labium with the front margin rather
        swollen and sausage-like. The
        single species has a highly
        characteristic appearance
        (Plate 25 *Nesticus*
        cellulanus) and genitalia
        which are easily
        identified with a lens

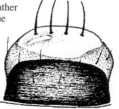

NESTICIDAE p. 296

Labium with the front
  margin not, or hardly,
  swollen

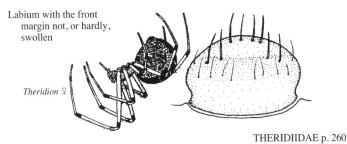

Theridion ♀

THERIDIIDAE p. 260

17. Maxillae much longer than broad (since they often project
      ventrally, you may need to view them slightly from
      behind). Most species spin orb webs; some spin no web as
      adults   TETRAGNATHIDAE p. 298

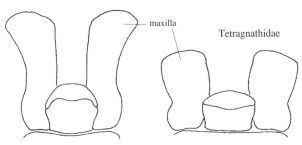

maxilla

Tetragnathidae

Maxillae not, or scarcely, longer than broad   18

18. Small spider (adults 1.5–3mm); abdomen globular, almost
      completely spherical; distinctly silver with reticulations
      and other marks. Femur I, viewed from the side, twice as
      thick as femur IV. A single rare species (Plate 25
      Theridiosoma gemmosum). (Check maturity and *all*
      characters; small spiderlings of some orb-weavers bear
      some resemblance and other species may have *some* of
      these features.) Web is a horizontal orb web pulled taut
      so that it resembles an umbrella turned inside out (p. 68).
                                          THERIDIOSOMATIDAE p. 297

    Spider, although perhaps with some of these characters, not
      having them all   19

19. Viewed from in front, clypeus height generally less than
     twice the diameter of an anterior eye (except in *Cercidia
     prominens*, Plate 28). Chelicerae usually with a lateral
     condyle but no stridulating ridges. Tarsi with three claws
     and auxiliary foot claws (see 12, above) Spinners of orb
     webs

ARANEIDAE p. 310

lateral condyle

Araneidae

Viewed from in front, clypeus height generally greater than
twice the diameter of an anterior eye (except in *Tapinopa
longidens* and *Poeciloneta variegata*, Plate 30).
Chelicerae often with stridulating ridges laterally, but no
lateral condyle. Tarsi with three claws, but no auxiliary
foot claws. Some species have a clear abdominal pattern
and spin sheet webs which they run on the underside of;
others have a unicolorous grey-black abdomen ('money
spiders') and some of these spin tiny sheet webs.

LINYPHIIDAE p. 339

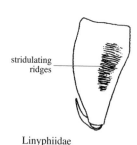

stridulating
ridges

Linyphiidae

Egg Sacs

Once the female has laid a batch of eggs, an attempt is made to protect them from the elements, and from predators and parasites. Perhaps the simplest protection is given in *Scytodes* (p. 93) and *Pholcus* (p. 98) where the female ties the eggs in a loose bundle of fine threads and carries them around. These spiders live inside buildings and are not exposed to the elements. Other species, with a nomadic lifestyle, make substantial silk egg sacs which they carry around with them. Such sacs may be opened periodically and given fluid from the mother's mouth; they may also be turned regularly, oriented towards the sun if in need of heat, and finally may be opened by the female to allow the spiderlings to escape. In the Lycosidae (Plates 16–18, p. 209) the egg sac is attached to the spinners and, later, the newly hatched spiderlings spend their first week of life clustered together on their mother's abdomen. The Pisauridae (Plate 19, p. 236) carry their large egg sac under the front of the body, holding it with chelicerae and palps. Before the young hatch, their mother spins a silk nursery tent (see Webs p. 66), hangs the sac up inside, and stands guard near the base. Later, she opens the sac when the young are ready to emerge. Some nocturnal wanderers and tube-dwellers make their egg sacs within the tube or a silken cell and remain with the sac until the young emerge, often caring for them until they themselves die. Many other species (e.g. of the families Zoridae, Oxyopidae, Thomisidae) fasten their egg sacs down and stand guard over them. Many of the Theridiidae guard their egg sacs or roll them about; many such sacs are pale and spherical, some coloured blue or strangely shaped (Plate 25). *Theridion bimaculatum* and the tiny *Theridion bellicosum* both carry their relatively huge white egg sac attached to the spinners, as does *Nesticus cellulanus* (Nesticidae, p. 296). Many of the Linyphiidae may be found with their egg sacs which, again, vary in shape, size and number; some are plastered down in the form of a flat sheet, others spherical and woolly and some papery with a fried-egg shape. Many are abandoned, the female laying several batches in different sites. Some of the Araneidae guard their egg sacs for a while, but many females die in the autumn, soon after laying, and the eggs are left unattended until they hatch the following spring. It follows then that some egg sacs are identifiable by means of the female which is carrying or guarding them. Other sacs may have been abandoned deliberately, or the female may have died. Many of these are not particularly distinctive and cannot be reliably identified unless the eggs are hatched and reared. However, a number of egg sacs, some deliberately abandoned, have a highly distinctive appearance and are identifiable, at least to genus level, in the field. Indeed, the egg sacs of *Ero* and *Agroeca* are more often seen than the spiders.

Species of *Clubiona* (p. 124) have a highly characteristic way of folding a leaf tip to form a strong foundation structure for their silken cell. Although the female is

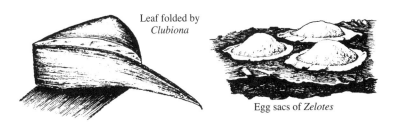

Leaf folded by
Clubiona

Egg sacs of *Zelotes*

always sealed in the cell with her egg sac, she will usually make a very rapid escape if the cell is opened.

The egg sacs of *Zelotes* (p. 110) are usually found stuck down under stones. They have a characteristic dome or nipple shape with crinkled edges and the female smooths and consolidates the outer layers, using the chelicerae and digestive juices, to give a papery appearance. The female usually remains with the egg sacs but, as with *Clubiona*, runs off at high speed as soon as the stone is lifted.

The stalked egg sacs of *Agroeca* (p. 136) are more commonly seen than the spiders, despite the fact that they are usually camouflaged with earth particles. The female spins a thick silk stalk attached to vegetation and then broadens this out to form a platform and walls. The eggs are laid in this cavity and the sac completed, a separate lower chamber being left for the moulting spiderlings. When finished, the sacs themselves are white, appearing like an inverted wineglass in some species, or more elongate in others. However, unless disturbed, the female will repeatedly carry particles of earth up the plant stem and stick them on to the sac until it is thoroughly plastered and brown.

Egg sacs with a much longer, thinner stalk are made by species of *Ero* (p. 257); *E. cambridgei* and *E. furcata* make spherical or pear-shaped sacs, whilst those of *E. tuberculata* are more elongate. As with *Agroeca*, they are more often seen than the spiders and occur in a wide variety of situations such as on vegetation, the underside of overhanging rocks and on the bark of trees. The egg sacs themselves are of whitish or beige silk, but outside this is a tangle of coarse, wiry silk which is yellow or reddish in colour. The thickness of this looped wiry covering, results from many strands being fused together. The construction of the stalk is puzzling in some cases. Egg sacs which hang

Egg sacs of *Agroeca* and *Ero*

Agroeca   with earth particles

Ero

vertically on a long thin stalk are merely following gravity. The construction of those with short thick stalks at a considerable angle is easy to fathom (and in some cases the vegetation may have moved after construction). But *Ero* sometimes produces sacs on a thin, springy stalk sticking straight out horizontally from tree trunks.

The diminutive *Theridiosoma* (p. 297) makes tiny egg sacs (2–3mm) with thin stalks which are usually fairly long. These are often suspended on vegetation much higher up than the web, which is amongst low plants.

Tetragnatha females (p. 301) attach their egg sacs to leaves, usually near water. Whilst the underlying silk is whitish, this is topped with knobbly greyish-green silk and looks like mould or a fragment of bird-droppings.

The huge flask-shaped sac of *Argiope* (p. 338) is brown, with an uneven papery surface. The upper part is made first, by spinning a disc of silk, extending it downwards and creating a shallow cylinder. The female, hanging upside down, fills this with the mass of eggs which are then covered with silk. Outside this she applies further coverings of silk, fashioned into the flask shape, which turn brownish. Usually the female and her web will be close by, but sacs are sometimes found alone.

Particularly common by the sea shore are the egg sacs of *Erigone arctica* ('money spiders', p. 345). These appear like miniature fried eggs, and are pale pinkish-brown in colour with papery, crinkled edges. Clusters of them are fastened under stones, wood and other shoreline debris and may be periodically submerged in sea water.

A selection of other egg sacs

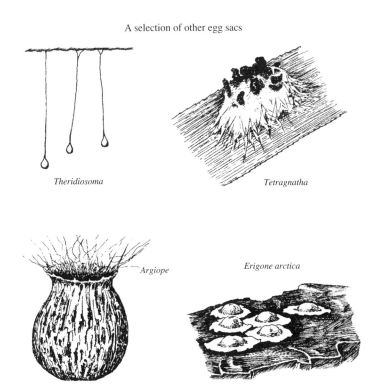

Theridiosoma

Tetragnatha

Argiope

Erigone arctica

Finally, although the abandoned egg sacs of some Araneidae are fairly unremark-able spherical structures, the emergence of the spiderlings of *Araneus diadematus* (p. 317) on a warm spring day is commonly followed by a flurry of interest. The fuzzy ball of orange spiders, with black triangles on their backs, appears to 'explode' and disappear on the slightest disturbance as the nursery cluster scatters radially.

Spiderlings of *Araneus diadematus* clustered in a ball (top) which on a slight disturbance 'explodes' and disappears (bottom) as spiderlings disperse radially

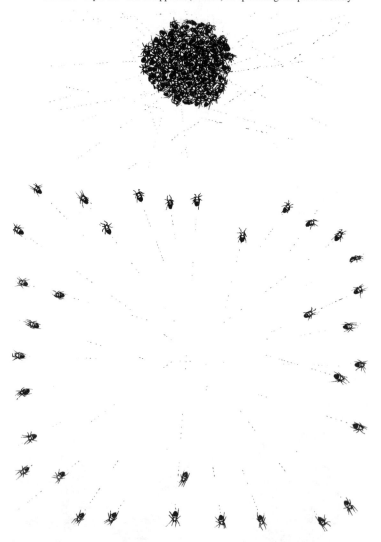

Webs

General Introduction

Apart from the construction of webs, spiders use silk in a variety of other ways: for the production of egg sacs (p. 57); for wrapping and immobilizing prey; for constructing retreats in which to shelter, moult or lay eggs; for air travel (p. 20); for sperm webs (p. 22); as safety lines when jumping, or dropping to escape; in draglines marked with pheromones (p. 19). Silk is a protein substance in the form of very fine threads of high tensile strength, and is produced by the spinners. The different silk glands, within the abdomen, produce several types of silk which may be variously combed, polished or provided with adhesive droplets. When silk strands are severed, as when detaching strands or removing a portion of web, this is achieved by the action of digestive juices produced from the mouthparts, rather than by cutting. These juices are sometimes used to fuse silk threads as in polishing or toughening the surface of egg sacs. The protein of silk can be rapidly recycled by the spider and this is particularly important for those species building orb webs with adhesive threads. Orb webs are quickly damaged by flying prey and bad weather, and the droplets of glue lose their adhesiveness after a day or two. The old web is eaten before a new one is made and, whilst this often occurs each night or early morning, fresh construction can be seen at any time of day when webs are damaged. Cribellate silk remains adhesive for much longer and in genera such as *Amaurobius*, the web is a permanent structure which is extended a little further each night. Many of the sheet weavers have permanent webs which may be gradually extended. They suffer much less damage, since prey either falls or crawls on to the sheet, and any holes are simply patched up.

The webs described below are silken constructions which act, with one exception, specifically as snares for prey. They show great variation in structure, are constructed in a wide variety of situations and allow the capture of diverse prey, which may be flying, crawling, jumping, large, small, diurnal or nocturnal. Within a given species, no two webs are ever the same; even the webs of an individual will vary and depend on the nature and extent of the surrounding support and the age of the individual.

When looking at webs in the field, two items of equipment are sometimes useful. Firstly, a plant-mister (capable of producing a very fine spray) is of value for revealing fine webs which might otherwise escape notice, and for showing up the full extent of web structures. Secondly, a tuning-fork is useful when spiders are ensconced in tubes or retreats; touching the web with the vibrating prongs will mimic prey activity, and frequently cause the spider to appear.

The Webs

Atypus (Atypidae p. 76) digs a hole up to 50cm deep which is lined with silk. This extends above the surface to form a silken tube, about 8cm long, which is tethered at its tip by a few silk strands and covered with particles of earth. It resembles a half buried root and is very difficult to spot at first; if you find one, then in all probability there will be others around. Free draining, light or sandy soil is essential, usually on unshaded, south-facing slopes. The part underground is often extended and may come to resemble a sock, with a heel and foot. Well-used or disturbed tubes sometimes have the aerial portion lying completely flat on the ground. Prey crawling or landing on the tube is seized from within, the spider's fangs piercing the tube wall

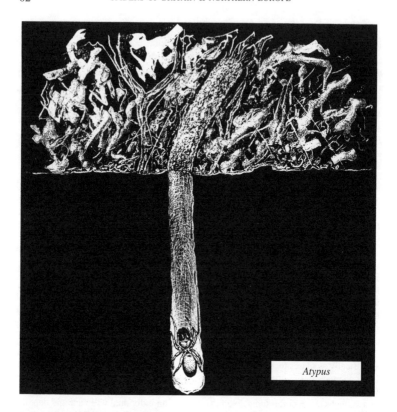

Atypus

and grabbing and stabbing the victim. The bruised and subdued prey is then pulled into the tube and the hole patched up.

Eresus (Eresidae p. 78) excavates a short, silk-lined burrow, usually on south-facing heathery slopes. On the surface, a roof-like sheet of bluish cribellate silk extends from one side of the tube margin to the ground and surrounding vegetation.

Amaurobius (Amaurobiidae p. 78) webs are very commonly seen around holes in walls, fence-posts and the bark of trees. The irregular lace-like threads are added to each night and are distinctly bluish when fresh. The woolly, cribellate silk produced by the cribellum (p. 41) is combed out and laid on to single strands. Visit the web at night with a torch to see this operation; try a tuning fork in the daytime to see the spider. The adhesive nature of these cribellate webs can be compared with Velcro, or goosegrass on your jumper, the prey providing the hooks and spines. *Titanoeca* (Titanoecidae p. 81) webs are similar, but are found at ground level under stones and amongst leaf-litter and other detritus.

Dictyna (Dictynidae p. 83) spins less obviously cribellate silk and the commonest species are found in webs on dry, dead heads of vegetation. Other species are found on the walls of buildings or amongst detritus on the sea shore. Other members of the family make webs on the living leaves of bushes and trees.

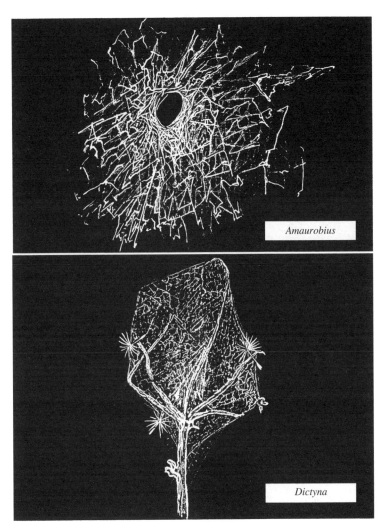

Amaurobius

Dictyna

Oecobius (Oecobiidae p. 89) also spins cribellate silk, but the web, about 30mm in diameter, is more noteworthy for its circular or star-shaped appearance and is made, indoors, on flat surfaces or in corners. The spider sits on the surface, under cover of the web and, when disturbed or catching prey, runs extremely quickly.

Hyptiotes (Uloboridae p. 90) is commonly called the 'triangle spider' because of the shape of its web. The four long threads forming the triangle are joined by a series of threads which have fuzzy cribellate silk applied to them. The thread from the apex of the triangle is held taut by the spider on a nearby twig. Prey hitting the triangle

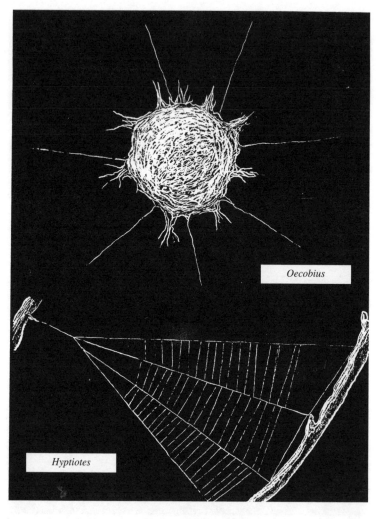

Oecobius

Hyptiotes

becomes increasingly entangled as the spider repeatedly slackens and tightens the structure and gradually advances to wrap the insect securely. In the same family of cribellate spiders, *Uloborus* (p. 90) spins a more or less horizontal orb web with adhesive, fuzzy silk applied to the spirals. In addition, there is usually an irregular white band of silk across the web each side of the hub which is commonly called a 'stabilimentum'. The spider hangs upside down at the hub in line with the stabilimentum and is thus effectively camouflaged.

Segestria (Segestriidae p. 96) has a tubular retreat in holes in walls and the bark of trees and within piles of stones and logs. From the opening of the retreat a

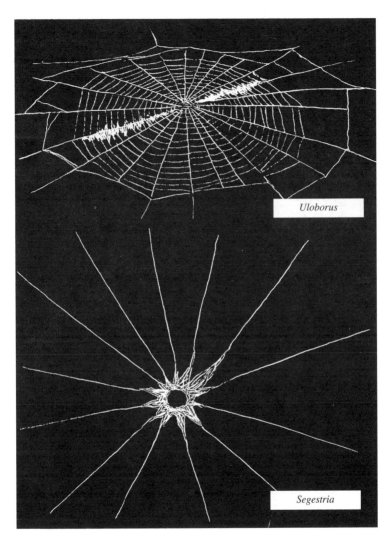

Uloborus

Segestria

number of strong threads extend radially and act as signal lines from potential prey to the spider within.

Pholcus (Pholcidae p. 98) spins a three-dimensional web of fine criss-cross threads inside houses, often in corners at ceiling level. The spider hangs upside down and if disturbed will shake and gyrate so rapidly as to become but a blur. *Psilochorus* also spins an open tangled web, often in cellars; over time, and with use and the continued addition of threads, a sheet develops in the web.

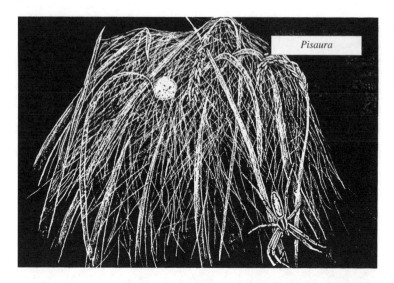

Pisaura

Pisaura (Pisauridae p. 236) is a hunter and does not spin a web for snaring prey. However, the nursery tent built by the female is so large, conspicuous and common that it seems wise to include it here. The egg sac is hung up in the tent and the female stands guard on the outside. Later on, the tent will contain spiderlings and the remnants of the egg sac. *Dolomedes* makes a similar tent but is a far less common species.

The Agelenidae (p. 240) have a tubular retreat from which extends a collar or sheet. *Tegenaria* and *Agelena* make large sheets which are sometimes slightly funnelled. In *Agelena* there are many vertical threads above the sheet which arrest flying or jumping prey. The spiders run on the upper surface of the sheet and their tarsal trichobothria seem to enable them to 'hear' prey or potential predators even before the web is actually touched. *Coelotes* also has a silken tubular retreat but usually this is surrounded only by a collar of white silk. Since the species lives right down at ground level, under stones and logs, a sheet might be difficult to produce anyway. Occasionally, when the ground has sloped suddenly below the retreat, I have seen the collar extended to form a small sheet. *Textrix* is extremely versatile in its use of different habitats and the webs made are a reflection of this. If undisturbed, in a corner indoors, it can make a large funnelled sheet from one side of a long retreat. On a barn floor with a thin covering of straw it makes a short, vertical retreat with a sheet-like collar symmetrically around the opening. In holes in walls the sheet is much smaller and asymmetrical, or absent. A variety of web shapes are made on vegetation but a tube is always present. On the sea shore or on scree there may be no web, and almost everywhere else the species is commonly found running rapidly in sunshine looking every bit like a wolf-spider with long spinners.

Most Theridiidae (p. 260) spin a tangled three-dimensional web of some description. Some (e.g. *Episinus* p. 261) have a very reduced web, and others (e.g. *Dipoena, Euryopis, Robertus*) either hunt and throw silk over the victim or rely on a very small number of random threads to alert them to the presence of prey. Some of these threads may have sticky droplets at the end; prey caught on these droplets struggles,

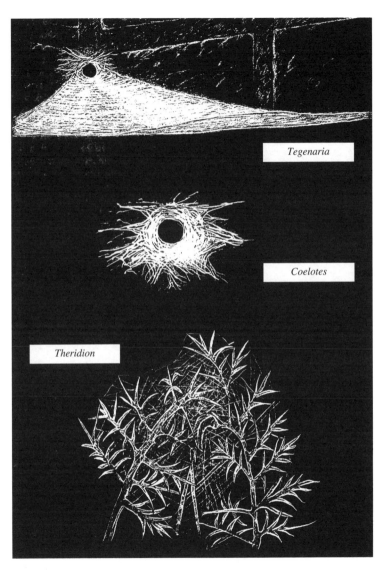

Tegenaria

Coelotes

Theridion

breaks the lower attachment of the silk strand and finds itself suspended in mid-air. Other genera use a larger number of these gummed threads attached loosely to the ground. Many species of *Theridion* spin a considerable tangle of criss-cross threads which, with use, may develop into quite a dense structure centrally and usually incorporates a retreat for egg-laying. The full extent and complexity of many

of these webs can be difficult to see, except on damp mornings. Using a plant mister causes the whole structure to emerge like magic.

Theridiosoma (Theridiosomatidae p. 297) makes a small orb web, the radii of which are joined in groups of two or three before converging at the centre. The spider sits at the centre, facing away from the web, holding the central suspending thread taut. The whole web is pulled up into the shape of an umbrella turned inside-out.

The Tetragnathidae (p. 298) all spin orb webs, with the exception of *Pachygnatha* which are ground-living and only spin webs as juveniles. The main characteristic of these webs lies in the hub, which has a hole in the centre. This hole is made by the spider neatly removing the central knot of silk (formed by the ends of the radii during construction) with its mouthparts; the size of hole usually corresponds to the span of the third and fourth pair of legs. This takes literally a couple of seconds and is carried out as soon as the web is completed, the spider then taking up a position in the centre of the web. If the spider is disturbed during these last moments, the hub may be left intact and not removed later. The webs of tetragnathids, particularly *Meta*, thus do occasionally have closed knotty hubs, but these are unlike the spun lattice in the centre of araneid webs. There is no specially strengthened signal line leading to a retreat, but a spider which has been moving frequently in and out of the web may have beaten a regular path along a thread to the underside of a nearby leaf. The webs of

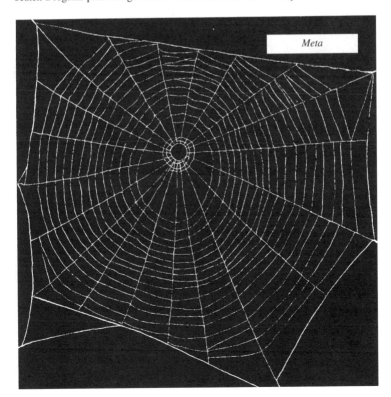

Meta

Tetragnatha species and those of *Meta merianae* are very fine, open structures with relatively few radii and widely spaced spirals. They are usually found near water, or at least in damp areas (shaded, damp areas in the case of *M. merianae*). They are built at night, and seem principally to catch small gnats and other Nematocera which emerge from the water in swarms. Whilst I have seen spiderlings of *Tetragnatha* rush into the web to catch tiny insects and adults to attack larger insects, the swarms of gnats sometimes found plastered to an adult's web seem to attract little or no attention from the occupant. The chelicerae of adult *Tetragnatha* are greatly enlarged for their role in mating perhaps making it both difficult and impractical to deal with such small prey items individually. The web seems here to be functioning as a trawl net, the whole lot eventually being hauled in and the silk protein plus gnats digested together. The webs of *Meta segmentata* and *M. mengei* have more radii and spirals and are rather small when compared with the size of the spider. They may be found in great abundance almost anywhere, if there are adequate structures to support a web, and the spider will usually be seen in the centre of the web with the four hind legs spanning the hole. *M. mengei* generally occurs in spring/summer, *M. segmentata* in summer/autumn; 'm' before 's' conveniently commits this to memory.

The Araneidae (p. 310) all spin orb webs, (mostly almost vertical, occasionally horizontal), usually with a stronger signal thread leading from the hub to a retreat situated

Araneus

above and to one side. The spider waits in the retreat with a front leg on the signal thread. Those species which add a camouflaging band of silk to the web wait for prey at the hub in line with the band. Once the araneid web is completed, the central knot of threads is removed, as in the Tetragnathidae, but the hole is then filled with a lattice of threads; *Cercidia prominens* is an exception and leaves the hub open; both this species and *Zilla diodia* sit in the centre of the web and there is no signal thread. The webs of *Araneus* are often very large, particularly in relation to the size of the spider and in most species there are many radii and close-set spirals. There is a free area between the hub and the main spirals, the threads of the latter having sticky droplets along their length. *Araniella* species spin smaller orb webs but, when spun within the convexity of a single leaf, they may be much smaller, of fewer threads, and hardly describable as an orb. *Zygiella* species spin a highly characteristic web with an open sector, completely free of spirals. (The spider turns to spin the spiral in the opposite direction each time it reaches this area.) Within this sector, a strong signal thread passes to the retreat. The webs of *Zygiella x-notata* are the easiest to find since they occur on the outside of most window frames and are spun at all times of the year. A tuning fork will usually summon the occupant. *Zygiella atrica* spins a similar web on vegetation, but the slightest

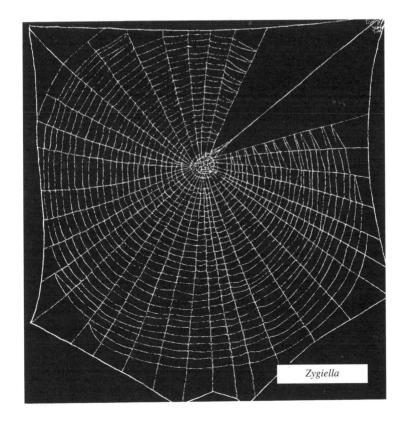

Zygiella

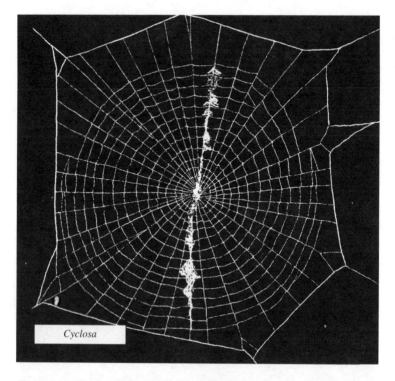

Cyclosa

disturbance will cause the spider to drop down rapidly from its retreat on a silk line. Other species spin their webs on tree trunks or rock faces and it is clear that the free sector is necessary because of the two-dimensional nature of the support. *Zygiella atrica* may partly or completely fill the free sector with silk. This seems mainly to occur in the autumn, when retreats with egg sacs are placed further back in vegetation and the signal thread runs backwards and clear of the spiral. The web of *Cyclosa conica* is usually found on evergreen foliage in shaded spots and usually has an irregular band of silk running across it with the spider sitting inconspicuously at the centre. Some of these webs, often in sheltered situations, seem to have a relatively long life, and the spider gradually adds undigested fragments of prey to this 'stabilimentum'. *Argiope* builds a much larger web, amongst grasses and other low vegetation, which has a zig-zag band of silk and more elaborate silking of the hub region.

The Linyphiidae (p. 339) spin sheet webs which differ from those of the Agelenidae in that, firstly, they have no retreat and, secondly, that the spider runs upside-down on the lower surface. Some of the money spiders spin tiny sheets over the slightest depression in the ground. *Tapinopa* spins a large sheet near ground level which looks as though slugs have traversed it and many other linyphiids spin sheets near ground level or in low vegetation. *Drapetisca socialis* spins a web, on the bark of trees, which is so incredibly fine as to be invisible; all one can make out is that the spider's legs are not quite touching the bark; the species also hunts on bark. The most

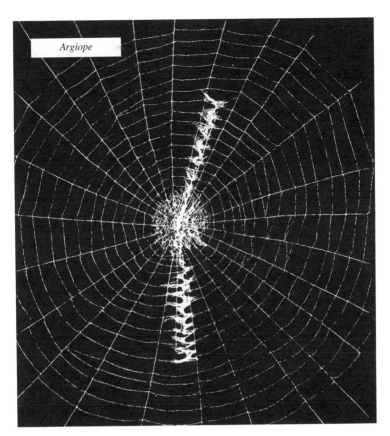

Argiope

common and conspicuous web of all must be that of the ubiquitous *Linyphia trian-gularis* which, in summer and autumn, must surely occur on every shrub and tree in the region. Larger webs are very slightly domed and, above the sheet, there are numerous vertical and scaffolding threads. Prey hitting these threads drops on to the sheet and is grabbed by the spider from below. The much rarer *Neriene radiata* spins a remarkably domed sheet with a dense superstructure of fine, criss-cross threads.

Whilst in the vast majority of cases the occupant of any web will also be its maker, there are exceptions. Misting a gorse or holly bush in summer or autumn will reveal a vast number of different webs, all in close proximity and with adjacent threads intermingling. One is left wondering how the spiders keep within their own web territory. Sometimes they stray and occasionally steal from other webs, and complex interactions occur between species. Prey stealing is most easily observed with *Theridion sisyphium*, a species very commonly found alongside *Linyphia triangularis*. The irregular threads of the theridiid web may frequently invade the

Linyphia triangularis

Neriene radiata

superstructure of a *Linyphia* web below. Although the *Linyphia* keeps to the underside of its web, the *Theridion* and its young frequently descend to take prey caught in threads just above the sheet. The *Linyphia* also frequently benefits when prey, temporarily caught in a *Theridion* web, drops down on to its sheet. The tiny, pink *Oonops pulcher* is frequently found in the webs of *Amaurobius fenestralis* where it catches small insects as well as scavenging on the remains of larger prey. Pirate spiders of the genus *Ero* specialize in deliberately and aggressively invading the webs of other spiders, surreptitiously mimicking the activity of prey, and then attacking the web owner.

Web Construction

No account has yet been given of the methods of web construction and many people ask how, in particular, an orb web is made. In the briefest account possible, the orb weaver forms a bridge line, either by trailing silk or floating it until it catches on something. This is then reinforced and, from its midpoint, another strand is dropped and pulled taut to form a Y-shape. This Y constitutes the hub and three radii; it is then framed and more radii added. A widely spaced temporary spiral is started at the hub and continued to the periphery of the web. From the periphery, the spider retraces its steps, using the temporary spiral as a guide, and lays down the sticky spiral, usually more closely spaced than the first one. The direction of the spiral may change occasionally and it stops short of the hub, leaving a free zone. Aggregations of silk at the hub are then removed and the hole is either left or filled with silk. The extreme brevity of the above account is a quite deliberate attempt to get the reader to investigate further – maybe by reading some of the books listed in the Bibliography (p. 375), but preferably by *watching webs being made*!

SUB-ORDER ORTHOGNATHA (MYGALOMORPHAE)

The name Orthognatha means 'straight jawed' and refers to the chelicerae which project straight forwards from the carapace. At rest, the fangs are folded in line with the long axis of the body; they open and move in a vertical plane, the action being rather like that of a pick-axe. Indeed, many species use the chelicerae for digging burrows, as well as for grabbing, piercing and crushing prey. Members of this sub-order are commonly referred to as mygalomorphs, and the large hairy mygalomorphs are the so-called 'tarantulas' – now frequently seen in pet shops. Hairy mygalomorphs (Theraphosidae), trap-door spiders (Ctenizidae) and funnel-web mygalomorphs (Dipluridae) are native to warmer, mostly tropical areas and the sub-order is represented in our region only by the purse-web spiders (Atypidae). In addition to the chelicerae, other features shared by these spiders include three-segmented posterior spinners and two pairs of book lungs.

FAMILY ATYPIDAE

Genus *Atypus*

Two members of the Atypidae occur in the region, both in the genus *Atypus*; illustrations of the main characters appear in the Family Key (p. 40). The common name of 'purse-web spider' is misleading in that the web (p. 62) is more like a sock, partly buried in a deep hole with a shorter, closed tube of silk above ground. The aerial portion of the tube is camouflaged with earth particles and has the appearance of a partly buried root. Prey landing on this is seized from within and pulled into the tube. Most of the spider's life is spent within the tube and wandering activity is confined largely to dispersing spiderlings and adult males searching for the tubes of females. Spiderlings take about four years to reach maturity; females may then live for several years longer. The adult male seeks out the tube of a female, taps on the walls and, if the female is receptive, is allowed inside. Mating occurs, in the autumn, within the tube and the spiders cohabit for a few months, until the male dies and is eaten. The egg sac is strung up in the tube and the eggs hatch the next summer; the spiderlings eventually disperse in the following spring. The general appearance of these spiders is such that even small spiderlings can easily be assigned to the genus.

Atypus affinis Eichwald 1830   Plate 1
Description ♀, 10–15mm (to 18mm including chelicerae); ♂, 7–9mm (to 12mm with chelicerae). Male has relatively longer legs and a much slimmer abdomen; the

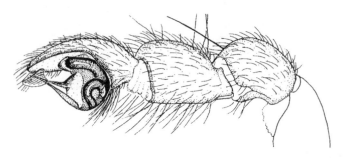

latter has a dorsal scutum covering the anterior two-thirds. In both sexes the posterior spinners are of three roughly equal segments. No epigyne. Male palpal organs relatively small.

Habitat Within tubular web (p. 62), the greater part of which is underground. Friable sandy or chalky soil is necessary to allow burrowing; south-facing slopes with unshaded low vegetation are preferred. The species is often found in substantial colonies. **Maturity** Females adult throughout the year; males in autumn.

Distribution Mainly southern England; rarer and more local further north, but has been recorded from Scotland. Widespread in Europe as far north as Denmark.

△ *Atypus piceus* (Sulzer 1776)
Description Very similar to *A. affinis* but usually a little darker. Both sexes distinguished by long terminal segment of posterior spinners which is longer than the other two segments together. Male palpal organs are an additional aid to identification.
Habitat and Maturity Similar to *A. affinis*
Distribution Absent from Britain. Probably widespread in Europe; recorded from Holland, France and Germany.

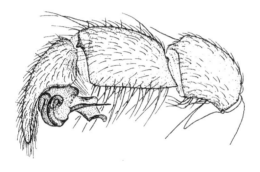

SUB-ORDER LABIDOGNATHA (ARANEOMORPHAE)

All other spiders in the region belong to this sub-order and have chelicerae which operate in a pincer-like fashion. Three groups are generally recognized for purposes of identification:

Cribellate spiders (which have a cribellum and a calamistrum) includes the families Eresidae, Amaurobiidae, Titanoecidae, Dictynidae, Oecobiidae, and Uloboridae.

Haplogyne spiders (which have only six eyes, simple male palpal organs and no epigyne in adult females) includes the families Oonopidae, Scytodidae, Dysderidae and Segestriidae.

Entelegyne spiders (which have eight eyes, more complex male palpal organs and an epigyne in adult females) constitute all the other families in the region.

FAMILY ERESIDAE

Genus *Eresus*

Only one species, *Eresus cinnaberinus*, occurs in the region. Illustrations of the main characters appear in the Family Key (p. 41). The name 'ladybird spider', recently imposed on the species, relates only to the adult male; the 'lady' is black and velvety, as are subadult males. The web is a silk-lined tube in the ground with a roof of cribellate silk (p. 62) in which the spiders remain. Only spiderlings and adult males are likely to be found wandering. Like *Atypus,* the species is slow to mature and females are long-lived. The brightly coloured male has a very short adult life.

Eresus cinnaberinus (Olivier 1789) (=*E. niger* (Petagna))　　　　　　　Plate 1
Description ♀, 8–16mm; ♂, 6–11mm. Both sexes, and immatures, are easily recognised by the large domed head and the arrangement of the eyes. Adult males are particularly conspicuous. British specimens lack the red hairs on legs III and IV. Examination of genitalia unnecessary.
Habitat South-facing, sheltered, heathery slopes in an excavated, silk-lined tube with a roof of cribellate silk.
Maturity Females throughout the year, males in autumn and spring.
Distribution Protected by law in Britain; very rare, and rediscovered in one Dorset site in 1979. Also rare in Europe, but occurs as far north as Denmark.

FAMILY AMAUROBIIDAE

Genus *Amaurobius*

Five species occur in the region, all in the genus *Amaurobius*. (One of the species is sometimes assigned to the genus *Callobius*).The main characters of the family are illustrated in the Family Key (p. 42). The cribellum is divided in two by a fine ridge and the calamistrum on metatarsus IV has two rows of bristles. Both of these structures are reduced or absent in adult males. Ranging in size from 4 to 15mm, all species spin lacy webs of cribellate silk (see Webs, p. 63) which is combed by the calamistrum and laid on to monofilament threads. This flocculent silk is faintly blue when fresh; insect spines and hairs adhere to it strongly. Most species construct a retreat within holes in walls and tree bark, with the web extending around the entrance; they and other species also occur under stones and logs and in leaf-litter. All species are nocturnal in their web spinning; visiting the webs with a torch at night will provide a demonstration of the method used. Prey is captured at all times of the day and a tuning fork usually elicits a good response. Males mature in late summer and autumn and wander in search of females. Having located a web, the male will strum the threads rapidly with the palps; some species vibrate the abdomen as well. Eggs are laid in a sac within the retreat; females frequently die and are eaten by the spiderlings before they disperse. Males have a slimmer abdomen and longer legs than females, but the abdominal patterns are similar in both sexes. The species are broadly similar in general appearance but are easily separated, often with a hand lens, by the female epigynes and male palpal tibiae (viewed from outside or above). Overall size may also aid identification in some cases.

Amaurobius fenestralis (Stroem 1768)
Description ♀, 7–9mm; ♂, 4–7mm. Female illustrated above epigyne. Epigyne similar to that of *A.erberi*, but spermathecae not extending much beyond anterior

margin. Male palpal tibia, from above, with both apophyses more or less equally broad and blunt.

Habitat Bark of trees, fallen logs, leaf-litter, under stones and also on plants with stiff, dense foliage. Under bark, particularly of fallen logs, sometimes associated with colonies of *Oonops pulcher* (p. 91).

Maturity Females adult for most of the year, males in late summer and autumn.

Distribution Common and widespread throughout the region.

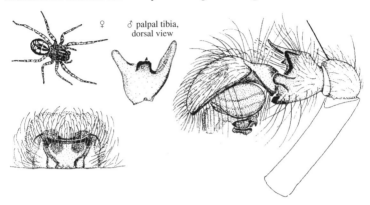

Amaurobius similis (Blackwall 1861)   Plate 1

Description ♀, 9–12mm; ♂, 6–8mm. Epigyne easily distinguished by dark sloping marks anteriorly. Male palpal tibia, from above, with one apophysis thin and curved, but of the same length as the other.

Habitat Holes in walls, fences, window frames, particularly in and around houses. Also occurs away from houses in similar situations to *A. fenestralis*.

Maturity Females adult for most of the year, males late summer and autumn.

Distribution Common and widespread throughout the region.

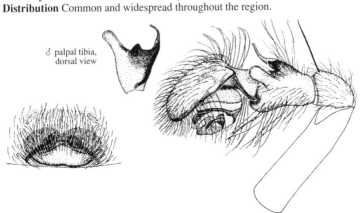

Amaurobius ferox (Walckenaer 1830)   Plate 1

Description ♀, 11–15mm; ♂, 8–10mm. Female similar to male but has larger abdomen and the markings may be very dusky and ill-defined. Central part of epigyne with a dark triangle pointing backwards. Male palpal organs conspicuously white, even to the naked eye. Palpal tibia with one apophysis broad and blunt, the other short and hooked.

Habitat Similar to *A. similis*, but more often under stones and logs in the north of the region.

Maturity Females found adult most of the year, males autumn and spring.

Distribution Widespread throughout the region, but less common than *A. similis* and *A. fenestralis*.

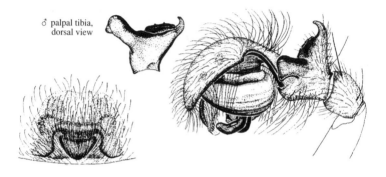

♂ palpal tibia, dorsal view

△ *Amaurobius erberi* (Keyserling 1863)

Description ♀, 8–11mm; ♂, 6–8mm. Very similar to *A. similis* and *A. fenestralis* in general appearance. Epigyne distinguished from that of *A. fenestralis* by the outlines of the spermathecae which extend well ahead of the anterior margin. Male palpal tibia similar to that of *A. similis* but, from above, the thin apophysis is longer. In most species there is a short, blunt apophysis between the longer ones; in *A. erberi* this is longer and joined to the outside apophysis so that the latter appears forked.

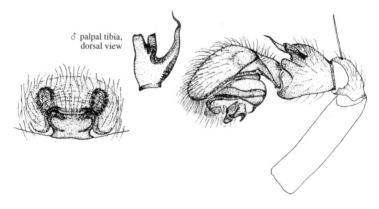

♂ palpal tibia, dorsal view

Habitat Generally under stones and logs and in leaf-litter.
Maturity Females probably throughout the year, males in autumn.
Distribution Absent from Britain, but could easily have been overlooked. Widespread in Europe.

△ *Amaurobius claustrarius* (Hahn 1833) (= *Callobius c.* (Hahn))
Description ♀, 9–12mm; ♂, 6–8mm. Female illustrated alongside epigyne and palp. Epigyne and male palpal tibia easily distinguished from the other species.
Habitat Usually under stones, more frequently on higher ground.
Maturity Autumn.
Distribution Absent from Britain. Widespread in Europe but only frequent on higher ground and mountains.

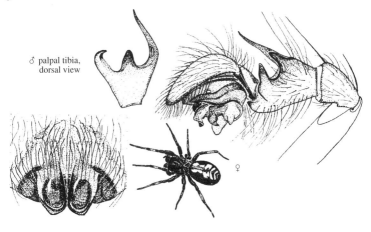

♂ palpal tibia, dorsal view

♀

△ FAMILY TITANOECIDAE
△ Genus *Titanoeca*

This family is represented in the region by two closely related species in the genus *Titanoeca*. These cribellate spiders have a calamistrum on metatarsus IV which comprises a single row of bristles and extends along most of its length. Females have a brownish abdomen with no markings; the male of one species is clearly marked with two pairs of white blotches. The spiders have a retreat under stones, in leaf-litter or on low vegetation and the open-meshed cribellate web extends around the opening. Males tug at the threads of the female's web to announce their presence prior to mating. The female remains with the egg sac in the retreat. The species are distinguishable by their genitalia (microscope), size, and male abdominal markings.

△ *Titanoeca quadriguttata* (Hahn 1833) (= *T. obscura* (Walckenaer))   Plate 1
Description ♀, 5–7mm; ♂, 4.5–5mm. Both sexes illustrated in colour. Larger than *T. psammophila*. Epigyne and male palpal organs distinctive as is the palpal tibia viewed from above.
Habitat Under stones and logs, amongst leaf-litter and in low vegetation.

Maturity Spring.
Distribution Absent from Britain. Widespread and common throughout Europe.

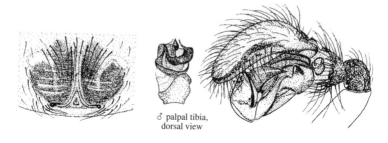

♂ palpal tibia,
dorsal view

△ *Titanoeca psammophila* Wunderich 1993
Description ♀ ♂, 3–4mm. This recently discovered species is smaller than *T. quadriguttata* and the males lack the paired white spots on the abdomen. Epigyne, palpal organs and palpal tibia easily distinguishable.
Habitat and Maturity Probably similar to *T. quadriguttata*.
Distribution Only recently discovered in SW Germany.

♂ palpal tibia,
dorsal view

FAMILY DICTYNIDAE

The cribellate spiders in this family are all less than 4mm in length and have a calamistrum on metatarsus IV comprising a single row of bristles. By far the commonest species belong to the genus *Dictyna*, of which seven are described. Three species of *Lathys* and three of *Nigma* are also included here. The genera *Argenna* and *Altella* are excluded from this guide, being mostly rare, small and indistinctly marked (they occur at ground level under stones). The commonest species within the family is *Dictyna arundinacea*. It spins a cribellate web in the heads of plants and on gorse bushes and heather (Webs, p. 63); it seems to prefer dry, dead vegetation or hard-leaved bushes. The dense weave of the cribellate web might well trap too much moisture if spun on rapidly transpiring leaves; this would encourage mould growth on the considerable number of prey remains and be a risk to the egg sacs. The web is a permanent structure which is added to daily and it becomes dense near the centre, where the retreat is made. The male vibrates his legs on the web and approaches to touch the female before mating; this takes place in the summer. Males have the inner margins of the chelicerae bowed outwards slightly and this allows grasping of the female chelicerae during mating. The two sexes spend several weeks together, until the male dies and is then sometimes eaten. The egg sacs are made within the web which, by this time, is full of all sorts of debris.

Key to the Genera

1.	Anterior median eyes roughly the same size as anterior laterals	2
	Anterior median eyes much smaller than anterior laterals	*Lathys* p. 87
2.	Carapace dark brown to black, marked with white hairs; abdomen brownish to black, often with a pattern, and light hairs which give a greyish bloom	*Dictyna* p. 83
	Carapace paler brown with light patches along the margins; abdomen yellow, green or red	*Nigma* p. 86

Genus *Dictyna*

The seven species described here are all small spiders with a brownish or black body patterned with light hairs. The hairs generally impart a greyish bloom but frequently get rubbed off as the spider ages. Because of this, and normal variation, abdominal patterns are not a very reliable guide to identification and examination of the genitalia is required. This is sometimes possible in the field using a spi-pot and ×20 lens or field microscope but the hairs may obscure the epigyne; with preserved specimens and a microscope identification is easy. The web is similar in all species and has already been discussed. The two sexes are very similar in general appearance (males having a smaller abdomen) and are often found together.

Dictyna arundinacea (Linnaeus 1758)   Plate 1
Description ♀, 2.5–3.5mm; ♂, 2–3mm. Epigyne with two shallow, circular openings which are relatively large and close together. Male palpal tibia with short bifid apophysis dorsally; a thick spiralled process points backwards from the palpal organs.
Habitat Web in heads of dry, often dead plants and on gorse and heather.
Maturity spring to late summer.
Distribution By far the commonest species of the genus. Widespread throughout the region.

Dictyna pusilla Thorell 1856
Description ♀, 1.5–2.5mm; ♂, 1.5–2mm. Small size of adults often helpful in identification. Epigyne openings relatively small, slightly oval and close together. Male

palpal tibia with a relatively long bifid apophysis dorsally; spiralled process arising from palpal organs smaller than in *D. arundinacea*.

Habitat and Maturity Very similar to *D. arundinacea*.

Distribution Rather uncommon throughout Britain and Europe; perhaps more frequent in the north of the region where it may be locally abundant.

Dictyna major Menge 1869

Description ♀, 3–3.5mm; ♂, 2.5–3mm. In both sexes, the dark midline mark in the front half of the abdomen is distinctly trifid at its posterior end. Relatively large size sometimes a useful guide to identification, as is the habitat. Epigyne openings small and close together with relatively long horizontal ridges on each side. Male palpal tibia with fairly blunt apophysis (arising near joint with patella) which bears two small, blunt projections.

Habitat Sandy shores, of sea or inland water, under dried seaweed and other detritus and amongst low vegetation; sometimes occurs at fairly high altitude along shores of lochs. **Maturity** Spring and summer.

Distribution Rare in Britain, only recorded from a very few localities in Scotland. Essentially a northern species (range extends to Greenland and Alaska) with a very local distribution in northern Europe.

Dictyna uncinata Thorell 1856

Description ♀, 2.25–2.75mm; ♂, 2–2.5mm. Very similar to *D. arundinacea*. Epigyne openings small and widely separated. Male palpal tibia with long, pointed, bifid dorsal apophysis arising near joint with patella; a second large blunt ventral apophysis arising near joint with cymbium.

Habitat and Maturity Very similar to *D. arundinacea*.

Distribution Fairly common and widespread throughout Britain and Europe but much less frequent in the north.

Dictyna latens (Fabricius 1775) Plate 1
Description ♀, 2.5–3.5mm; ♂, 2–2.5mm. Both sexes very dark brown to black with rows of white hairs on the carapace and white hairs on the sides of the abdomen forming a pattern. Epigyne with large, well-separated openings. Male palpal tibia with barely visible, bifid tooth-like projection dorsally; a small process points backwards from the palpal organs.
Habitat Most frequent on heather and gorse, but also on other low vegetation.
Maturity Spring and summer.
Distribution Uncommon but widespread in Britain; rare in the north. Also widespread in Europe, but rare or absent in the north.

△ *Dictyna civica* (Lucas 1850)
Description ♀, 3–3.5mm; ♂, 2.5–3mm. Resembles *D. arundinacea* in general appearance. Epigyne very distinctive. Male palpal tibia with short, bifid, tooth-like apophysis dorsally.
Habitat Greyish-blue cribellate web almost exclusively on walls of buildings.
Maturity Spring.
Distribution Absent from Britain. Widespread in Europe but not recorded from Scandinavia.

△ *Dictyna ammophila* Menge 1871

Description ♀ ♂, 1.5–2mm. Abdomen dark with little or no pattern. Epigyne very distinctive. Male palpal tibia with no apophyses; palpal organs of distinctive shape.
Habitat At ground level under stones, in detritus on sand dunes.
Maturity Spring and early summer.
Distribution Absent from Britain. Very local distribution, possibly throughout Europe.

Genus *Nigma*

These spiders were previously assigned to the genus *Heterodictyna*. Three species are described and all have a light or greenish-brown carapace with light patches around the margins. The abdomen is either yellow-green (sometimes marked with red) or entirely reddish in colour. They all occur on bushes and trees; the spiders are usually well camouflaged and the fairly insignificant cribellate web is often spun within a slightly curled leaf. Mating occurs in the summer; males have transverse ridges and swellings on the front of the chelicerae, near the base, which are held by the female chelicerae during mating. The genus is readily identified in the field, but separation of the species often requires microscopy. The colours fade on preservation.

Nigma puella (Simon 1870)   Plate 2

Description ♀, 2.5–3mm; ♂, 2–2.75mm. General appearance of both sexes highly characteristic, but males occasionally pale yellow. Epigyne ill-defined but with small, circular openings. Male palp has a relatively large tooth on the patella and the structures projecting back from the palpal organs are of characteristic shape.
Habitat Cribellate web on leaves of bushes and trees. **Maturity** Spring and summer.
Distribution Very locally distributed in the south of England and Wales. Apparently rare or absent from the rest of the region but recorded from southern Europe, Canaries and Madeira.

△ *Nigma flavescens* (Walckenaer 1830)

Description ♀, 2.5–3.5mm; ♂, 2.25–2.5mm. Carapace lacks the dark marks present in *N. puella* and the female abdomen lacks the distinct red spot or stripe. Abdomen of both sexes greyish-pink with lighter mottling and sometimes a series of larger pale spots. Epigyne very indistinct, but openings relatively closer to epigastric fold. Male palpal patella with smaller tooth than *N. puella* and structures of a slightly different shape projecting back from the palpal organs.

Habitat Mainly on foliage of low vegetation. **Maturity** Spring and summer.

Distribution Almost certainly absent from Britain; not rediscovered since the single record from Durham in 1909. Uncommon or rare in Europe and absent from the north of the region.

Nigma walckenaeri (Roewer 1951)

Description ♀, 4–5mm; ♂, 3–4mm. Females almost entirely green with light margins to the carapace and light hairs on the abdomen which form a vague pattern of chevrons and light sides. Males similar, but with yellow-brown carapace and legs. Epigyne with large, oval openings. Male palpal patella with very small tooth; structures projecting back from palpal organs of characteristic shape.

Habitat Web and retreat generally on fairly large leaves.

Maturity Summer and autumn.

Distribution Recorded only from the south-east of England where it has a very local distribution. Absent or rare in northern parts of Europe but frequent locally in southern parts of the region.

Genus *Lathys*

The three species described are small spiders with the anterior median eyes much smaller than the rest. The commonest species has clear black markings on the carapace and legs and is recognisable in the field. Examination of the genitalia requires a microscope. They spin small cribellate webs on vegetation or at ground level and little is known of their biology. Males are similar to females but have a smaller, slimmer abdomen.

Lathys humilis (Blackwall 1855)   Plate 2

Description ♀, 2–2.5mm; ♂, 1.75–2mm. The legs are very clearly annulated with black in this species. Epigyne and male palp distinctive; the palpal tibia is more easily distinguished from that of *L. nielseni* if viewed from above.

Habitat Cribellate web on bushes and trees with small, hard leaves (heather, gorse, box, yew). **Maturity** Spring and summer.
Distribution Rather locally distributed in England and Wales; commoner in the south, with very few records from Scotland. Widespread throughout Europe, but not recorded from Scandinavia.

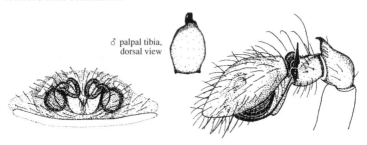

♂ palpal tibia, dorsal view

Lathys nielseni (Schenkel 1932)
Description ♀ ♂, 1.6–2mm. Appears like a pale, newly moulted specimen of *L. humilis*. Legs with only faint darkening at the ends of each segment. Epigyne easily distinguished from other species, but often rather pale. Apophysis on male palpal patella distinct from that of *L. humilis* when viewed from above.
Habitat Under stones and amongst leaf-litter, grass tussocks, moss etc. in damp habitats. **Maturity** Spring and summer.
Distribution Recorded from several sites in southern England. Possibly widespread in Europe with some records from high ground.

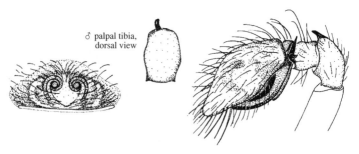

♂ palpal tibia, dorsal view

Lathys puta (O.P.-Cambridge 1863) (= *L. stigmatisata* (Menge))
Description ♀, 2.25–2.75mm; ♂, 2mm. Carapace with markings like those of *L. humilis*, but less well defined. Legs brownish with no markings. Abdomen greyish-brown with no clear pattern. Epigyne with a pair of closely set, circular openings. Male palpal patella with no apophysis; a spiralled process extends upwards and backwards from the palpal organs.
Habitat Under stones, often on dry land with sparse vegetation. (Note: any other small, uniformly coloured cribellates found under stones are likely to belong to the

genera *Argenna* and *Altella*.) **Maturity** Spring and summer.
Distribution Recorded from a very few sites, near the coast, in southern England.
Widely but locally distributed throughout most of Europe but rare or absent from
Scandinavia.

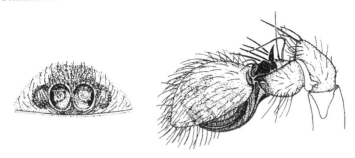

FAMILY OECOBIIDAE
Genus *Oecobius*

A single species of the family Oecobiidae, genus *Oecobius*, occurs in the region. It
is a cosmopolitan species, widely introduced throughout the world, and in cooler
regions lives inside buildings. The main characters of this cribellate species are given
in the Family Key (p. 41) and include the presence of a cribellum, a calamistrum on
metatarsus IV with a double row of bristles, and a large, two-jointed anal tubercle
fringed with long hairs. The web is flat, circular and about 30mm across; eventually
it assumes a star shape (Webs, p. 64). The spider runs very rapidly when disturbed.
For many years the species has been incorrectly identified as *Oecobius annulipes*
Lucas 1846, a closely similar species from Africa.

Oecobius navus Blackwall 1859 (**Not** *O. annulipes* Lucas) Plate 2
Description ♀ ♂, 2–2.5mm. This small spider has an unmistakable appearance even
to the naked eye; closer examination will reveal the other characteristic features and
the structure of the genitalia.
Habitat Indoors, in buildings and hothouses. Web (p. 64) made on flat surfaces or
corners of walls etc. The spider sits on the wall (or other surface) under cover of the
web and runs very rapidly out if catching prey or if disturbed.
Maturity Possibly all year.

spinners, cribellum and anal
tubercle from below

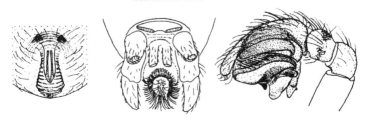

Distribution Known to be established in the Natural History Museum, London. It would be very surprising if this were the only colony in the country and it may have been overlooked elsewhere. This cosmopolitan species has been widely introduced throughout Europe but is only able to survive indoors.

FAMILY ULOBORIDAE

This cribellate family is represented in the region by just two species, in separate genera. The strange arrangement of the eyes and the calamistrum are illustrated in the Family Key (p. 42). The family is unique in having no poison glands; they rely completely on the cribellate silk and very elaborate wrapping to immobilise prey before feeding. The two genera spin entirely different snares which are also unique amongst spiders.

Genus *Uloborus*

Uloborus walckenaerius Latreille 1806   Plate 2

Description ♀, 3.5–6mm; ♂, 3–4mm. Both sexes illustrated in colour; eye arrangement illustrated in Family Key (p. 42). The carapace and abdomen are both furnished with white hairs; those on the abdomen form lines of tufts which curve upwards and are more easily seen in profile. Identifiable in the field with a lens; examination of the genitalia affords confirmation.

Habitat Spins horizontal orb web on low plants, particularly heather. Web (p. 65) has a band of silk running across it; the spider hangs below, at the hub, in line with the band of silk. **Maturity** Summer.

Distribution Rare and very locally distributed in southern England. Widespread but locally distributed in Europe and not recorded from Scandinavia.

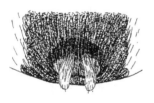 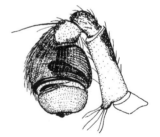

Genus *Hyptiotes*

Hyptiotes paradoxus (C.L. Koch 1834)   Plate 2

Description ♀, 5–6mm; ♂, 3–4mm. Both sexes illustrated in colour; eye arrangement illustrated in Family Key (p. 42). Colour usually ginger-brown but may be darker and some parts of the abdominal pattern may be black. Female has a very hunched appearance and there may be a pair of small tubercles on the upper part of the abdomen. Male palps quite remarkable in size. Easily identifiable with a lens.

Habitat Spins triangular snare on evergreen trees and shrubs (especially yew and box). Web (p. 64) is a triangle formed by four strands of silk with cribellate silk running across. A thread runs from the apex of the triangle and is held taut by the spider sitting on a nearby twig. Prey is entangled when the spider repeatedly slackens

and tightens the snare, finally advancing to wrap it securely.
Maturity Spring and summer.
Distribution Very locally distributed, mainly in southern England. Widespread but
local distribution in Europe, but rare or absent in the north of the region.

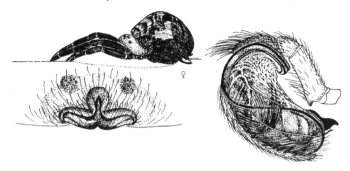

FAMILY OONOPIDAE
Genus *Oonops*

The two members of the Oonopidae are both small, pink spiders of the genus
Oonops. They have six oval eyes, closely arranged in a group which is almost as wide
as the head (see Family Key, p. 43). They are nocturnal wanderers and spend the daytime in a loose silken cell. Eggs are laid in the cell, just two to each batch. As with
all haplogyne spiders, there is no epigyne and the male palpal organs are simple. The
two sexes are very similar in general appearance. They have a highly characteristic
way of walking; a slow, groping, measured progression is suddenly interrupted by a
dash of great speed.

Oonops pulcher Templeton 1834   Plate 2
Description ♀ ♂, 1.2–2mm. Generally pink but may be paler, and yellowish, or
quite a deep red colour. Both sexes distinguished from *O. domesticus* by the four
pairs of ventral spines on the tibia of leg I. Male palpal organs with a long, fine embolus.
Habitat Under bark, stones and leaves, sometimes in the webs of *Amaurobius* and
Coelotes species. Only rarely found indoors. **Maturity** Spring to Autumn

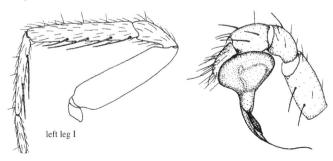

left leg I

Distribution Widespread but local distribution throughout Britain; may be abundant in some woodland sites. Widespread in Europe, but apparently not recorded from Scandinavia.

Oonops domesticus de Dalmas 1916
Description ♀ ♂, 1.2–2mm. Indistinguishable from *O. pulcher* in general appearance but both sexes have five pairs of ventral spines on tibia I. Male palpal organs with a simpler tip and no long embolus.
Habitat Within houses and other buildings. It may be found when renovating or even reroofing your house; otherwise its presence is established by getting up at 3 or 4a.m. and examining walls and ceilings. By a strange coincidence my first sight of *O. domesticus* in our present home was when illustrating the species, at 4a.m., and it ran across the illustration! **Maturity** Throughout the year.
Distribution Widespread throughout Britain and Europe.

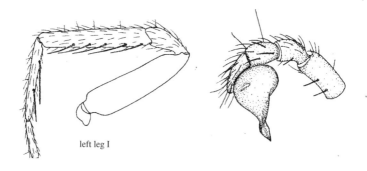

left leg I

FAMILY SCYTODIDAE

Genus *Scytodes*

The single species representing the family Scytodidae, genus *Scytodes*, is frequently called the 'spitting spider'. It has a highly characteristic appearance, one feature of which is the domed carapace. This accommodates a pair of enormous two-lobed glands, the front lobe producing poison, and the rear lobe a gummy glue substance. The glands are connected by ducts to the holes near the tip of each fang. By the sudden contraction of muscles, these glands are compressed and a spray of glue and poison shoots from the fangs. A additional 'shotgun' effect is provided by the fangs moving rapidly in and out creating an oscillating spray. This is used on insects, at a distance of 10mm or more, and very effectively sticks the victim down with zig-zags of glue and poison. The spider then advances and bites. *Scytodes* occurs only indoors in this part of the world and is a nocturnal wanderer with a very slow, measured gait. There is no web and the female carries her bundle of eggs under the body. Being a six-eyed haplogyne spider (Family Key, p. 43), there is no epigyne and the male palpal organs are simple. Males and females are very similar in general appearance; the male palpal organs are so small and thin that you will need to look very closely to distinguish the sexes.

Scytodes thoracica Latreille 1804   Plate 3
Description ♀, 4–6mm; ♂, 3–5mm. General appearance unmistakable. There is no epigyne and the male palpal organs are simple with a long, tapering embolus.
Habitat Inside houses and other buildings. **Maturity** Spring to autumn.
Distribution Southern Britain; as far north as the Midlands but probably increasing its range. Widespread in Europe, but rare or absent from the far north.

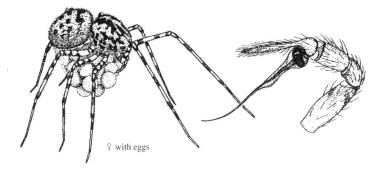

♀ with eggs

FAMILY DYSDERIDAE

This family of six-eyed haplogyne spiders is represented in the region by two genera, with two species in each. The eye arrangement is illustrated in the Family Key (p. 44). They are all rather elongate and the abdomen has no pattern or clear markings. Two pairs of tracheal spiracles are present, just behind the epigastric fold. There is no epigyne, and the male palpal organs are relatively simple.

Key to the Genera and Species

1. Carapace reddish-brown. Size of adult spider 7–15mm   2

    Carapace dark brown or black. Size of adult spider
    5–7mm   *Harpactea hombergi* p. 95

2. Chelicerae conspicuously large, projecting anteriorly and
    divergent. Femur IV with 0–3 dorsal spines near the base   3

    Chelicerae smaller. Femur IV with 8–10 dorsal spines   *Harpactea rubicunda* p. 95

3. Femur IV with 1–3 dorsal spines near base   *Dysdera crocota* p. 94

    Femur IV with no dorsal spines   *Dysdera erythrina* p. 94

Genus *Dysdera*

The two species in this family have a distinctly reddish carapace and legs, but this feature is also shared with *Harpactea rubicunda*. The chelicerae are long, projecting and divergent and have impressive fangs. This is an adaptation for catching and eating woodlice, which most spiders either reject or are unable to tackle. They are nocturnal wanderers, spending the daytime in a silken cell in which the female also lays her eggs. The two sexes are very similar in general appearance, the male having a slimmer abdomen.

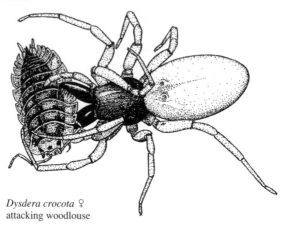

Dysdera crocota ♀
attacking woodlouse

Dysdera crocota C.L. Koch 1838 (= *D. crocata* C.L. Koch)
Description ♀, 11–15mm; ♂, 9–10mm. This impressive-looking spider is identical in appearance to *D. erythrina* (Plate 3) but is distinguished by the greater size of adults, by having 1–3 spines on femur IV and by the male palpal organs. It might however be confused with *Harpactea rubicunda* which has more femoral spines and smaller chelicerae.
Habitat Under stones, logs, and other debris (often in gardens) in slightly damp but warm habitats also favoured by woodlice. **Maturity** Probably all year.
Distribution Widespread in Britain, but commoner in the south and not extending far into Scotland. Widespread in Europe, but not recorded from Scandinavia.

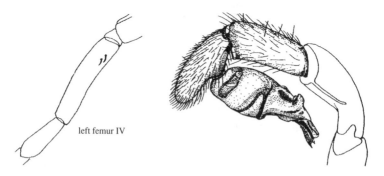

left femur IV

Dysdera erythrina (Walckenaer 1802)   Plate 3
Description ♀, 9–10mm; ♂, 7–8mm. Smaller than *D. crocota*, with no dorsal spines on femur IV and different male palpal organs.

Habitat and maturity As for *D. crocota*.
Distribution Similar to *D. crocota* but extending rather less far into the north of the region.

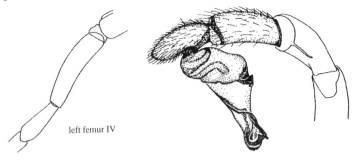

left femur IV

Genus *Harpactea*

The two species in this genus are, like *Dysdera*, nocturnal hunters and in the daytime are found in a silken cell wherein also the eggs are laid. Their chelicerae are not particularly large or specially adapted and the prey consists of a wide variety of invertebrates. The two sexes are similar in general appearance, but males have a particularly slim, tubular abdomen.

Harpactea hombergi (Scopoli 1763)   Plate 3
Description ♀, 6–7mm; ♂, 5–6mm. Male similar to female but with a very slim, tubular abdomen. Distinguished from *H. rubicunda* by smaller size, darker coloration, fewer spines on femur IV and by the male palpal organs.
Habitat Under bark and stones and in other detritus. **Maturity** Possibly all year.
Distribution Widespread throughout Britain and Europe and fairly common.

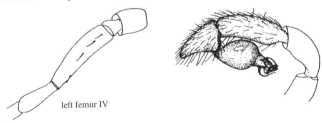

left femur IV

Harpactea rubicunda (C.L. Koch 1838)
Description ♀, 8–12mm; ♂, 7–8mm. Greatly resembles the species of *Dysdera* but has smaller chelicerae and 8–10 dorsal spines on femur IV. Male palp characteristic.
Habitat Under stones and other debris in warm dry wasteland or grassland sites.
Maturity Probably spring and summer.
Distribution Discovered at several sites in south-east England. May have been overlooked in the past. Widespread in Europe, but more frequent in the south of the region.

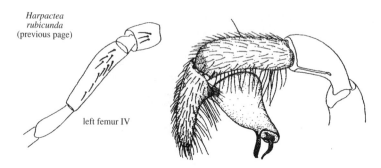

Harpactea rubicunda (previous page)

left femur IV

FAMILY SEGESTRIIDAE

Genus *Segestria*

The haplogyne spiders of the family Segestriidae are represented by three species in the region, all in the genus *Segestria*. They have six eyes, arranged in three groups of two (see Family Key, p. 44) and an elongate, cylindrical abdomen which has a clear pattern in two of the species. They all construct tubular retreats, within holes in walls and bark, from the entrance of which a number of strong threads radiate (see Webs, p. 65). The spider waits near the entrance, with the front legs on the rim of the opening, and will rush out to seize prey when the threads are disturbed. Prey is then dragged backwards by the spider into the retreat. All species have the first three pairs of legs directed forwards. Males resemble females closely but have a smaller, slimmer abdomen. There is no epigyne and the male palpal organs are simple. Eggs are laid within the retreat and the female remains with the young until they disperse. Sometimes she dies first and is eaten by the young.

Segestria senoculata (Linnaeus 1758)   Plate 3
Description ♀, 7–10mm; ♂, 6–9mm. Male similar to female, but with smaller, slimmer abdomen. There are three pairs of ventrolateral spines on metatarsus I. The male palpal organs taper to a long, thin embolus.
Habitat Holes in walls and bark; sometimes uses holes left by wood-boring insects. Also under stones, including scree and shoreline boulders.
Maturity Spring to autumn.
Distribution Widespread throughout Britain and Europe.

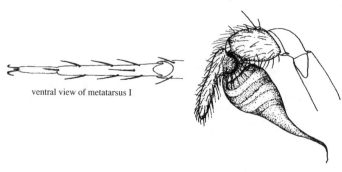

ventral view of metatarsus I

Segestria bavarica C.L. Koch 1843
Description ♀, 10–13mm; ♂, 9–11mm. Female illustrated alongside palp. Usually larger than *S. senoculata*. The central abdominal markings are usually narrower at the front with the dark patches further back being broken clearly into two halves. There is only one pair of ventrolateral spines on metatarsus I (as in *S. florentina*) and the male palpal organs taper to a rather blunt, bifurcate tip.
Habitat In Britain, under stones and in holes or crevices in walls and cliffs. In Europe, also in holes in the bark of forest trees. **Maturity** Spring to autumn.
Distribution In Britain confined to south and south-west England mostly in coastal sites. Widespread in Europe, not confined to the coast, and mainly found in holes in the bark of forest trees, especially in mountainous areas.

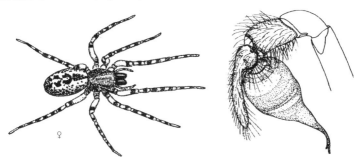

Segestria florentina (Rossi 1790)   Plate 3
Description ♀, 13–22mm; ♂, 10–15mm. The female is a very impressive spider with green iridescence on the chelicerae; the abdomen is usually almost black, but the pattern may be quite clear in immatures and males. The latter have a smaller, slimmer abdomen with slightly bronzed chelicerae. Metatarsus I has only one pair of ventrolateral spines. The male palpal organs taper to a relatively short, blunt embolus.
Habitat Holes in walls or under stones. **Maturity** Summer to autumn.
Distribution Southern England and Wales, usually near ports. Widespread in Europe, apart from the extreme north, and again often associated with ports.

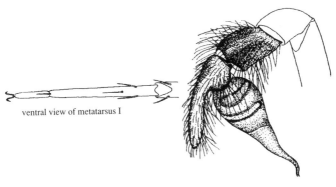

ventral view of metatarsus I

FAMILY PHOLCIDAE

Three species of Pholcidae occur in the region; the arrangement of the eyes and the very long legs, with false tarsal segments, are illustrated in the Family Key (p. 44). At this point, the complete novice might also refer to 'Spiders and their Near Relatives' (p. 10) just to make sure that the specimen *is* a spider, and not a harvestman! All species spin an open web of criss-cross threads; in Britain this is usually in houses and other buildings. The two genera are easily separated: *Pholcus* has a yellowish-grey, rather tubular abdomen with terminal spinners; *Psilochorus* has a globular, bluish abdomen and the spinners are set far forward, just behind the epigastric fold.

Genus *Pholcus*

The two species in the region are very similar in general appearance. They hang upside down in their random, open webs and, if disturbed, will shake and whirl their bodies in the web at such high speed that they become blurred. This is a defence mechanism against predators. Females carry their loosely wrapped eggs in the chelicerae. The sexes are of similar general appearance but males have a slimmer abdomen.

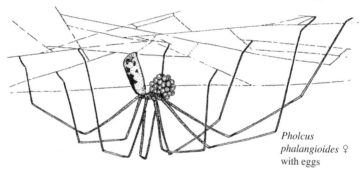

Pholcus phalangioides ♀ with eggs

Pholcus phalangioides (Fuesslin 1775)   Plate 3
Description ♀, 8–10mm; ♂, 7–10mm. Larger than *P. opilionoides* and also distinguishable by the form of the epigyne and the male palp.
Habitat In Britain always in rooms or cellars of buildings; in Europe may also be found in caves. **Maturity** Females all year, males spring and summer.

Distribution A cosmopolitan species. Found in most parts of Britain, but always indoors and commoner in the south. Widespread in Europe, but absent from the extreme north; mainly in buildings, but also in caves.

△ *Pholcus opilionoides* (Schrank 1781)
Description ♀ ♂, 3–5.5mm. Similar to *P. phalangioides*, but smaller and with distinctly different epigyne and male palpal organs.
Habitat Sometimes in buildings; usually in rock crevices and caves in warmer parts.
Maturity Females all year, males spring and summer.
Distribution Absent from Britain and the more northerly parts of Europe; commoner in warmer parts of the region.

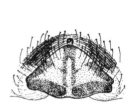 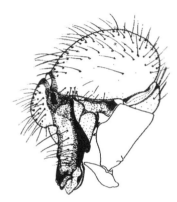

Genus *Psilochorus*

The single representative of this genus is similar to *Pholcus* in its web construction and method of carrying the egg sac. It will also whirl defensively, but does so less readily. Males closely resemble females.

Psilochorus simoni (Berland 1911)   Plate 3
Description ♀ ♂ 2–2.5mm. The bluish, globular abdomen, with spinners close to the epigastric fold, allow easy identification. The epigyne and male palp provide confirmation of identity.

 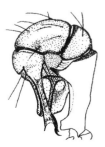

Habitat In buildings, usually in wine cellars. **Maturity** All year.
Distribution Widely distributed in Britain, France and Belgium and probably occurs elsewhere in the region.

FAMILY ZODARIIDAE

Genus *Zodarion*

Three members of the Zodariidae are described from the region, all in the genus *Zodarion*. They have the anterior spinners arising from a cylindrical projection and the median and posterior spinners much reduced in size; these, and the arrangement of the eyes, are illustrated in the Family Key (p. 46). The legs are rather slender and devoid of spines except for a single short one on femur I and II; the latter are darkened. They are fast-moving, ground-hunting species in which the abdomen is shiny black (or dark purplish-brown) on the upper surface, but pale yellow underneath. This reversed coloration affords some camouflage when combined with light reflecting from the upper side. The species appear rather ant-like when running and are found in the company of ants, upon which they feed exclusively. The two sexes are similar in general appearance. Females hang up their oval egg sac in a suitably protected niche and camouflage it with bits of debris. The species resemble one another closely, as do their genitalia. Previous confusion over the names and status of some species has now been resolved by R. Bosmans, to whom I am indebted for the loan of specimens.

Zodarion italicum (Canestrini 1868)   Plate 3
Description ♀, 2.1–4.3mm; ♂, 1.6–2.9mm. The epigyne is somewhat variable, but differs distinctly from the other species. The male palp is similar to that of *Z. gallicum*, but differs in the palpal organs, viewed from the side or below, and in the tibial apophysis, which appears broad and triangular when viewed from below.
Habitat Dry stony areas and old quarries. **Maturity** Spring and summer.
Distribution Well-established colonies in old quarries and wasteland in Essex. Possibly widespread in Europe, but occurs more to the north of the region - France, Belgium, Germany, Austria

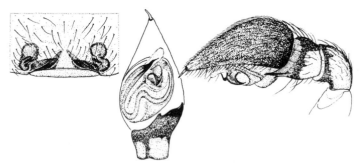

△ *Zodarion gallicum* (Simon 1873)
Description ♀, 2.2–3.6mm; ♂, 1.7–2.4mm. The validity and true identity of this species has only recently been demonstrated by R. Bosmans; it is similar to *Z.*

italicum in general appearance. The epigyne is distinctive, as are the male palpal organs, viewed from the side or below. The tibial apophysis, viewed from below, is narrower and less triangular than in *Z. italicum*.
Habitat Dry, sandy areas. **Maturity** Spring and summer.
Distribution Absent from Britain. In Europe, commoner to the south of the region - SE Fance, Corsica, Italy, Croatia and Slovenia

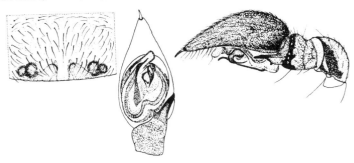

△ *Zodarion germanicum* (C.L. Koch 1837)
Description ♀, 4.5–5mm; ♂, 3–3.5mm. The epigyne of this species is quite distinctive as are the palpal organs and tibial apophysis.
Habitat Dry habitats in association with coniferous woodland in mountainous areas.
Maturity Spring and summer.
Distribution Absent from Britain. Recorded from Germany and France but may well occur elsewhere in the south of the region.

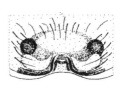 

FAMILY GNAPHOSIDAE

Forty-one species of the family Gnaphosidae are described here, in ten genera. They have cylindrical spinners, the anterior pair of which are slightly longer than the rest and separated from each other by roughly the diameter of one of them (see Family Key, p. 52). In most species, the posterior median eyes are oval, irregular or slit-like in shape. The spinners are not typical in the genus *Micaria* and the eyes are not typical in *Scotophaeus* and some *Zelotes* species. The majority of spiders in this family are greyish-brown to jet-black, the abdomen lacking a pattern and being furnished with short, sleek hairs. These are nocturnal hunters, spending the daytime in a silken retreat. A few gnaphosids are strikingly marked with lines or patches of shining white hairs and members of the genus *Micaria* are usually iridescent in sunlight. These are mainly diurnal hunters and *Micaria*, in particular, runs about very rapidly in bright sunshine. The sexes are of similar general appearance, males having a slimmer abdomen and, in *Drassodes*, enlarged chelicerae. Females of many species make their egg sac in a large silken cell in which they remain until the eggs are hatched. *Micaria* makes stiff, papery sacs within a cell but does not remain inside. *Zelotes* makes domed or nipple-shaped sacs of tough, papery silk which are attached to stones (see Egg Sacs, p. 57).

Identification to genus level is possible with a ×10 lens and some genitalia are large and distinctive enough to enable identification even to species level. However, many will require a ×20 lens, field microscope or even higher magnification to establish identity.

Key to the Genera

1. Trochanters, viewed from below, each with a notch. Abdomen mousy, brownish-grey with no pattern or clear markings

    Drassodes p. 104

    Trochanters without notches. Abdomen with or without markings   2

    If notched trochanters not fairly obvious with a lens then assume absent.

2. Posterior row of eyes recurved when viewed from above

    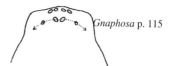
    Gnaphosa p. 115

    Posterior row of eyes straight or procurved   3

    If not easily seen with a lens, assume that eyes are straight or procurved.

3. Anterior median eyes noticeably larger than the others. Abdomen with sleek, grey, mousy hairs and no pattern.

    Scotophaeus p. 108

    Anterior median eyes same size or smaller than the rest. May or may not have abdominal markings   4

    If anterior eyes not seen fairly easily with lens, assume not larger than rest.

4. Anterior spinners, viewed from below, close together and scarcely projecting from the posterior end of the abdomen. Abdomen usually iridescent (depends on brightness of light) and often marked with lines or spots of white hairs

    Micaria p. 120

Anterior spinners, viewed from below, separated by the
width of one of them and projecting considerably beyond
the posterior end of the abdomen. Abdomen possibly
marked with white hairs or may lack markings; may be
shiny but not iridescent 5

5. Abdomen with very clear markings of light spots or bars 6

Abdomen without very clear markings; either unicolorous or
with ill-defined, dusky markings 8

6. Posterior median eyes reduced to
transverse slits *Callilepis* p. 119

Posterior median eyes oval or irregular (and arranged
obliquely) or circular 7

7. Abdomen marked dorsally with three pairs of
light oval patches *Phaeocedus* p. 119

Abdomen marked dorsally
with transverse bars as
well as light patches m *Aphantaulax* p. 117
and m *Poecilochroa* p. 117

Aphantaulax   *Poecilochroa*

8. Carapace markedly narrowed anteriorly with
total width of eye group less than one-
third of the maximum width of carapace
(except in *Zelotes rusticus*). Abdomen
usually black and sleek with the
branchial opercula contrastingly orange
or yellow (except in *Z. rusticus* q.v.) *Zelotes* p. 110

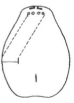

🕷 All the common *Zelotes* are recognizable, to the naked eye, by the narrow
head and elongate, sleek, black abdomen with spinners protruding like fingers.

Carapace not markedly narrowed anteriorly;
total width of eye group more than one-
third of the maximum width of carapace.
Abdomen may have some dusky
markings or a vague pattern *Haplodrassus* p. 105

Genus *Drassodes*

Several species occur in the region, the commonest and most widespread of which are described here. They have a rather mousy, grey-brown abdomen and superficially resemble some *Clubiona* species. However, they are easily distinguished by the long, tubular spinners and oval, rather squinty-looking posterior median eyes. They are distinguished from other gnaphosids by the notched trochanters. There are two dorsal spines on tibia IV which provides additional separation from *Haplodrassus*. The spinners are highly mobile, like fingers, and are employed to spin a broad swathe of silk around the legs of prey. They are all quite fierce nocturnal hunters, spending the day in a silk retreat. Females seal themselves in a silken cell with their egg sac. Identification of species is largely based on the epigynes and male palps but the male chelicerae (and, occasionally, size) are an additional aid. The structures can usually be made out with a strong lens or field microscope, but higher magnification may sometimes be required.

Drassodes lapidosus (Walckenaer 1802)
Description ♀ ♂, 9–18mm. Indistinguishable from *D. cupreus* (Plate 3) in general appearance. Epigyne distinguished by the relative width across the two pairs of spermathecae (narrower across anterior pair) and the relatively wide central tongue. Males identified by the arrangement of the three cheliceral teeth and by the form and proportions of the palp (longer and relatively thinner than in *D. cupreus*).
Habitat Under stones, in leaf-litter and amongst the base of grass tussocks. Often in very dry situations (e.g. scree). **Maturity** Females all year, males spring and summer.
Distribution Most old records unreliable and many refer to *D. cupreus* which overall is much commoner. However, it is widespread throughout the whole of Britain and Europe.

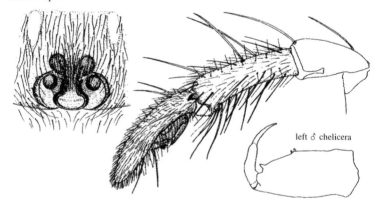

left ♂ chelicera

Drassodes cupreus (Blackwall 1834)   Plate 3
Description ♀ ♂, 9–18mm. Females distinguished from *D. lapidosus* by the epigyne in which the width across the anterior pair of spermathecae is greater than that across the posterior pair, and the central tongue is relatively narrow. Males distinguished by the arrangement of the three cheliceral teeth and by the form and proportions of the palp.

Habitat, Maturity and Distribution As for *D. lapidosus* but seems generally to be much commoner.

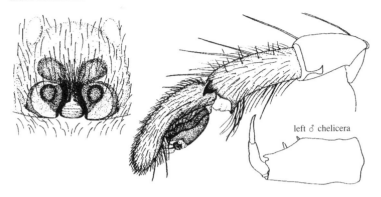

left ♂ chelicera

Drassodes pubescens (Thorell 1856)
Description ♀, 6–9mm; ♂, 4–6mm. Small size of adults generally separates this species from the previous two. Similar in general appearance but paler, as though newly moulted. Epigyne distinctive, male palpal tibia with a bifid apophysis and male chelicerae with three teeth arising from a common base.
Habitat Similar to *D. lapidosus* and *D. cupreus*, but my experience has been that it is more commonly found in grass tussocks in wooded areas and perhaps prefers damper habitats. **Maturity** Spring and summer.
Distribution Much less common, but widely distributed throughout the region.

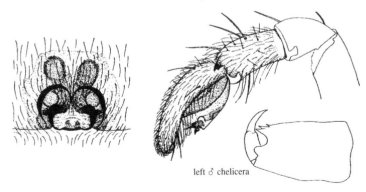

left ♂ chelicera

Genus *Haplodrassus*

Several species of *Haplodrassus* occur in the region, the most widespread of which are described here. They show some similarities to *Drassodes* but lack the notched trochanters and have no dorsal spines on tibia IV. In many species, the carapace has clear, dark markings and there may be a dusky abdominal pattern. However, the latter is variable and not a reliable guide to identification. Their habits and lifestyle are similar to those of *Drassodes*. The species can frequently be identified in the field since the epigynes and male palps are mostly large and conspicuous. Females which have mated may have irregular exudates or plugs within the epigyne openings, but this rarely obscures the main structure.

Haplodrassus signifer (C.L. Koch 1839)   Plate 4

Description ♀, 8–9mm, ♂, 6–8mm. Variable in colour; sometimes very dark. Abdomen sometimes with obscure chevrons and lighter orange-brown hairs. Epigyne and male palp very distinctive.

Habitat Under stones, at the base of grass tussocks, in moss and leaf-litter in a variety of situations. It seems to prefer dry habitats but these can often be found in slightly raised, dry patches within otherwise wet and boggy sites.

Maturity Spring to late summer.

Distribution Widespread throughout Britain and Europe and the commonest species of the genus.

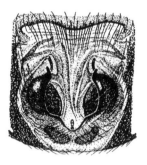 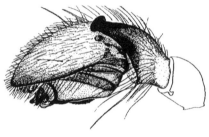

Haplodrassus dalmatensis (L. Koch 1866)   Plate 4

Description ♀, 4,5–6,5mm; ♂, 4–4.5mm. Smaller than *H. signifer* and with clearer markings. Epigyne and male palp distinctive.

Habitat Under stones and other detritus on heathland and by the coast.

Maturity Spring and summer.

Distribution Rare in Britain with a very local distribution mainly in south but extending to Midlands and North Wales. Widespread but local in northern Europe.

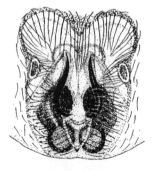 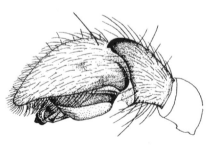

Haplodrassus silvestris (Blackwall 1833)
Description ♀, 8–10mm; ♂, 6.5–7.5mm. Very similar to *H. signifer* but easily distinguished by the epigyne and male palp.
Habitat In woods, under stones, bark of fallen logs and in leaf-litter.
Maturity Spring and summer.
Distribution Widespread in Britain but locally distributed and uncommon. Widespread throughout the rest of Europe.

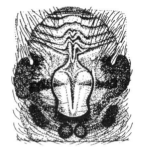 

Haplodrassus minor (O.P. -Cambridge 1879)
Description ♀, 4mm; ♂, 3.5mm. Similar to *H. signifer* but smaller, the adult size being a useful guide to identity. Epigyne and male palp distinctive but much smaller than in other species and difficult to see with a lens.
Habitat Dry coastal habitats such as shingle. **Maturity** Summer.
Distribution South and east coasts of England, but rare. Rare and locally distributed in Europe.

Haplodrassus soerenseni (Strand 1900)
Description ♀, 6–7mm; ♂, 4.5–5.5mm. Similar to *H. signifer* but smaller and readily distinguished by the epigyne and male palp.
Habitat Mainly coniferous woodland, amongst detritus and moss. **Maturity** Summer.
Distribution Scotland, in two areas of Caledonian pine forest; absent from the rest of Britain. Widespread in Scandinavia, but apparently absent from the rest of Europe.

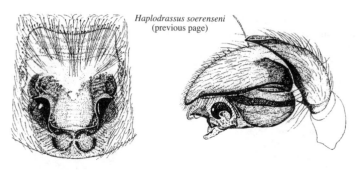

Haplodrassus soerenseni
(previous page)

Haplodrassus umbratilis (L. Koch 1866)
Description ♀, 6–7.5mm; ♂, 5–6mm. Similar to *H. soerenseni* and *H. signifer* but distinguished by the epigyne and male palp.
Habitat Dry stony areas often in heathland. **Maturity** Summer.
Distribution In Britain has only been found in the south of England. Widespread in Europe, including Scandinavia.

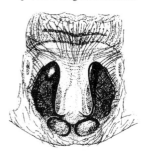

Genus *Scotophaeus*

The three species described in this genus are quite large spiders with a rather mousy, grey abdomen which lacks a pattern. They superficially resemble *Drassodes* but the anterior median eyes are larger than the rest and the posterior median are circular. The sexes are similar but males have a scutum on the upper surface of the abdomen (the latter varies in size in all species and is of no value in identification). They are nocturnal wanderers, mainly in and around houses, and have a distinct penchant for entomologists' setting boards! The epigynes are relatively small for the size of spider but are still large enough to be identified with a ×10 lens, as are the male palps.

Scotophaeus blackwalli (Thorell 1871)   Plate 4
Description ♀, 10–12mm; ♂, 8–9mm. Male similar to female but with small scutum on dorsum of abdomen. Readily identified by the epigyne and male palp, the latter having a relatively short, pointed tibial apophysis.
Habitat Exclusively within houses in the north of Britain, in and around houses in the south; in warmer parts of Europe, under bark and in holes in walls as well as in

houses. **Maturity** Females all year, males summer and autumn.
Distribution Widespread throughout Britain and Europe.

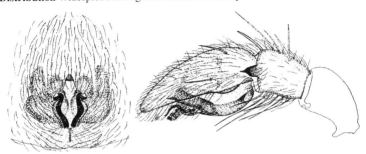

Scotophaeus scutulatus (L. Koch 1866)
Description ♀, 8–16mm, ♂, 7–11mm. Very similar to *S. blackwalli* but readily distinguished by the epigyne and male palp, the latter having a large tibial apophysis which has a dark ridge along its slightly hooked tip.
Habitat and Maturity Similar to *S. blackwalli*.
Distribution A single record from Colchester. Widespread in Europe.

△ *Scotophaeus quadripunctatus* (Linnaeus 1758)
Description ♀, 8–15mm; ♂, 7–10mm. Similar to *S. blackwalli* but easily distinguished by the epigyne and male palp, the latter having a broad tibial apophysis curving to a point.
Habitat and Maturity Similar to *S. blackwalli*.
Distribution Absent from Britain. Widespread in northern Europe.

Genus *Zelotes*

At least fifteen species of *Zelotes* occur in the region, of which twelve are described here. The genus has been divided by some workers to form several smaller genera. Whilst able to see the *differences* which suggest such subdivision, I am not sure that they outweigh the *similarities* or that the changes are useful taxonomically, although they are useful at a subgeneric level. The suggested new genera are indicated following each species name. Most *Zelotes* species are instantly recognizable by the narrowed front of the carapace, the sleek, black abdomen and the contrastingly yellow-orange branchial opercula. They are mostly nocturnal hunters and during the daytime are found under stones and detritus or amongst vegetation at ground level. Some species, particularly *Z. electus*, may be found running in sunshine. Females make domed, papery egg sacs with flat, often crinkled edges and these are stuck down on to the surface of stones (see Egg Sacs, p. 57). Females are often found with the sacs, but run off at high speed when the stone is turned over. The two sexes are similar in general appearance but males have a slimmer abdomen which usually has a small dorsal scutum. The epigynes are relatively large and well-defined, allowing identification with a lens in many cases. The male palps are all rather similar and microscopy will generally be required, the palp being viewed from exactly the right angle.

Zelotes pedestris (C.L. Koch 1837) (= *Trachyzelotes p.* (C.L. Koch))   Plate 4
Description ♀, 7–8mm; ♂, 4–6mm. Coxae, trochanters and femora darkened, the remaining segments being light brown. Chelicerae with a brush-like group of short, stout spines anteriorly – absent in other *Zelotes* in the region. Male similar to female, but with slimmer abdomen and a small black scutum dorsally. Epigyne distinctive, as are male palpal organs and tibial apophysis.
Habitat Under stones and amongst detritus. **Maturity** Spring and summer.
Distribution Southern England; often common on chalk grassland, but very locally distributed. Widespread in Europe.

 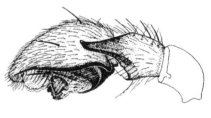

Zelotes lutetianus (L. Koch 1866) (= *Drassyllus l.* (L. Koch))
Description ♀, 5–7.5mm; ♂, 4–5mm. The branchial opercula are brownish and less striking in this species. Coxae, trochanters, femora, patellae and tibiae darkened, the remaining segments being paler. Male with brown abdominal scutum. Similar to *Z. pusillus*, but larger; epigyne differs in the shape of the anterior border and in the spherical spermathecae which are close together. Male palpal organs and tibial apophysis differ from those of *Z. pusillus* and the palpal tibia lacks the stout spines present in the latter species.

Habitat Under stones and detritus in marshy and coastal sites.
Maturity Spring and summer.
Distribution Widely distributed throughout Britain, but rare. Widespread in Europe.

Zelotes pusillus (C.L. Koch 1833) (= *Drassyllus p.* (C.L. Koch))
Description ♀, 4–5mm; ♂, 3–4mm. Very similar to *Z. lutetianus* but smaller; epigyne differs in the shape of the anterior border and in the oval spermathecae which are more separated. Male palpal organs and tibial apophysis differ from those of *Z. lutetianus* and the palpal tibia is furnished with a number of short, stout spines dorsally.
Habitat Under stones and detritus in dry situations, often heathland.
Maturity Spring and summer.
Distribution Widespread throughout Britain and not uncommon. Also widespread in Europe.

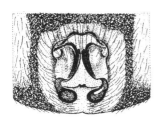 

△ *Zelotes villicus* (Thorell 1875) (= *Drassyllus v.* (Thorell))
Description ♀, 5–6mm; ♂, 4–5mm. Very similar to *Z. lutetianus*. Epigyne and male palpal organs distinctive; palpal tibia with pointed, bifid apophysis and stout spines.
Habitat Under stones and detritus; mainly dry habitats. **Maturity** Spring and summer.
Distribution Absent from Britain; widespread in Europe.

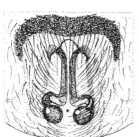 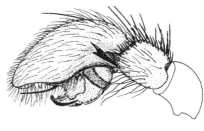

Zelotes praeficus (L. Koch 1866) (= *Drassyllus p.* (L. Koch))
Description ♀, 5–6mm; ♂, 4.5–5mm. This species is entirely black except for the branchial opercula and tarsi, which are contrastingly yellow-orange. Epigyne and male palp distinctive.
Habitat Under stones and detritus on dry, chalky ground. **Maturity** Spring and summer.
Distribution Uncommon and recorded only from the south of England. Widespread in Europe.

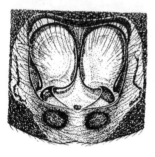
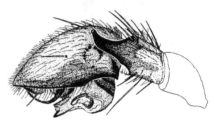

Zelotes rusticus (L. Koch 1872) (= *Urozelotes r.* (L. Koch))
Description ♀, 7–8.5mm; ♂, 6–6.5mm. Carapace and legs orange-brown; abdomen greyish-brown. Carapace less narrowed anteriorly, with width of eye group about one-third the maximum width of carapace. Epigyne and male palp distinctive.
Habitat Under stones and other detritus, often around houses.
Maturity Spring and summer.
Distribution Rare, with a very scattered distribution throughout England and Wales. Widespread but uncommon throughout Europe.

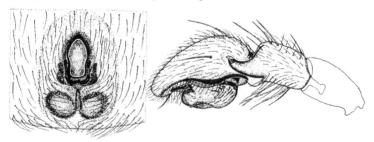

Zelotes latreillei (Simon 1878)   Plate 4
Description ♀, 7–8mm; ♂, 4.5–7.5mm. Whole spider black apart from branchial opercula which are orange; tarsi sometimes light, often dark. Abdomen of male has a small scutum. Epigyne and male palp distinctive.
Habitat Under stones and detritus in dry situations; also dry, raised patches of vegetation within marshy sites. **Maturity** Spring and summer.
Distribution The commonest species; widespread throughout Britain and Europe.

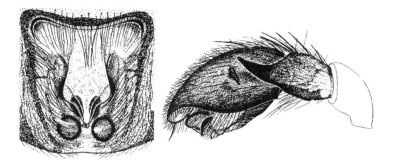

Zelotes longipes (L. Koch 1866) (= *Z. serotinus* (L. Koch))
Description ♀, 6–8mm; ♂, 5–6mm. Very similar to *Z. latreillei*. Distinguished by the epigyne and the male palpal organs and tibial apophysis.
Habitat On dry heathland; under stones and amongst moss and other vegetation at the base of heather; also dry coastal sites. **Maturity** Spring and summer.
Distribution Rare, but probably widely distributed in Britain; recorded from Scotland and Ireland, but most records from southern England. Widespread in Europe.

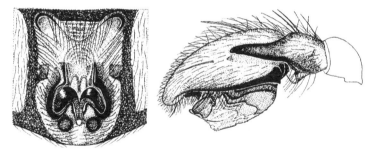

Zelotes petrensis (C.L. Koch 1839)
Description ♀, 6–7mm; ♂, 5–6mm. Very similar to *Z. latreillei*. Distinguished by the epigyne and the male palpal organs and tibial apophysis.

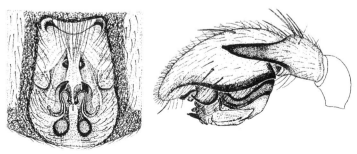

Habitat Under stones and amongst detritus on heathland.
Maturity Spring and summer.
Distribution Rare in Britain and recorded only from a few localities in southern and eastern England. Widely distributed in Europe.

Zelotes electus (C.L. Koch 1839)
Description ♀, 4–5.5mm; ♂, 3.5–4.5mm. Carapace reddish-brown to dark brown with dark markings. Abdomen dark brown to black, that of male with dorsal scutum. Easily distinguished from other species by the epigyne, male palpal organs and tibial apophysis; size sometimes helpful, as is habitat.
Habitat Coastal areas, mostly dunes; under stones and other detritus and amongst base of plants. Often found running in sunshine. **Maturity** Spring and summer.
Distribution Widespread around Britain, in coastal sites and in the Norfolk/Suffolk Breckland sandy heaths. Widespread in Europe but generally on sandy terrain.

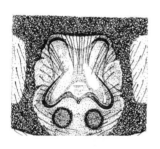 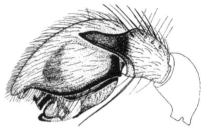

Zelotes apricorum (L. Koch 1876)
Description ♀, 6.5–9mm; ♂, 5–6mm. Very similar to *Z. latreillei* with epigyne and male palp very similar to those of *Z. subterraneus* (below), with which it was once confused. The epigyne is distinguished by the shape of the central area and the curvature of the dark margins around it. The male palp is distinguished by the tip of the embolus which has a broad, blunt apophysis above it.
Habitat Under stones and detritus and amongst dry vegetation in a variety of situations. **Maturity** Spring and summer.
Distribution Probably widespread in Britain but not very common; until recently, confused with *Z. subterraneus*. Widespread but uncommon in Europe.

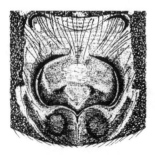 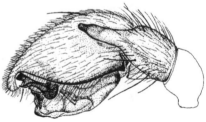

Zelotes subterraneus (C.L. Koch 1833)

Description ♀, 6.5–9mm; ♂, 5–6mm. Similar in all respects to *Z. apricorum* (above), with which it was once confused. Epigyne distinguished by the shape of the central area and the curvature of the dark margins around it (the widest part of the central area is closer to the spermathecae than in *Z. apricorum*). The male palp has a curved embolus with no apophysis above it.

Habitat, Maturity and Distribution Probably similar to *Z. apricorum* but sufficient data on their relative distribution not yet available.

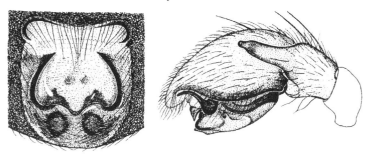

Genus *Gnaphosa*

There are fifteen species of *Gnaphosa* in the region, many of them confined to mountainous regions in Scandinavia. Four are described here but none of them is common. The most useful single character distinguishing them from other Gnaphosidae is the recurved row of posterior eyes. They are rather thickset spiders with a dull brownish-grey, hairy appearance and are generally found under stones and other detritus and amongst debris at the base of vegetation. They are mainly nocturnal in habits, but occasionally are found running in sunshine. The genus is identifiable in the field with a lens, and the tibial apophysis of the male palp is similarly recognizable. However, the epigynes are difficult to separate without a microscope. Of the species described, *G. leporina* is the commonest in Britain.

Gnaphosa lugubris (C.L. Koch, 1839)   Plate 5

Description ♀, 10–13mm; ♂, 9–12mm. Female similar to male, but with larger abdomen. Epigyne distinctive and less broad than that of *G. occidentalis*. Tibial

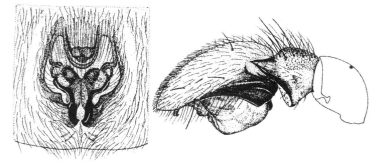

apophysis of male palp short and pointed. Tip of palpal organs, viewed from the side, with a hooked process.

Habitat Under stones and other detritus and amongst the base of vegetation in dry heathland and coastal; sometimes active in sunshine. **Maturity** Summer.

Distribution Rare, and recorded from a few sites in the southern half of England. Widespread in Europe.

Gnaphosa nigerrima L. Koch 1877

Description ♀,7.5–9mm; ♂, 6–7mm. This species is entirely black in the field and the carapace is very dark brown in preserved specimens. It is smaller than *G. lugubris* and *G. occidentalis*. The epigyne is distinctive and has a shorter scape than that of *G. leporina*. The tibial apophysis of the male palp is more narrowly pointed than in *G. lugubris* and not elongate as in *G. leporina*.The tip of the palpal organs lacks the hooked process and forms a blunt point.

Habitat Amongst moss in boggy areas. **Maturity** Summer.

Distribution Recently discovered at Wybunbury Moss, Cheshire, and possibly restricted to this one site in Britain. Widespread in northern Europe.

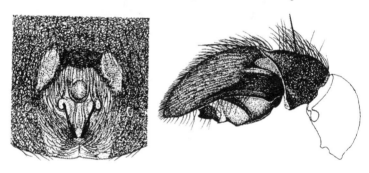

Gnaphosa occidentalis Simon 1878

Description ♀, 10–12mm; ♂, 9–11mm. Very similar to *G. lugubris*, but epigyne broader relative to the central tongue and the tibial apophysis of the male palp has a bifid tip.

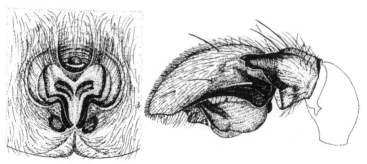

Habitat Under stones and detritus in dry habitats. **Maturity** Summer.
Distribution Recorded from one site in Cornwall. Widespread in Europe.

Gnaphosa leporina (L. Koch 1866)
Description ♀, 7–9mm; ♂, 5.5–7mm. Smaller than *G. lugubris* and *G. occidentalis* and with a less well-defined epigyne which has a longer scape than that of *G. niger-rima*. Tibial apophysis of male palp relatively long and pointed.
Habitat Damp heathland. **Maturity** Summer.
Distribution Widespread, but locally distributed in Britain and throughout Europe.

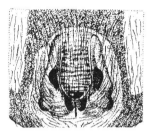 

△ Genus *Aphantaulax*

A single species occurs in the region and resembles *Zelotes*, but has a clear abdominal pattern similar to that of *Poecilochroa*. Although found under stones, these spiders are also active in the daytime. The two sexes are similar in general appearance.

△ *Aphantaulax seminiger* (Simon 1878)   Plate 4
Description ♀, 5.5mm; ♂, 4.5mm. The abdomen sometimes lacks the small pair of light spots just above the spinners. Legs sometimes more unicolorous. Epigyne and male palp distinctive.
Habitat Under stones and detritus or running in sunshine. **Maturity** Summer.
Distribution Absent from Britain. Recorded from the south and west of the region, but apparently absent from the north and east.

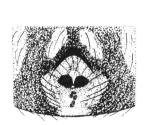 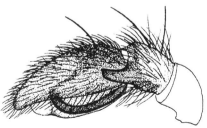

△ Genus *Poecilochroa*

Two species occur in the region, neither of them in Britain. The abdomen has a clear pattern of white hairs and the tarsi, metatarsi and (sometimes) tibiae are lighter in colour than the rest of the leg segments. They occur under stones and amongst detritus, but also on vegetation, and are frequently active in sunshine. The two sexes are similar in general appearance.

△ *Poecilochroa variana* (C.L. Koch 1839)   Plate 4

Description ♀, 6.5–9mm; ♂, 6–7mm. The abdominal pattern does vary a little; sometimes the paired light patches are reduced or absent and some of the white hairs may be rubbed off in older specimens. Femora black and rest of leg segments paler. Epigyne distinctive, as also is the male palp with its long tibial apophysis.

Habitat In dry, stony or sandy habitats; under stones, amongst detritus or running in sunshine. **Maturity** Spring and summer.

Distribution Absent from Britain. Widespread throughout Europe, including Scandinavia.

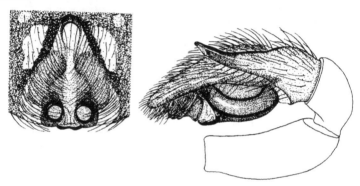

△ *Poecilochroa conspicua* (L. Koch 1866)

Description ♀, 7.5–8mm; ♂, 6mm. Resembles *P. variana* but the light triangle above the spinners is often absent and the legs are darkened more extensively with only the metatarsi and tarsi being paler. Epigyne distinctive; male palp with very short, hooked tibial apophysis and the femur curved and furnished with a blunt projection near its base.

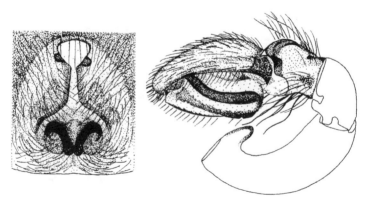

Habitat Bushes and the lower branches of trees, often with the retreat in a curled leaf.
Maturity Spring and summer.
Distribution Absent from Britain. Widespread throughout most of Europe, but absent from Scandinavia.

Genus *Phaeocedus*

A single species of this genus occurs in the region and has abdominal markings in the form of three pairs of light patches, but no continuous light bars. The eyes are oval, not slit-like as in *Callilepis* and only the femora of legs I and II are darkened. The species is active during the daytime and males, in particular, look rather ant-like.

Phaeocedus braccatus (L. Koch 1866)   Plate 4
Description ♀, 4.5–6.5mm; ♂, 4–5mm. Male similar to female but has clearer markings and an abdominal scutum. Epigyne and male palp distinctive.
Habitat Under stones, amongst detritus and leaf-litter and running in sunshine.
Maturity Spring and summer.
Distribution Rare, on chalk grassland, in the south of England. Widespread but rather rare in Europe, including Scandinavia.

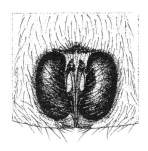 

Genus *Callilepis*

A single species occurs in the region and has an abdominal pattern made up of light hairs. The lenses of the posterior median eyes are partly sclerotized so that they appear as transverse slits. Legs I and II are slightly stouter and darker than the rest and are rather hairy. The species feeds on ants and is itself rather ant-like, in movements and appearance, when running in sunshine. The egg sac is similar to those made by *Zelotes* (p. 57) but is white and less papery.

Callilepis nocturna (Linnaeus 1758)   Plate 4
Description ♀, 3.5–6mm; ♂, 3–4.5mm. Male similar to female in general appearance. Epigyne and male palp distinctive.
Habitat Under stones and detritus, often in coniferous woodland; in Britain, recorded from a sandy, coastal site. Active in sunshine, often in the company of ants.
Maturity Spring and summer.
Distribution Recorded from one site in Devon. Widespread throughout Europe, including Scandinavia, where it is usually associated with coniferous woodland.

Callilepis nocturna (previous page)

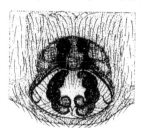

Genus *Micaria*

At least fifteen species of *Micaria* occur in the region of which eight are described here. By far the commonest and most widespread is *Micaria pulicaria*. They all have an iridescent abdomen, but this is more marked in some species than others and, as with all iridescence, is more obvious in bright sunlight. There have been some suggestions that *Micaria* and *Phurolithus* (Liocranidae) should be placed together in a separate family. I now consider this to be incorrect, and that *Micaria* is a gnaphosid; adaptive radiation in both families may have independently enabled these genera to exploit an active, diurnal lifestyle. Their markings partly render them less conspicuous, and, combined with the appearance when running, give a distinctly ant-like impression which may deter potential predators. *Micaria* may be found in detritus, under stones and at the base of vegetation, but in bright sunshine may be seen running about rapidly in a manic, ant-like fashion. Most species occur at ground level, but *M. subopaca* runs about on tree trunks. The spiders construct silken retreats under stones or bark, or at the base of vegetation. Females make their egg sacs within the retreat but do not remain permanently with them. The two sexes are similar in general appearance. The species can sometimes be identified with a ×15–20 lens on the basis of the epigyne and male palp combined with the size of the adult spider.

Micaria alpina L. Koch 1872
Description ♀ ♂, 2.7–4mm. Similar in general appearance to *M. pulicaria*. Epigyne distinctive; male palpal tibia shorter than cymbium, about the same length as patella, and with a relatively narrow tibial apophysis curved slightly downwards.
Habitat Mountains; under stones and detritus or running in sunshine.
Maturity Summer.

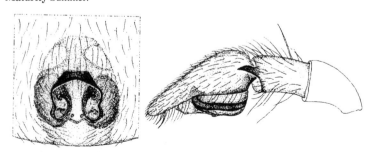

Distribution Rare in Britain and recorded only from Welsh mountains. Widespread in Europe in mountainous regions.

Micaria subopaca Westring 1861
Description ♀ ♂, 2.5–3.3mm. Similar in general appearance to *M. pulicaria*. Epigyne distinctive, with spermathecae much longer than broad. Male palpal tibia shorter than cymbium, longer than patella and with a narrow tibial apophysis which curves upwards. Palpal organs almost as long as cymbium.
Habitat Trunks of trees exposed to sunshine, particularly conifers near heathland.
Maturity Spring to Autumn.
Distribution Very locally distributed in parts of southern England, but specimens may then be quite numerous. Also recorded, in some numbers, in a Liverpool factory! In Europe appears restricted to Scandinavia and more northern parts.

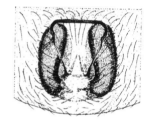

Micaria silesiaca L. Koch 1875
Description ♀, 4–5mm; ♂, 3.5–4mm. Similar in general appearance to *M. pulicaria* but white markings less distinct. Epigyne very distinctive. Male palpal tibia about the same length as patella, almost as long as cymbium, and with a very short tibial apophysis.
Habitat Dry, sandy terrain and heathland; under stones, at the base of heather and running in the open. **Maturity** Summer.
Distribution Recorded from a few sites in south and south-east England. Widespread in northern and eastern Europe.

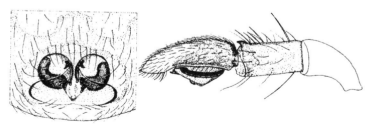

Micaria pulicaria (Sundevall 1832)   Plate 5
Description ♀, 2.7–4.5mm; ♂, 3–3.5mm. By far the commonest and most widespread species. Male similar to female in general appearance. Epigyne similar to those of *M. fulgens* and *M. formicaria*, but these are larger spiders. Male palpal tibia

much shorter than cymbium, slightly longer than patella, and with a short, broad-based, pointed apophysis.

Habitat Occurs, at ground level, in a wide variety of situations which are open to sunshine. May be found under stones and other detritus, amongst the base of grass tussocks and in leaf-litter. In sunny conditions it is often found running about.

Distribution Common and widespread throughout Britain and Europe.

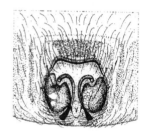

△ *Micaria fulgens* (Walckenaer 1802)   Plate 5
Description ♀, 4.5–6mm; ♂, 4.5–5.5mm. Male similar to female in general appearance. Carapace quite iridescent in this species, but the abdomen has only ill-defined broad bands. Chelicerae are iridescent (a feature not found in other Micaria in the region. Epigyne similar to that of *M. formicaria*, but the paired sclerotized ridges around the openings are smaller, with their concavity directed inwards; *M. formicaria* is also a larger spider, with clear markings as in *M. pulicaria*. The male palpal tibia is much shorter than the cymbium and has a small pointed apophysis as well as small, blunt projections dorsally.

Habitat Under stones, and running about, in dry, often sandy terrain; sometimes at high altitudes. **Maturity** Spring and summer.

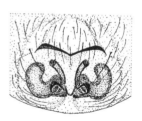
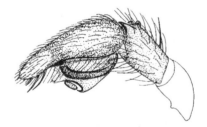

Distribution Absent from Britain. Widespread throughout Europe.
△ *Micaria formicaria* (Sundevall 1832)
Description ♀, 7–7.5mm; ♂, 4.5–5.7mm. Carapace as iridescent as that of *M. fulgens* with clear abdominal markings as in *M. pulicaria*. Epigyne similar to that of *M. fulgens*, but the paired sclerotized ridges around the opening are longer, with their concavity directed outwards. Similar to *M. romana* in this respect, but the latter has the anterior margin of the epigyne less wide and is a smaller spider. Male palpal tibia almost as long as cymbium, and with two small, pointed apophyses – the second being

smaller, and set dorsally and further back. Palpal organs and cymbium very slim.
Habitat Under stones, and running about, in dry, often sandy terrain. **Maturity** Summer.
Distribution Absent from Britain. Widespread throughout most of Europe.

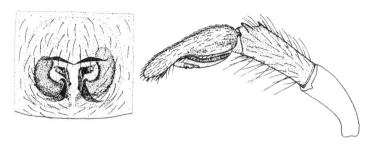

Micaria romana L. Koch 1866 (= *M. scintillans* (O.P.-Cambridge))　　　Plate 5
Description ♀, 4.5–5mm; ♂, 3.5–4.5mm. Female similar to *M. pulicaria* but almost
always larger. Epigyne with the sclerotized anterior margin relatively less wide than
in *M. fulgens* and *M. formicaria*. Male palpal tibia almost as long as cymbium, and
with a single, pointed, slightly hooked apophysis. Palpal organs and cymbium not as
slim as in *M. formicaria*, which is a larger spider.
Habitat Under stones or running about in warm, dry habitats. **Maturity** Summer.
Distribution Recorded only from sites near the south coast in England. In Europe,
seems confined to France and western and southern regions.

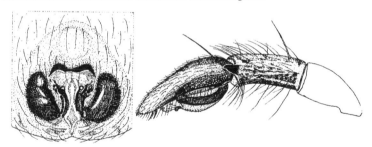

△ *Micaria dives* (Lucas 1846) (= *Micariolepis d.* (Lucas))　　　Plate 5
Description ♀, 2.5–4mm; ♂, 2–3.5mm. This small spider lacks any definite white

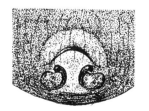

lines on the abdomen, but the whole body is dotted with iridescent squamose hairs which glint as pinpoints of coloured light. Epigyne and palp rather small, but the latter is relatively very long for the size of spider. The patella and tibia together are roughly twice as long as the cymbium.

Habitat Under stones and detritus, and running about, in dry habitats with good exposure to the sun. **Maturity** Spring and summer.

Distribution Absent from Britain and Scandinavia. Uncommon in the rest of the region, becoming more frequent towards middle and southern Europe.

FAMILY CLUBIONIDAE

This family is represented in the region by thirty-five species in two genera. Twenty-four of the most widespread species are described here. The family Liocranidae (p. 136) was once regarded as a subfamily of the Clubionidae but it is now generally agreed that it warrants separate status. The characters distinguishing this family from the Liocranidae include the relatively large width of the eye group and the labium, which is appreciably longer than broad (see Family Key, p. 53). Although many species superficially resemble the Gnaphosidae, they lack the widely set cylindrical spinners and have circular posterior median eyes. The abdomen is sometimes a dull brownish- or reddish-grey with a mousy pubescence; other species have well-defined patterns or markings. They are mainly nocturnal hunters and spend the daytime in a silk cell which may be under stones and bark, or amongst vegetation. Some occur in fairly dry habitats at ground level, similar to those favoured by most gnaphosids. Others are found only in damper situations or higher up on bushes and trees. In the majority of cases, the female spins a silk cell in which she remains with the egg sac. Frequently this cell is constructed by rolling or bending a leaf to form a cavity and then silking the edges together (see Egg Sacs, p. 57). There should be no difficulty in identification to genus level with a hand lens and some species can be identified by the epigyne and male palp in this way. A ×20 lens or field microscope may be necessary with others and in a few cases higher magnification will be required.

Key to the Genera

Leg IV the longest. Carapace with a clear foveal mark in the midline   *Clubiona* p. 124

Leg I clearly the longest. Carapace with no foveal mark   *Cheiracanthium* p. 133

Genus *Clubiona*

Nineteen species of *Clubiona* are described here. The carapace generally lacks any well-defined markings, but there may be radiating lines from the fovea, and some reticulations in the head region. Many have little in the way of abdominal markings and are of a greyish- or reddish-brown colour with a covering of silky hairs. Others have a clear pattern and a representative range of species appears on Plate 5. Males have a slimmer abdomen and sometimes slightly longer chelicerae, but otherwise resemble females.

Clubiona corticalis (Walckenaer 1802)   Plate 5
Description ♀, 7–10mm; ♂, 6–10mm. Clear abdominal pattern in both sexes. Epigyne and male palp easily recognisable with a lens.

Habitat Under bark, stones and detritus; often near houses.
Maturity Spring and summer.
Distribution Absent from Scotland and the extreme north of England; widespread elsewhere but commoner in the south. Widespread throughout northern Europe.

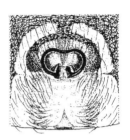 

Clubiona reclusa O.P.-Cambridge 1863
Description ♀, 6–9mm; ♂, 5–6mm. Abdomen uniformly reddish-brown, with slightly darker cardiac mark. This and the following three species have very similar genitalia requiring higher magnification for identification. The epigyne is variable but the wrinkles curve the whole way around and the posterior margin usually forms a shallow V or U. The male palpal organs are distinctive as also is the barbed tibial apophysis.
Habitat Amongst low vegetation and detritus in a wide range of habitats. Egg sac and female often found on vegetation in curled leaves.
Maturity Spring and summer.
Distribution Common and widespread throughout Britain and northern Europe.

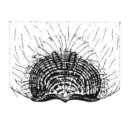 

Clubiona subsultans Thorell 1875
Description ♀, 5–7mm; ♂, 4–7mm. Abdomen generally with markings similar to those of *C. corticalis* (Plate 5), but these less well defined and reddish-brown in colour. Epigyne with transverse folds, behind which are a pair of clear areas followed by a protrusion carrying the openings. Male palpal organs distinctive as also is the barbed tibial apophysis.
Habitat Under bark and stones, amongst pine needles and moss. **Maturity** Summer.
Distribution Recorded from areas of Caledonian pine forest in northern Scotland, where it is not infrequent; absent from the rest of Britain. Widespread in Scandinavia and most of Europe but absent from the south.

Clubiona subsultans (previous page)

Clubiona stagnatalis Kulczynski 1897

Description ♀, 6–8mm; ♂, 5–7mm. Abdomen uniformly reddish-brown with darker cardiac mark. Epigyne with curved wrinkles which do not reach the posterior border. The openings are set widely apart and on each side there is a distinct dark mark. Male palpal organs and barbed tibial apophysis distinctive.

Habitat In moss and under detritus and on leaves of low vegetation, usually in damp situations. **Maturity** Spring and summer.

Distribution Common and widespread throughout Britain and northern Europe.

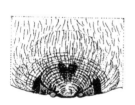 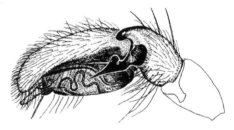

Clubiona norvegica Strand 1900

Description ♀, 5–8mm; ♂, 4–5mm. Abdomen uniformly reddish-brown with slightly darker cardiac mark. Epigyne with openings fairly close together and bulging slightly beyond the posterior border. Wrinkles transverse in the midline but curving round to posterior margin. Male palpal organs and barbed tibial apophysis distinctive.

Habitat Amongst moss and leaf-litter, under stones and other detritus, in a variety of mainly damp habitats. **Maturity** Spring and summer.

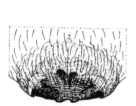 

Distribution Recorded from several sites in northern England and Scotland. Most European records are from Scandinavia.

Clubiona caerulescens L. Koch 1867 (= *C. coerulescens* L. Koch)
Description ♀, 6–9mm; ♂, 5–7mm. Abdomen brownish with slightly longer, silkier pubescence than in other species. Epigyne and male palp identifiable with a lens in the field.
Habitat On or under low vegetation in fairly dry habitats.
Maturity Summer and autumn.
Distribution Rare, but widely distributed throughout Britain. Widespread but uncommon in northern Europe.

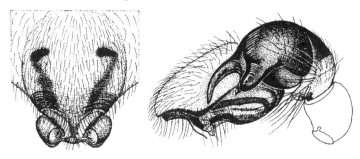

Clubiona pallidula (Clerck 1757)
Description ♀, 7–11mm; ♂, 6–8mm. Abdomen dark purplish-brown with no markings. Epigyne and male palp distinctive; sometimes discernible with a lens.
Habitat Chiefly on bushes and trees, but also under bark and occasionally in leaf-litter. **Maturity** Summer.
Distribution Widespread but local distribution throughout the region.

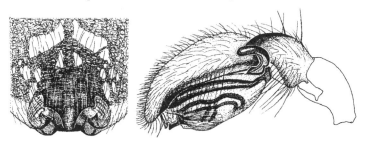

Clubiona phragmitis C.L. Koch 1843
Description ♀, 7–11mm; ♂, 5–10mm. Abdomen greyish- or reddish-brown with silky pubescence. Chelicerae relatively large and dark. Epigyne and male palp distinctive and often discernible with a lens.
Habitat On vegetation, generally in marshy habitats but sometimes on sand dunes.

Female spins a retreat, for herself and the egg sac, in the heads of reeds.
Maturity Spring and summer.
Distribution Widespread but local distribution throughout Britain and northern
Europe.

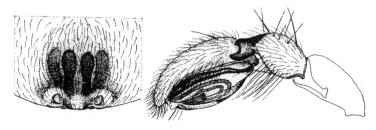

Clubiona terrestris Westring 1851
Description ♀, 6–7mm; ♂, 5–6mm. Abdomen yellowish- to reddish-brown with
reddish-brown cardiac mark. Epigyne and male palp distinctive; often discernible
with a lens, but a little care is needed to avoid confusion with *C. lutescens*.
Habitat Amongst low vegetation and leaf-litter, and under bark and stones; usually
in fairly dry habitats. **Maturity** Spring to autumn.
Distribution Common and widespread throughout the region.

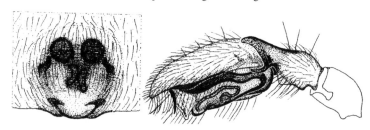

Clubiona neglecta O.P.-Cambridge 1862
Description ♀, 6–8mm; ♂, 4–6mm. Abdomen reddish-brown with slightly darker
cardiac mark. Epigyne and male palp distinctive; epigyne usually not sufficiently
well defined to allow identification with a lens.

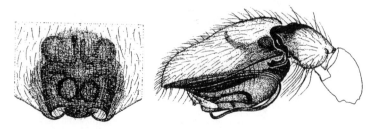

Habitat Amongst low vegetation, in leaf litter and under stones and bark in a variety of situations. **Maturity** Summer.
Distribution Widely distributed throughout the region, but not particularly common.

Clubiona frisia Wunderlich & Schuett 1995
(Previously known as *C. similis* L. Koch 1867 but recently described as a new species, separate from *C. similis*. The latter species is widespread in northern Europe but has not been recorded from Britain.)
Description ♀, 5–7mm; ♂, 5–6mm. Abdomen reddish-brown with slightly darker cardiac mark. Male palp discernible with a lens but epigyne requires higher magnification.
Habitat At the base of vegetation on sandhills and also on hilly or mountainous terrain. **Maturity** Spring and summer.
Distribution Recorded from several coastal sites in south-east England where it has been found amongst clumps of marram grass on sandhills. Widespread throughout northern Europe where it has previously been confused with *C. similis*.

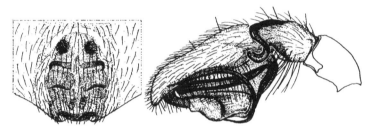

Clubiona lutescens Westring 1851   Plate 5
Description ♀, 6–8mm; ♂, 4–6mm. Male similar to female but with slimmer abdomen. Apart from *C. corticalis* and *C. subsultans*, the foregoing species all have a similar general appearance to this. Epigyne and male palp distinctive and often discernible with a lens; care is needed to avoid confusion with *C. terrestris*.
Habitat On low vegetation, bushes and trees, often in damp habitats.
Maturity Spring to autumn.
Distribution Uncommon in Scotland; common and widespread throughout the rest of the region.

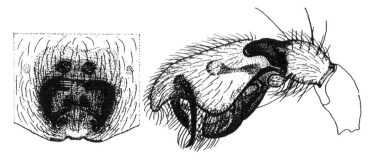

Clubiona comta C.L. Koch 1839 (= *C. compta* C.L. Koch)   Plate 5
Description ♀, 3.5–6mm; ♂, 3–5mm. Highly characteristic general appearance; the only other species which resembles it is *C. genevensis*. The abdominal pattern is similar to that of *C. corticalis*, but the latter species is larger and the markings are never reddish. Epigyne and male palp discernible with a lens, despite small size of spider.
Habitat On leaves of bushes, trees and plants such as ivy; also under bark.
Maturity Spring and summer.
Distribution Common and widespread throughout the region.

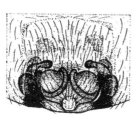 

Clubiona brevipes Blackwall 1841
Description ♀, 4.5–7mm; ♂, 4–6mm. Abdomen reddish-brown, sometimes with a darker cardiac mark and often with reticulations and lighter spots. Epigyne and male palp usually discernible with a lens, although the epigyne may sometimes be ill-defined.
Habitat Usually on the leaves of trees and bushes, but occasionally found under bark. **Maturity** Spring and summer.
Distribution Common and widespread throughout the region.

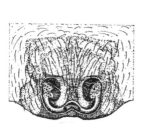 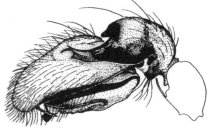

Clubiona trivialis C.L. Koch 1843
Description ♀, 4–4.5mm; ♂, 3.5–4mm. Abdomen uniformly reddish-brown with faint darker cardiac mark. Male palp discernible with a lens, especially the spade-like tibial apophysis. Epigyne similar to the four species following below, but none of these has a uniformly red-brown abdomen.
Habitat On or at the base of low plants and heather, and on gorse and under stones, usually in dry situations and often on higher ground. **Maturity** Spring to autumn.
Distribution Fairly frequent and widely distributed throughout the region.

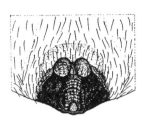 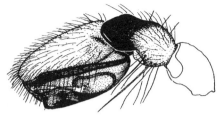

Clubiona juvenis Simon 1878
Description ♀, 5–6mm; ♂, 4–5mm. The carapace is almost oblong in appearance, with the midpoint of the carapace scarcely wider than the head. The abdomen is pale yellowish (darker in males) with a red-brown cardiac mark and a covering of silky hairs. The male palp is discernible with a lens, especially the broad, hooked tibial apophysis. The epigyne is similar to *C. trivialis* and the three species following below, but these have different markings and none has an oblong carapace.
Habitat In marshland, amongst vegetation and leaf-litter; also on sand dunes.
Maturity Summer.
Distribution Recorded from a very few marshy localities in the south and east of England and from dunes in the south-east of Ireland. Rare, but possibly widespread in Europe, with records from France and Switzerland.

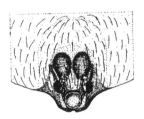 

Clubiona genevensis L. Koch 1866
Description ♀, 3.5–4.5mm; ♂, 3–3.5mm. Abdomen with a clear red-brown pattern similar to that of *C. comta* (Plate 5). Epigyne and male palp easily distinguished from those of *C. comta* with a lens. Those species with similar epigynes to *C. genevensis* lack the clear abdominal pattern.

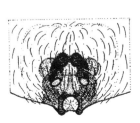 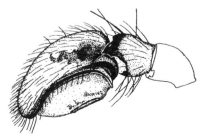

Habitat Under stones or amongst low vegetation in mainly dry, sandy habitats.
Maturity Spring and summer.
Distribution Recorded from a very few localities on the south and south-west coast
of England and from Scilly, Ramsey, and Skokholm islands. Widespread throughout
northern Europe but uncommon, except locally.

Clubiona diversa O.P.-Cambridge 1862   Plate 5
Description ♀, 4–5mm; ♂, 3–4mm. Males closely resemble females in the abdominal markings; the pale yellow abdomen with reddish midline marks and reddish tip
are very noticeable to the naked eye. The epigyne and male palp are usually discernible with a lens; the abdominal markings distinguish the species from those
described above, and the adult size usually separates it from *C. subtilis*, below.
Habitat In the south of England it appears to favour drier habitats and is locally common on chalk grassland. In the north of England and Scotland it is extremely common amongst moss in boggy areas. **Maturity** Spring to autumn.
Distribution Widespread in Britain, but perhaps commoner in the north. Widespread
in northern Europe.

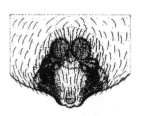

Clubiona subtilis L. Koch 1867
Description ♀, 3–4.5mm; ♂, 2.5–3mm. Abdomen yellowish-brown, slightly darker
than *C. diversa* with a darker reddish-brown cardiac mark which is broader at the
front of the abdomen. Usually suffused with reddish-brown at the tip of the abdomen.
Males a little darker than females. These markings, together with the overall adult
size and the epigyne and male palp, should enable identification in the field.
Habitat Amongst moss and low vegetation in damp habitats.
Maturity Spring to autumn.
Distribution Widespread, but generally less common than *C. diversa*; commoner in
the south of England. Widespread in northern Europe.

Genus *Cheiracanthium*

Eight species of *Cheiracanthium* occur in the region of which five are described here. They are easily distinguished from species of *Clubiona* by having the first pair of legs the longest and lacking a clear foveal mark in the midline of the carapace. The spiders are usually found in a silk retreat during the daytime; this is usually on vegetation, but may be under stones. Mating usually occurs within the retreat and the female subsequently makes a large silk cell, on vegetation or under stones, in which she remains with the eggs. Males resemble females in most respects, but have a slimmer abdomen and markedly elongated chelicerae. The epigynes and male palps are all very similar but readily distinguished and, if taken together with the abdominal markings and overall size, should allow identification in the field.

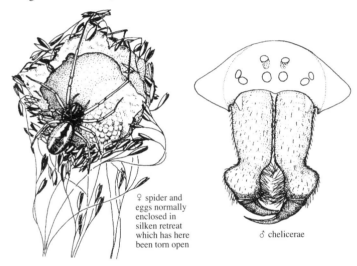

♀ spider and eggs normally enclosed in silken retreat which has here been torn open

♂ chelicerae

Cheiracanthium erraticum   *Cheiracanthium oncognathum*

Cheiracanthium erraticum (Walckenaer 1802)   Plate 6

Description ♀, 6–9mm; ♂, 5–6.5mm. Abdomen greyish-brown at the sides with clear reddish median stripe flanked by pale yellow stripes; male similar, but abdomen slimmer and chelicerae longer. The epigyne has a circular opening which

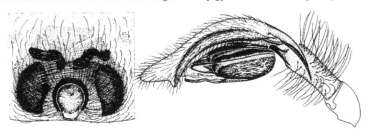

is relatively small when compared with the spermathecae and the overall width of the epigyne. The cymbium of the male palp has a distinct ventral projection near the tip, and a sharply pointed spur (extending back over the tibia) at the opposite end.
Habitat On low plants (grasses, heather etc.). Females and egg sacs typically found in a silken cell interwoven with bent grass heads or leaves.
Maturity Spring and summer.
Distribution By far the commonest member of the genus; widespread throughout the region.

Cheiracanthium pennyi O.P.-Cambridge 1873

Description ♀, 6–7mm; ♂, 5–6mm. Very similar to *C. erraticum* in general appearance. Epigyne has a much broader opening which is not circular and which is much wider than either of the spermathecae. The cymbium of the male palp lacks a ventral projection near its tip and the long cymbial spur is blunter at its tip, and broader at its base, than in *C. erraticum*.
Habitat and Maturity Similar to *C. erraticum*.
Distribution Very rare in Britain and only recorded from a few sites in southern England. Not recorded from Scandinavia; widespread but uncommon in the rest of the region.

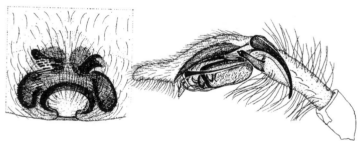

Cheiracanthium virescens (Sundevall 1833)

Description ♀, 5–9mm; ♂, 5–7mm. Abdomen greenish-brown to rusty brown with no other clear markings apart from a slightly darker cardiac mark. The epigyne opening forms more of an arch than a circle, the spermathecae are relatively smaller than in *C. erraticum*, and two pairs of ducts are visible. The cymbium of the male palp has a very small ventral projection near its tip and the cymbial spur is more slender, and directed more downwards, than in *C. erraticum*.

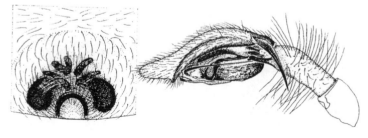

Habitat Dry, sandy habitats; under stones and on low vegetation, such as heather.
Maturity Spring and summer.
Distribution Widely distributed throughout Britain and northern Europe but rather uncommon.

△ *Cheiracanthium punctorium* (Villers 1789)   Plate 6
Description ♀, 10–15mm; ♂, 7.5–12mm. Male as illustrated; female greenish-brown with slightly darker cardiac mark; chelicerae smaller than in the male. Both this and the following species are larger than the three described above. The opening of the epigyne is frequently heart-shaped; even when the anterior border has a smooth curvature the posterior margins curve inwards. The ducts, when visible, also differ from those of *C. oncognathum*. The male palp differs from that of *C. oncognathum* in the shape of the cymbium, the shorter cymbial spur and the palpal organs.
Habitat On grasses and bushes in damp clearings or wasteland.
Maturity Summer and autumn.
Distribution Absent from Britain, but widespread throughout the rest of northern Europe.

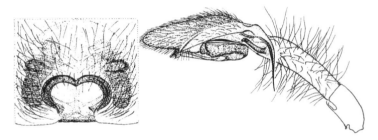

△ *Cheiracanthium oncognathum* Thorell 1871
Description ♀, 11–13mm; ♂, 9–10mm. Very similar in general appearance, and size, to *C. punctorium* but the male is instantly recognisable by the conspicuous swellings on the enlarged chelicerae, as illustrated (p. 133). The opening of the epigyne is an arch which is joined to the posterior margin by more or less straight sides. The male palp has the cymbium turned up at its tip, and the cymbial spur is much longer than in *C. punctorium*.
Habitat and Maturity Similar to *C. punctorium*.
Distribution Absent from Britain. Widespread throughout the rest of northern Europe with the possible exception of Belgium and Holland.

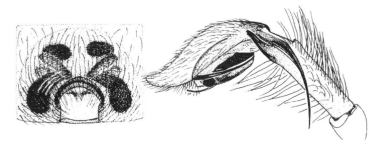

FAMILY LIOCRANIDAE

This family is represented in the region by seventeen species in six genera. Fourteen of the most widely distributed species are described here. The family Liocranidae was once regarded as a subfamily of the Clubionidae but is now given separate status. The characters distinguishing this family from the Clubionidae include the relatively narrow width of the eye group and the labium, which is roughly as broad as it is long. Many species have clear markings on the carapace as well as an abdominal pattern or markings. They are mainly nocturnal hunters but *Phrurolithus* species are adapted for an active diurnal lifestyle. Whilst some guard their egg sac, some species of *Agroeca* suspend theirs on stalks, camouflage them with mud, and abandon them (see Egg Sacs, p. 58).

Key to the Genera

1.	Posterior row of eyes, viewed from above, slightly recurved	2
	Posterior row of eyes, viewed from above, straight or procurved	3
2.	Adult spider 2.8–4mm long; tibia I and II with five pairs of ventral spines; metatarsus I and II with three pairs of ventral spines	*Apostenus* p. 141
	Adult spider 5.5–10.5mm long; tibia I and II with four pairs of ventral spines; metatarsus I and II with one pair of ventral spines	*Liocranum* p. 142
3.	Posterior row of eyes more or less straight. Abdomen marked with white patches and bars. Carapace usually with rows of white hairs radiating from the fovea. Rather ant-like in appearance. Epigyne of female broad and swollen; male palp with a long, broad, hooked tibial apophysis. Tibia I with four or five pairs of ventral spines; metatarsus I with two to three pairs of ventral spines	*Phrurolithus* p. 143
	Posterior row of eyes markedly procurved. General appearance not as above	4
4.	Tibia I with six to ten pairs of ventral spines. Posterior median eyes further from each other than from posterior lateral eyes	*Scotina* p. 139
	Tibia I with two pairs of ventral spines. Posterior eyes more or less equidistant	5
5.	Metatarsus I and II with three pairs of ventral spines	*Agroeca* p. 136
	Metatarsus I and II with two pairs of long ventral spines	*Agraecina* p. 139

Genus *Agroeca*

The five representatives of this genus are rather similar in general appearance. The carapace usually has clear dark marks (lines, wedges or loops) radiating from the fovea and the abdomen usually has a vague pattern of bars or chevrons. They are generally found amongst low vegetation and amongst moss, leaf-litter and other detritus, but some species occur in marshland or on sand dunes. The egg sacs of *A. brunnea* and *A. proxima* are placed on a stalk and camouflaged with earth (see Egg

Sacs, p. 58). The genus is readily identifiable with a lens and in some cases identification to species level will be possible in this way. However, higher magnification will be required for reliable identification in the majority of cases.

Agroeca brunnea (Blackwall 1833) Plate 6
Description ♀, 7–8mm; ♂, 6–7mm. Male similar to female but generally darker and with a slimmer abdomen. Epigyne and male palp relatively large and usually discernible with a lens, but care is needed to distinguish the species from *A. lusatica* (below).
Habitat Amongst low vegetation, moss, and leaf-litter in damp habitats, often in or near woodland. **Maturity** Summer to late autumn.
Distribution Widely distributed throughout Britain and northern Europe but fairly uncommon, the egg sacs being seen more frequently than the spiders.

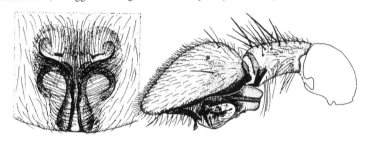

Agroeca lusatica (L. Koch 1875)
Description ♀, 6–7mm; ♂, 5–6mm. General appearance like that of *A. proxima* (Plate 6). Epigyne with relatively smaller ducts than in *A. brunnea* and with the curved opening narrower than the outside width of the ducts. Male palp with a narrower tibial apophysis than in *A. brunnea* and with different palpal organs which do not project backwards as far as in that species.
Habitat Sandhills, and also moss and detritus in woodland.
Maturity Summer to late autumn.
Distribution Recorded in England from sandhills in Kent. Widespread but uncommon in northern Europe.

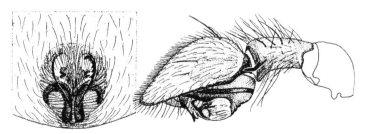

Agroeca proxima (O.P.-Cambridge 1871) Plate 6
Description ♀, 5.5–7.5mm; ♂, 4–5.5mm. Eyes more or less equal-sized (cf. *A. inopina*). Male similar to female but with slimmer abdomen. The J-shaped ducts in the epigyne are characteristic, together with the straight ducts, angled together, in the

posterior half. The male palpal tibia has an apophysis which curves slightly upwards and is rounded below.

Habitat Amongst low vegetation, leaf-litter and moss often in fairly dry habitats, including heathland and woodland clearings.

Maturity Females most of the year, males late summer to autumn.

Distribution Widely distributed throughout Britain and northern Europe and the commonest of the species. The egg sacs are seen more frequently than the spiders.

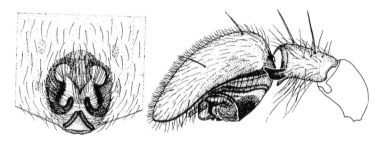

Agroeca inopina O.P.-Cambridge 1886

Description ♀, 4.5–7.5mm; ♂, 3–4.5mm. Median eyes equal-sized but smaller than laterals. Similar in general appearance to *A. proxima*. Epigyne with long, curved ducts in posterior half. Tibial apophysis of male palp with a small projection on the upper surface; smoothly rounded below.

Habitat On sandhills and in woodland, amongst low vegetation and in leaf-litter.

Maturity Summer to late autumn.

Distribution Locally distributed in southern England and south Wales. Widespread in northern Europe, but apparently not in Scandinavia.

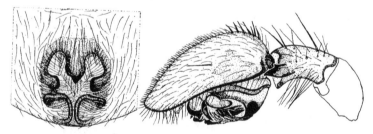

Agroeca cuprea Menge 1873 (= *Agroeca pullata* Thorell 1875)

Description ♀, 4–5mm; ♂, 3.5–4mm. Anterior median eyes smaller than posterior medians and smaller than the laterals. Similar to *A. proxima*, but usually much darker. The epigyne has J-shaped ducts as in *A. proxima*, but the ducts posterior to these are smaller and set at a shallower angle. The epigyne is often partly or completely obscured by a dark, irregular exudate, much more than in the other species. Tibial apophysis of male palp smooth on its upper surface, but with an angled protrusion below. **Habitat** In sandy areas, often with grass and heather, and in wood-

land amongst moss and under stones. **Maturity** Spring and summer.
Distribution Very locally distributed near the coast of south and south-east England.
Widespread in Europe.

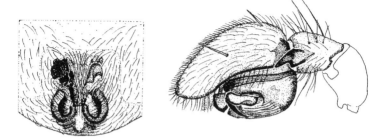

Genus Agraecina

This genus differs from *Agroeca* (in which it has formerly been included) by having
only two pairs of ventral spines on metatarsus I and a rather different epigyne and
male palp.

Agraecina striata (Kulczynski 1882) (= *Agroeca s*. Kulczynski)   Plate 6
Description ♀, 4.5–5.5mm; ♂, 3–3.5mm. The abdominal markings and the slight
darkening of tibia and metatarsus I and II are usually characteristic. Male similar to
female, but with a slimmer abdomen. The epigyne varies slightly, in that the ducts
may be further apart. The male palpal organs are distinctive, as also is the long tibial apophysis.
Habitat Under stones and amongst detritus in marshy areas; also in damp woodland
sites. **Maturity** Summer.
Distribution Rather rare and recorded from south and south-east England and the
south-west of Ireland. Widespread but rare throughout northern Europe.

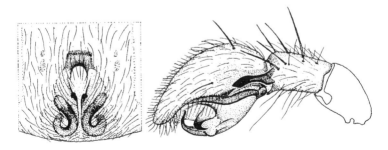

Genus *Scotina*

The three species of *Scotina* in the region are distinguished from *Agroeca* and
Agraecina by the six to ten pairs of ventral spines on tibia I. These are easily seen with
a lens. The carapace is darker than in *Agroeca* but sometimes has light median and

lateral bands. The femora are usually lighter in colour than the rest of the leg segments, especially those of legs I and II. These spiders live and hunt at ground level and are usually found amongst moss and leaf-litter, or at the base of grass tussocks. They are generally uncommon or rare spiders and little is known of their biology. They all have rather similar epigynes and male palps but these can easily be distinguished with a microscope. The two commonest species are generally separable by their markings.

Scotina celans (Blackwall 1841)   Plate 6
Description ♀, 4–4.75mm; ♂, 2.5–3mm. Male similar to female, but with slimmer abdomen. The light median and lateral bands on the carapace are characteristic of this species, as also is the reddish abdomen (this may however be partly obscured by hairs). The epigyne has relatively large, broad ducts; the paired spermathecae, in the posterior part, may not always be visible. The palpal organs and the arrangement of ducts are characteristic, as also is the tibial apophysis.
Habitat Amongst moss, leaf-litter and grass tussocks in woodland, often in damp habitats; also on chalk grassland.
Maturity Females all year, males in late summer and autumn.
Distribution Uncommon but widespread in Britain; commoner in the south. Widespread in northern Europe.

 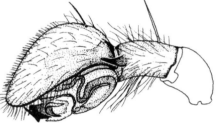

Scotina gracilipes (Blackwall 1859)
Description ♀ ♂, 2.5–3.5mm. Carapace uniformly dark brown to black and lacking the light markings present in *S. celans*. Abdomen similar to that of *S. celans* but usually darker. Darkening of tibiae, metatarsi and tarsi of legs I and II is more pronounced than in *S. celans*. The epigyne has relatively small and widely separated

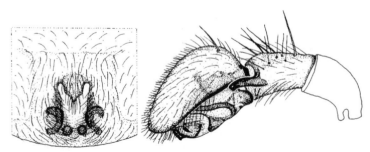

ducts and a pair of small spermathecae is usually visible. The male palpal organs and tibial apophysis are distinctive.

Habitat Usually in drier, often heathland habitats, but also in woodland.

Maturity Females all year, males in late summer and autumn.

Distribution Widespread in Britain, but uncommon and locally distributed. Widespread in northern Europe.

Scotina palliardi (L. Koch 1881)

Description ♀ ♂, 2.5–3.5mm. Carapace usually dark brown; occasionally there may be very obscure light bands as in *S. celans*; sometimes there is a narrow dark border which is never present in *S. celans*. The abdomen is generally darker than in *S. celans* and legs I and II have more pronounced darkening of the tibia, metatarsus and tarsus. The ducts in the epigyne are narrower, relative to the size of the spermathecae, and are closer together than in *S. gracilipes*. The male palpal organs and tibial apophysis are distinctive.

Habitat Amongst moss, grass, heather and leaf-litter on chalk grassland and heathland.

Maturity Spring to autumn.

Distribution Rare in Britain and only recorded from a small number of sites in southern England. Widespread but generally uncommon in northern Europe.

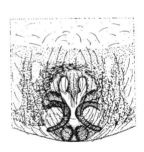 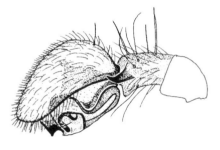

Genus *Apostenus*

A single species occurs in the region and, like *Liocranum*, has the posterior row of eyes recurved. It differs from *Liocranum* in being smaller and in having five pairs of ventral spines on tibia I and II and three pairs of ventral spines on metatarsus I and II.

Apostenus fuscus Westring 1851   Plate 6

Description ♀, 3–4mm; ♂, 2.8–4mm. Male similar to female but the carapace is relatively narrower in the head region, and the slimmer abdomen has an indistinct scutum on the anterior part, dorsally. The epigyne and male palp are distinctive.

Habitat Amongst moss and undergrowth and under stones in woodland. Also amongst heather and, in Britain, on coastal shingle.

Maturity Spring to autumn.

Distribution Recorded from shingle in Kent. Widespread in northern Europe.

Apostenus fuscus (previous page)

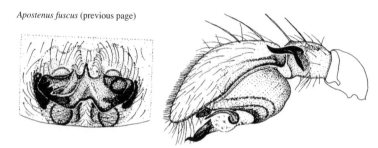

Genus *Liocranum*

Two species occur in the region, only one in Britain. They have slightly recurved eyes, like *Apostenus*, but are larger and have fewer ventral spines on tibia and metatarsus I and II. Both species occur in dry habitats, under stones and detritus, and occasionally are found indoors. The epigynes and male palps are discernible in the field and the species can also be separated by the abdominal markings and, usually, by size.

Liocranum rupicola (Walckenaer 1830)   Plate 6
Description ♀, 6–8.5mm; ♂, 5.5–6mm. Male similar to female, with slimmer abdomen and a clear pattern. Epigyne distinctive. Male palp with a small, hooked tibial apophysis. The palpal patella (not fully shown in the illustration) is longer than the tibia.
Habitat Under stones and detritus in dry situations and occasionally indoors.
Maturity Spring to autumn.
Distribution Mainly southern England and south Wales but occasionally found further north and recorded from Ireland. Widespread in northern Europe.

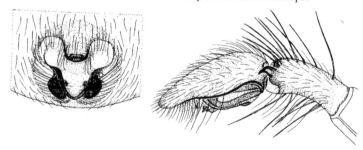

△ *Liocranum rutilans* (Thorell 1875)
Description ♀, 8–10.5mm; ♂, 8mm. Both the carapace and the abdomen are uniformly brownish with no pattern. Epigyne distinctive. Male palp with a long tibial apophysis; palpal patella much shorter than tibia.
Habitat and Maturity Similar to *L. rupicola*.
Distribution Absent from Britain. Widespread in northern Europe.

Genus *Phrurolithus*

Four species occur in the region, two of which are described here. They are small spiders, rather ant-like in appearance and movement, and are diurnal hunters. In warm, sunny conditions they run about very rapidly and somewhat resemble species of *Micaria*, although completely lacking the iridescence of these species. The abdomen is marked with patches and lines of white hairs and males have a shiny, dorsal abdominal scutum covering the entire abdomen. The epigynes and male palps are relatively large and are often discernible with a lens.

Phrurolithus festivus (C.L. Koch 1835)   Plate 6
Description ♀ ♂, 2.5–3mm. Female similar to male but with a larger abdomen, more clearly marked with white hairs. Epigyne and male palp distinctive, the latter having a very long, broad, tibial apophysis curving ventrally around the side.
Habitat Under stones and detritus and amongst leaf-litter and moss in a variety of situations, both damp and dry; occasionally in the company of ants. Runs about rapidly in the open in sunny conditions. **Maturity** Spring and summer.
Distribution Widely distributed and fairly common throughout Britain and northern Europe.

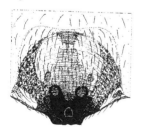
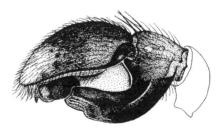

Phrurolithus minimus C.L. Koch 1839
Description ♀, 2.5–3.5mm; ♂, 2–2.5mm. Similar to *P. festivus*, but less clear abdominal markings, sometimes reduced to a single pair of light spots anteriorly. Epigyne and male palp distinctive, the latter having a narrower and more hooked tibial apophysis than *P. festivus*.

Habitat and Maturity Similar to *P. festivus*.

Distribution Rare in Britain and recorded from a few chalk grassland sites in the south of England. Widespread but uncommon in northern Europe.

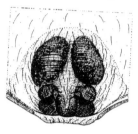 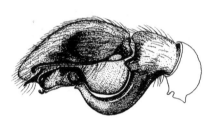

FAMILY ZORIDAE

Genus *Zora*

There are seven species of this family represented in the region. All are in the genus *Zora* and four of the most widespread species are described here. The carapace is rather narrowed in front and the characteristic arrangement of the eyes has been given in the Family Key (p. 47). The species are all very similar in general appearance, being yellowish with distinctive brown markings. Males are similar to females but have a slimmer abdomen, often with more clearly defined markings. They hunt actively in the daytime on low vegetation and at ground level, but can also be found in moss, leaf-litter and under stones and other detritus. The female fixes her white, flat egg sac to a stone or a leaf and stands guard directly over it. Whilst the genus is readily identifiable with a lens, the epigynes and male palps are small and so similar that higher magnification is required for the determination of species.

Zora spinimana (Sundevall 1833)   Plate 7

Description ♀, 5–6.5mm; ♂, 4.5–5mm. Male similar to female but with slimmer, more clearly marked abdomen. Epigyne with a pair of spermathecae in the posterior half which are each larger than the opening. This feature also applies to *Z. silvestris*, but this species has a different shape to the opening and to the ducts on each side. *Z. silvestris* also has only two pairs of ventral spines on metatarsus I and II whereas all other species have three pairs. Male palp distinguished by the palpal organs and the tibial apophysis. Males of *Z. spinimana* can also be distinguished from all the other

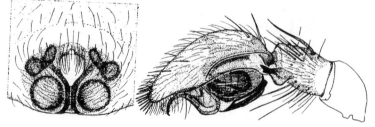

species by the presence of a pad or brush of dense, short, grey-brown hairs on the under surface of coxa IV.
Habitat Amongst moss, leaf-litter and detritus in woods and hedgerows and in a wide variety of other situations; also running on vegetation.
Maturity Spring to autumn.
Distribution Widespread and common throughout the region.

Zora armillata Simon 1878
Description ♀, 4–6.5mm; ♂, 3.5–4mm. Similar to *Z. spinimana* but with fewer dark markings on the legs. Epigyne with a relatively large opening and distinctively shaped spermathecae and ducts. Male palpal organs and pointed tibial apophysis distinctive, and the lack of a brush of hairs on coxa IV provides additional separation from *Z. spinimana*.
Habitat Fens and marshy areas or wet areas of heathland.
Maturity Spring to Autumn.
Distribution Recorded from a small number of sites in the south and east of England. Recorded from Sweden and France, but apparently also rare in northern Europe.

Zora nemoralis (Blackwall 1861)
Description ♀, 3.5–5.5mm; ♂, 3–4mm. Similar to *Z. spinimana* but slightly darker with the dark marking sometimes a more greyish brown. Epigyne with a relatively large opening which is usually heart-shaped, and relatively small spermathecae. Male palpal organs distinctive, and the blunt tibial apophysis is much broader at its tip than in *Z. silvestris*.
Habitat Woodland, and grass and heather in woodland clearings.
Maturity Spring to autumn.
Distribution Rather locally distributed; uncommon in Scotland and the north of England, rare in Wales and the south of England. Widely distributed throughout northern Europe.

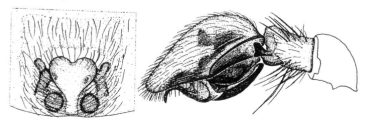

Zora silvestris Kulczynski 1897

Description ♀, 3.5–4mm; ♂, 3–4mm. Similar to *Z. spinimana* but more greyish brown in overall appearance. Only two pairs of ventral spines on metatarsus I and II whereas the other species have three pairs. Epigyne has a small opening of characteristic shape, and relatively large spermathecae. Male palpal tibia with a blunt apophysis which is not broadened at its tip.

Habitat On or beneath heather. **Maturity** Spring to autumn.

Distribution Recorded from a very few sites in south-east England. Probably widespread in north-eastern Europe but not apparently recorded from the south-west of the region.

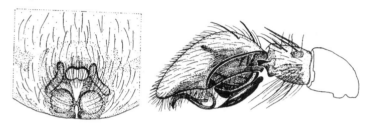

FAMILY ANYPHAENIDAE

Genus *Anyphaena*

A single member of the Anyphaenidae, genus *Anyphaena*, occurs in the region. The spider is distinctively marked and the tracheal spiracles are easily visible halfway between the spinners and the epigastric fold (see Family Key, p. 48). The species lives and hunts on the leaves of trees and bushes. Males vibrate the abdomen on the surface of a leaf in order to attract the female's attention prior to mating. The female attaches the egg sac to a curled leaf and remains on guard with it in a flimsy silk cell. By this time, the abdomen of the female has become rather slim and the colour darkened to an almost uniform grey-brown. The species is easily identified with a lens in the field, both by its general appearance and by the epigyne and male palp.

Anyphaena accentuata (Walckenaer 1802)   Plate 7

Description ♀, 4.5–7.5mm; ♂, 4–6.5mm. Both sexes are illustrated and have an unmistakable appearance. Females on egg sacs are usually slimmer and darker and may have the markings completely obscured. Epigyne and male palp distinctive.

Habitat On the leaves of trees and bushes.
Maturity Early summer, females to autumn.
Distribution Widely but locally distributed throughout Britain and northern Europe. Where it does occur, there are usually large numbers together.

FAMILY HETEROPODIDAE

The names Sparassidae and Eusparassidae have previously been used for this family which contains just one species, genus *Micrommata*, in the region.

Genus *Micrommata*

The single species in the region has a striking appearance. Both sexes have a green carapace and legs (duller in the male) and the eyes are ringed with white hairs. Females have a bright green abdomen with the cardiac mark outlined in yellow. Subadult males resemble females in general appearance but when moulted into maturity have a yellow abdomen marked with scarlet bands. Spiderlings are straw-coloured, often spotted with pink, but are still recognisable by the white rings around the black eyes. These spiders catch their prey in low vegetation, largely by waiting and grabbing rather than by pursuit. The female makes a substantial cell, for herself and the egg sac, by joining together leaves of bushes or trees.

Micrommata virescens (Clerck 1757) (= *M. roseum* (Clerck))   Plate 7
Description ♀, 10–15mm; ♂, 7–10mm. Both sexes are illustrated and are of unmistakable appearance. Epigyne and male palp also very distinctive.
Habitat On low vegetation in damp, sheltered woodland clearings.
Maturity Late spring to autumn; adult males only for a short season in summer.
Distribution Widespread throughout Britain but generally rare in the north and uncommon in the south; recently recorded from Colonsay. Widespread throughout northern Europe but generally uncommon.

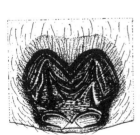 

FAMILY THOMISIDAE

Sixty-two species of the family Thomisidae are known from the region, in fourteen genera. Of these, fifty-one species are described here. The family falls into two groups, the Misumeninae (or Thomisinae) and the Philodrominae, and these have been elevated to family status in recent years (the Thomisidae and Philodromidae). I remain wholly unconvinced of the validity of this move and feel that there are insufficient consistent features to allow the erection of clearly separable families. It appears to me that the differences between the Misumeninae and Philodrominae are far outweighed by their similarities. These spiders are inherently diverse and, even within the two groups, the genera show wide variation in general appearance, epigynes and male palpal organs.

The great diversity of form and colour shown by the Thomisidae relates to their exploitation of a wide variety of habitats and their often remarkable capacity for camouflage, sometimes even to the extent of slowly changing colour. Illustrations on a white background (see Colour Plates 7 to 11) show quite strikingly marked spiders of different colours and shapes. It may be difficult to imagine that, in their natural surroundings, many are easily overlooked and some are almost invisible unless they move! The majority of species are rather crab-like in appearance, have the first two pairs of legs longer than the rest, and can walk sideways, as well as forwards and backwards. For this reason they are sometimes called 'crab spiders'. None of the species spins a web for snaring purposes; the majority sit and wait for prey which they grab with the front pairs of legs, but others are more active hunters. The Misumeninae lie in wait for prey, and only have claw tufts and scopulae on the metatarsi and tarsi of legs III and IV; these anchor the spider to the substrate leaving legs I and II to act as traps. The Philodrominae are more active hunters and have claw tufts and scopulae on the metatarsi and tarsi of all legs. Those species which wait camouflaged in flowers, and ambush visiting insects, have venom which is apparently highly toxic to insects such as bumble bees, which are much larger than the spiders themselves. When an insect approaches the flower, the spider opens wide the first two pairs of legs, and may also subtly realign itself with the prey. Only when the victim is definitely within grasp do the legs fold around, although there may be some almost imperceptible movement as it gets close and perhaps wanders away again. Once gripped, it is bitten and quickly dies from the poison. Similar tactics are used by many other species which wait, suitably camouflaged, on vegetation and at ground level. Species of *Philodromus* also do this but, in addition, will actively pursue their prey. Thomisids have small chelicerae with no large teeth, and prey is sucked dry, rather than mashed up, leaving a perfectly formed husk.

In some genera there is great disparity in size and markings between males and females. Mating often involves the male touching and stroking the female who may adopt a submissive posture with legs drawn in. In *Xysticus* species, the female seems to fall into a torpid state and the male walks over and around her cephalothorax and flexed legs, trailing silk as he goes, and tying up her front end before mating. Other species have a much briefer mating, with little ceremony. Females usually stand guard over their eggs, but frequently die before the spiderlings emerge. The egg sacs themselves may be rather flat, silk structures fastened to vegetation, or take the form of a woolly ball or papery sac which is guarded on vegetation, on bark or at ground level under stones. In many species the male palps have the cymbium and palpal organs rather discoid in shape and slightly flattened dorsoventrally. The majority of the important identification features are visible only from below and, for comparative purposes, a ventral view is illustrated for all species. Identification of males is possible in the field with many species, the male spider being slightly compressed in the spi-pot once the palps have been extended (see p. 34). The following key separates the genera, but a glance at the colour plates (7 to 11) may help in the interpretation of couplet 1. I have tried to use only those characters which are easily seen with a lens in the field.

Key to the Subfamilies and Genera

1. Femora of legs I and II considerably stouter than those of
    legs III and IV, Subfamily Misumeninae (p. 152)   2

    Femora of legs I and II scarcely stouter than those of legs III
    and IV, Subfamily Philodrominae (p. 169)   13

2. Whole spider covered thickly with long,
    pale hairs and pale spines   △ *Heriaeus* p. 157

    Spider with only short hairs; spines, if present, are dark   3

3. Abdomen distinctly triangular, being
    widened and truncated behind.   4

    Abdomen possibly wider behind, but
    more rounded; may be globular
    oval, or pointed behind   5

    Thomisus ♀

4   Lateral eyes on a pronounced conical
    protuberance which projects beyond
    each anterior and posterior lateral eye   *Thomisus* p. 152

    Thomisus head
    from in front

    Lateral eyes on separate shallow tubercles   *Pistius* p. 153

5. Abdomen with a single blunt
    tubercle posteriorly,
    above the spinners   △ *Tmarus* p. 153

    Abdomen globular, oval or slightly pointed behind, but
    lacking a tubercle   6

6. Trapezium formed by the four median eyes longer than broad
    (view at an angle of about 45° between dorsal and front
    views so that both pairs of eyes are square on)   7

    Trapezium formed by the four median eyes square, or
    broader than long   8

7. Spider yellowish, or earthy-brown, often
   with marbled markings; sometimes
   black and covered with particles of
   earth. Never green. Numerous
   short, club-shaped hairs may be
   present on the head, but no long
   bristles

Ozyptila p. 164

Female and subadult spiders green with brown
   abdominal pattern. Male less obviously
   green, but with long bristles on head

Diaea p. 156

8. Anterior median eyes closer to the anterior laterals than to
   each other and considerably smaller than the anterior
   laterals (view from in front)   9

   Anterior eyes roughly equidistant and more equal in size   10

9. Whole of spider markedly flattened
   dorsoventrally. Carapace dark
   brown with white around the
   eyes. Abdomen dark brown
   with conspicuous white
   wrinkles, which extend from
   the sides over the hind part and
   impart a shrivelled appearance

△ *Coriarachne*
p. 158

Spider not markedly flattened. Carapace
   marked with broad lateral bands,
   within which is a roughly triangular
   area running back from the eyes.
   Sides of abdomen often
   wrinkled but this not
   extending over the hind
   part. Abdomen often with a
   pattern of triangles and bars

Xysticus p. 158

10. Anterior median eyes roughly
      the same distance
      apart as are the
      posterior median
      eyes

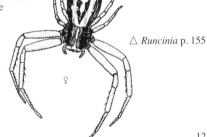

♀

Misumena p. 154

     Anterior median eyes closer together
      than posterior median eyes   11

11. Carapace with a continuous, transverse,
      white bar running between the lateral
      eyes on each side, through the
      posterior median eyes, and
      extending to a small tubercle
      laterally

△ *Runcinia* p. 155

♀

     Eyes on light tubercles, but no
      continuous light bar   12

12. Abdomen with broad, black, dentate folium;
      sides pale yellow to orange-red.
      Carapace and legs dark brown to
      black

△ *Synaema* p. 156

♀

     Carapace and legs green and
      abdomen with brown and
      white pattern *or*, carapace
      and legs brown and
      abdomen with green,
      white and brown markings

△ *Misumenops* p. 155

♀

13. Posterior row of eyes, viewed from
    above, only slightly recurved,
    the eyes being equidistant, or
    the medians a little closer to
    the laterals than to each
    other   *Philodromus* p. 169

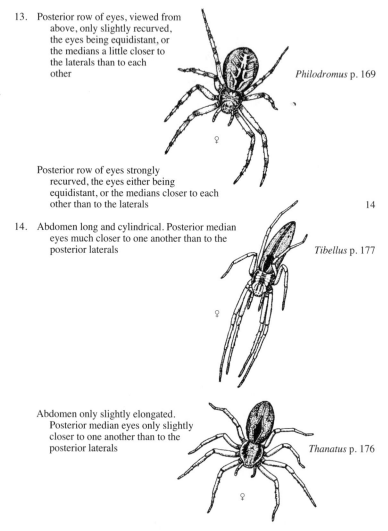

   Posterior row of eyes strongly
    recurved, the eyes either being
    equidistant, or the medians closer to each
    other than to the laterals   14

14. Abdomen long and cylindrical. Posterior median
    eyes much closer to one another than to the
    posterior laterals   *Tibellus* p. 177

   Abdomen only slightly elongated.
    Posterior median eyes only slightly
    closer to one another than to the
    posterior laterals   *Thanatus* p. 176

Subfamily Misumeninae
Genus *Thomisus*

Only one species of *Thomisus* occurs in the region and it is easily identified by the
protuberances which carry the lateral eyes, together with the shape of the abdomen.
The colour of the female's abdomen varies and may be white, yellow or various
shades of pink. Individual spiders can slowly change colour to match their surroundings. The spider typically sits amongst the pink blooms of heather and waits
for prey.

Thomisus onustus Walckenaer 1806   Plate 7
Description ♀, 6–7mm; ♂, 2.5–3.5mm. Colour of female may be white, yellow or various shades of pink. The much smaller male is less variable in colour. The epigyne is often rather ill-defined. The male palp, viewed from below, is distinctive.
Habitat On flowers, especially heather. **Maturity** Summer.
Distribution Southern England. Widespread in northern Europe, but less common in the north of the region.

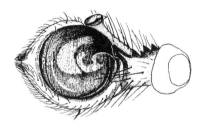

Genus *Pistius*

A single species occurs in the region. Like *Thomisus,* it has a triangular abdomen, but the whole spider is brownish and the lateral eyes are on shallow tubercles.

Pistius truncatus (Pallas 1772)   Plate 7
Description ♀, 7–9mm; ♂, 4–5mm. Female similar to the male illustrated, but with a larger abdomen, which is often of a lighter more reddish-brown colour and less shiny. Epigyne distinctive, as is male palp viewed from below.
Habitat In woodland; on bushes, lower branches of trees. Overwinters under bark and within dead wood. **Maturity** Summer.
Distribution Very rare in Britain. First recorded in 1896; the second record was from woodland in Kent in 1985. Widespread in Europe but rather uncommon.

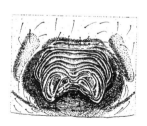
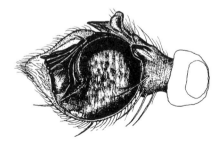

△ Genus *Tmarus*

The single species in the region has a highly characteristic appearance, with a single tubercle on the posterior end of the abdomen. Its cryptic pose on twigs, with the front legs stretched out in front, is very similar to that adopted by *Tibellus* (Philodrominae).

△ *Tmarus piger* (Walckenaer 1802)   Plate 7
Description ♀, 5–6mm; ♂, 3.5–4mm. Male very similar to female but with a slimmer abdomen and a smaller abdominal tubercle. Epigyne and male palp distinctive.
Habitat Twigs and branches of conifers and bushes. Typical cryptic position (illustrated) is with front legs outstretched along a twig and abdomen resembling an old leaf stump. **Maturity** Summer.
Distribution Absent from Britain. Recorded from most of northern Europe, but absent from Scandinavia and generally commoner in the south of the region.

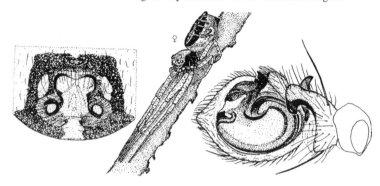

Genus *Misumena*

The single species in the region sits in flowers, usually white or yellow, and ambushes visiting insects in the same manner as *Thomisus*. It is similarly able to slowly change colour and the female may be white, yellow or greenish, with or without red spots or stripes. I have once seen a faintly slate-blue specimen on blue flowers. The male differs markedly from the female.

Misumena vatia (Clerck 1757)   Plate 8
Description ♀, 9–11mm; ♂, 3–4mm. Female may be white, yellow or greenish and the red stripes may be reduced to spots or absent. The much smaller male is less variable. Epigyne small and indistinct. Male palp distinctive when viewed from below.
Habitat On flowers, especially white and yellow blooms. **Maturity** Summer.
Distribution England and Wales; commoner in the south. Widespread in northern Europe but commoner in the south.

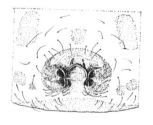
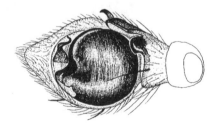

△ Genus *Misumenops*

The single species in the region has similar habits to *Thomisus* and *Misumena* but waits for prey on the leaves of bushes where it appears quite inconspicuous. The male is smaller than the female and differs substantially in appearance.

△ *Misumenops tricuspidatus* (Fabricius 1775)   Plate 8

Description ♀, 5–6mm; ♂, 2.5–3.5mm. Both sexes have a highly distinctive appearance. Epigyne small and indistinct. Male palp distinctive when viewed from below.
Habitat On leaves of bushes. **Maturity** Summer.
Distribution Absent from Britain. Widespread in northern Europe, but not recorded from Scandinavia.

△ Genus *Runcinia*

There is one species in the region and it waits for prey on bushes, flowers and grasses. The male is darker and much smaller than the female, but both sexes have the distinctive white band across the eye region.

△ *Runcinia grammica* (C.L. Koch 1837) (= *R. lateralis* (C.L. Koch))   Plate 8

Description ♀, 4–6mm; ♂, 2.5–3.5mm. Both sexes have a highly distinctive appearance. Epigyne small and indistinct. Male palpal organs remarkably small, but distinctive when viewed from below.
Habitat Bushes, flowers and grasses. **Maturity** Summer.
Distribution Recorded from France and commoner in central Europe.

 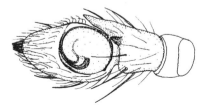

△ Genus *Synaema*

The single species in the region has an unmistakable appearance and ambushes prey on tall plants and bushes.

△ *Synaema globosum* (Fabricius 1775) — Plate 8

Description ♀, 6–8.5mm; ♂, 3–4mm. The lighter parts of the abdomen may be a much paler yellow than illustrated, or orange-red. Male very similar, but abdomen smaller and darker, with markings occasionally obscured. Epigyne distinctive, as also is male palp viewed from below.

Habitat Usually on umbellifers but may occur on other flower heads, tall vegetation and bushes. **Maturity** Summer.

Distribution Absent from Britain. Widespread in northern Europe, but not extending into Scandinavia.

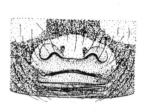 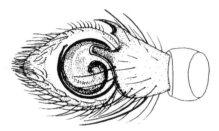

Genus *Diaea*

Only one species of *Diaea* occurs in the region and it catches prey on the leaves of bushes and trees.

Diaea dorsata (Fabricius 1777) — Plate 8

Description ♀, 5–6mm; ♂, 3–4mm. Males are similar to females but have a brownish carapace and the legs are greenish-brown, spotted with brown. The abdominal folium is also darker in males. Epigyne small but distinctive as is male palp, viewed from below.

Habitat On the leaves of bushes and trees (box, yew, oak, conifers).
Maturity Summer.

Distribution Locally distributed, mainly in the southern half of England. Widespread in northern Europe, but commoner in the south of the region.

 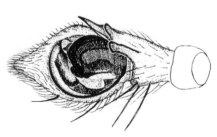

△ Genus *Heriaeus*

Five species of *Heriaeus* occur in Europe, of which two are described here. They are strikingly hairy, green spiders which sometimes have red markings in the anterior midline of the abdomen. The long hairs and spines are white, or very pale green, and these spiders are very well camouflaged on the hairy stems of grasses and other vegetation where they wait for prey.

△ *Heriaeus hirtus* (Latreille 1819)   Plate 8

Description ♀, 7–9mm; ♂, 4–5mm. The reddening of the cardiac mark may be more, or less, than illustrated. Male similar to female but with a slimmer abdomen which is pale yellow and usually has a reddish cardiac mark. Epigyne rather pale, but has an almost circular tongue. Male palp, viewed from below, similar to that of *H. melloteei* but differs in the tibial apophyses and the arrangement of the ducts.

Habitat On hairy vegetation. **Maturity** Summer.

Distribution Absent from Britain. Absent from Scandinavia; recorded from Belgium, France and Germany.

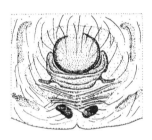 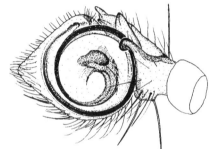

△ *Heriaeus melloteei* Simon 1886 (= *H. oblongus* Simon)

Description ♀, 6–8mm; ♂, 4–5mm. Similar to *H. hirtus* but the female has a much more oval, slightly elongated abdomen with three longitudinal white bands and, occasionally, red cardiac markings. The epigyne, although pale, is distinct from that of *H. hirtus*. The male palpal organs, from below, differ in the arrangement of the coiled ducts and in the tibial apophyses.

Habitat and Maturity Similar to *H. hirtus*.

Distribution Absent from Britain. Recorded from France and Germany.

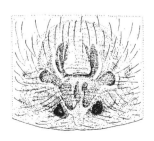 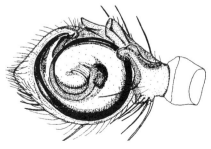

△ Genus *Coriarachne*

The single European species in this genus has a very flattened, wrinkled, rather dried-up appearance. The extreme flattening allows the spider to get into very narrow spaces under bark and stones.

△ *Coriarachne depressa* (C.L. Koch 1837)   Plate 9

Description ♀ ♂, 4–5mm. Male very similar to female in general appearance. The white wrinkles on the abdomen are very striking and there are paired black sigilla and other depressions. The eye region contrasts markedly with the dark carapace. Epigyne and male palpal organs distinctive. It is interesting to compare the epigyne and palpal organs with those of *Misumena* and *Heriaeus* and contrast these similarities with the huge differences in the general appearance of these spiders, which are adapted to different lifestyles.

Habitat Under bark and stones, in leaf-litter and detritus; sometimes on conifers.
Maturity Spring and summer.
Distribution Absent from Britain. Widespread throughout northern Europe, but rare.

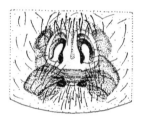 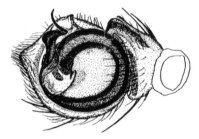

Genus *Xysticus*

Of the seventeen European species of *Xysticus*, twelve of the most widespread are described here. They bear some resemblance to the genus *Ozyptila* but have the median ocular trapezium square or broader than long. The head region is generally furnished with fairly long spines whereas *Ozyptila* has shorter, club-shaped hairs. The abdominal patterns in *Xysticus* tend to be made up of triangles and bars, whereas *Ozyptila* generally have rounded marbling and swirls. The majority of species occur on low vegetation or at ground level, but *X. lanio* is generally found on bushes and the lower branches of trees. Mating involves the female adopting a submissive posture, with the legs drawn in, and the male spinning a silk veil over carapace and legs before lifting the rear of the abdomen and applying the palps to the epigyne. The smooth, flattish, white egg sac is attached to low vegetation and guarded by the female, who often dies before the spiderlings emerge.

The colour illustrations (Plate 9) show the range of markings in the genus and also the differences between the sexes. However, it should be remembered that colours and markings are quite variable, even within a single species, and frequently approximate to the spider's surroundings. A specimen of *X. cristatus* found at ground level will look similar to the illustration; specimens from heather are often paler, with a distinct pink or lilac hue; others may be very much darker. Although the genus is readily identifiable with a lens, identification to species level does require examination of the epigyne and male palp. The epigynes vary quite a lot in the depth of colour and degree of sclerotization. Some are discernible with a ×10 lens, but most will require a field microscope or even higher magnification for certain identification. The male palpal organs are much less variable.

Xysticus cristatus (Clerck 1757)   Plate 9
Description ♀, 6–8mm; ♂, 3–5mm. Both sexes are illustrated. The central triangle on the carapace ends in a well-defined dark point near the fovea (cf. *X. audax*, below). Epigyne and male palp similar to those of *X. audax* (see below).
Habitat On bushes, low vegetation or at ground level in a variety of situations.
Maturity Spring and summer.
Distribution The commonest and most widespread species, occurring throughout Britain and northern Europe.

 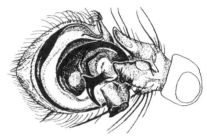

Xysticus audax (Schrank 1803)
Description ♀, 6–8mm; ♂, 3–5mm. Very similar to *X. cristatus* but the central triangle on the carapace does not extend quite as far back and does not end in a well-defined point. This seems to be a reliable distinguishing feature between these two species, but does not separate *X. audax* from the other members of the genus. In the epigyne of *X. audax*, the curvature of the openings, around from the central septum, is slightly irregular. In *X. cristatus* the oval openings have smoothly curved margins. The form of the T-shaped apophysis and of other structures in the palpal organs allows easy identification.
Habitat and Maturity Similar to *X. cristatus*, but tends to occur more frequently on higher vegetation such as gorse and heather.
Distribution Common and widespread throughout Britain and northern Europe.

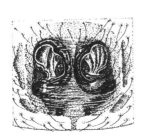 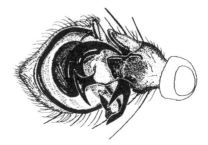

Xysticus kochi Thorell 1872
Description ♀, 6–8mm; ♂, 4–5mm. Similar to *X. cristatus* and only distinguishable by the epigyne and male palpal organs which are distinctive.
Habitat and Maturity Similar to *X. cristatus*.
Distribution Widely distributed throughout Britain and northern Europe but appreciably less common than *X. cristatus*.

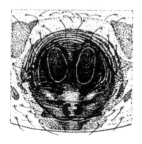 

Xysticus erraticus (Blackwall 1834)   Plate 9
Description ♀, 6–8mm; ♂, 4–5mm. Both sexes are illustrated. Females may be much paler than in the illustration and then superficially resemble *Ozyptila atomaria* and *O. trux*, which occur in the same type of habitat. Epigyne and male palp distinctive.
Habitat Almost always at ground level, typically amongst the base of grass tussocks or under stones and detritus. **Maturity** Spring to autumn.
Distribution Widespread throughout Britain and northern Europe and fairly common in the appropriate habitat.

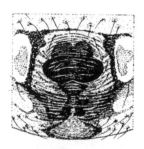 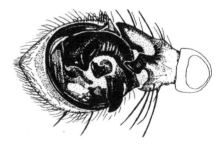

Xysticus lanio C.L. Koch 1835
Description ♀, 6–7mm; ♂, 4–5mm. This species has a definite reddish hue, particularly on the sides of the abdomen, and a triangle on the head region of the carapace which is less well defined than in *X. cristatus* and does not end in a dark point. The epigyne has a pair of bulging structures, on each side of the septum, which are sometimes dark in colour, but occasionally very pale. The apophyses in the male palpal organ are distinctive.

Habitat In woodland, on bushes and the lower branches of trees.
Maturity Late spring and summer.
Distribution Widely distributed in Britain, but commoner in the south. Widespread and fairly common throughout northern Europe.

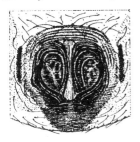 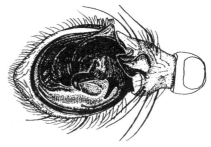

Xysticus ulmi (Hahn 1831)
Description ♀, 5–8mm; ♂, 3–4mm. Similar in general appearance to *X. cristatus* but the abdomen is slightly more elongated. Epigyne and male palpal organs distinctive.
Habitat Almost always in damp, marshy habitats amongst low vegetation. Females guarding egg sacs are often found near the top of higher plants.
Maturity Spring and summer.
Distribution Widespread but local distribution throughout Britain and northern Europe.

 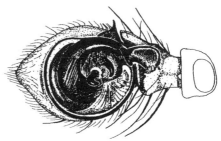

Xysticus bifasciatus C.L. Koch 1837   Plate 9
Description ♀, 7–10mm; ♂, 6–7mm. Female similar to the male, but with a larger abdomen and paler, less well-defined markings and lacking the darkening of the femur and patella of legs I and II. Epigyne with a roughly circular opening; depth of colour variable. The male is usually identifiable by the large size alone, but the palpal organs are distinctive.
Habitat Usually in short, chalk grassland with good exposure to the sun; amongst the grass and under stones. **Maturity** Spring and summer.
Distribution Widely distributed but very uncommon in Britain. Widespread throughout northern Europe.

Xysticus bifasciatus (previous page)

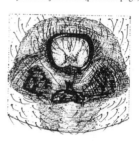
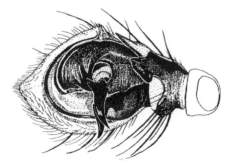

Xysticus luctator L. Koch 1870
Description ♀, 7–10mm; ♂, 6–7mm. Very similar in size and appearance to *X. bifasciatus*. The opening of the epigyne is larger than in that species and is usually wider posteriorly. The male palpal organs are very distinctive.
Habitat Amongst heather on dry heathland and in leaf-litter and under dead wood.
Maturity Spring to autumn.
Distribution Extremely rare in Britain; only recorded from three sites in the south of England (only three males and two females in total since 1854). Fairly widespread in northern Europe, but generally rare.

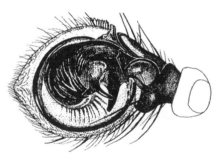

Xysticus sabulosus (Hahn 1832)   Plate 9
Description ♀, 7–9mm; ♂, 5–6mm. Both sexes are illustrated. Some specimens are much darker, almost black. Epigyne and male palpal organs distinctive.

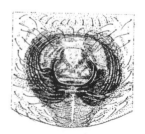
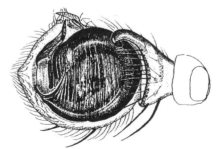

Habitat Usually on dry ground (sand or gravel) but occasionally on low heathland vegetation. **Maturity** Summer and autumn.
Distribution Widespread but uncommon throughout Britain and northern Europe.

Xysticus luctuosus (Blackwall 1836)
Description ♀, 7–8mm; ♂, 4–5mm. Similar to *X. cristatus* but markings less well defined, particularly in the male which is almost uniformly dark brown. The median ocular trapezium is roughly square in this species (cf. *X. acerbus*, below). The epigyne and male palp are distinctive.
Habitat On low plants and bushes in wooded areas. **Maturity** Summer and autumn.
Distribution Widespread in Britain, but rare; a little more frequent in the south. Widespread but rather uncommon in northern Europe.

 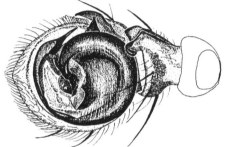

Xysticus acerbus Thorell 1872
Description ♀, 7–8mm; ♂, 4–5mm. Very similar to *X. luctuosus* in having very ill-defined markings. The median ocular trapezium is clearly broader than long and this helps identification, together with the distinctive epigyne and male palpal organs.
Habitat Most records are from grassland. **Maturity** Summer and autumn.
Distribution Rare in Britain and recorded from a few sites in southern England and South Wales. Widespread but generally rare in northern Europe.

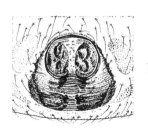 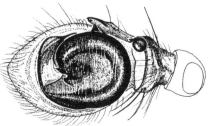

Xysticus robustus (Hahn 1832)   Plate 9
Description ♀, 7–10mm; ♂, 5–6mm. The appearance of the male is unmistakable. The female has a more greyish carapace and legs and a grey-brown abdomen largely devoid of markings. Epigyne and male palp distinctive.

Habitat At ground level, mainly under stones and boulders but also amongst grass, heather. **Maturity** Summer to autumn.

Distribution Rare in Britain and recorded from a very few sites in southern England. Widespread but generally uncommon in northern Europe.

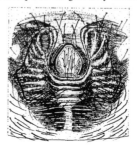 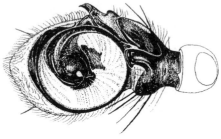

Genus *Ozyptila* (= *Oxyptila*)

Twelve species of *Ozyptila* occur in Europe, of which nine are described here. They differ from *Xysticus* in having the median ocular trapezium longer than broad and have clavate (club-shaped) hairs, rather than pointed spines, on the carapace. Similar hairs are often present on the legs and abdomen. The abdominal pattern, when present, is made up of more rounded figuring and swirls, rather than the triangles and bars found in *Xysticus*. As with that genus, the two sexes often differ substantially in their markings. Little is known of the biology of these spiders. During the daytime they are usually found at ground level – under stones or deep within the base or roots of vegetation. They are very slow in their movements and are easily overlooked when sieving vegetation or litter over a sheet. Quite some time may elapse between them landing on the sheet, legs drawn in and feigning death, and the resumption of painfully slow movement. During the night, some species move up into vegetation and may be swept with a net. Careful searching of vegetation with a torch sometimes reveals them climbing upwards, almost tortoise-like, to the heads of grasses and other vegetation. The egg sacs are often of papery silk and are guarded by the female under stones or within detritus at the base of vegetation. The female epigynes vary a little bit in shape, and quite a lot in the depth of colour and degree of sclerotization. The male palpal organs and tibial apophyses are less variable and are highly distinctive. Identification to species level is sometimes possible with a ×25 field microscope but, in many instances, higher magnification will be required.

The following three species are very dark (sometimes black), clothed liberally with clavate hairs, and sometimes covered with particles of earth.

Ozyptila blackwalli Simon 1875

Description ♀, 3–4mm; ♂, 2–3mm. Both sexes are of an almost uniform dark grey-brown colour, marked with black spots and some black bars on the abdomen. The carapace has a pale central band. The whole spider is clothed with a large number of conspicuous clavate hairs. The M-shaped swelling in the centre of the epigyne is usually reddish in colour and this, together with the long, projecting tibial apophysis on the male palp, readily separates the species from the two other uniformly dark species – *O. scabricula* and *O. nigrita*.

Habitat Under stones and in undergrowth in dry situations.
Maturity Spring and summer.
Distribution Rather rare in Britain and restricted to southern England. Absent from Scandinavia and more frequent in the south and west of the region.

 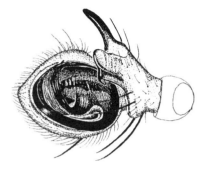

Ozyptila scabricula (Westring 1851)
Description ♀, 3–4mm; ♂, 2–3mm. Very similar to *O. blackwalli*, often even darker and lacking the median band on the carapace. Clothed with a large number of clavate hairs and usually covered with particles of earth, which obscure everything. Epigyne and male palpal organs distinctive, the latter having an apophysis rather like a crab's claw arising from the centre.
Habitat Under stones, amongst undergrowth in sandy areas, heathland, and on vegetation in breckland. **Maturity** Spring to autumn.
Distribution Widely but very locally distributed across the south of England and Wales, and generally very rare. Widespread but uncommon in northern Europe.

 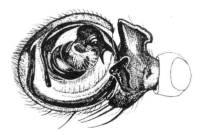

Ozyptila nigrita (Thorell 1875) (NB *O. claveata* (Walckenaer) = a *nomen dubium*)
Description ♀, 3–4mm; ♂, 2–3mm. Very similar to *O. blackwalli* and *O. scabricula*, but easily distinguished by the epigyne and male palpal organs.
Habitat On short, chalk grassland, and also under stones and amongst moss in coniferous woodland. **Maturity** Summer.
Distribution Rare in Britain; in southern counties of England, usually near the coast and occasionally abundant on chalk grassland. Widespread in northern Europe, but generally uncommon.

Ozyptila nigrita (previous page)

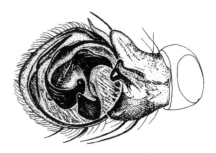

The remaining species are generally lighter in colour and have fewer clavate hairs.

Ozyptila sanctuaria (O.P.-Cambridge 1871)   Plate 10
Description ♀, 3–4mm; ♂, 2–3mm. Male darker than female with femora I and II almost black. Epigyne and male palpal organs distinctive, the male palp having no long tibial apophysis on the outer side.
Habitat In undergrowth, grass tussocks, sometimes on chalk or marl.
Maturity All year, but males not found in winter.
Distribution Widespread from North Wales and central England southwards; commoner in the south, where it may be abundant on chalk grassland, but generally rare. Absent from Scandinavia, and most European records are from the west of the region (Belgium, France).

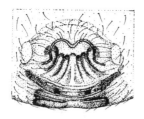
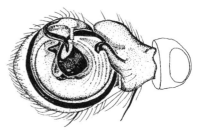

Ozyptila praticola (C.L. Koch 1837)   Plate 10
Description ♀, 3–4mm; ♂, 2.5–3mm. Female less clearly marked than the male illustrated. Both sexes have the sternum distinctively marked with a longitudinal

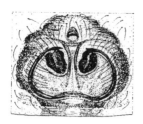
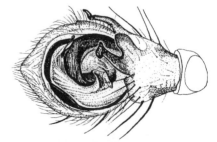

dark line, and dark lines radiating from the centre to the margin between each coxa; a similar pattern is sometimes present in *O. brevipes*. The epigyne is distinctive and one of the tibial apophyses of the male palp has a spiralled tip.

Habitat In moss, undergrowth and detritus in a variety of situations, on low vegetation and hedgerows; and in coniferous woodland, on the lower branches of trees and under bark. **Maturity** Spring and summer; females possibly all year.

Distribution Widespread in England, recorded from Wales, but much commoner in the south. Widespread in northern Europe.

Ozyptila trux (Blackwall 1846)
Description ♀, 4–5mm; ♂, 3–4mm. Very similar in general appearance to *O. atomaria*. The epigyne has a broad tongue anteriorly, but this is sometimes very pale and poorly sclerotized. The structures behind and to the side of this are similarly variable, but are quite distinct from those of *O. atomaria* and *O. simplex*. The male palpal organs are distinctive, and the pointed outer tibial apophysis is shorter than that of *O. simplex* and quite different from that of *O. atomaria*.

Habitat At ground level, amongst grass tussocks, leaf-litter, moss and detritus in a variety of situations. Often higher up on vegetation at night. **Maturity** All year.

Distribution Common and widespread throughout Britain and northern Europe.

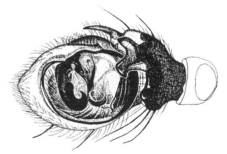

Ozyptila simplex (O.P.-Cambridge 1862)   Plate 10
Description ♀, 4–5mm; ♂, 3–4mm. Both sexes are illustrated but are somewhat variable in the depth of colour and in the markings. The sternum sometimes has dark spots on the margin, opposite each coxa and in the posterior midline. The epigyne has a narrower tongue than that of *O. trux* and differently shaped structures behind

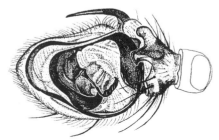

and to the side of it. The male palpal organs are distinctive and the outer pointed apophysis is longer and thinner than in other species.

Habitat Amongst the base of plants and in detritus, usually in sandy habitats. Sometimes found higher up on low vegetation. **Maturity** Spring to autumn.

Distribution Commoner in the south of England, but recorded in Wales and Scotland. Absent from Scandinavia, but widespread throughout the rest of northern Europe.

Ozyptila atomaria (Panzer 1801)   Plate 10

Description ♀, 4–6mm; ♂, 3–4mm. Both sexes are illustrated and may be darker or lighter in colour than shown. The epigyne has a narrow tongue and the structures on either side of it are distinctive. The male palpal organs are distinctive, as also is the spade-like tibial apophysis arising from a socket.

Habitat At ground level, amongst grass tussocks, leaf-litter, moss and detritus in a variety of situations. Often found higher on vegetation at night. **Maturity** All year.

Distribution Common and widespread throughout Britain and northern Europe.

 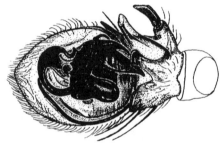

Ozyptila brevipes (Hahn 1826)

Description ♀, 3–4mm; ♂, 2–3mm. Male has similar markings to those of *O. praticola*; female has a brownish carapace and a pale abdomen marked with brown or black bars. The sternum frequently has markings similar to those of *O. praticola*, but they usually consist of a dark spot opposite each coxa and a dark mark in the posterior midline. Epigyne and male palpal organs distinctive; the outer, pointed tibial apophysis is occasionally slightly twisted at its tip, giving it a slight resemblance to that of *O. praticola*.

Habitat Amongst the base of vegetation, detritus and moss; in marshy areas and on chalk grassland. **Maturity** Summer and autumn.

Distribution Commoner in the south of England and Wales; recorded further north, but not from Scotland. Widespread in northern Europe.

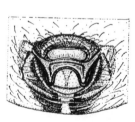 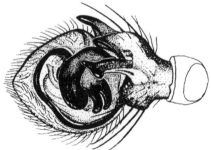

Subfamily **Philodrominae**
Genus *Philodromus*

Seventeen species of *Philodromus* occur in the region, of which thirteen are described here. The legs are fairly long, with the femora of legs I and II scarcely thicker than those of legs III and IV. Legs I and II are slightly longer than III and IV; sometimes they are very much longer, especially in some males. The abdomen is usually oval (quite elongate in some males) but in some species (e.g. *P. margaritatus*) it is shaped like those of *Xysticus* and *Misumenops*. Colours and markings are often cryptic and the degree of camouflage can be quite amazing. *Philodromus fallax* (Plate 11) is extremely difficult to spot on sand dunes and individuals can change their depth of colour to suit different backgrounds. *Philodromus margaritatus* is frequently pale green when on this colour of lichen and the body and legs are often held so that they closely follow the contours of the substrate – almost as though the spider is pressing itself into the lichen and bark. The specimen illustrated on page 175 was pale lichen-green and I frequently had difficulty finding it on quite a small piece of lichen-covered bark. It turned quite white (within 24 hours) on white cloth, later changed to a much more obvious green on green felt, and finally turned greyish on its (second) egg sac. It is interesting that some of the camouflage effect is lost in photographs, presumably because the photographic emulsion registers colour in a different way from the human eye.

Males and females of *Philodromus* sometimes differ greatly in their appearance (e.g. *P. dispar*, Plate 10), but in other species the sexes may be very similar, apart from the male having a slimmer abdomen and darker, more concentrated markings. Although sometimes adopting a motionless, camouflaged posture and grabbing prey which ventures near, philodromids can run very rapidly in pursuit of prey, or to escape. Their sure-footedness is aided by the tarsal and metatarsal scopulae on all legs (less developed in adult males). Courtship and mating appear to be very brief in this genus. Egg sacs usually have a woolly or gauze-like exterior and females stand guard directly over them in foliage or on bark. Sometimes particles of sand (*P. fallax*) or bits of vegetation (*P. histrio*) are used to disguise the egg sacs. Sometimes leaves are drawn together with silk, or a covering is provided by spinning a sheet of silk. Females of *P. aureolus* frequently lose most of their abdominal markings when guarding egg sacs, appearing beige with brown sides. Other species also slowly change colour after the final egg sac is made – some make at least two egg sacs within a few weeks. A few species have a very distinctive appearance in the field, but many are so similar and variable that examination of the epigyne and male palp is required. This is sometimes possible with a field microscope, but higher magnification will be required in many cases. Some species have been confused or unrecognized until relatively recently, and their distribution status is uncertain.

Philodromus dispar Walckenaer 1826   Plate 10
Description ♀, 4–5mm; ♂, 4mm. The disparity in appearance between the sexes gives the species its name. The female illustrated has a relatively slim abdomen and it may become as distended as that illustrated for *P. cespitum* (Plate 10), and *vice versa*. The male is identifiable in the field, and the epigyne is usually discernible with a lens.
Habitat On low vegetation, bushes and the lower branches of trees.
Maturity Spring and summer.
Distribution Widespread in England and Wales, but commoner in the south; apparently absent from Scotland. Widespread throughout northern Europe.

Philodromus dispar (previous page)

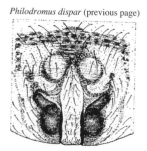
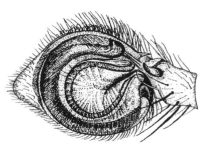

Philodromus aureolus (Clerck 1757)   Plate 11.

Description ♀, 5–6mm; ♂, 4mm. Female very similar to *P. dispar* and *P. cespitum* (Plate 10) in general appearance, but may have a uniformly pale yellow or beige abdomen. The male is iridescent in good light and may be darker than illustrated. The epigyne is variable, but is distinguished from that of *P. praedatus* by the lack of transverse ridges in the front part of the opening. The male is identified by the form of the ducts and other structures in the palpal organs and by the tibial apophyses.

Habitat On low vegetation, bushes and the lower branches of trees.

Maturity Spring and summer.

Distribution Common and widespread throughout Britain and northern Europe.

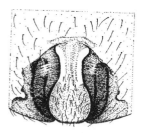
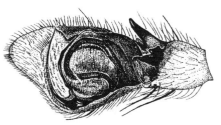

Philodromus praedatus O.P.-Cambridge 1871

Description ♀, 5–6mm; ♂, 3.5–4mm. Very similar in general appearance to *P. aureolus* and *P. cespitum*. Epigyne distinguished from that of *P. aureolus* by the transverse, sclerotized ridges in the anterior part of the opening. The male is identified by

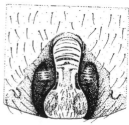
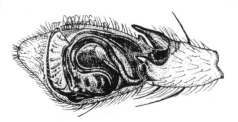

the form of the ducts and other structures in the palpal organs and by the tibial apophyses.

Habitat Most records are from the lower branches of trees, particularly oak.

Maturity Spring and summer.

Distribution Uncertain. Fairly widespread in the south of England, with some records from the north. Probably widespread in northern Europe.

Philodromus cespitum (Walckenaer 1802)   Plate 10

Description ♀, 5–6mm; ♂, 4mm. The female illustrated has a distended abdomen; other specimens may appear like the female of *P. dispar* (Plate 10). Male similar to that of *P. aureolus* (Plate 11). Epigyne distinctive. Male distinguished by the form of the ducts and other structures in the palpal organs and by the tibial apophyses.

Habitat, Maturity and Distribution Similar to *P. aureolus*; equally common.

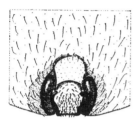 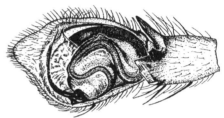

Philodromus longipalpis Simon 1870

Description ♀, 5–6mm; ♂, 3.5–4mm. Both sexes very similar in general appearance to *P. aureolus* and *P. cespitum*. Epigyne distinctive. Male distinguished by the form of the ducts and other structures in the palpal organs, and by the tibial apophyses.

Habitat Bushes and trees. **Maturity** Probably spring and summer.

Distribution Uncertain. Recorded from the south of England but may have been overlooked elsewhere. Possibly widespread in northern Europe.

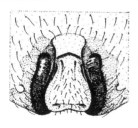 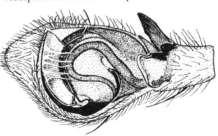

Philodromus buxi Simon 1884

Description ♀, 5–7mm; ♂, 4mm. Both sexes very similar to *P. aureolus* and *P. cespitum*. Epigyne very distinctive, as also are the male palpal organs and tibial apophyses.

Habitat Bushes and trees. **Maturity** Spring and summer.
Distribution Rare in Britain and recorded from one locality in the south of England.
Absent from Scandinavia; recorded from France and possibly more frequent in the
south and west of the region.

 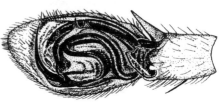

Philodromus collinus C.L. Koch 1835
Description ♀, 4–6mm; ♂, 3–4mm. Very similar in general appearance to *P. aure-olus* and *P. cespitum*, but the abdomen is usually marked with a midline band of white
hairs which tapers to the spinners. Epigyne distinctive, with more spherical sper-mathecae than in *P. cespitum* and being less elongate than *P. buxi*. The male is dis-tinguished by the form of the ducts and other structures in the palpal organs and by
the tibial apophyses.
Habitat On the lower branches of trees, particularly conifers. **Maturity** Summer.
Distribution Uncommon in Britain and recorded from sites in the south and south-east of England. Widespread throughout northern Europe.

Philodromus fallax Sundevall 1833   Plate 11
Description ♀, 4.5–6mm; ♂, 4–5mm. Male similar to the female but often a little
darker and with a slimmer abdomen. Depth of colour and markings vary, and closely

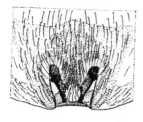 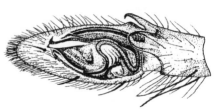

match the sandy habitat upon which it is superbly camouflaged. The epigyne is rather ill defined and usually obscured by light hairs. The male palpal organs are distinctive.
Habitat On sandy ground; usually on sand dunes or amongst marram, but also on sandy river banks. **Maturity** Spring and summer.
Distribution Widely but locally distributed around the coasts of England and Wales. Widespread throughout northern Europe.

Philodromus histrio (Latreille 1819)   Plate 11
Description ♀, 6–7mm; ♂, 5–6mm. Very distinctively marked. The male is similar to the female, but has a slimmer, slightly darker abdomen. At first sight the species may be confused with *Oxyopes heterophthalmus* (Oxyopidae, Plate 15), but that species (also occurring on heather) has very long leg spines and a different eye arrangement. The epigyne is extremely variable but generally recognisable. The male palpal organs are distinctive.
Habitat Low vegetation, usually heather. The female encloses the egg sac within a substantial covering of silk and dried heather shoots. **Maturity** Spring and summer.
Distribution Widespread throughout the whole of Britain but very locally distributed and generally rare. Widespread throughout northern Europe.

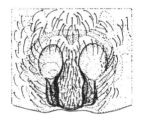 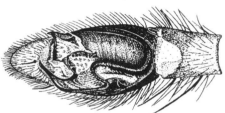

Philodromus emarginatus (Schrank 1803)
Description ♀, 5–6mm; ♂, 4–5mm. Similar to *P. aureolus* and *P. cespitum* but with less well-defined markings and an overall greyish, pinkish-brown colour. Epigyne and male palp very distinctive.
Habitat On heather and the lower branches of conifers. **Maturity** Summer.
Distribution Widespread throughout the whole of Britain but very locally distributed and generally uncommon. Widespread throughout northern Europe.

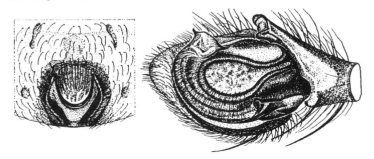

Philodromus albidus Kulczynski 1911

Description ♀, 3.4–5mm; ♂, 3–3.5mm. This rather small species is similar in general appearance to the female of *P. dispar* (Plate 10) but is paler. Until recently, it has been confused with *P. rufus* (below). The openings of the epigyne have lightly sclerotized edges, the anterior arches of which do not extend beyond the outlines of the curved ducts, when viewed directly from above. The curvature of the opening in the midline also differs from that in *P. rufus*. In the male palpal organs, the fine tip of the embolus, and the adjacent conductor, scarcely project beyond the edge of the cymbium, and the looped duct extends less than half-way from the base of the palpal organs to the tip.
Habitat On bushes and the lower branches of trees. **Maturity** Summer.
Distribution Rather rare; recorded from the more southern and eastern counties of England. Possibly absent from Scandinavia and most records are from western parts of northern Europe.

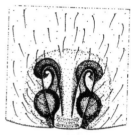 

△ *Philodromus rufus* Walckenaer 1826

Description ♀, 4–6mm; ♂, 3.3–4mm. Very similar to *P. albidus*, but often suffused with red, particularly in the male. However, the reddish coloration is not reliable and rapidly fades in specimens preserved in alcohol. The epigyne is distinguishable from that of *P. albidus* by the lightly sclerotized openings, the anterior arches of which extend beyond the outlines of the curved ducts, when viewed directly from above. The curvature of the opening in the midline also differs from that in *P. albidus*. In the male palpal organs, the fine tip of the embolus, and the adjacent conductor, project beyond the edge of the cymbium, and the looped duct extends to about half-way from the base of the palpal organs to the tip.
Habitat and Maturity Similar to *P. albidus*.
Distribution Absent from Britain. Probably widespread throughout northern Europe, including Scandinavia.

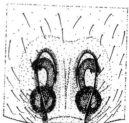 

Philodromus margaritatus (Clerck 1757)   Plate 11

Description ♀, 5–6mm; ♂, 4–5mm. Colour and markings variable in both sexes. Background colour may be white, greyish or greenish and may be mottled with dark spots or, in the female, entirely pale dorsally with broad black bands on the front and sides. The epigyne and male palp are characteristic. (Note: Two other species, with closely similar epigynes and male palps, occur in Europe – *P. fuscomarginatus* (De Geer) and *P. poecilus* (Thorell). *P. poecilus* also closely resembles *P. margaritatus*

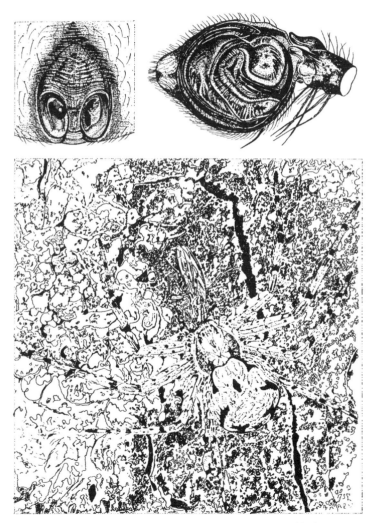

Philodromus margaritatus ♀ with prey on lichen-covered bark

in general appearance, but the femora and patellae of legs I and II are marked with a black band ventrally.)

Habitat On the bark (and sometimes leaves) of lichen-covered trees. **Maturity** Summer.
Distribution Rare in Britain; recorded from a number of counties across the most southerly part of England and from several areas of Caledonian pine forest across northern Scotland. Widespread throughout northern Europe.

Genus *Thanatus*

Seven species of *Thanatus* occur in the region, the four most widespread of which are described here. The abdomen is oval, slightly elongate, and has a pronounced dark cardiac mark in all species. They occur at or near ground level, amongst low vegetation. Some species occur in sandy habitats, others in damp or boggy situations. These spiders are generally rather rare and little is known of their biology.

Thanatus striatus C.L. Koch 1845   Plate 11
Description ♀, 4–5mm; ♂, 3–4mm. Male very similar to female but with a slimmer abdomen and slightly darker markings. The spider is clothed with rather coarse black hairs. The epigyne and male palpal organs are distinctive.
Habitat In grassland on dry, sandy soil, on dunes, and also on wet heathland and in fens. **Maturity** Spring and summer.
Distribution Rare, but widespread in England and Wales. Widespread throughout northern Europe, but generally uncommon.

△ *Thanatus sabulosus* (Menge 1875)
Description ♀, 4–5.5mm; ♂, 3–4mm. Very similar in size and general appearance to *T. striatus*. Epigyne and male palpal organs distinctive.
Habitat Generally in dry situations; amongst heather and other vegetation in sandy

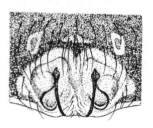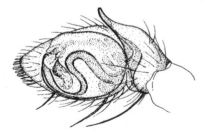

habitats; sometimes under stones and on rocky ground. **Maturity** Spring and summer.
Distribution. Absent from Britain and Scandinavia. Widespread throughout the rest
of northern Europe.

Thanatus formicinus (Clerck 1757)   Plate 11
Description ♀, 7–12mm; ♂, 5–7mm. Male similar to that of *T. arenarius* (Plate 11).
Epigyne and male palpal organs distinctive.
Habitat Wet heathland; amongst moss and the base of grasses and heather; some-
times in drier, sandy habitats. **Maturity** Early spring and summer.
Distribution Rare in Britain and recorded from three sites in southern England.
Widespread but uncommon throughout northern Europe.

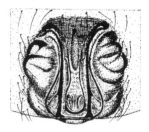 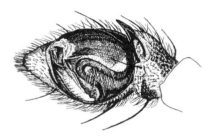

△ *Thanatus arenarius* Thorell 1872   Plate 11
Description ♀, 6mm; ♂, 5mm. Female similar to *T. formicinus* (Plate 11), but
smaller. Epigyne and male palpal organs distinctive.
Habitat At ground level in a variety of both wet and dry habitats.
Maturity Summer and autumn.
Distribution Absent from Britain. Widespread throughout northern Europe.

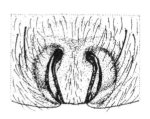 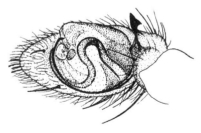

Genus *Tibellus*

Two species of *Tibellus* occur in the region. They have an elongated appearance and
have the habit of extending their legs along grasses and plant stems, as illustrated on
the spine of this book. Their straw coloration renders them inconspicuous on dried
vegetation, where they ambush passing insects. *Tmarus piger* (Misumeninae, p. 154)
adopts a similar posture on twigs, as do species of *Tetragnatha* (Tetragnathidae,
p. 305) on grasses. The latter are easily distinguished from *Tibellus* by their large
chelicerae. Males are similar to females, but have a shorter, slimmer abdomen and

are often darker in colour. Courtship and mating are relatively brief. The female attaches her egg sac near the top of grasses and other vegetation and stands guard over it. Abdominal markings, and the number of paired dark spots, are variable. Identification of the species requires examination of the epigyne and male palpal organs. This can sometimes be achieved with a lens, but higher magnification is usually required. Note: subadult females of both species have a pair of dark marks in the epigyne region not unlike the epigyne of *T. oblongus*, but they lack the other sclerotized structures.

Tibellus maritimus (Menge 1875)
Description ♀, 8–10mm; ♂, 7–8mm. Very similar to *T. oblongus* in general appearance. Epigyne and male palpal organs distinctive, the latter having a screw-like embolus.
Habitat On long grasses; on coastal dunes, but also inland.
Maturity Summer.
Distribution Widespread throughout Britain, but slightly less common than *T. oblongus*. Widespread throughout northern Europe.

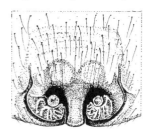 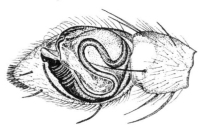

Tibellus oblongus (Walckenaer 1802)   Plate 11
Description ♀, 8–10mm; ♂, 7–8mm. Male similar to female but with a smaller, slimmer abdomen. Epigyne and male palpal organs distinctive.
Habitat Similar to *T. maritimus*, but commoner inland and in damper habitats.
Maturity Summer.
Distribution Common and widespread throughout Britain and northern Europe.

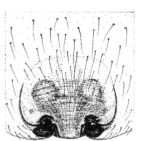 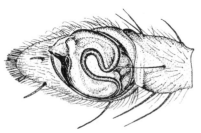

FAMILY SALTICIDAE

The square-fronted carapace, with four large, forward-facing eyes, makes members of this family easily recognizable in the field (see Family Key, p. 45), even though some are quite small spiders. In warm, sunny weather they are extremely active creatures and are able to jump, either to catch prey or to escape. Although popularly called 'jumping spiders' they are not alone in having this ability; members of the Lycosidae, Clubionidae, Oxyopidae and Agelenidae (*Textrix*) can also jump, and frequently do so in order to avoid capture or to get from one leaf to the next. Salticids use the third and/or fourth pairs of legs for jumping. Before leaping, the spider attaches a silk thread to the substrate and draws in the hind legs. The flexor muscles are then relaxed and the legs suddenly extended hydraulically, whereupon the spider leaps a few centimetres forward with a safety-line attached. Compared with fleas and grasshoppers, the salticids are relatively poor jumpers but some small species, such as *Attulus saltator* can achieve distances of over twenty times their own length. The eyes of salticids have a greater range of movement than our own, elaborate focusing, binocular vision and are probably sensitive to colour as well as to polarized light. The smaller eyes, further back on the carapace, are able to detect movement, but less detail; if something enters the rear or side field of vision the spider jumps around to focus the large front eyes upon it. This is easily demonstrated, and the spider will often raise up the front end of the cephalothorax to get a better look at you. The Salticidae are hunting spiders, stalking prey which comes within their vision and finally leaping on to it. Many species are clothed with coloured, shining or iridescent hairs, with the eyes attractively fringed, and males frequently have enlarged, coloured front legs and decorated palps. These find use, in conjunction with the great visual acuity, in elaborate courtship displays when legs and palps are waved semaphore-style as the male moves rhythmically about in front of the female. Females remain guarding their egg sacs within a silken cell, which the young spiderlings leave as soon as they are capable of an independent existence.

Around seventy-five salticid species are recorded from Europe, in forty-three genera; most of the four thousand or so known species in this family occur in warmer parts of the world and the colours and markings of many of these are quite spectacular. Since the patterns and markings are largely made up of coloured hairs, these spiders appear markedly different when immersed in alcohol for preservation. Forty-three species are described here, in twenty genera. In the following key to the genera, I have used only those characters which are visible with a lens in the field.

Key to the Genera

1. Spider distinctly ant-like in appearance and movement   2

     Spider not obviously ant-like   4

2. Head abruptly raised from thoracic part of carapace, with width across posterior lateral eyes as wide as, or wider than, thorax. Female with the palpal tarsus flattened; male with greatly enlarged chelicerae   *Myrmarachne* p. 206

Head more smoothly raised from thoracic part of carapace,
    with width across posterior lateral eyes less than width of
    thorax. Female palpal tarsus not flattened; male chelicerae
    not unduly enlarged   3

3. Legs I considerably stouter than the rest; tibia I oval in cross-
        section, appearing thicker when viewed from the side.
        Size of adult spider 3–4mm.   *Synageles* p. 205

    Legs I only slightly stouter than the rest; tibia I more or
        less circular in cross-section, appearing of the same
        thickness from the side as from above. Size of adult
        spider 6–7mm   △ *Leptorchestes* p. 205

4. Spider with largely black and white markings,
        which form broad oblique bands on the
        abdomen. Tibia and metatarsus
        I without ventral spines (rarely,
        one metatarsal spine)   *Salticus* p. 183

    Spider possibly with some black and white
        markings (and possibly with a white line
        on the front of the abdomen) but not forming a series of
        broad, oblique bands   5

5. Distance *between* posterior lateral eyes
        appreciably greater than width *across*
        anterior lateral eyes   6

                                        Ballus
                                        carapace

    Distance between posterior lateral eyes
        the same or less than width across
        anterior lateral eyes   8

6. Legs pale yellow, with clear black streaks on
        some segments and usually additional
        black spots or annulations   *Ballus* p. 193

    Legs darker and with less clear markings   7

7. Abdomen brownish with a clear pattern
        comprising a white median band, broken
        into spots at the rear, and with a white
        line extending around the sides from
        the first spot   *Pellenes* p. 192

Abdomen dark, with a metallic glint and no
    pattern. Femur and tibia of leg I
    greatly enlarged   *Bianor* p. 194

                              ♂

8.   Posterior lateral eyes, viewed from the side or
      directly above, situated roughly mid-way
      between the front and rear margins of
      the carapace. Size of adult spider
      2–3mm   *Neon* p. 193

      Posterior lateral eyes closer to the front
      margin of the carapace than to the rear   9

9.   Dense brush of hairs (scopula) on tarsus I to well over half its
      length. This much less developed on tarsus IV   10

      Scopula on tarsus I less obvious (or absent) and only present
      near the tip. Less obvious difference between tarsus I and IV   11

10. Abdomen of female as wide as long; mottled
      with black and white to form a vague
      pattern. Carapace of male with two
      U-shaped rows of hairs on the
      head; black abdomen with light
      longitudinal band   *Aelurillus* p. 204

                        ♀

      Abdomen more oval, slightly pointed
      behind. Pattern, in female, of two
      longitudinal brown stripes on a pale
      background. Abdomen of male
      much darker and glossy, with
      stripes less obvious   *Phlegra* p. 204

                        ♀

11. Abdomen with broad, continuous black
      median stripe, tapering to a point near
      the spinners. Sides of the abdomen
      brownish in the female, bright red in
      the male   △ *Philaeus* p. 202

                        ♀

Abdomen possibly with an interrupted median line of dark
   spots or triangles; if dark band present, then not tapering
   to a point near the spinners   12

12. Sternum roughly oval; narrow at the front
      with the front margin only about the
      same width as the labium. Coxae I
      separated by not much more
      than the diameter of one
      of them   *Marpissa* p. 188

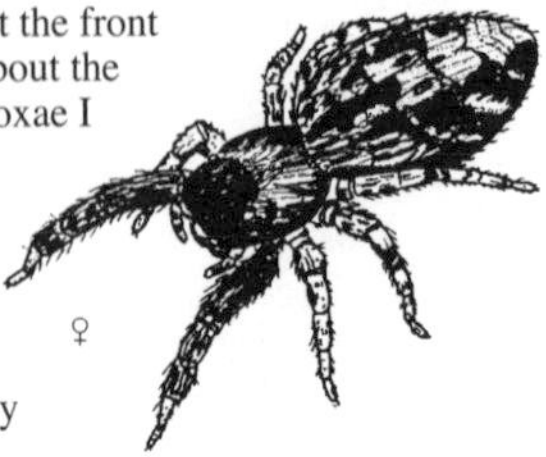

♀

     Sternum not so narrow anteriorly   13

13. Total length of patella and tibia of leg IV scarcely greater than
      that of leg III   14

     Total length of patella and tibia of leg IV appreciably greater
      than that of leg III   16

14. Size of adult spider 2–3mm   *Euophrys aequipes* p. 197

     Size of adult spider 5–8mm   15

15. Patella of leg I longer than tibia IV.
      Abdomen *either* with two or three
      pairs of white spots posteriorly

♀   △ *Dendryphantes* p. 191

     or with oblique white lines   △ *Eris* p. 191

     Patella of leg I the same size as, or shorter
      than, tibia IV   *Evarcha* p. 202

♀

16. Tibia IV about three times as long as
      tibia III   *Attulus* p. 201

♀

Tibia IV about twice as long as tibia III

Sitticus p. 199

♀

Tibia IV about 1¼ to 1½ times as
long as tibia III

17

17. Carapace and abdomen blackish, often with a
metallic sheen. Abdomen often with a
thin white band around the front end
and, occasionally, one or two paired
spots of white hairs. Legs often
contrastingly pale yellow with
black streaks

Heliophanus p. 185

♀

Spider not like this

18

18. Abdomen oval and elongate in both sexes. Leg I
noticeably enlarged. Carapace brownish with
margin of light hairs and possibly a median
band of light hairs. Abdomen of female
with a pair of broad, brown longitudinal bands enclosing lighter
chevrons; sides lighter and clothed in
light hairs. Abdomen of male darker,
but with a pair of longitudinal light
bands of white hairs

♀

△ *Pseudicius* p. 192

Abdomen not particularly elongate (except in
some males); pattern variable but usually
of spots, triangles, bars or chevrons
and may be very clear or very dark
and obscure. Males may have leg I
slightly enlarged and possibly dark
and iridescent

Euophrys p. 195

♀

Genus *Salticus*

Four species of *Salticus* are recorded from the region and three are described here.
Salticus scenicus (Plate 12) is the most commonly noticed salticid in the region; the
black and white striped appearance of this spider has, in Britain, given rise to the
common name of 'zebra spider'. This name could of course apply to the other species
of *Salticus* and, although the Danes refer to the spider as the 'zebraedderkoppen', in
Germany it is called the 'Harlekinspringspinne'. *S. scenicus* most commonly occurs
on the outside walls of houses, and only becomes fully active in the sunshine and
when the bricks or stones have been warmed. Evidence of the spider's activities can
often be seen in the form of criss-cross draglines over the surface of the wall; if the

weather is inclement, the spider itself will be hidden away within a suitable crevice. On a warm, sunny day, *Salticus* will be found hunting on the wall and will raise its eyes up to watch your approach. It will readily take prey held in fine forceps – greenfly or other aphids are easy to catch and hold in this way and provide a certain amount of satisfaction for the giver as well as for the recipient! Adult males of *Salticus* have enlarged, projecting chelicerae and these are used in sparring contests between rival males. Courtship involves a certain amount of legwork on the male's part, but is less balletic than in some other genera. The genus is readily identifiable in the field and the epigynes and the tibial apophyses on the male palp are often discernible with a lens.

Salticus scenicus (Clerck 1757)   Plate 12
Description ♀, 5–7mm; ♂, 5–6mm (including chelicerae). The pattern of white hairs does vary quite a bit and sometimes there may be brownish hairs present on the abdomen in addition to the black ones. The brightness of the pattern and any iridescence will vary with the degree of sunlight. The epigyne and male palp are distinctive.
Habitat Mainly on the walls and fences of houses and gardens, but occasionally found away from human habitations on rocks, fence posts and the bark of trees.
Maturity Summer.
Distribution Widespread and common throughout Britain and northern Europe.

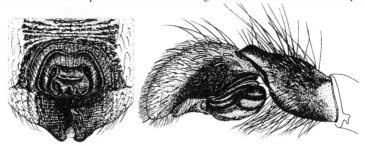

Salticus cingulatus (Panzer 1797)
Description ♀, 5–7mm; ♂, 5–6mm (including chelicerae). Similar to *S. scenicus*, but the abdomen usually has more white hairs arranged to form black and white triangles and chevrons in the rear half. Epigyne and male palp distinctive.

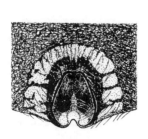

Habitat Almost always on the trunks and lower branches of trees; sometimes fence posts. **Maturity** Summer.
Distribution Much less common than *S. scenicus*, but widespread throughout Britain and northern Europe.

Salticus zebraneus (C.L. Koch 1837)
Description ♀, 3–4mm; ♂, 3–3.5mm (including chelicerae). Similar to *S. scenicus*, but generally smaller and with less noticeable white stripes – sometimes there is just a sprinkling of white hairs. Epigyne distinctive and the tibial apophysis of the male palp is relatively much larger than in *S. cingulatus*. Take care not to confuse this spade-like apophysis with that of *Sitticus pubescens* (p. 199).
Habitat On tall plants and bushes and on trees, particularly conifers.
Maturity Summer.
Distribution Generally very rare in Britain but recorded from a number of localities in south-east England where it is mainly found on the trunks of pine trees, sometimes in abundance. Widespread in northern Europe, but much less common than the previous two species.

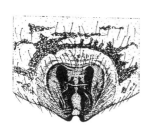 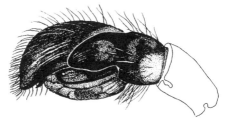

Genus *Heliophanus*

Eleven species of *Heliophanus* occur in Europe, of which six are described here. The females of many species are easily recognized in the field by the combination of a black body with pale greenish-yellow legs, which are sometimes streaked with black. In both sexes there is usually a thin line of white hairs around the front end of the abdomen and in some species there are other spots of white hairs further back. Males tend to have much darker, brownish legs and the body is usually more iridescent or metallic in appearance. The majority of species occur on low vegetation, being found in the undergrowth in poor weather but very active near the top of plants in sunshine. The epigynes can sometimes be discerned with a lens, but higher magnification is often required. The male palps are highly distinctive, but the main problem here lies in arranging the first leg so that it does not obscure the palpal femur and its apophyses.

Heliophanus cupreus (Walckenaer 1802)   Plate 12
Description ♀, 5–6mm; ♂, 3.5–4mm. Male as illustrated. Female very similar in general appearance to *H. flavipes* (Plate 12), but is easily distinguished by the legs, which have black streaks along both sides of the femur and tibia of all four pairs of legs. The abdomen sometimes has one or two light patches of hairs in the posterior half. The epigyne is distinctive, but many specimens have the opening obscured by

irregular, reddish exudates. The male palp has distinctive apophyses on the femur and tibia.

Habitat On, or at the base of, low vegetation in a variety of situations.

Maturity Spring and summer.

Distribution Common and widely distributed throughout Britain and northern Europe.

Heliophanus flavipes Hahn 1832   Plate 12

Description ♀, 5–6mm; ♂, 3.5–4mm. Female as illustrated; the legs usually have black markings on femora III and IV. Male similar to that of *H. cupreus*. Epigyne distinctive, as also are the apophyses on the femur and tibia of the male palp.

Habitat, Maturity and Distribution Similar to *H. cupreus*.

Heliophanus dampfi Schenkel 1923

Description ♀, 3.2–5mm; ♂, 3–3.5mm. Very similar in general appearance to *H. flavipes*, but generally smaller. In the female, coxa IV has a striking black mark dorsally, and there is usually a smaller mark on coxa III. The rest of the legs are yellow or orange with only a few streaks of black on the femora. Males have the femora and tibiae of all legs streaked with black. Epigyne distinctive, as also are the femoral and tibial apophyses on the male palp.

Habitat On low vegetation, and in undergrowth and moss, in bogs.
Maturity Spring and summer.
Distribution In Britain, recorded from raised bogs in Scotland and Wales. Widespread in northern Europe.

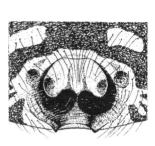

△ *Heliophanus tribulosus* Simon 1868
Description ♀, 4.5–6mm; ♂, 3–4mm. Similar to *H. flavipes*; the abdomen usually has a pair of light spots posteriorly, which may join to form a narrow band. Epigyne distinctive, as also are the apophyses on the femur and tibia of the male palp.
Habitat and Maturity Similar to *H. cupreus*.
Distribution Absent from Britain and Scandinavia. Widespread throughout the rest of northern Europe.

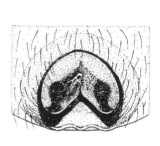
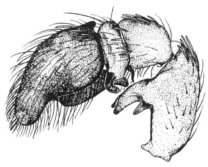

Heliophanus auratus C.L. Koch 1835
Description ♀, 4.5–5mm; ♂, 3.5–4.5mm. Similar in general appearance to *H. flavipes* and *H. cupreus*. The epigyne is distinctive. The bifid femoral apophysis on the male palp is similar to that of *H. melinus*, but the latter species has an additional blunt femoral apophysis towards the inside, different tibial apophyses, different markings on the abdomen, and is generally larger.
Habitat On shingle; amongst sparse vegetation and running on shingle in sunshine.
Maturity Summer.
Distribution In Britain recorded only from coastal shingle in Essex. Absent from Scandinavia, but widespread in central and southern Europe.

Heliophanus auratus (previous page)

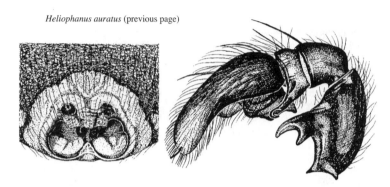

△ *Heliophanus melinus* L. Koch 1867

Description ♀, 6–7mm; ♂, 4mm. Similar in general appearance to *H. flavipes* and *H. cupreus*, but both sexes distinguished by having a pair of longitudinal rows of white hairs on the abdomen as well as the transverse white line at the front. The epigyne is distinctive and the male palp has distinctive femoral and tibial apophyses.

Habitat and Maturity Similar to *H. cupreus*.

Distribution Was recorded once in the south of England in 1870, but not now considered to occur in Britain. Absent from Scandinavia, but possibly widespread in the south of the region.

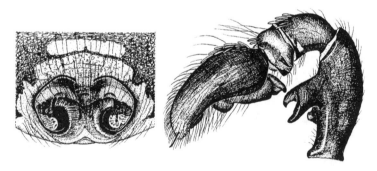

Genus *Marpissa*

Of the five European species of *Marpissa*, four are described here. They all have an elongate abdomen and leg I is stouter and darker than the rest. Males use these legs in courtship displays, raising them in the air and moving from side to side, before approaching to touch the female. Egg sacs are placed in a silken cell, under bark and stones or on vegetation, and guarded by the female. Of the three British species, *M. radiata* has in the past been confused with *M. pomatia*, and *M. nivoyi* was at one time assigned to a separate genus, *Hyctia*.

Marpissa muscosa (Clerck 1757)   Plate 12

Description ♀, 8–10mm; ♂, 6–8mm. Male similar in general appearance to the female, but with a smaller abdomen. The whole spider has a very furry appearance and is rather flattened dorsoventrally. The epigyne has a rather thick, dark central opening in the form of an incomplete ring and the ducts are distinct from those of the other species. The male palpal organs and tibial apophysis are distinctive.

Habitat On the bark and lichen of trees and fences with a silk cell in crevices underneath. **Maturity** Spring and summer, but females perhaps all year.

Distribution Uncommon but fairly widespread in England; more frequent in the south and east. Widespread in northern Europe.

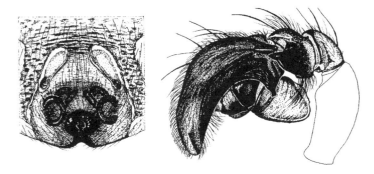

Marpissa radiata (Grube 1859)

Description ♀, 8–10mm; ♂, 6–7mm. Similar in shape to *M. muscosa* but the abdomen has a yellow-brown midline band flanked by a pair of blackish stripes; the whole abdomen is furnished with light hairs. In males, the abdomen may be almost uniformly black. The epigyne is distinguished by the relatively small, arched opening and the extensive ducts. The male palp is distinguished from that of *M. pomatia* by the shape of the cymbium, the palpal organs and by the tibial apophysis.

Habitat Fens and marshy areas, damp heathland and woodland. Egg sac usually placed in the heads of vegetation, such as reeds. **Maturity** Summer.

Distribution Rare in Britain but frequent in the fens and broads of East Anglia and also recorded from heathland in Somerset. Widespread throughout northern Europe but fairly uncommon.

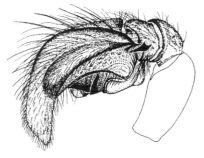

△ *Marpissa pomatia* (Walckenaer 1802)

Description ♀, 8–10mm; ♂, 6–7mm. Similar in shape to the previous species. The head region of the carapace is black and the thoracic part yellow, with broad, dark lateral bands and a dark midline band. There is a golden median band on the abdomen and the legs are yellow, streaked with black. The epigyne has an almost circular opening which forms a complete ring and is less heavily sclerotized than in *M. muscosa*. The male palp differs from that of *M. radiata* in the shape of the cymbium, the palpal organs, and the tibial apophysis.

Habitat and Maturity Similar to *M. radiata*.

Distribution Absent from Britain and Scandinavia. Widespread in the rest of northern Europe but apparently quite rare.

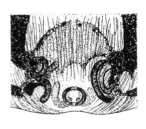
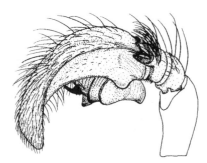

Marpissa nivoyi (Lucas 1846)   Plate 12

Description ♀, 4–6mm; ♂, 4–5mm. Male similar to the female but darker. The shape of the abdomen, the large first pair of legs, and the habit of sometimes running backwards give it the appearance of a large pseudoscorpion. The epigyne and male palp are distinctive.

Habitat Amongst marram on coastal dunes; or in marshy areas, sometimes inland.

Maturity Summer to autumn.

Distribution Rare in England, South Wales and southern Ireland, the majority of records being from the coast. Absent from Scandinavia and recorded from Belgium, Holland, France and areas to the south of the region.

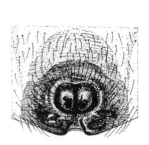
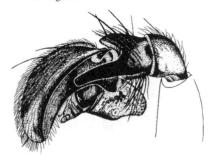

△ Genus *Dendryphantes*

Two species of *Dendryphantes* occur in Europe, one of which is described here. A third species, previously known as *D. nidicolens*, is now assigned to the genus *Eris* (below).

△ *Dendryphantes rudis* (Sundevall 1832) Plate 12

Description ♀, 5–6mm; ♂, 4.5–5mm. Male similar to female but with a smaller, darker abdomen which has a more metallic lustre. The epigyne and male palp are distinctive.

Habitat On the branches and trunks of trees, particularly conifers. Female places the spherical white egg sac amongst pine needles. **Maturity** Summer.

Distribution Absent from Britain. Widespread in northern Europe.

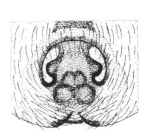 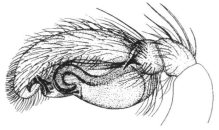

△ Genus *Eris*

One species of *Eris* occurs in Europe; it was once included in the genus *Dendryphantes*.

△ *Eris nidicolens* (Walckenaer 1802) Plate 12

Description ♀, 5–6mm; ♂, 4.5–5mm. Female similar to the male illustrated with a larger abdomen, dark bands, and oblique white lines. The epigyne and male palp are distinctive.

Habitat On the branches and trunks of trees. **Maturity** Summer.

Distribution Absent from Britain. Uncommon in northern Europe but possibly widespread; more common in the south of the region and in the Mediterranean.

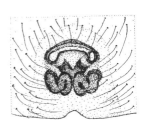 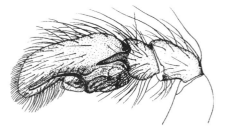

Genus *Pellenes*

Three species of *Pellenes* occur in Europe, the most widely distributed of which is described here.

Pellenes tripunctatus (Walckenaer 1802)   Plate 12
Description ♀, 6–6.5mm; ♂, 4–5mm. The two sexes are similar in general appearance with a distinctive abdominal pattern. The epigyne and male palp are distinctive.
Habitat Recorded from sparsely vegetated shingle beaches in England, but in Europe it is found on grasses, bushes and at ground level in clearings and meadows and a variety of other habitats. **Maturity** Summer.
Distribution Rare in Britain and recorded only from the east coast of Kent. Widespread in northern Europe.

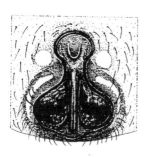 

△ Genus *Pseudicius*

A single species of *Pseudicius* occurs in Europe. It bears a superficial resemblance to *Marpissa muscosa* but is only half the size and has leg I less obviously darkened.

△ *Pseudicius encarpatus* (Walckenaer 1802)   Plate 13
Description ♀, 4.5–5.5mm; ♂, 3.5–5mm. Both sexes are illustrated and have a highly distinctive appearance. Epigyne and male palp distinctive.
Habitat In woodland, amongst leaf-litter and moss as well as on the bark of trees.
Maturity Summer.
Distribution Absent from Britain. Widespread throughout most of Europe but generally uncommon.

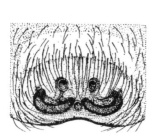 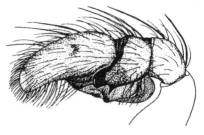

Genus *Ballus*

A single species of *Ballus* occurs in northern Europe and it has a highly characteristic appearance.

Ballus chalybeius (Walckenaer 1802) (= *B. depressus* (Walckenaer))   Plate 13
Description ♀, 4.5–5mm; ♂, 3–4mm. The pale legs, streaked and annulated with black, are very noticeable in the field. The male has a darker, rough-textured carapace and a reddish-brown abdomen which often lacks any clear pattern. The femur and tibia of leg I are much stouter than in the female, and are dark brown to black with a pronounced metallic lustre. The epigyne and male palp are also distinctive.
Habitat Almost entirely on broadleaved bushes and trees, particularly oaks. The female attaches her egg sac to a leaf and guards it under a tent of silk.
Maturity Late spring and summer.
Distribution Rather locally distributed in England and Wales, and much commoner in the south of England. Widely distributed in northern Europe.

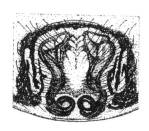 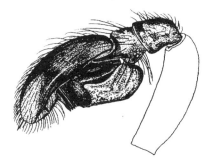

Genus *Neon*

Four species of *Neon* occur in the region and the two most widespread species are described here. They are found in leaf-litter and moss and, despite their small size, are readily identifiable to genus level with a lens. The epigynes are relatively large for the size of spider and females are sometimes identifiable to species level with a lens.

Neon reticulatus (Blackwall 1853)   Plate 13
Description ♀, 2–3mm; ♂, 2–2.5mm. Some specimens are a darker greenish-grey in overall colour with subdued markings which may only be visible in bright sunlight; others are paler than illustrated. Males are generally darker; the head has a metallic lustre, the abdominal pattern is sharper and the tibia and metatarsus of leg I are black. The epigyne is easily distinguished from that of *N. valentulus* by the relatively small arched openings and large spermathecae. The male palp requires microscopy and more care, but the palpal organs and tibial apophyses are distinctive and the cymbium lacks the ventral lip present in *N. valentulus*.
Habitat The spider occurs in two distinct habitats: in leaf-litter (often quite dry) in woodland, and within moss in open, damp, boggy habitats.
Maturity Males spring to autumn; females all year.
Distribution Widespread and common throughout Britain and northern Europe and often abundant locally.

Neon reticulatus (previous page)

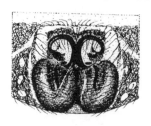
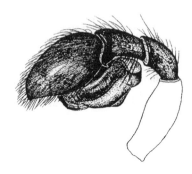

Neon valentulus Falconer 1912
Description ♀, 2–3mm; ♂, 2–2.5mm. Similar to *Neon reticulatus* but generally much darker. Leg I is frequently entirely dark brown or black in both sexes, apart from the coxa and tarsus. The other legs are strikingly annulated with black. The epigyne has relatively large arches around the openings when compared with the size of the spermathecae. The male palpal organs and tibial apophysis differ from those of *N. reticulatus* and the cymbium has a small ventral lip.
Habitat Amongst grass and moss in fens. **Maturity** Summer.
Distribution Rare in Britain and restricted to a few fens in East Anglia. Also fairly rare in northern Europe, but possibly widespread, with records from Sweden, Germany and the Netherlands.

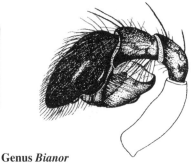

Genus *Bianor*
There is only one species of *Bianor* in the region; it is a small dark spider with a metallic sheen and has leg I noticeably dark and swollen.

Bianor aurocinctus (Ohlert 1865) (= *B. aenescens* (Simon))
Description ♀, 3.2–4mm; ♂, 3–3.5mm. The male is illustrated next to the palp; the femur and tibia of leg I are dark and greatly swollen and this is further exaggerated by the thick covering of black hairs. The carapace and abdomen are very dark brown with a coppery sheen. The first legs are not quite as swollen in the female, but are still an obvious feature. The epigyne and male palp are very distinctive.
Habitat Amongst short vegetation (grass, heather) and amongst stones.
Maturity Spring to autumn.
Distribution Rare in Britain; fairly widespread throughout England but with an extremely local distribution. Similarly widespread but rare in northern Europe.

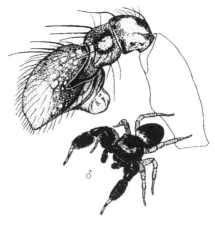

Genus *Euophrys*

Eleven species of *Euophrys* occur in northern Europe of which eight are described here. They are fairly small spiders, 5mm or less in length, and many have attractive markings. Males frequently have the first pair of legs darkened, and frequently iridescent, and these are employed in courtship displays, being waved aloft as the female is approached. The egg sac in many species is loosely attached under a stone or piece of detritus and is guarded by the female. Many of the epigynes are of similar general appearance as are the male palps, and in both cases are often obscured by a liberal covering of hairs. However, they are readily identifiable with a microscope.

Euophrys frontalis (Walckenaer 1802)   Plate 13
Description ♀, 3–5mm; ♂, 2–3mm. Both sexes are illustrated. The first pair of legs are black in the male and have a greenish-blue iridescence; the male also has fringes of bright orange hairs around the anterior eyes. The general appearance of this species is similar to that of *E. herbigrada* (below) and microscopy is required to distinguish their epigynes and male palps. The ducts in the epigyne, and the lightly sclerotized structures around the opening, are reliably identifiable from the illustration. The male palpal organs differ slightly from those of *E. herbigrada*, the tibial apophysis is darker and much longer, and the palpal tibia has a group of thick white hairs dorsally.
Habitat Amongst low vegetation, leaf-litter and detritus and under stones in woodland and on open ground. **Maturity** Spring and summer; females to late autumn.

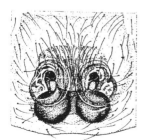

Distribution The commonest species of the genus; widespread throughout Britain and northern Europe.

Euophrys herbigrada (Simon 1871)
Description ♀, 3–4mm; ♂, 2.5mm. Very similar to *E. frontalis* in general appearance, but darker, with the black component of the abdominal pattern being relatively larger. The female has a similar pattern to that illustrated for the male of *E. frontalis* (with a larger abdomen) and has a band of white hairs across the clypeus. The male is darker than that of *E. frontalis*. The ducts in the epigyne are distinctive and the dark tip of the sclerotized arch, near the opening, is characteristic. The male palp has a very short, pale, tibial apophysis and lacks the long white hairs present in *E. frontalis*.
Habitat Most records are from coastal grassland. **Maturity** Summer.
Distribution Probably under-recorded and confused with *E. frontalis*, but much rarer than the latter species. Possibly widespread in England, although most early records are from the south-west coast. Possibly widespread in northern Europe.

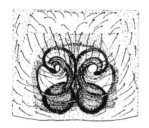 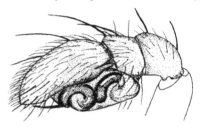

Euophrys petrensis C.L. Koch 1837
Description ♀♂, 3mm. The female is almost entirely dark brown to black, sometimes with a few white and orange hairs which, on the abdomen, are disposed to form vague chevrons. The male is similarly dark, but has bright orange hairs around the anterior eyes and over the whole of the front face of the carapace. The male palpal tibia is furnished thickly with long white hairs, which also contrast markedly with the rest of the spider. The epigyne and male palp are distinctive.
Habitat Under stones and on low vegetation in a variety of habitats; in coastal localities and at much higher altitudes in mountainous areas.
Maturity Spring and summer; females sometimes to autumn.
Distribution Very locally distributed, and commoner in the south of England; also recorded from high ground in Cumbria and from Ireland. Widespread throughout northern Europe.

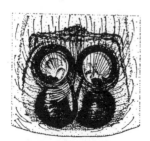 

Euophrys aequipes (O.P.-Cambridge 1871) Plate 13
Description ♀, 2–3mm; ♂, 2–2.5mm. Apart from its small size and general appearance, this species can be distinguished by the total length of patella and tibia of leg III which is roughly the same as that of leg IV. Both sexes frequently have a sparse covering of dull yellow hairs. The male is very similar to the female, but femur I is darkened and the inner surface of the femur, patella, tibia and metatarsus of leg I is black with a green-blue iridescence. The epigyne and male palp are distinctive.
Habitat Amongst stones on warm, stony or sandy banks. **Maturity** Summer.
Distribution Locally distributed, with most records from the south of England; has been recorded from Scotland. Widespread throughout northern Europe.

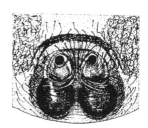 

Euophrys erratica (Walckenaer 1826)
(= *Pseudeuophrys callida* (Walckenaer)) Plate 13
Description ♀ ♂, 3–4mm. Both sexes are illustrated. The female has pale yellow palps and the male palp has the femur and patella pale yellow. The species is very similar to *E. lanigera*. The abdominal pattern in females of *E. erratica* has a dark, inverted Y in the front half followed by dark chevrons; in *E. lanigera* the colour is usually reversed, with the inverted Y and the following chevrons being lighter than the surrounding abdomen. The epigyne and male palp are distinctive.
Habitat On walls and amongst rubble and stones.
Maturity Summer; females to autumn.
Distribution Widely, but locally distributed throughout Britain. Widespread throughout northern Europe.

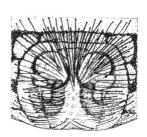 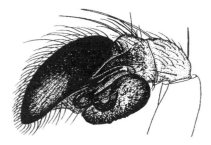

Euophrys lanigera (Simon 1871)
Description ♀, 4–5mm; ♂, 3.5–4mm. Very similar to *E. erratica* but with the light and dark colours in the abdominal pattern reversed and usually forming an inverted

Y of light hairs in the front half, followed by light chevrons. The epigyne and male palp are distinctive although the tibial apophysis of the male palp shows some variation.

Habitat Around human habitations; sometimes in gardens, but usually higher up on walls and roofs, occasionally venturing indoors.

Maturity Spring and summer; females all year.

Distribution Widespread in England and probably under-recorded. Absent from Scandinavia and appears to be commoner in the more western parts of northern Europe.

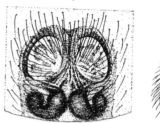 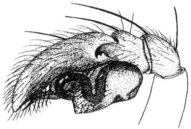

Euophrys browningi Millidge & Locket 1955 (possibly = *E. obsoleta* (Simon 1868))

Description ♀, 3–3.5mm; ♂, 2.5–3mm. Similar in general appearance to *Sitticus caricis* (Plate 14), the male being darker. The epigyne and male palp are distinctive, but possibly the same as European specimens of *E. obsoleta*; I have not yet seen sufficient material to formally relegate *E. browningi* to a junior synonym of *E. obsoleta*.

Habitat On shingle beaches; running in the open, and within empty whelk shells.

Maturity Spring to autumn.

Distribution In Britain restricted to coastal shingle in the south-east of England. Not recorded elsewhere, but quite possibly widely distributed in Europe under the name of *E. obsoleta*.

 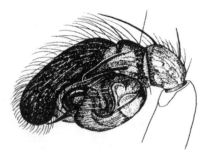

Euophrys thorelli Kulczynski 1891

Description ♀, 2.3–2.5mm; ♂, 1.9–2.3mm. Very similar in general appearance to *E. aequipes*, but the total length of the patella and tibia of leg III is less than that of leg IV. The legs are pale yellow, annulated with black, and the male does not have

femur I blackened. The epigyne and male palp are small but distinctive.
Habitat At ground level, amongst stones and low vegetation. **Maturity** Summer.
Distribution Recently discovered in Kent. Widespread in northern Europe.

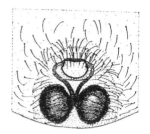

Genus *Sitticus*

Eleven species of *Sitticus* are known from Europe and four of the most widespread
are described here. They have a rather dull brown or greyish-black appearance, but
many species are attractively marked with light hairs. The epigynes and male palps
of some species are very similar to one another and are usually obscured by hairs.
The general appearance and habitat are helpful in identification.

Sitticus pubescens (Fabricius 1775)   Plate 14
Description ♀, 4–5mm; ♂, 4mm. Male similar to the female illustrated but with a
smaller abdomen. In both sexes, the number and distribution of the white patches is
variable. The epigyne and male palp are distinctive in this species and are usually
discernible with a lens.
Habitat Usually around human habitations; on walls and fences and occasionally
indoors. Sometimes under stones and on fence posts and tree trunks away from
houses. **Maturity** Summer; females throughout the year.
Distribution Widespread, but rather locally distributed throughout England and
parts of Wales. Widespread throughout northern Europe.

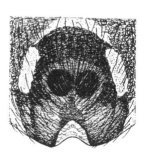

Sitticus floricola (C.L. Koch 1837)   Plate 14
Description ♀, 4.5–6mm; ♂, 4–4.5mm. Male similar to female, but having a
smaller abdomen. Epigyne covered in white hairs and often difficult to see unless
these are rubbed off. Male palp similar to that of *S. rupicola*, but has a broad lip

extending further from the margin of the cymbium and a differently shaped tibial apophysis.
Habitat In wet, swampy areas; in *Sphagnum* moss and on, or at the base of, vegetation. Occasionally in drier leaf-litter. Females make their egg sacs in the heads of plants. **Maturity** Spring to autumn.
Distribution Generally rare; very locally distributed and recorded from sites in England, Scotland and Ireland where it is sometimes abundant. Widespread and commoner in northern Europe.

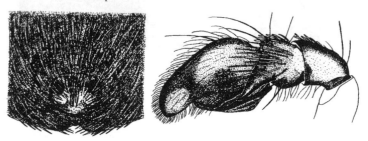

Sitticus inexpectus (Logunov & Kronestedt 1997)
Note: Recently described as a new species, separate from Sitticus rupicola (C.L. Koch 1837) with which it had been confused. The latter species does not occur in Britain.)
Description ♀, 6–7mm; ♂, 4–5mm. Very similar to *S. floricola* but the paired light patches on the abdomen are smaller and less elongate. The epigyne is obscured by light hairs. The male palp has a smaller lip on the cymbium and also differs from that of *S. floricola* in the tibial apophysis.
Habitat On shingle beaches, and amongst scree and rocks in mountainous areas.
Maturity Summer to autumn.
Distribution In Britain, recorded only from coastal shingle in the south and east of England. Widespread but uncommon in northern Europe.

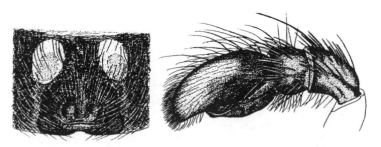

Sitticus caricis (Westring 1861)   Plate 14
Description ♀ ♂, 3–4mm. Male similar to female but has a smaller abdomen. Some specimens, of either sex, may be marked more strikingly with orange and white hairs; others may be darker with a purple, metallic sheen. The epigyne is distinctive,

and is furnished with rather coarse, black hairs. The male palp has very little in the way of a lip extending from the margin of the cymbium.
Habitat Amongst moss and low vegetation in swampy areas.
Maturity Summer to autumn.

Distribution Rather uncommon; widely distributed in England, Ireland and Wales, but commoner in south-east England.

Genus *Attulus*
The single European species of *Attulus* is a small spider, resembling species of *Sitticus* but having longer fourth legs, larger and fewer teeth on the claws of the fourth legs, and the ability to jump relatively large distances.

Attulus saltator (Simon 1868)
Description ♀, 3–4mm; ♂, 3mm. The female is illustrated next to the epigyne, below. The carapace is black with light hairs in the midline, the abdomen brownish and marked with patches of light hairs. The legs are yellowish-brown with faint annulations and a covering of light hairs. The male is similar, but the tibia and metatarsus of leg I are usually darker. The epigyne and male palp are distinctive.
Habitat In sandy habitats. **Maturity** spring to autumn.

Distribution In Britain confined mainly to dunes around the coasts of England and Wales, but has occurred inland. Widespread throughout northern Europe, but generally uncommon.

△ Genus *Philaeus*

A single species of *Philaeus* occasionally occurs in northern Europe and is of distinctive appearance, the two sexes being very dissimilar in colour.

△ *Philaeus chrysops* (Poda 1761)   Plate 14
Description ♀ ♂, 7–12mm. Both sexes are illustrated; the tapering median band on the abdomen is distinctive in both males and females. Epigyne and male palp distinctive.
Habitat Amongst stones, rocks and low vegetation, sometimes at fairly high altitude. **Maturity** Summer.
Distribution Absent from Britain and much of northern Europe. Recorded from much of France but commoner in warmer, more southerly parts of Europe.

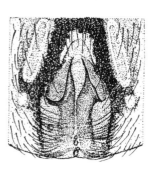 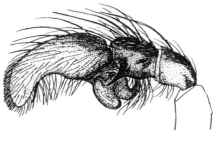

Genus *Evarcha*

Of the four European species of *Evarcha*, three of the most widespread are described here. The two sexes are, in most species, very different in their general appearance. Courtship is frequently quite energetic with the male waving the first pair of legs as he approaches. Females make their egg sacs in dried, rolled-up leaves or within several bunched shoots of vegetation. The species can usually be identified from their general appearance; the epigynes and male palpal tibiae are sometimes discernible with a lens, and easily distinguished with higher magnification.

Evarcha falcata (Clerck 1757) (= *E. flammata* Clerck)   Plate 14
Description ♀, 6–8mm; ♂, 5mm. Both sexes are illustrated and have a characteristic appearance. Some females are more greyish than illustrated, and the dark spots

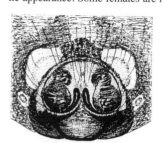 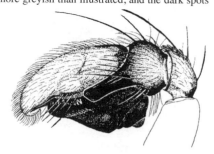

and light hairs are a little variable. The epigyne has the openings larger than the dark posterior portion. The male palp has a relatively long tibial apophysis.
Habitat In woodland, on the lower branches of trees and on vegetation such as heather and gorse in clearings. **Maturity** Spring to autumn.
Distribution Fairly common and widespread throughout Britain and northern Europe.

Evarcha arcuata (Clerck 1757) Plate 14
Description ♀, 6–8mm; ♂, 5–6mm. Both sexes are illustrated and are of distinctive appearance. The male illustrated has hardly any chevrons visible on the abdomen; occasionally they are a little more pronounced, but even then are partly obscured by the metallic sheen. The epigyne has smaller openings relative to the size of the dark posterior part. The male palp has a relatively short, blunt tibial apophysis.
Habitat On low vegetation, such as heather, often in damp situations.
Maturity Summer.
Distribution Locally distributed in southern counties of England. Widespread throughout northern Europe.

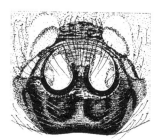 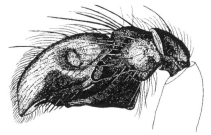

△ *Evarcha laetabunda* (C.L. Koch 1846)
Description ♀, 6–7mm; ♂, 5mm. The female of this species broadly resembles *E. arcuata*, but the abdominal pattern is made up of dark brown lines on a pale, sometimes almost white background. The male is similar but slightly darker. The epigyne is very distinctive and the male palp has a spade-like tibial apophysis.
Habitat On low vegetation, often in fairly dry situations. **Maturity** Summer.
Distribution Absent from Britain. Widespread in northern Europe, but rare (or absent) in Scandinavia.

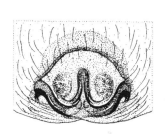 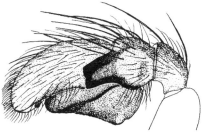

Genus *Aelurillus*

A single species of *Aelurillus* occurs in Europe. The two sexes differ considerably in their appearance but both are recognisable in the field. They are excellent jumpers.

Aelurillus v-insignitus (Clerck 1757)   Plate 15

Description ♀, 6–7mm; ♂, 4–5mm. Both sexes are illustrated next to the epigyne and male palp, below. The female lacks the inverted U-shaped rows of hairs on the head and has a less pronounced light, median stripe on the abdomen. The markings in the female are made up of light grey, black and brownish hairs. The epigyne and male palp are distinctive, the latter being furnished thickly with yellowish-brown hairs.

Habitat In open heathland areas, and on stony ground; sometimes on high ground. Highly active in sunshine. **Maturity** Spring to autumn.

Distribution Locally distributed in the southern counties of England, but has been recorded from Scotland. Widespread throughout northern Europe.

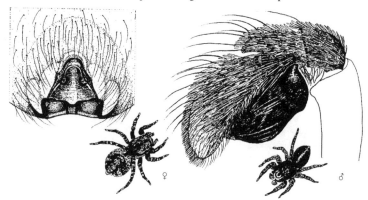

Genus *Phlegra*

Of the three European species of *Phlegra*, one is described here, and both sexes have a very distinctive appearance.

Phlegra fasciata (Hahn 1826)   Plate 15

Description ♀, 6–7mm; ♂; 5–6mm. Both sexes are illustrated; the male has a very glossy abdomen with a more obscure pattern. The epigyne and male palp are also distinctive.

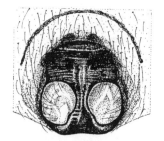

Habitat Amongst low vegetation on sandhills and on shingle.
Maturity Summer, females to autumn.
Distribution Rare in Britain and recorded from a very few stretches of coastline in southern England. Fairly widespread but uncommon in northern Europe.

Genus *Synageles*

Two species of *Synageles* occur in Europe, one of which is described here. Like *Myrmarachne* and *Leptorchestes* (below), these spiders are impressive ant mimics, both in appearance and in their movements.

Synageles venator (Lucas 1836)   Plate 15
Description ♀, 3.5–4mm; ♂, 3mm. The female is similar to the male, but sometimes a little paler. Epigyne and male palp distinctive.
Habitat On coastal sandhills and in fens; in Europe it sometimes occurs on cultivated land amongst low vegetation and on hedges and trees.
Maturity Summer to autumn, possibly later.
Distribution Locally distributed in the south and east of England and south Wales. Widespread in northern Europe.

△ Genus *Leptorchestes*

The single species of *Leptorchestes* in the region is also an impressive ant mimic. It is a larger spider than *Synageles venator*, and does not have the first pair of legs enlarged to the same extent. It differs from *Myrmarachne formicaria* in not having the head region sharply differentiated from the thorax, in the male not having enlarged chelicerae, and in the female not having flattened palps.

△ *Leptorchestes berolinensis* (C.L. Koch 1846)   Plate 15
Description ♀♂, 5–7mm. The female is very similar to the male illustrated. Epigyne and male palp very distinctive.

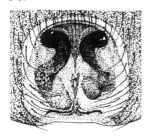
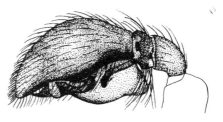

Habitat On sunny walls and on the bark of trees. **Maturity** Summer to autumn. **Distribution** Absent from Britain. Absent from Scandinavia, but fairly widespread elsewhere in northern Europe.

Genus *Myrmarachne*

One species of *Myrmarachne* occurs in Europe and is distinguished from the genera *Synageles* and *Leptorchestes* by the sharply raised and demarcated head region, the flattened palps in the female, and the greatly enlarged chelicerae in the male. The species both looks and walks like an ant.

Myrmarachne formicaria (DeGeer 1778)   Plate 15
Description ♀, 5–6mm; ♂, 5.5–6.5mm (including chelicerae). Both sexes are illustrated. The epigyne and male palp are also distinctive.
Habitat Amongst low vegetation in a sunny position, under stones and amongst moss. **Maturity** Summer.
Distribution Very locally distributed in the south and east of England. Widespread throughout northern Europe.

FAMILY OXYOPIDAE

Only one genus, *Oxyopes*, occurs in the region and all three north European species are described. The hexagonal arrangement of the eyes, and the long leg spines, are illustrated in the Family Key (p. 45). They are long-legged, diurnal, hunting spiders, capable of running very rapidly on low vegetation and also jumping on their prey. This has earned them the common name of 'lynx spiders'. Although their eyes are much smaller than those of the Salticidae and Lycosidae, their vision is obviously acute enough to enable them to recognise potential prey, or a mate, from three or four inches away. Courtship is not unlike that seen in the salticids and lycosids, visual recognition being followed by the male waving his palps and legs as he approaches, first to touch, and then to mate. Females place their rather flat-looking, discoid egg sacs near the top of low vegetation and stand guard over them.

The family and genus are readily identifiable in the field, although the markings and habitat of *Philodromus histrio* (p. 173) could lead to momentary confusion with *Oxyopes heterophthalmus* at first sight. The epigynes and male palps allow easy identification to species level and are usually discernible with a lens.

Oxyopes heterophthalmus ♀ on egg sac

Oxyopes heterophthalmus Latreille 1804   Plate 15
Description ♀, 5–8mm; ♂, 5.5–6.5mm. The male is very similar to the female illustrated, but is sometimes an almost uniform deep, reddish-brown colour. The epigyne has a much broader tongue than that of *O. ramosus* and the male palp has large and conspicuous tibial apophyses which are not present in the other two species.
Habitat On dry, mature heathland on south-facing slopes. The spider hunts on and amongst heather and the female guards the egg sac near the top of plants.
Maturity Summer.
Distribution Rare in Britain and restricted to a few small heathland sites in Surrey, where it can be abundant. Absent from Scandinavia, but widespread in France, the Netherlands and in southern Europe.

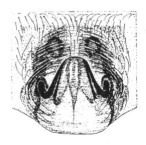

△ *Oxyopes lineatus* Latreille 1806   Plate 15

Description ♀, 6–6.5mm; ♂, 4–5mm. This species is much paler than *O. heterophthalmus* and the female is usually paler than the male illustrated. In both sexes, a pair of dark stripes usually runs from the anterior median eyes, down over the clypeus, and along the front of the chelicerae. The epigyne is narrower than in the other two species, with the spermathecae set relatively far out to the sides. The male palp is much slimmer than in the other species and has a single, small tibial apophysis.
Habitat Low vegetation, bushes and the lower branches of trees. **Maturity** Summer.
Distribution Absent from Britain and Scandinavia. Widespread in France, the Netherlands and in southern Europe.

△ *Oxyopes ramosus* (Panzer 1804)

Description ♀, 6–10mm; ♂, 6mm. This species is very similar to *O. heterophthalmus* but females are often darker on the sides of the abdomen, which has three oblique, light marks extending laterally and a broader midline mark of light hairs extending almost to the spinners. The epigyne is broad, but the central tongue narrower than in *O. heterophthalmus*. The male palpal organs are more bulbous than in the other two species and there are small tibial apophyses and a pointed apophysis on the patella.
Habitat On heather, other low vegetation and bushes. **Maturity** Summer.
Distribution Absent from Britain. Widespread throughout northern Europe, including Scandinavia.

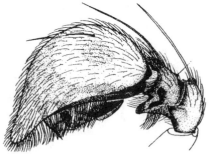

FAMILY LYCOSIDAE

The family Lycosidae is represented in Europe by eighty-one species in eight genera. The characteristic arrangement of the eyes is illustrated in the Family Key (p. 46) and in the Key to the Genera, below. They are all hunting spiders, mostly at ground level but occasionally on low vegetation. Some make silk-lined burrows in which they spend part of their time and *Aulonia* makes a flimsy sheet web with a tubular retreat. Although most species are brownish in overall coloration, many are attractively marked. Although some parts of the markings and patterns are in the cuticle, this is frequently reinforced or modified by the dense, coloured hairs with which these spiders are clothed. In some cases, the pattern may be almost entirely due to light and dark hairs and this effect is largely lost when the spider is immersed in alcohol for preservation. On warm sunny days, large numbers of lycosids may be seen running rapidly on the ground. This, together with their brown, furry appearance, has given rise to the common name of 'wolf spiders'. Many species, particularly of *Trochosa*, are also active at night and their eyes reflect back the light of a torch, particularly if the latter is worn on, or held close to, one's head. In addition to their ability to run at speed, most species can also jump; this is most noticeable in species such as *Pardosa nigriceps,* which hunts on low vegetation and is adept at leaping from leaf to leaf. The males of many species have their palps furnished with dense black hairs, and others have the first pair of legs conspicuously modified. Lycosids have good eyesight and, having first located a female by her pheromones, the male waves the modified legs and palps about in front of her in a courtship display, prior to mating. The females of some genera (*Arctosa, Trochosa* and *Alopecosa*) excavate small burrows where they remain, with their egg sacs, until the spiderlings emerge. However, in the majority of species, the egg sac is attached to the spinners and carried around by the female (Plates 16, 18, and illustrations in text). The egg sac in some species is spherical and white or beige in colour; in other species it is lenticular, with a pale seam, and brownish or green-blue in colour. Females with egg sacs are extremely conspicuous as they run about. The egg sac is periodically removed from the

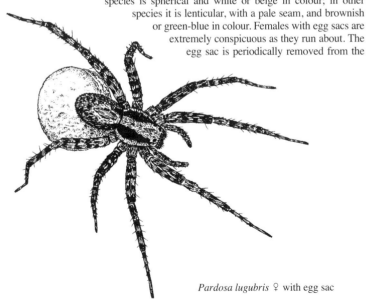

Pardosa lugubris ♀ with egg sac

Pardosa amentata ♀ with young

spinners, turned around and then reattached. Females frequently open the sac, introduce fluid from their mouthparts on to the developing eggs, and then reseal it with silk. Some species periodically dip the sac in water and most will orient themselves so that the bundle of developing eggs gets the optimum exposure to the warmth of the sun. Those living in burrows will periodically expose the egg sac near the entrance. Females parted from their sacs will readily carry small pellets of paper, or similar sized objects, around instead. When the spiderlings are ready to emerge, they rely on the female to open the sac for them. Once out, the spiderlings climb on to their mother's abdomen and are carried around by her for the first week or so. At this stage, the female appears, to the naked eye, to have a fuzzy, irregularly-shaped abdomen. The empty egg sac is usually discarded at this stage, but occasionally it is reattached to the spinners and carried around in addition to the young. I once found a female *Pardosa pullata* carrying young and a *full* egg sac, and wondered at the time whether she had fostered the spiderlings or appropriated the sac from another female – either being a possibility with these spiders.

Although these spiders are easily identified to family level in the field, one member of the Agelenidae, *Textrix denticulata* (p. 242, Plate 19) does appear very similar and may also be found running rapidly on the ground. However, this species does have conspicuously long posterior spinners which are easily visible to the naked eye. The genera are identifiable with a lens, and the general appearance allows some to be identified to species level. However, most species will require examination of the epigyne and male palp to be certain of their identity. Some of the epigynes are identifiable with a lens; others are either too small to be seen properly, or difficult to separate from closely similar structures in related species. In these cases, higher magnification is necessary. It is worth noting that subadult females of some species, particularly *Trochosa*, do have a small sclerotized structure in the epigyne region. This is very much smaller than the adult epigyne and is of a different shape. The male palpal organs are usually more difficult to see in the field; many species will require the use of a microscope, although the spi-pot and field microscope are always worth a try. The characters used in the Key to the Genera are all visible with a lens.

Key to the Genera

1. Patella of palps white in both sexes *Aulonia* p. 235

   Patella of palps not white 2

2. Height of clypeus at least twice the
   diameter of an anterior lateral eye
   (view head from in front) 3

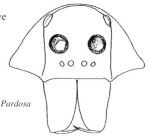

Pardosa

   Height of clypeus narrower than twice the
   diameter of an anterior lateral eye 4

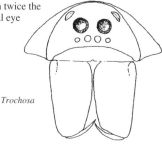

Trochosa

3. Head, viewed from in front, with almost vertical sides.
   Metatarsus IV at least as long as patella and tibia IV
   together. Tibia I with two to three pairs of ventral spines *Pardosa* p. 213

   Head, viewed from in front, with more sloping sides.
   Metatarsus IV shorter than patella and tibia IV together.
   Tibia I with four pairs of ventral spines *Hygrolycosa* p. 222

4. Carapace with well-defined, almost straight-sided, median
   light band extending from between the eyes back to the
   posterior edge of the carapace. This band is sometimes
   constricted at the midpoint and and is usually reinforced
   by a covering of light hairs. Few, if any, dark markings
   within this band 5

   Median light band, if present, less well defined and seldom
   reinforced by light hairs. (If an irregular median band of
   light hairs is present, then this not extending to rear of
   carapace.) If light band is present, then it contains a pair
   of dark longitudinal bars, which may be joined to form a V 6

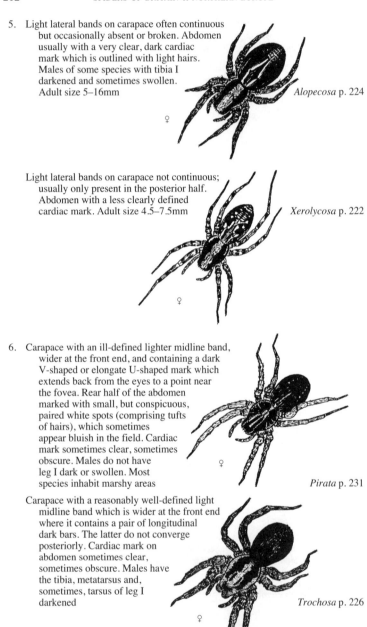

5.   Light lateral bands on carapace often continuous but occasionally absent or broken. Abdomen usually with a very clear, dark cardiac mark which is outlined with light hairs. Males of some species with tibia I darkened and sometimes swollen. Adult size 5–16mm

♀

Alopecosa p. 224

   Light lateral bands on carapace not continuous; usually only present in the posterior half. Abdomen with a less clearly defined cardiac mark. Adult size 4.5–7.5mm

Xerolycosa p. 222

♀

6.   Carapace with an ill-defined lighter midline band, wider at the front end, and containing a dark V-shaped or elongate U-shaped mark which extends back from the eyes to a point near the fovea. Rear half of the abdomen marked with small, but conspicuous, paired white spots (comprising tufts of hairs), which sometimes appear bluish in the field. Cardiac mark sometimes clear, sometimes obscure. Males do not have leg I dark or swollen. Most species inhabit marshy areas

♀

Pirata p. 231

   Carapace with a reasonably well-defined light midline band which is wider at the front end where it contains a pair of longitudinal dark bars. The latter do not converge posteriorly. Cardiac mark on abdomen sometimes clear, sometimes obscure. Males have the tibia, metatarsus and, sometimes, tarsus of leg I darkened

Trochosa p. 226

♀

Carapace without a definite light median band, but there
may be some light hairs and irregular light markings.
Legs often spotted or clearly annulated. Abdominal
pattern quite variable; cardiac mark usually clear. Some
species have tufts of light hairs making up the pattern,
but not like the small paired spots in *Pirata*   *Arctosa* p. 228

Genus *Pardosa*

Spiders of the genus *Pardosa* make up the largest number of lycosid species in the
region and are also the most abundant and common. Of the thirty-nine European
species, sixteen of the most widespread in northern Europe are described here.
The majority of species are found running rapidly on the ground in warm, sunny
conditions, but on cold, dull days are more likely to be found by sieving leaf-
litter, detritus and moss. *Pardosa nigriceps* is usually found hunting on low vegetation, but it too will seek shelter at ground level in inclement weather. Females
become very conspicuous from late May or early June onwards, when they
begin carrying round their egg sacs. These are lenticular, brown or greenish-blue
in colour and have a paler seam. After two or three weeks the sac is opened by
the female. The young clamber on to her abdomen where they travel around in a
fuzzy bundle for about another week before dispersing. One or two more egg
sacs may be made during the course of the season, even though most males may
have died off by this time.

Although a few species of *Pardosa* have a fairly characteristic general appearance,
the majority can only be identified by the form of the epigyne and male palpal organs.
Patterns and markings within the cuticle are reinforced or modified by light and dark
hairs. The overall appearance of individuals of *Pardosa* species can vary greatly,
both between and within different populations. In males, the density and length of
hairs on the first leg and palp are also highly variable. In the past, some of these differences have led to species being split up, to form separate species, or subspecies.
Whilst some of these 'species' are now recognized as being different *races*, with
intermediate forms, others have not yet been fully accepted as such. The situation is
rather like that found with the Carrion Crow (*Corvus corone corone*) and the Hooded
Crow (*Corvus corone cornix*). *P. agrestis* and *P. purbeckensis* are still sometimes
regarded separately but are considered here as one species, *P. agrestis* which grades
into a race, form or subspecies, known as *purbeckensis*. Intermediates occur and considerable variation occurs even within isolated populations.

Whilst the epigynes are readily identifiable, the male palpal organs often require
examination from below, as well as from the side. **Two structures in the palpal
organs are of particular value and are indicated on the figures for *P. agricola***
(next page). When viewed from below, there is an elongate projection with a tooth
at its base; this is called the median apophysis (M) and it is also visible when the palp
is viewed from the side. To the right of this, in the illustration, is a smaller structure
called the terminal apophysis (T), which is sometimes visible in side view; it is larger
in some species and insignificant in others.

Pardosa agricola (Thorell 1856)   Plate 16
Description ♀, 5.5–8mm; ♂, 4.5–6.5mm. Male similar to the female illustrated, but
usually darker. Both sexes may be lighter, and more greyish than illustrated, or
darker and more like *P. amentata* in appearance. The midline mark on the carapace
is usually widened behind the eyes. The epigyne is generally identifiable with a lens.

The male palpal organs have a relatively long median apophysis and the terminal apophysis is fairly broad and bears two teeth.

Habitat On coastal shingle, on the banks of streams, rivers and lakes, and occasionally on sand dunes. **Maturity** Spring to autumn; males only to mid-summer.

Distribution Widespread throughout Britain; on shingle beaches in the south, but by rivers and lakes in the north. Widespread in northern Europe.

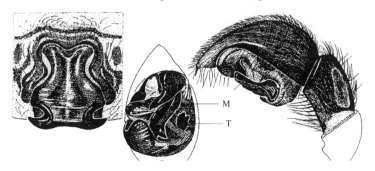

Pardosa agrestis (Westring 1862)   Plate 16

Description ♀, 6–9mm; ♂, 4.5–7mm. Variable in general appearance and may resemble either *P. agricola* or *P. monticola*. The female illustrated is of the form or race *purbeckensis*. Males are similar but may have long hairs on the metatarsus and tarsus of leg I. The epigyne is easily seen with a lens, but is similar to that of *P. monticola*. The width across the projecting tips at the rear of the tongue is greater than 0.48mm and *P. agrestis* is almost always a larger spider than *P. monticola*. The median apophysis of the male palpal organs is relatively short, and the terminal apophysis is a single tooth which curves in towards the median apophysis.

Habitat Mud-flats and the shores of estuaries where it usually is of the form *purbeckensis* and sometimes regarded as a separate species. It also occurs in a form which has the carapace resembling that of *P. agricola*, and this occurs alongside *purbeckensis* and, rarely, inland.

Maturity Spring to autumn; males only to mid-summer.

Distribution Widespread throughout Britain, but mainly coastal where it is usually abundant locally. Widespread throughout northern Europe.

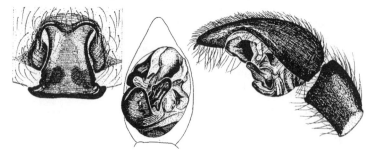

Pardosa monticola (Clerck 1757) Plate 16
Description ♀, 4–6mm; ♂, 4–5.5mm. Usually as illustrated, but the carapace may sometimes have the median band wider behind the eyes, as in *P. agricola,* and/or the lateral light bands broken. Male similar to female. Epigyne discernible with a lens; similar to that of *P. agrestis*, but width across the posterior tips of the tongue less than 0.48mm and *P. monticola* is almost always smaller than *P. agrestis*. The median apophysis of the male palp is relatively thinner and longer than in *P. agrestis* and the terminal apophysis is a small tooth which curves outwards, away from the median apophysis.
Habitat Open areas with short, often sparse vegetation.
Maturity Spring to autumn; males only to early summer.
Distribution Widespread throughout Britain and northern Europe; fairly common, but rather locally distributed.

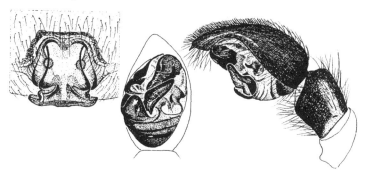

Pardosa palustris (Linnaeus 1758)
Description ♀, 4.5–6mm; ♂, 4.5–5.5mm. Very similar in general appearance to *P. monticola* (Plate 16). Epigyne discernible with a lens. Median apophysis of male palpal organs relatively short; the terminal apophysis is quite large, with a jagged edge, and projects conspicuously below the margin of the cymbium when viewed from the side.
Habitat Mainly open heathland.
Maturity Spring to autumn; males only to early summer.
Distribution Widespread throughout Britain and northern Europe. Fairly common, but rather locally distributed.

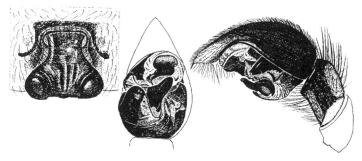

△ *Pardosa bifasciata* (C.L. Koch 1834)　　　　　　　　　　　　　　Plate 16
Description ♀, 5–6mm; ♂, 4–5mm. Male similar to the female illustrated, but rather darker. Epigyne distinctive, sometimes discernible with a lens. Male palpal organs distinctive and unlike those of the other species.
Habitat On dry, sandy or stony ground.
Maturity Spring to late summer; males only to mid-summer.
Distribution Absent from Britain. Widespread in northern Europe but generally uncommon.

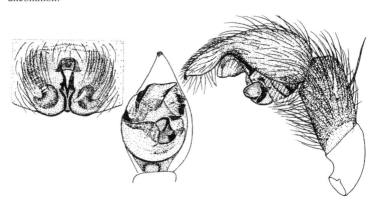

Pardosa pullata (Clerck 1757)　　　　　　　　　　　　　　　　　Plate 16
Description ♀, 4–6mm; ♂, 4–5mm. The male generally has a clear midline mark on the carapace and often a clear cardiac mark – like the illustration of *P. proxima* but without the lateral bands on the carapace. Epigyne distinguishable with a lens. Male palp distinguished from *P. prativaga* and *P. sphagnicola* by the lack of a hooked tip on the end of the tarsus, and from *P. fulvipes* by the general form of the palpal organs and the lack of a distinct bulge on the palpal patella.
Habitat Found in a very wide variety of situations.
Maturity Spring to autumn; males only to mid-summer.
Distribution Ubiquitous. One of the commonest species of the genus in Britain. Common and widespread in northern Europe.

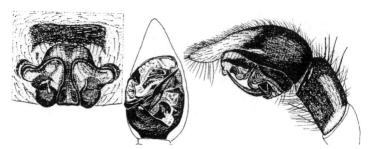

Pardosa prativaga (L. Koch 1870)
Description ♀, 4–6mm; ♂, 4–5mm. Very similar to *P. pullata* but the legs are more clearly annulated and the abdomen has clearer markings, due to patches of light hairs. Epigyne similar to those of *P. fulvipes* and *P. sphagnicola* but easily distinguished by the arches and the sclerotized area anterior to these. The male palpal tarsus has a hooked tip, and is distinguished from *P. sphagnicola* by the general form of the palpal organs and by the longer median apophysis which reaches beyond the edge of the cymbium.
Habitat and Maturity Similar to *P. pullata* and often found with this species.
Distribution Less common than *P. pullata* but widely distributed throughout Britain and northern Europe.

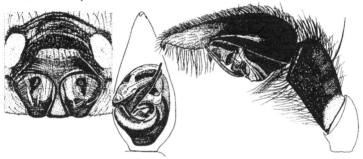

△ *Pardosa fulvipes* (Collett 1875)
Description ♀, 5–6mm; ♂, 4.5–5mm. Very similar to *P. pullata* but with paler legs which are often contrastingly pale yellow. Epigyne distinguished from *P. pullata* by the form of the arches, and from *P. sphagnicola* by the width of the posterior part relative to the width of the central tongue. The male palp does not have a hooked tip to the tarsus, and also differs in the form of the palpal organs and in having a distinctly bulbous patella (illustrated in outline only).
Habitat Grassland. **Maturity** Early summer to autumn; males only to mid-summer.
Distribution Absent from Britain. Recorded from Scandinavia and Germany.

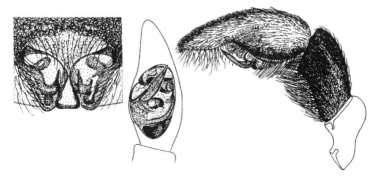

△ *Pardosa sphagnicola* (Dahl 1908)

Description ♀, 5–6mm; ♂, 4.5–5mm. Not unlike *P. pullata* but the abdomen usually has paired white spots (tufts of hairs). In view of the habitat, could be confused with *Pirata piraticus* (Plate 18) at first sight. Epigyne distinguished from *P. pullata* by the form of the anterior arches, and from *P. fulvipes* by the width of the posterior part relative to the central tongue. The male palp has the tarsal tip hooked and concave dorsally. The median apophysis does not reach beyond the edge of the cymbium.

Habitat On moss and amongst low vegetation in damp or marshy habitats.

Maturity Spring to late summer; males only to mid-summer.

Distribution Absent from Britain. Recorded from Scandinavia, Germany and the Netherlands.

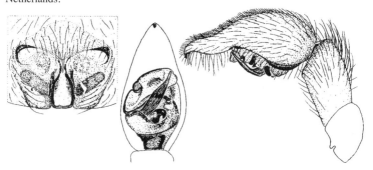

Pardosa amentata (Clerck 1757)   Plate 16

Description ♀, 5.5–8mm; ♂, 5–6.5mm. Male similar to the female illustrated but generally darker, with clearer markings, and the palps are usually conspicuously black. Epigyne sometimes discernible with a lens but could be confused with that of *P. hortensis* (which has a narrower anterior arch) and higher magnification is often required. The male palp is black and covered densely with dark hairs, although these are not quite as long as in *P. nigriceps*. The shape of the median apophysis is characteristic and the terminal apophysis is relatively thin, hooked, and pointing away from the median apophysis.

Habitat Like *P. pullata*, it is found in a wide variety of habitats and is equally common. **Maturity** Spring to autumn; males only up to mid-summer.

Distribution Common and widespread throughout Britain and northern Europe.

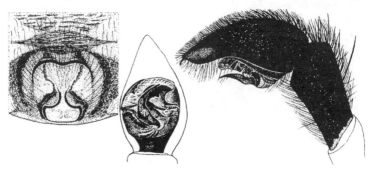

Pardosa nigriceps (Thorell 1856)   Plate 16
Description ♀, 5–7mm; ♂, 4–5mm. Female very similar to the male illustrated, but has a larger abdomen and the light yellow bands on the carapace are even more striking. Epigyne discernible with a lens as also is the male palp which is densely furnished with long black hairs. The median apophysis is distinctively shaped and the terminal apophysis relatively long and pointing towards the median apophysis.
Habitat Usually found hunting on low vegetation and bushes (e.g. heather and gorse), but may also be collected at ground level.
Maturity Spring to late summer; males up to early summer.
Distribution Common and widespread throughout Britain and northern Europe.

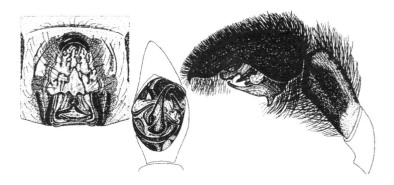

Pardosa lugubris (Walckenaer 1802)
Description ♀, 5–6mm; ♂, 4–5mm. The female and egg sac are illustrated on p. 209; although similar to *P. pullata*, the median band on the carapace is usually clearly marked with light hairs and this is even more distinct in the male. The epigyne can usually be discerned with a lens. The male palp may also be identifiable with a lens since the tarsus is particularly long and projects considerably beyond the palpal organs. The distinctive median apophysis and small tooth-like terminal apophysis require higher magnification.
Habitat In or near woodland; usually on the edges or in clearings.
Maturity Spring to late summer; males to early or mid-summer.
Distribution Common and widespread throughout Britain and northern Europe.

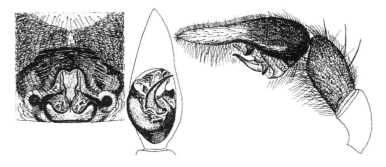

Pardosa hortensis (Thorell 1872)   Plate 16
Description ♀, 4.5–6mm; ♂, 3.5–4.5mm. Female sometimes more greyish-brown
than illustrated; male darker but with paler legs and fewer annulations. The epigyne
is not easily discerned with a lens and can look similar to that of *P. amentata*; at
higher magnification, it is easily distinguished by the relatively narrow arch anteriorly. The tibia and tarsus of the male palp are black, but with relatively shorter hairs
than in *P. amentata* and *P. nigriceps*. The latter species has an entirely different
appearance, but both have prominent, elongate median apophyses, the absence of
which can be seen with a lens in *P. hortensis*. *P. hortensis* is also usually smaller than
P. amentata.
Habitat Occurs in a variety of situations, in woodland clearings, open ground and
on beaches. **Maturity** Spring to late summer; males only to early summer.
Distribution More frequent in the southern half of England; widely, but locally distributed with few records from Scotland. Apparently absent from Scandinavia, but
widespread throughout the rest of northern Europe.

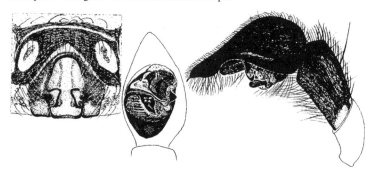

Pardosa proxima (C.L. Koch 1847)   Plate 16
Description ♀, 5.5–6.5mm; ♂, 4.5–5mm. Female similar to the male illustrated, and
not unlike the illustration of *P. monticola*, although the lateral bands on the carapace
are usually broken into three parts. The epigyne can sometimes be discerned with a
lens, but higher magnification is often necessary. It is similar to the epigyne of *P.
paludicola*, but that species is a much larger spider and its epigyne is almost twice
the size (the illustrations are not to scale). The male palp, like that of *P.*

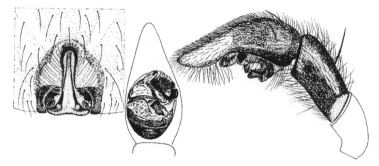

hortensis, lacks a prominent, elongate median apophysis. It is not usually as dark as in *P. hortensis*, and the two species differ in size and general appearance.
Habitat Usually on grassland, often in damp situations.
Maturity Spring, females to summer.
Distribution Recorded from Wales and the southern half of England. Uncommon and locally distributed. Apparently absent from Scandinavia. Probably widespread in the rest of northern Europe, but most records from the west of the region.

Pardosa trailli (O.P.-Cambridge 1873)
Description ♀, 7–8.5mm; ♂, 6.5–7mm. This species is similar to *P. amentata* but is much darker, often lacks clear markings, and is usually larger. The epigyne and male palp are very distinctive and identifiable with a lens.
Habitat On mountains, usually on scree slopes. **Maturity** Late spring to autumn.
Distribution On mountains in Wales, northern England, Scotland, and on St Kilda. This is mainly a Scandinavian species and is apparently absent from the rest of northern Europe.

Pardosa paludicola (Clerck 1757)
Description ♀, 8–9mm; ♂, 7mm. Similar to *P. amentata* in general appearance, but larger and much darker, with few markings. The epigyne is similar in shape to that of *P. proxima* but about twice the size and discernible with a lens. The male palp is distinguishable from that of *P. amentata* by having a more prominent downward-pointing tooth at the base of the median apophysis. The latter does not project forwards and downwards to a fine point as in *P. amentata*, but is shorter, with an upward-curving tip.

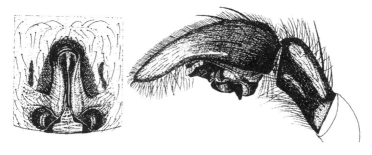

Habitat It has been recorded from grassy woodland clearings, in grassland near a pond, and in a fen. **Maturity** Spring to autumn; possibly all year.
Distribution Rare in Britain and recorded from a very few sites in the southern half of England. Probably widespread in northern Europe, but most records are from the north of the region.

Genus *Hygrolycosa*

There is only one European species of *Hygrolycosa* and it has an unmistakable appearance. The female carries her egg sac like species of *Pardosa*; the sac itself is beige with a rather wide, white seam.

Hygrolycosa rubrofasciata (Ohlert 1865)   Plate 17
Description ♀, 5.5–6mm; ♂, 5–5.5mm. Females may have a paler carapace and legs than illustrated and most males are a little darker, but otherwise similar. The clear brown spots are distinctive only on the femora of females. In males the legs are a darker brown from the coxae to the midpoint of the tibiae, with obscure markings. The epigyne is small and difficult to see because of a covering of light hairs. The male palp is easily recognizable and has a rather bulbous tibia.
Habitat In fens and in damp areas of woodland. **Maturity** Summer.
Distribution Very uncommon and locally distributed. Recorded from a number of sites in central, southern and eastern England where it is sometimes abundant. Commoner and widespread in the rest of northern Europe.

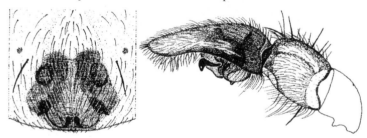

Genus *Xerolycosa*

Two species of *Xerolycosa* occur in Europe and are described here. They have an almost parallel-sided light band on the carapace which is furnished with light hairs. This gives them a slight resemblance to *Pardosa lugubris*, but the head is not so elevated or straight-sided. They are smaller than species of *Alopecosa*, and have thinner legs; the lateral bands on the carapace are confined to the rear half and are partly composed of white hairs. The leg tarsi each have a short row of four trichobothria (long and short, arranged alternately). The egg sac is generally white.

Xerolycosa nemoralis (Westring 1861)
Description ♀, 4.5–7.5mm; ♂, 4.5–6mm. Similar to *X. miniata* in general appearance, but the median band on the carapace is usually slightly narrower at the rear end and gradually broadens towards the head region. The light lateral bands in the rear half of the carapace are composed mainly of white hairs, which may gradually get rubbed off. Both sexes are distinctly pinkish-red in colour and males usually have a

broad midline band of pinkish-grey hairs on the front half of the abdomen. The openings of the epigyne are relatively larger than in *X. miniata* and of a different shape. The structures projecting from the male palpal organs differ from those of *X. miniata*.

Habitat Heathland, chalk grassland and woodland clearings.

Maturity Summer to autumn; males to late summer.

Distribution Very locally distributed in the south and south-east of England, but may then be abundant. Widespread in northern Europe.

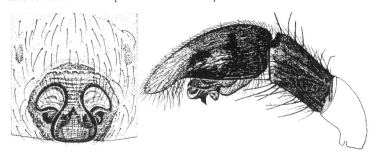

Xerolycosa miniata (C.L. Koch 1834) Plate 17

Description ♀, 5.5–6.5mm; ♂, 4.5–5.5mm. Male similar to the female; in both sexes, the lateral bands on the carapace are due to pigmentation in the cuticle as well as to hairs, and the light median band may be more obvious on the head than illustrated. The colour varies from a slightly pinkish brown to a more sandy grey. Generally, both sexes have a more speckled, sandy appearance than *X. nemoralis* and this renders them inconspicuous on sand. The epigyne has relatively smaller openings than in *X. nemoralis* and they also differ in shape. The structures projecting from the male palpal organs differ from those of *X. nemoralis*.

Habitat In dry, sandy habitats.

Maturity Spring to late summer; males to midsummer.

Distribution Locally distributed on sand dunes around the coast of Britain, including parts of Scotland. Widespread in northern Europe.

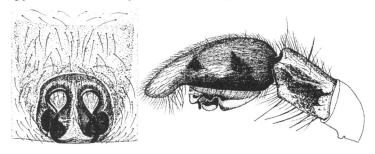

Genus *Alopecosa*

Seventeen species of *Alopecosa* are known to occur in Europe and four of the most widespread species are described here. They have a clear light median band on the carapace, accentuated by white hairs, and have fairly stout legs which are sometimes darkened or swollen in males. The cardiac mark on the abdomen is clearly defined. Females remain with their egg sac in a burrow and periodically expose the sac to sunlight near the opening. They are identifiable in the field.

Alopecosa pulverulenta (Clerck 1757)   Plate 17
Description ♀, 6.5–10mm; ♂, 5–8mm. Both sexes are illustrated. The male has slight darkening of tibia I, but the latter is not swollen or furnished with long hairs. The epigyne is similar to that of *A. cuneata* but the narrowest part of the central tongue is over half the maximum width of the opening and sometimes almost fills it. The female of *A. cuneata* has clearer abdominal markings. The male palpal organs are similar to those of *A. cuneata,* but the lack of swelling or long dark hairs on the tibia of leg I readily separates the species from both *A. cuneata* and *A. barbipes*.
Habitat Open areas of heathland, grassland and cultivated land.
Maturity Spring to autumn; males to mid-summer.
Distribution Common and widespread throughout Britain and northern Europe.

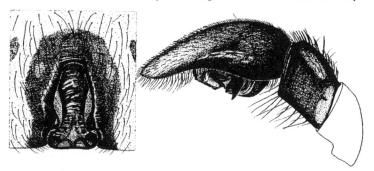

Alopecosa cuneata (Clerck 1757)   Plate 17
Description ♀, 6–8mm; ♂, 6–7.5mm. The female has similar abdominal markings to the male illustrated, the cardiac mark being outlined more clearly than in *A.*

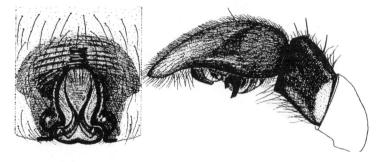

pulverulenta and the conspicuous light band continuing to the spinners. Note the short, swollen tibia I in the male, which allows identification in the field. The epigyne is similar to that of *A. pulverulenta* but smaller, and the narrowest point of the central tongue is only about one-third of the maximum width of the opening.
Habitat Mainly on chalk grassland and dunes.
Maturity Spring to late summer; males to mid-summer.
Distribution Rather locally distributed and uncommon; most records are from southern England, but it does occur in the north. Widespread throughout northern Europe.

Alopecosa barbipes (Sundevall 1833) Plate 17
Description ♀, 8–12mm; ♂, 7.5–9mm. Female similar to the male illustrated, but having a larger abdomen and no modification of tibia I. Note the points extending laterally from the cardiac mark. The epigyne is usually discernible with a lens, and the male is identifiable in the field by the swollen tibia I which is longer and less bulbous than in *A. cuneata*. Both tibia and metatarsus I are darkened and furnished with long hairs. (Note: The species has been confused with *A. accentuata* (Latreille 1817) which occurs in southern central Europe. The males of this species lack the dense black hairs on tibia and metatarsus I.)
Habitat Open heathland and grassland.
Maturity Spring to autumn.
Distribution Rather locally distributed, but widespread throughout Britain. Widespread in northern Europe.

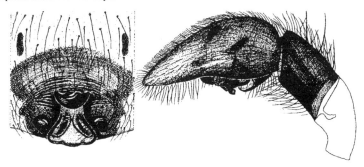

Alopecosa fabrilis (Clerck 1757) Plate 17
Description ♀, 13–16mm; ♂, 10–12mm. Female similar to the male illustrated but with a larger abdomen. Males of this species do not have leg I modified. The large size and general appearance of this spider enable easy identification in the field. The epigyne is visible with a lens as also are the male palpal organs.
Habitat Dry sandy heathland where the female digs a burrow in soil or under stones.
Maturity Autumn to late spring.
Distribution Rare in Britain and recorded from two localities in southern England. Widespread throughout northern Europe and a little more common.

Alopecosa fabrilis (previous page)

Genus *Trochosa*

Four species of *Trochosa* occur in Europe, all of which are described here. Like *Alopecosa*, they are robust spiders but lack the very clear median band of light hairs on the carapace. The median band is wider towards the front of the carapace and contains a pair of dark bars. They are nocturnal hunters and during the day are found in undergrowth and amongst moss and detritus. Females make shallow burrows where they seem to spend most of the day with their white or beige egg sacs. They may be seen carrying the egg sac around at night and occasionally I have seen this in the daytime on rather dull days. Identification can be narrowed down to two groups of two species by the cardiac mark, which may be of the same colour as the rest of the abdomen (*T. terricola, T. spinipalpis*) or distinctly paler (*T. ruricola, T. robusta*). The epigynes are rather small relative to the size of the spider and both these and the male palps require a microscope for reliable identification. Most subadult females of *Trochosa* have a small, sclerotized structure in the epigyne region which can cause confusion for the novice; it is quite unlike the adult epigyne.

Trochosa ruricola (DeGeer 1778) Plate 17
Description ♀, 9–14mm; ♂, 7–9mm. The female has a larger abdomen than the male illustrated, but the pale cardiac mark is as clear. The male has the tibia, metatarsus and tarsus of leg I darkened. This species has similar markings to *T. robusta* (below) but is usually smaller. The epigyne has relatively thin anterior arches which curve around more tightly at the sides than in *T. robusta*. The dark marks anterior to the arches are also different in the two species. The male palp, like that of *T. robusta*, has a claw at

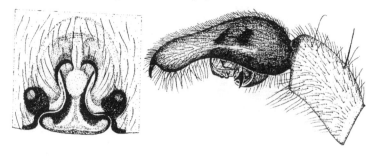

its tip; in *T. ruricola* this claw is of about the same size as the median apophysis in the palpal organs. Also, the tip of the palp is more bulbous than in *T. ruricola*.
Habitat Under stones and detritus and amongst moss in a variety of (usually) damp habitats. **Maturity** All year.
Distribution Widespread and common throughout Britain and northern Europe.

Trochosa robusta (Simon 1876)
Description ♀, 11–20mm; ♂, 9–18mm. Both sexes very similar in markings to *T. ruricola*; usually larger but there is overlap in size. The epigyne has relatively thick anterior arches which curve in less tightly at the sides than in *T. ruricola*. The dark marks anterior to the arches are also different. The claw at the tip of the male palp is smaller than the median apophysis projecting from the palpal organs, and the palpal tip is less bulbous than in *T. ruricola*.
Habitat Mostly on dry chalk grassland. **Maturity** All year.
Distribution Rare in Britain, but widely distributed in England. Apparently absent from Scandinavia, but widespread throughout the rest of northern Europe.

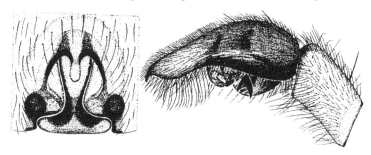

Trochosa terricola Thorell 1856   Plate 17
Description ♀, 7–14mm; ♂, 7–9mm. This species (and *T. spinipalpis*, below) has a reddish abdomen in which the cardiac mark is of the same colour as the rest of the abdomen. Males have the tibia and metatarsus of leg I darkened, but not the tarsus. The epigyne has thicker anterior arches than that of *T. spinipalpis*, different markings above the arches and differently shaped spermathecae on each side. The wide, posterior part of the central tongue also differs from that species in the shape of the tip on each side. The tip of the male palp is more bulbous than in *T. spinipalpis* and

lacks the group of stout spines on the under surface of the tibia.

Habitat and Maturity Similar to *T. ruricola*.

Distribution Widespread throughout Britain and northern Europe and generally even commoner than *T. ruricola*.

Trochosa spinipalpis (F.O.P.-Cambridge 1895)

Description ♀, 9–11mm; ♂, 8–10mm. Both sexes very similar in general appearance to *T. terricola*. The epigyne has rather thin anterior arches, different markings anterior to these, and a different shape to the spermathecae on each side. The sides of the posterior part of the central tongue are shaped like the tip of a Dutch clog. The tip of the male palp is not bulbous and the tibia has a group of stout spines on the under surface.

Habitat and Maturity Similar to *T. ruricola* and *T. terricola*.

Distribution Widespread in Britain and northern Europe. Much less common than *T. terricola* but part of the rarity may be due to misidentification and under-recording.

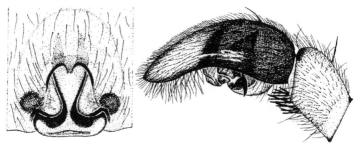

Genus *Arctosa*

Nine species of *Arctosa* are found in Europe, six of which are described here. Two of the species have previously slipped in and out of the genera *Trochosa* and *Tricca*. The carapace usually lacks a definite median band, but there may be a light area behind the eyes, or some irregular light markings and, rarely, a substantial covering of light hairs. The legs are usually clearly spotted or annulated with black. Males resemble females in general appearance and lack modification of the first pair of legs. Most species make burrows in sand, or under stones and amongst detritus and moss, but are frequently seen hunting in the open during the daytime. The epigynes and male palps are easily identified with a microscope, but are not easily seen with a lens, partly because they are often obscured by hairs. However, the species can be identified in the field by size and general appearance.

Arctosa perita (Latreille 1799)   Plate 18

Description ♀ ♂, 6.5–9mm. The colour of this species varies considerably; some are paler and more yellowish, others darker. Specimens on burnt heathland and colliery spoil-heaps may be almost completely black. The male is similar to the female illustrated, but has a slimmer abdomen. However, most specimens will be easily recognizable by their size and general appearance. Identity can be confirmed by examination of the epigyne and male palp.

Habitat Usually on light, sandy soil, both on coastal dunes and inland on dry heath-land. The colour matches the habitat and the spider is very difficult to spot when standing still with its legs outstretched. **Maturity** Spring to autumn.
Distribution By far the commonest species; widespread throughout Britain and northern Europe.

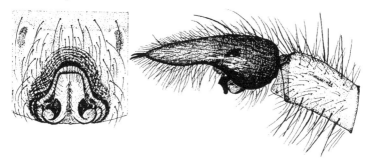

Arctosa leopardus (Sundevall 1833)   Plate 18
Description ♀, 8.5–9.5mm; ♂, 6.5–7mm. The appearance is characteristic; the male is very similar, but the abdomen may be almost black with a conspicuous yellow cardiac mark. The epigyne and male palp are distinctive.
Habitat Amongst moss and detritus in marshy areas. It may be found within a silk tube in moss or detritus, or running in the open. **Maturity** Spring to late summer.
Distribution Widespread throughout Britain, but very locally distributed and generally uncommon. Widespread in northern Europe.

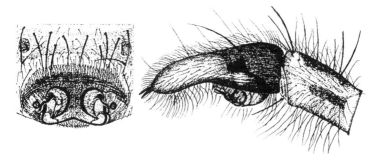

Arctosa cinerea (Fabricius 1777)   Plate 18
Description ♀, 12–17mm; ♂, 12–14mm. The male is similar to the female illustrated and both vary somewhat in colour. This varies from pale grey to fairly dark brown, and the covering of light hairs may be more or less obvious than illustrated. Sometimes the cardiac mark is lighter and surrounded by more obvious black markings. The epigyne and male palp are distinctive, but the size of this spider, its general appearance, and its habitat, make identification an easy matter.

Habitat On riverbeds and lakesides; in a silk-lined burrow under stones, where it may be submerged for long periods of time. **Maturity** Possibly all year.
Distribution Recorded from Wales, Ireland, northern England and Scotland, but absent from the south. Widespread throughout northern Europe with the possible exception of the Netherlands.

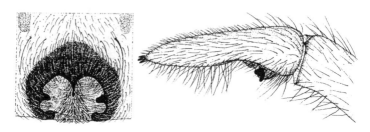

Arctosa fulvolineata (Lucas 1846) (= *Trochosa f.* (Lucas))
Description ♀, 10–12mm; ♂, 7.5–8.5mm. This species has a similar appearance to that of *A. leopardus*, but is larger. The abdomen has a much clearer, yellow cardiac mark and is brown with dark patches which may form a pair of longitudinal dark bands. The epigyne and male palp are characteristic.
Habitat On saltmarshes; under stones and lumps of mud, amongst matted detritus and within cracks in dried mud. **Maturity** Possibly all year.
Distribution This rare species is recorded from a few saltmarshes around the Solent and on the coast of East Anglia where it is sometimes numerous. Recorded from France, Switzerland and in southern Europe.

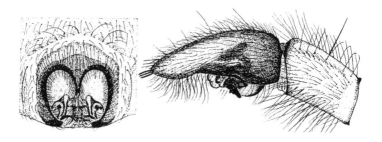

Arctosa alpigena (Doleschall 1852) (= *Tricca a.* (Doleschall))   Plate 18
Description ♀, 9–10mm; ♂, 7–8mm. Female similar to the male illustrated, but has a larger abdomen. The dark markings on the carapace are distinctive, as is the white cardiac mark on the abdomen. The epigyne and male palp are also distinctive but the general appearance and habitat should enable identification in the field.
Habitat On mountains above 1000m, in silk tubes within matted vegetation; only occasionally seen running in the open. **Maturity** Summer to autumn.
Distribution Rare in Britain and confined to the Cairngorms and adjacent areas. Fairly widespread in northern Europe, in the appropriate habitat.

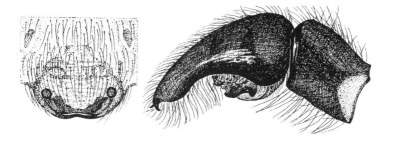

△ *Arctosa lutetiana* (Simon 1876) (= *Tricca l.* (Simon)) Plate 18
Description ♀ ♂, 5.5–8mm. Female similar to the male illustrated, but having a larger abdomen. The light hairs on the carapace are characteristic, as is the pale cardiac mark on the abdomen and the series of light chevrons. The epigyne and male palp are also distinctive.
Habitat Amongst detritus and low vegetation in sandy habitats.
Maturity Summer to autumn.
Distribution Absent from Britain and Scandinavia. Widespread in Belgium, France, Germany and Switzerland.

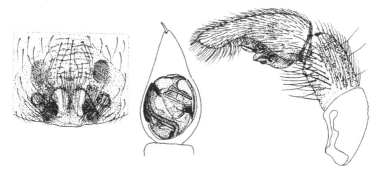

Genus *Pirata*

Eight species of *Pirata* are known to occur in Europe and are described here. The carapace often has an elongate U-shaped mark running from behind the eyes to a point near the fovea. The margins of the carapace may be fringed with white hairs. Most species have the abdomen marked with small, paired white patches. These are tufts of hairs and often appear slightly bluish. All but one of the species inhabit wet, marshy areas and, as well as hunting on the surface of mosses, are adept at running across water and catching insects on or just below the surface. They construct silk tubes leading from the surface of moss down towards the water level. The egg sacs are white, spherical, and have a narrow seam. Females carrying egg sacs are very conspicuous when running about on the surface of moss. They will also push the egg sac up to the tube entrance and hold it there in sunlight, whilst staying cooler themselves. Males are very similar to females in general appearance; leg I is not modified and only in *P. latitans* is there any appreciable darkening of segments. The genus is readily identifiable with a lens, but most of the epigynes, and all of the male palps, will require higher magnification. Size and general appearance is of use in narrowing down the species, but cannot be relied on entirely for identification.

Pirata piscatorius (Clerck 1757)
Description ♀, 5–10mm; ♂, 4.5–8.5mm. In life, this spider appears almost completely black with a white margin to the carapace and paired white spots on the abdomen. The carapace is dark red-brown in preserved specimens with few clear markings and just the margins fringed with white hairs. The dark brown abdomen usually has a paler cardiac mark, on closer inspection, as well as the white spots. The epigyne can sometimes be discerned with a lens, but the structures may be too dark. With higher magnification, the epigyne and male palpal organs are readily identifiable. **Habitat** Marshy areas. **Maturity** Spring and summer.
Distribution Rather uncommon; very locally distributed but probably widespread throughout Britain and northern Europe.

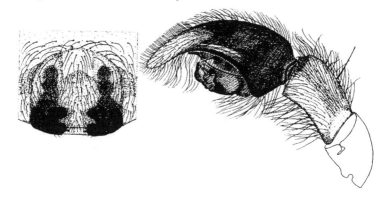

Pirata piraticus (Clerck 1757)　　　　　　　　　　　　　　　　　Plate 18
Description ♀, 4.5–9mm; 4–6.5mm. The yellow cardiac mark is clear in this species and is outlined by white hairs. White hairs are also present on the sides of the

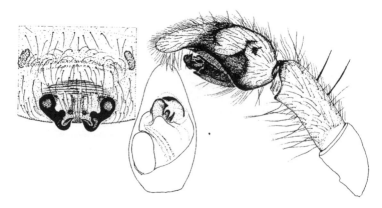

abdomen, and as paired spots, and around the carapace margins. The species is similar in general appearance to *P. tenuitarsis*. The epigyne of *P. piraticus* has the dark structures leading from the spermathecae to the posterior margin angled at about 45°. The male palp is distinguished from that of *P. tenuitarsis* by the palpal organs viewed from the side, or from below.
Habitat Damp habitats and marshes. **Maturity** Spring and summer.
Distribution Common and widespread throughout Britain and northern Europe.

Pirata tenuitarsis Simon 1876
Description ♀, 4.5–8mm; ♂, 4–6mm. This species is very similar to *P. piraticus* and is only reliably identified by the epigyne and male palp. The epigyne is usually less sclerotized and the spermathecae are set at a much shallower angle to the posterior margin. The male palpal organs are distinguishable viewed from the side or below.
Habitat Sphagnum bogs. **Maturity** Spring and summer.
Distribution Uncertain in Britain since the species has only been recognized here since 1980. Less common than *P. piraticus*. Widespread in northern Europe.

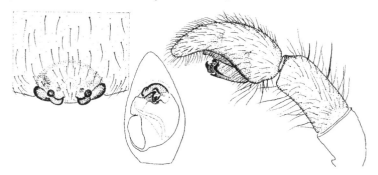

Pirata hygrophilus Thorell 1872   Plate 18
Description ♀, 5–6.5mm; ♂, 4.5–5.5mm. This species is usually darker than *P. piraticus* and occasionally appears almost black in life, with paired white spots on the abdomen. The epigyne is relatively large and distinctive and can often be discerned with a lens. The male palp is distinctive.
Habitat Damp habitats and marshes. **Maturity** Spring and summer.
Distribution Common and widespread throughout Britain and northern Europe.

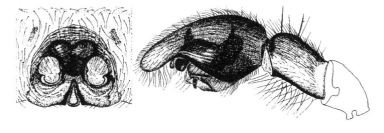

△ *Pirata insularis* Emerton 1885 (= *P. piccolo* Dahl)
Description ♀ ♂, 2.8–3.7mm. This species resembles *P. hygrophilus* but is much smaller. The epigyne and male palp are distinctive.
Habitat Damp habitats and bogs. **Maturity** Spring and summer.
Distribution Absent from Britain. Recorded from Scandinavia and Germany.

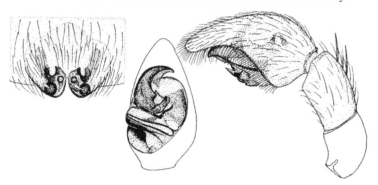

Pirata uliginosus (Thorell 1856)
Description ♀, 5–6mm; ♂, 4–5mm. Very similar in general appearance to *P. hygrophilus*; the epigyne and male palp are much smaller but are easily identifiable at higher magnification.
Habitat Generally occurs in drier habitats than do the other species.
Maturity Spring and summer.
Distribution Widespread, but much less common than *P. piraticus* and *P. hygrophilus*. Widespread in northern Europe.

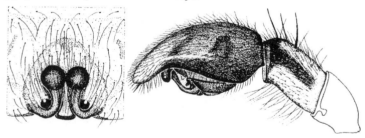

Pirata latitans (Blackwall 1841)   Plate 18
Description ♀, 4–5mm; ♂, 2.5–4.5mm. This spider has an obscurely marked brown carapace and an almost uniform velvety brown abdomen, with paired white spots and white hairs on the sides. The epigyne and male palp are small, but distinctive at higher magnification.
Habitat Damp habitats and bogs. **Maturity** Spring and summer.
Distribution Generally uncommon and locally distributed. Most records are from the southern half of Britain. Fairly widespread in northern Europe but not recorded from Scandinavia.

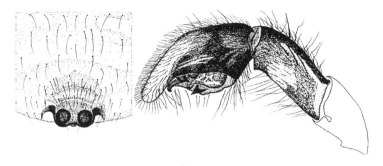

△ *Pirata knorri* (Scopoli 1763)
Description ♀, 6–8.5mm; ♂, 5–6.5mm. Similar in general appearance to *P. hygrophilus*; often larger, but reliably distinguished only by the appearance of the epigyne and male palp.
Habitat Damp areas in woodland and often alongside streams.
Maturity Spring and summer.
Distribution Absent from Britain and Scandinavia. Widespread throughout the rest of northern Europe.

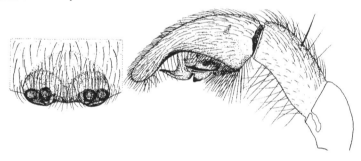

Genus *Aulonia*

There is one species of *Aulonia* in Europe and its appearance is so characteristic that even immature specimens are identifiable. It makes a small silk retreat at ground level with a flimsy web around the opening. The spider may also be found running actively in sunshine.

Aulonia albimana (Walckenaer 1805)   Plate 18
Description ♀, 3.5–4.5mm; ♂, 3–3.5mm. Both sexes are of similar general appearance; the white palpal patellae contrast markedly with the black tibiae and tarsi and with the black femora of the first pair of legs. The epigyne and male palp are distinctive.
Habitat In grass and moss and amongst stones, in situations which are sheltered and sunny. **Maturity** Spring and summer.
Distribution Currently known to exist in just one site on the Isle of Wight. Widespread in northern Europe, but commoner in the south of the region.

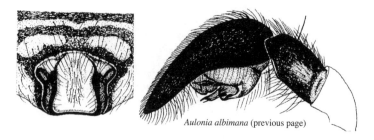

Aulonia albimana (previous page)

FAMILY PISAURIDAE

This family is represented in northern Europe by three species in two genera. They are fairly large spiders with long but robust legs; the arrangement of the eyes is illustrated in the Family Key (p. 47). They have good vision and are very active hunters, either on vegetation or on the surface of water. When at rest or sensing prey, they often extend the first and second legs and hold them together, straight out at an angle. *Pisaura* does this on vegetation, sitting quite still with the first pairs of legs held up, and seems almost like a dog sniffing the air. *Dolomedes* often holds the front legs together, touching the ground, when carrying the egg sac, but spreads them out on the surface of water when sensing prey. The Pisauridae make quite large egg sacs which are carried underneath the body. I have never seen any threads running between the sac and the spinners, and the large bundle of eggs is held firmly in place solely by the grip of the chelicerae and backward pressure from the palps. Before the spiderlings emerge, the egg sac is attached to low vegetation and a tent of silk is spun over and around it. The egg sac is partially opened by the female who then stands guarding the nursery tent near its base. *Pisaura* often makes more substantial tents than *Dolomedes* (although some are quite small) and, after mid-summer, these are often seen in great abundance on low vegetation (see Webs, p. 66). The two genera are easily distinguished by their general appearance: *Pisaura* has a light midline stripe on the carapace and a slim, tapering abdomen; *Dolomedes* has light lateral stripes on the carapace and abdomen, and the latter is more or less oval in shape.

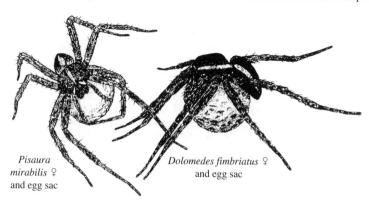

*Pisaura
mirabilis* ♀
and egg sac

Dolomedes fimbriatus ♀
and egg sac

Genus *Pisaura*

The single species, *Pisaura mirabilis,* is sometimes called the 'nursery web spider' in Britain. This common name is used in other countries but is applied, more correctly, to both *Pisaura* and *Dolomedes*. Different common names, for both the family and the species, are used in other parts of Europe (e.g. 'rovedderkopper' in Denmark, 'Raubspinne' in Germany). The spider hunts on low vegetation and on the ground. Courtship is interesting in this species, the male presenting the female with wrapped prey as a diversion whilst he mates with her.

Pisaura mirabilis (Clerck 1757)   Plate 19
Description ♀, 12–15mm; ♂, 10–13mm. The colour varies from grey to yellowish-orange to quite a dark brown and the abdominal markings may be very striking or absent. Males are similar to females but have a smaller abdomen which is generally clearly marked. Immatures are easily recognized and the epigyne and male palp are distinctive and discernible with a lens.
Habitat Grassland, heathland, and in woodland clearings. The nursery web is illustrated on p. 66. **Maturity** Summer.
Distribution Common and widespread in Britain and northern Europe.

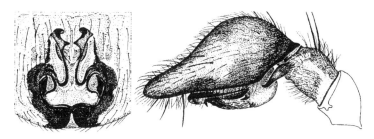

Genus *Dolomedes*

The two European species of *Dolomedes* are commonly called 'raft spiders' in Britain; the name 'fishing spiders' is used in other countries and this is more appropriate since the spiders do not make rafts. The spiders are found in damp habitats, usually swamps with permanent pools of water. Prey is hunted on the surface of moss and other low vegetation, and also on the surface of water. The spider sits on vegetation at the edge of pools, with the front legs resting on the surface of the water. It is thus able to detect insects, tadpoles and sometimes small fish, which are pulled out of the water and devoured. The spider will also run out some distance across the surface of the water to capture prey. If threatened, the spiders will crawl down aquatic vegetation and remain submerged there, sometimes for almost an hour. Courtship involves the male waving the front legs in a prolonged approach to mating, but there is no wrapping of prey as a diversionary tactic. When the young emerge from their nursery tent and disperse, they often exploit higher and drier habitats than the adults, and may be found in bushes and trees.

Dolomedes fimbriatus (Clerck 1757)   Plate 19
Description ♀, 13–20mm; ♂, 9–16mm. The male is similar to the female illustrated, but has a smaller abdomen. The epigyne is usually discernible with a lens and the

central area has a covering of hairs. The male palp is identifiable with a lens by the shape of the tibial apophysis which is pointed and of a different shape from that of *D. plantarius*.

Habitat Swampy areas, usually with pools of water. **Maturity** Spring and summer. **Distribution** Widespread throughout Britain, but very locally distributed and commoner in the south of England. Widespread in northern Europe.

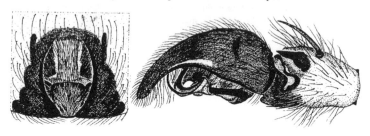

Dolomedes plantarius (Clerck 1757)

Description ♀, 13–20mm; ♂, 10–16mm. Very similar to *D. fimbriatus* but sometimes a little paler and with less well-defined stripes. The epigyne is discernible with a lens and lacks the light hairs in the central area, which can obscure the structures in *D. fimbriatus*. The male palp is identifiable with a lens by the form of the tibial apophysis, which is bifid, with a larger, flat tip and a small, pointed tooth.

Habitat and Maturity Similar to *D. fimbriatus*.

Distribution Protected by law in Britain. Only known from fens in Norfolk and Suffolk and from one site in East Sussex. The species is widespread in northern Europe, but less common than *D. fimbriatus*.

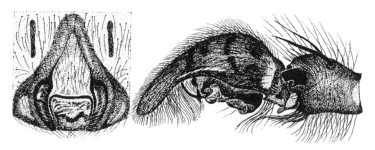

FAMILY ARGYRONETIDAE

Genus *Argyroneta*

The single species in this genus is the well-known 'water spider' and is the only spider known to live an almost entirely submerged, aquatic existence. The tracheal spiracles are situated just behind the epigastric fold and legs III and IV are furnished with long, fine hairs in marked contrast to legs I and II (see Family Key, p. 48). The disparity in hairiness between front and rear legs is easily visible with a lens and quite

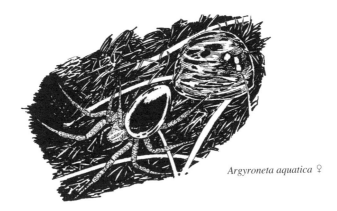

Argyroneta aquatica ♀

small immatures can be thus identified. Occasionally, spiderlings are found wandering amongst waterside vegetation; their identity can be confirmed by placing them on water, whereupon they will dive straight down. *Argyroneta aquatica* is an underwater hunter, swimming and moving with ease amongst vegetation and preying on a range of aquatic invertebrates. The spider constructs a retreat amongst underwater vegetation which is filled with air, carried down from the surface, and comes to resemble a diving bell. Once filled, the oxygen levels within are maintained by diffusion with the surrounding water and by bubbles of oxygen from aquatic vegetation. Prey is taken to the retreat for consumption since the external digestion practised by spiders is not possible in water; occasionally, prey is taken above the surface. Out of the water, the spider has a mousy, dark grey abdomen; when submerged, the air trapped on the surface of the hairs give it the appearance of quicksilver. Whilst moulting takes place on vegetation near the water surface, most other activities are under water. Mating and egg-laying take place in the bell and females remain there over the winter.

Argyroneta aquatica (Clerck 1757)   Plate 19
Description ♀, 8–15mm, sometimes over 20mm; ♂, 9–12mm. The carapace has a row of very short, dark hairs in the midline. Males are very similar to females in general appearance. The epigyne and male palp are distinctive.
Habitat In vegetated fresh water where there is little current. **Maturity** All year.
Distribution Widespread throughout Britain and northern Europe. Very locally distributed, but then often abundant.

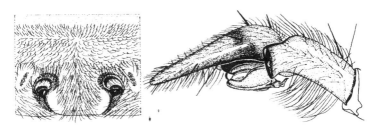

FAMILY AGELENIDAE

The taxonomy of this family is in a fluid state; several genera have been moved to and from different families in recent years. Many of the arguments are subjective, different interpretations are possible, and it may be some time before a consensus is reached. In order to facilitate reference to earlier literature, I have continued to treat the family in its traditional form. When referring to some more recent literature, it may be helpful to note the current, tentative position: *Coelotes* moved to Family Amaurobiidae; *Mastigusa* (= *Tetrilus*) and *Cicurina* moved to Family Dictynidae; *Cryphoeca* and *Tuberta* moved to Family Hahniidae. That is the position at the time of writing, but it may have changed by the time you read this!

Of the twenty-eight north European species here considered in the family Agelenidae, twenty-one species, in eight genera, are described below. The majority of species have the posterior spinners clearly longer than the anteriors and of two segments. The tarsus of each leg has a series of trichobothria which increase in length towards the end of the segment – this character is present in the few species which have rather short spinners (see Family Key, p. 49). These spiders are sometimes called 'cobweb spiders' in Britain, but this name is also commonly used for the Family Theridiidae (p. 260). The origins of the word 'cob' are obscure, but amongst other things it is applied to small, roundish pieces of coal. The webs of domestic *Tegenaria* species are more extensively developed in undisturbed cellars, including coal cellars, where they accumulate a good deal of dust. The name 'funnel weavers' is widely used in some countries (and in Germany 'Trichterspinnen', Denmark 'tragtspindere'). The name 'funnel-web spiders' has also been used in Britain, but this common name has long been used for a group of notoriously poisonous Australian mygalomorphs.

The Agelenidae spin a tubular retreat from which extends either a small collar of silk, or a small to large sheet, which may be slightly funnel-shaped (see Webs, p. 66). The spiders run on the upper surface of the sheet to catch prey which has landed on it. Sometimes there is a superstructure of threads, and insects hitting this fall down on to the sheet. Prey is then dragged back into the retreat for consumption. Courtship varies between genera. It may involve tapping on the female's web, seizing her fairly quickly and mating on the sheet; other species may mate away from the retreat/web and there may be considerable stroking, with the female entering a torpid state. The egg sac is made within the retreat, and males often remain with their mates, eventually dying of old age. Males resemble females in general appearance but have a slimmer abdomen and, in most cases, relatively longer legs.

The genera, and some species, are identifiable with a lens. Other species will require higher magnification, the critical features of the epigynes and male palps being too small to distinguish with a lens.

Key to the Genera

1. Terminal segment of posterior spinners clearly visible; almost
   as long as, or longer than, basal segment   2

   Terminal segment of posterior spinners much shorter than
   basal segment   6

2. Posterior row of eyes strongly recurved (viewed from above).
   Posterior spinners conspicuously long   *Textrix* p. 242

   Posterior row of eyes slightly recurved, straight, or procurved   3

3. Posterior row of eyes strongly procurved; anterior row of
   eyes slightly procurved — *Agelena* p. 241

   Posterior row of eyes very slightly procurved, straight or
   slightly recurved — 4

4. Head region of carapace rather narrowed. Legs fairly long
   relative to body size — 5

   Head region of carapace broad. Legs fairly short and stout
   relative to body size — *Coelotes* p. 248

5. Posterior row of eyes slightly recurved. Head region
   distinctly paler than the rest of the carapace — △ *Histopona* p. 248

   Posterior row of eyes straight or slightly procurved. Head
   region of same depth of colour as the rest of the carapace
   (i.e. background colour, not dark markings) — *Tegenaria* p. 243

6. Abdomen pale grey-brown; mousy with no pattern or
   markings — *Cicurina* p. 251

   Abdomen with a pattern, or at least some markings — 7

7. Carapace with clear, dark, radiating streaks. Abdominal
   pattern clear. Legs with dark annulations. Adult size
   2.5–3mm — *Cryphoeca* p. 252

   Carapace with no clear dark markings; abdominal pattern
   less well-defined. Legs without annulations. Adult size
   3–3.5mm — *Mastigusa* p. 250

Genus *Agelena*

There are two European species in this genus and both make quite large sheet webs, with a superstructure of threads and a tubular retreat. The webs are spun amongst grass and heather and occasionally a little higher on bushes such as gorse. Prey is generally taken back to the retreat entrance for consumption. Mating occurs on the web and the two sexes live together for a few weeks. The egg sac is suspended in a silk chamber and the female remains with the eggs until she dies.

Agelena labyrinthica (Clerck 1757) — Plate 19

Description ♀, 8–12mm; ♂, 8–9mm. Male similar to the female illustrated but with a slimmer abdomen and relatively longer legs. The epigyne is discernible with a lens

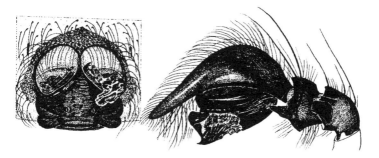

but may have variable amounts of exudate in and around the openings. The male palpal organs are also distinctive, as are the apophyses on the tibia and patella, and are usually discernible with a lens.

Habitat In large sheet web with retreat amongst low vegetation and bushes.
Maturity Summer.
Distribution Not recorded from Scotland or northern Ireland; widespread in England and Wales but much commoner in the south. Widespread in northern Europe.

△ *Agelena gracilens* C.L. Koch 1841
Description ♀, 7–10.5mm; ♂, 5–8.5mm. Similar to *A. labyrinthica* in general appearance, but easily distinguished by the epigyne and the male palpal organs and tibial and patellar apophyses.
Habitat Similar to *A. labyrinthica*. **Maturity** Summer to autumn.
Distribution Absent from Britain and the north of the region. Widespread in France and central Europe, but commoner in the south and in the Mediterranean.

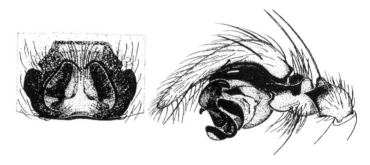

Genus *Textrix*

Three species of *Textrix* occur in Europe, but only one is common and widespread in the north. The spider usually makes a tubular retreat, with a small collar of silk or an extensive sheet around the entrance (see Webs, p. 66). It is frequently found running very rapidly on the ground or amongst stones on hot, sunny days and appears very much like a wolf spider (Lycosidae) with very long spinners. Mating involves the male taking hold of the female and then stroking her, whereupon she falls into a submissive, torpid state. I have seen females remain in this state for almost an hour after the male has finished mating. The egg sac is made in the retreat; females sometimes remain with the eggs, sometimes disappear. This spider is easily identifiable with a lens, both by general appearance and by the epigyne and male palp.

Textrix denticulata (Olivier 1789)   Plate 19
Description ♀ ♂, 6–7mm. The male is very similar in general appearance to the female illustrated. Epigyne and male palp also distinctive.
Habitat Amongst stones and stone walls, by the sea and on higher ground, on low vegetation and bushes, and running on warm dry ground. It occurs equally in open countryside and within houses; in parts of northern England and Scotland it is a very common house spider. **Maturity** Males in summer, females all year.
Distribution Widespread and common throughout Britain and northern Europe.

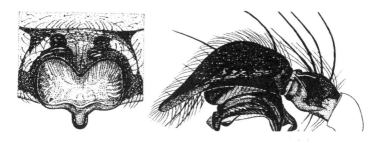

Genus *Tegenaria*

Eleven species of *Tegenaria* are known to occur in northern Europe and ten of these are described here. Most of the species make sheet webs which extend from a tubular retreat; these sheets may gradually attain a considerable size when in relatively undisturbed corners of cellars, garages and sheds (see Webs, p. 67). Webs are generally smaller when outside, and exposed to the elements and disturbance, and may be very much reduced in species living at ground level amongst stones. Females of those species living in houses are known to live for several years as adults. Males are very similar to females in general appearance but have a slimmer abdomen and much longer legs. Those large species which share our homes with us spend most of their time unobtrusively in their webs. However, in late summer and autumn, the long-legged males wander about in search of females, sometimes dashing across the carpet, sometimes becoming trapped in the bath. Males live with their mates for some weeks, but eventually die of old age and are eaten by the female. Females remain with the egg sac until the spiderlings emerge and disperse. Some epigynes and palps are too small to be seen properly with a lens. Others are quite large, but the differences between related species are small, and higher magnification will be required for accurate identification.

Tegenaria duellica Simon 1875 (= *T. gigantea* Chamberlin & Ivie)　　　Plate 19
Description ♀, 11–16mm; ♂, 10–14mm. The illustrations show the differences between the sexes, particularly the long legs of the male. (The five species following below are very similar to this and are only distinguishable by their epigynes and male palps.) The epigyne and male palp are similar to those of *T. saeva* and some specimens may appear intermediate, perhaps because of hybridization. The pointed processes on the epigyne come more suddenly to a point, and the anterior arch is

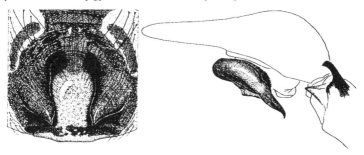

more sclerotized and better defined at the sides than in *T. saeva*. The structure projecting from beneath the palpal organs has a longer, broader tapering tip and is not as angular on its upper surface as that of *T. saeva*. The tibial apophysis is not reliable for separating the species.

Habitat Within houses, sheds, garages and in gardens; also under stones, in crevices in tree trunks and rocks away from houses in the south.

Maturity Males late summer and autumn; females all year.

Distribution Widespread in Britain, possibly more frequent in the east, but previously confused identity necessitates much more collection of material before the relative distribution of *T. duellica* and *T. saeva* can be ascertained. Widespread in northern Europe.

Tegenaria saeva Blackwall 1844

Description Size and general appearance as for *T. duellica*, above. The pointed processes on the epigyne narrow more gradually to a point, and the anterior arch is less well defined at the sides than in *T. duellica*. The structure projecting from beneath the palpal organs has a shorter, narrower, tapering tip and is more angular on its upper surface than in *T. duellica*.

Habitat, Maturity and Distribution Similar to *T. duellica*.

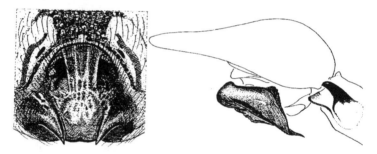

Tegenaria atrica C.L. Koch 1843

Description Size and general appearance as for *T. duellica*, above. The circular bodies near the anterior arch are closer together and not as recessed as in the previous two species, and the elongate dark marks on either side of the opening are characteristic. The structure projecting from below the palpal organs is smoothly curved on its upper surface and abruptly angled downwards, tapering to a point.

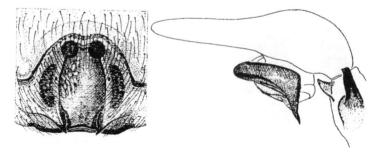

Habitat and Maturity Similar to *T. duellica*.
Distribution Recorded from northern England, Scotland and Ireland. Widespread in northern Europe.

Tegenaria parietina (Fourcroy 1785)
Description ♀, 11–20mm; ♂, 10–17mm. Similar in general appearance to *T. duellica* but has longer legs, particularly in males. The epigyne is similar to that of *T. ferruginea* but of different proportions. The male palpal organs and tibial apophysis are distinctive.
Habitat Sometimes in houses, but usually in very old buildings; outdoors in more southerly parts of Europe. **Maturity** Males late summer and autumn, females all year.
Distribution Much less common, with most records from the southern and eastern counties of England and eastern Ireland. Not recorded from Wales or Scotland. Widespread in northern Europe but generally uncommon.

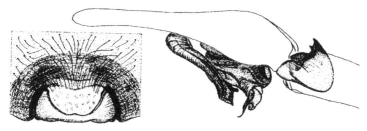

△ *Tegenaria ferruginea* (Panzer 1804)
Description ♀, 11–14mm; ♂, 9–11mm. Similar to *T. duellica* and *T. parietina* but the abdomen has a distinctly reddish median band similar to that illustrated in *Textrix denticulata* (Plate 19). The epigyne is similar to that of *T. parietina* but is of different proportions. The male palpal organs and tibial apophysis are distinctive.
Habitat In holes and crevices in overhanging banks, crevices in tree trunks in woodland and in barns and derelict buildings.
Maturity Males in summer, females all year.
Distribution Absent from Britain. Widespread in northern Europe but commoner in the south.

Tegenaria agrestis (Walckenaer 1802)
Description ♀, 10–15mm; ♂, 7–10mm. Similar in general appearance to *T. duellica*. The epigyne and male palp are very distinctive and discernible with a lens. **Habitat** Amongst vegetation and under stones in grassy areas, waste ground and alongside railway tracks. Sometimes under stones and bark in wooded areas. Not normally indoors in Europe. **Maturity** Males in late summer and autumn, females possibly all year.
Distribution In Britain it is increasing its range northwards, but does not normally occur in houses. It was accidentally introduced into North America, first discovered there in 1930, and since the 1960s has become one of the commonest house spiders in the Pacific Northwest. The colder North American winters are probably responsible for it moving into houses, but in this habitat it bites humans with little provocation and has earned the title of 'Aggressive House Spider'. I await its arrival inside houses in northern Scotland with interest; it is perhaps most likely to arrive in houses adjacent to railway lines since the species is often abundant in trackside debris and could easily hitch a ride northwards. The species is widespread in northern Europe.

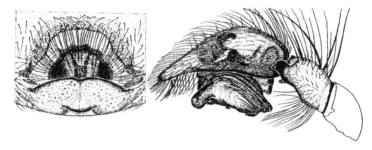

Tegenaria domestica (Clerck 1757)   Plate 19
Description ♀, 9–10mm; ♂, 6–9mm. Males similar to the female illustrated but have a slimmer abdomen and longer legs. The markings are variable; sometimes darker than shown, and sometimes the spider is uniformly yellowish-grey. The epigyne is distinctive, but usually not clearly discernible with a lens. The male palpal organs and tibial apophyses are distinctive and usually are discernible with a lens. **Habitat** Houses. **Maturity** All year.
Distribution A cosmopolitan species; widespread and common in Britain and Europe.

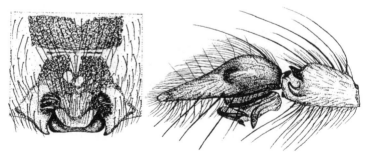

Tegenaria silvestris L. Koch 1872
Description ♀, 5–7mm; ♂, 5–6mm. Similar to *T. duellica* but much smaller. The abdomen sometimes has a brown midline band, on each side of which are pairs of pale brownish-yellow patches. Epigyne and male palp distinctive, but not easily distinguished with a lens.
Habitat Under bark, logs, stones and detritus, often in woodland.
Maturity Males summer and autumn, females all year.
Distribution Widespread in England and Wales; not uncommon but rather locally distributed. Widespread throughout northern Europe.

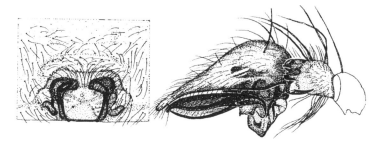

Tegenaria picta Simon 1870
Description ♀, 6–7mm; ♂, 5.5–6mm. Similar to *T. duellica* but much smaller and with fainter abdominal markings which may be slightly reddish in the midline. The epigyne and male palpal organs are distinctive but not easily distinguished with a lens.
Habitat Amongst stones and low vegetation in a variety of habitats, including woodland and mountains. **Maturity** Spring to autumn.
Distribution First recorded in Britain in 1982 from chalk pits in West Sussex. Possibly widespread in the southeast of England. Not recorded from Scandinavia; widespread but uncommon throughout the rest of northern Europe.

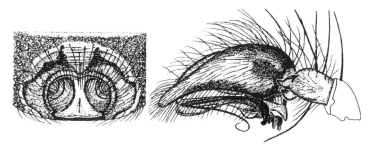

△ *Tegenaria campestris* C.L. Koch 1834   Plate 19
Description ♀, 6–7mm; ♂, 5–5.5mm. Male similar to the female illustrated, but with a slimmer abdomen and longer legs. Epigyne and male palp distinctive, the latter sometimes being discernible with a lens.

Habitat Amongst stones and low vegetation in a variety of habitats.
Maturity Summer to autumn, females possibly all year.
Distribution Absent from Britain and Scandinavia. Widespread in the rest of northern Europe, but generally uncommon.

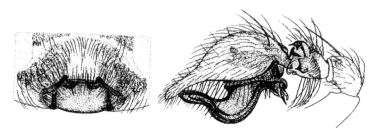

△ Genus *Histopona*

Several species of *Histopona* are known from southern and eastern Europe but only one occurs in northern Europe. It has sometimes been included in the genus *Tegenaria,* which it much resembles in appearance and biology. The carapace of this spider is conspicuously pale in the head region and the epigyne and male palp are very distinctive and usually identifiable with a lens.

△ *Histopona torpida* (C.L. Koch 1843)　　　　　　　　　　　　　　　Plate 20
Description ♀, 5.5–6.5mm; ♂, 4.5–6mm. Female similar to the male illustrated, but with a larger abdomen and shorter legs. The epigyne has a rather pale appearance. The male palpal organs are very distinctive, the embolus is very long and there are apophyses on the patella as well as on the tibia.
Habitat Amongst stones, logs, and cavities in tree trunks; often in woodland.
Maturity Spring to autumn.
Distribution Absent from Britain and Scandinavia. Widespread throughout the rest of northern Europe.

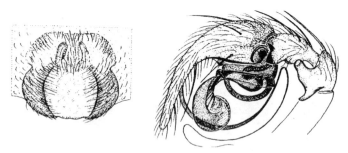

Genus *Coelotes*

Three species of *Coelotes* are known to occur in northern Europe, with several more species described from eastern and southern Europe. They have a fairly robust appearance, with relatively short, stout legs, a rather broad head region, and strong-looking chelicerae. All species construct a tubular, silk-lined burrow under stones and logs, and a collar of silk is spun around the opening (see Webs, p. 67). The eggs are laid within the tube, and the female remains with the spiderlings, feeding them by regurgitation and by sharing large prey items. Eventually she dies and is herself consumed by the spiderlings before they disperse. Details of the epigynes and male palps are sometimes sufficiently discernible with a lens, but higher magnification will often be required.

Coelotes atropos (Walckenaer 1830)   Plate 20
Description ♀, 9–13mm; ♂, 7–9mm. Both sexes are illustrated. The epigyne is similar to that of *C. terrestris* but the dark lateral borders are more curved and broaden anteriorly. There is a less well-defined arch anterior to these dark marks. On each side of the opening there is a blunt projection; these are further away from the anterior margin than in *C. terrestris*. The male palpal organs, tibial apophysis and patellar apophysis are readily distinguishable.
Habitat Under stones and logs in woodland, moorland and in mountainous areas.
Maturity Spring and summer, females to late autumn.
Distribution Most of England and Wales, but commoner in the north; largely replaced by *C. terrestris* in the south-east of England. Widespread in northern Europe.

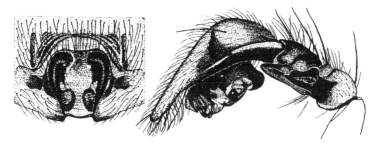

Coelotes terrestris (Wider 1834)
Description ♀, 9–13mm; ♂, 7–10mm. Very similar to *C. atropos* in general appearance; abdomen usually darker at the front end, with a lighter cardiac mark within the

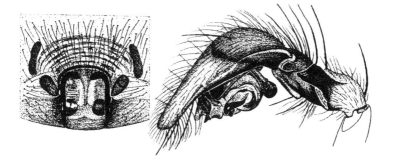

midline stripe. The dark marks, on each side of the epigyne opening, almost form the sides of a square and scarcely broaden anteriorly. There is a thin sclerotized arch anterior to these dark marks. On each side of the opening, the blunt projections are situated closer to the anterior margin than in *C. atropos*. The male palpal organs, tibial apophysis and patellar apophysis are readily distinguishable.

Habitat Under stones and logs in similar situations to *C. atropos*.

Maturity Spring and summer, females to autumn.

Distribution Widespread, but generally much less common, apart from in the southeast of England, where it replaces *C. atropos*. Widespread in northern Europe.

△ *Coelotes inermis* (L. Koch 1855)   Plate 20

Description ♀, 7–12mm; ♂, 6–10mm. Very similar to *C. atropos*, but the clear dark midline mark is absent and there are light chevrons, broken into paired light patches anteriorly. The epigyne and male palp are distinctive, the latter lacking a large patellar apophysis.

Habitat Under stones and within moss and leaf-litter, often in damp woodland habitats. **Maturity** Spring to autumn.

Distribution Absent from Britain. Widespread in northern Europe.

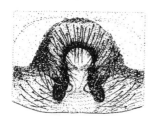 

Genus *Mastigusa*

The two European species in this genus were formerly assigned to the genus *Tetrilus*, and for a short time to *Tuberta*. They differ from each other only in the size and arrangement of the eyes and it seems likely that the two forms represent separate races, rather than species. For the moment, and until intermediates are found, it is simpler to regard them as separate species. Both species are associated with ants' nests, particularly in ancient woodland sites with relict oaks. Where the trees have completely gone, the species survive on open, rocky terrain provided that there are well-established ant colonies. The species live with the ants and the egg sacs are placed in galleries, often deep within the nests; the latter may be in tree stumps or under boulders. Specimens may also be found, away from ant nests, in grass tussocks, leaf-litter and under bark. Overmature, relict woodland and dead timber are not always fully appreciated, and in public places there is always concern over falling branches. However, such sites support a very rich invertebrate fauna. Although relatively small, these spiders can be identified to genus level with a lens. The male has enormous palpal organs which curve back over the carapace and the female has a relatively large epigyne. The abdominal markings are usually characteristic in both sexes.

Mastigusa macrophthalma (Kulczynski 1897)   Plate 20
Description ♀ ♂, 3–3.5mm. Both sexes are illustrated; the male palps are quite
remarkable structures. The distance between the eyes in the posterior row is equal
to, or not much more than, the diameter of each eye (cf. *M. arietina*, below).
Habitat In ants' nests, often in association with dead wood in ancient woodland.
Found with the ant species *Lasius brunneus* (Latreille), *L. fuliginosus* (Latreille), *L.
umbratus* (Nylander), *Formica fusca* Linnaeus and *F. rufa* Linnaeus. Specimens may
also be found amongst low vegetation, leaf-litter and under bark.
Maturity Probably all year.
Distribution Generally rare, but the habitat may influence recording. Recorded from
the Midlands, south and south-west England, and south Wales. European records are
from Austria, Belgium, France, Hungary, Poland, Portugal and Yugoslavia.

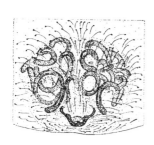
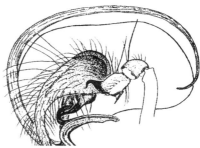

Mastigusa arietina (Thorell 1871)
Description Size, general appearance, epigyne and male palp as for *M. macroph-
thalma*, above. Distinguished by the much smaller eyes; the distance between the
eyes in the posterior row is at least twice the diameter of each eye.
Habitat Similar to *M. macrophthalma* but only recorded from the nests of the ants
L. brunneus and *L. fuliginosus*. **Maturity** Probably all year.
Distribution Rare, and recorded from Surrey, Berkshire and Cumberland. Fairly
widespread in Europe.

Genus *Cicurina*

The single European species in this genus has a mousy, greyish-pink abdomen which
lacks a pattern. It makes a small sheet web at ground level in damp habitats. The egg
sac is sometimes covered with particles of detritus or prey remains, and the female
stays with it in the retreat.

Cicurina cicur (Fabricius 1793)   Plate 20
Description ♀ ♂, 5–7mm. Male similar to female illustrated but has a smaller
abdomen. The epigyne and male palp are distinctive and the latter is usually discernible with a lens.
Habitat In damp, often dark habitats. In woodland, amongst moss and low vegetation and under stones and logs. In damp cellars, culverts, covered drains and caves.
Maturity Probably all year.
Distribution Generally rather rare in Britain with records from the south, north and
east of England. Widespread in northern Europe.

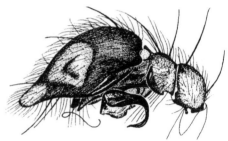

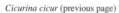
Cicurina cicur (previous page)

Genus *Cryphoeca*

Only one species of *Cryphoeca* occurs in northern Europe but another three occur to the south and east of the region. The spider sometimes spins a small sheet web, but often there is only a flimsy tubular retreat and even this may be absent or easily over-looked. The long posterior spinners are easily visible in males, but are less obvious in females. Nevertheless, the Family Key will have directed you to the illustrations on Plate 20, and the species is readily identifiable with a lens.

Cryphoeca silvicola (C.L. Koch 1834)   Plate 20
Description ♀ ♂, 2.5–3mm. Both sexes are illustrated and consideration of size and general appearance makes identification an easy matter. The depth of colour of the abdomen does vary somewhat. (Note: There is another very rare species, *Tuberta maerens* (O.P.-Cambridge 1863) which is very similar to *C. silvicola* in general appearance, lives on the bark of trees, and measures only 2mm in both sexes. It has an entirely different epigyne and male palp.) The epigyne and male palp of *C. silvicola* are distinctive, although too small to be discerned with a lens. If an adult specimen measuring only 2mm is found, with a different epigyne and male palp, reference should be made to other literature (see Bibliography, p. 375).
Habitat In woodland, amongst leaf-litter (broadleaves and pine needles), under bark, in holes and crevices in bark. Also on high ground amongst stones, many of these sites having long ago been cleared of trees.
Maturity Males spring to autumn, females all year.
Distribution Widely distributed in Britain, but much less common in the south of England and rare or absent in the south-east of England. Often extremely abundant in woodland, moorland and mountainous areas in the north of England and Scotland. Widespread in northern Europe.

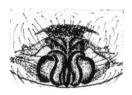

FAMILY HAHNIIDAE

This family contains ten European species in two genera, but is sometimes considered also to include the genera *Cryphoeca* and *Tuberta*. Six of the most widespread species are described here. They are small spiders, 3mm or less in length, and make small sheet-webs at ground level amongst stones, moss, and across small impressions in the ground. I have never seen any kind of retreat and the spiders hunt on the surface of the web. Despite their small size, the transversely arranged row of spinners is easily visible with a lens and the position of the tracheal spiracles is also usually discernible (see Family Key, p. 45). The epigynes and male palps are very small and require higher magnification to identify the species, although the epigyne of *Hahnia montana* is identifiable with a lens by its overall shape.

Key to the Genera

Tracheal spiracles situated half-way between spinners and
   epigastric fold. Carapace and legs a distinctly orange-brown
   colour (except in very newly moulted specimens)   *Antistea* p. 253

Tracheal spiracles situated slightly closer to the spinners than
   to the epigastric fold. Carapace and legs generally a more
   greyish brown, occasionally pale yellow or almost black   *Hahnia* p. 254

Genus *Antistea*
There is only one European species in this genus.

Antistea elegans (Blackwall 1841)   Plate 21
Description ♀ ♂, 2.5–3mm. This species has a highly characteristic general appearance; the male is similar to the female illustrated, but has a smaller abdomen. The epigyne and male palp are distinctive, the latter having a prominent apophysis on the femur.
Habitat In wet habitats, with a small sheet web in moss or other low vegetation, or across depressions in the ground. **Maturity** Summer, females to autumn.
Distribution Widespread throughout Britain and northern Europe in suitable habitats.

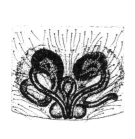
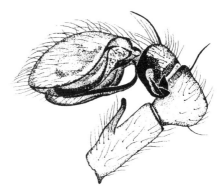

Genus *Hahnia*

Nine species of *Hahnia* are known to occur in Europe and five of the most wide-spread are described here.

Hahnia montana (Blackwall 1841)

Plate 21

Description ♀, 1.8–2mm; ♂, 1.5–1.8mm. Male similar to the female but with a smaller abdomen, as illustrated for *H. nava*. Some specimens may have a slightly paler abdomen than illustrated. The epigyne is distinctive and the pinkish-brown spermathecae are discernible with a lens. The male palpal organs are distinctive, as is the tibial apophysis, and the patellar apophysis is relatively short and not shaped like a crochet hook, as it usually is in three of the species below.

Habitat Amongst leaf-litter and detritus in woods; occasionally amongst grass and low vegetation away from woods. **Maturity** All year.

Distribution The commonest species of the genus; widespread throughout Britain and northern Europe.

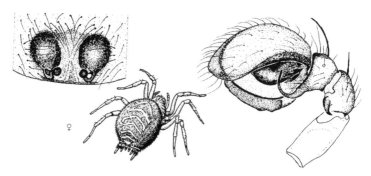

Hahnia nava (Blackwall 1841)

Plate 21

Description ♀ ♂, 1.5–2mm. Female similar to the male illustrated, but with a larger abdomen. The dark carapace and almost black abdomen are generally characteristic in the field, but occasional specimens may be almost as pale as the illustration of *H. montana*. The epigyne is highly distinctive. The male palp is similar to those of *H. helveola* and *H. pusilla* (which are invariably paler species) but differs in the form of the curved tibial apophysis and in the patellar apophysis. These do vary a little and

Continued after the colour plates.

COLOUR PLATES

The preparation of these colour plates required very careful planning in order to present the maximum amount of visual information; two aspects were of particular importance. Firstly, the spiders depicted vary in actual size from less than 2mm to over 20mm. Secondly, the legs of spiders form a very significant part of their overall appearance and vary greatly in size and appearance.

I decided to illustrate all species to roughly the same size, unless the legs were exceptionally long. This allows an equal amount of detail to be included on each species, irrespective of the actual size. The actual *adult* size range for each species depicted is given on the facing caption page, and careful note of this should be taken when comparing with specimens. The size of a spider is measured from the front of the carapace to the rear end of the abdomen and excludes the chelicerae. A millimetre scale is given on each caption page, but you will find it much easier if you incorporate a scale on your spi-pot (p. 33). Recognizable immatures will generally be smaller than the sizes given; a check for maturity precedes the Family Key (p. 38).

I also decided to include all of the legs in order to convey a complete impression. In many cases, this necessitated considerable intertwining of legs – great fun to do, but a little nail-biting as each colour plate neared completion! Remember that the legs are highly mobile and spiders will often stand with them drawn up. Species which hang upside-down beneath webs never appear as illustrated when on their webs; these attitudes are conveyed by the line drawings in the text.

Finally, remember that individual spiders of any species may vary (sometimes considerably) in colour and markings and the size of the abdomen will depend upon the sex, how well fed the spider is and, in females, whether eggs are developing. Significant likely colour variation is indicated on the caption pages and more detailed description appears in the text. Remember, too, that the amount of light will sometimes greatly affect the appearance – a spider which is lively and iridescent in bright sunshine may look as dull as ditchwater on an overcast day.

The symbol △ before a family or species indicates that it does not occur in the British Isles.

Plate 1

Sub-order Orthognatha (Mygalomorphae)

Massive, forward-projecting chelicerae articulated for up-and-down (pick-axe) movement of the fangs. Only one family in the region.

Atypidae p. 76

Spiders living within a closed tube, mostly buried below ground; the aerial portion of the tube is camouflaged with earth to resemble a part-buried root. Massive chelicerae, small eye group, three-segmented posterior spinners and two pairs of book lungs.

    1. *Atypus affinis* Eichwald Female 10–15mm (to 18mm including
    chelicerae) p. 76

Sub-order Labidognatha (Araneomorphae)

Chelicerae articulated for inward and outward (pincer) movement of the fangs. All other spiders in the region belong to this sub-order.

Cribellate Spiders

Spiders with a cribellum, anterior to the spinners, which produces fine, woolly silk; this is combed out by the calamistrum on metatarsus IV.

Eresidae p. 78

Spiders living within a silk-lined tube buried in the ground; above the tube is a roof of cribellate silk. Massive domed head, eight small eyes – four grouped in the anterior midline and one at each 'corner'.

    2a. *Eresus cinnaberinus* (Olivier) Male 6–11mm p. 78
    2b. *Eresus cinnaberinus* (Olivier) Female 8–16mm p. 78

ALSO KNOWN AS A LADYBIRD SPIDER.

Amaurobiidae p. 78

Spiders living in a tubular retreat within holes in walls or bark etc. A web of lacy, faintly bluish, cribellate silk extends around the tube entrance. Cribellum divided in two by a fine ridge; calamistrum comprising two rows of bristles (reduced or absent in males).

    3. *Amaurobius similis* (Blackwall) Female 9–12mm p. 79
    4. *Amaurobius ferox* (Walckenaer) Male 8–10mm p. 80

△ **Titanoecidae** p. 81

Spiders living at ground level in a retreat under stones or in detritus, with a cribellate web extending around the opening. Calamistrum relatively long and comprising a single row of bristles (reduced or absent in males).

△ **5a.** *Titanoeca quadriguttata* (Hahn) Male 4.5–5mm p. 81
△ **5b.** *Titanoeca quadriguttata* (Hahn) Female 5–7mm p. 81

Dictynidae p. 82

Spiders making cribellate webs on vegetation, often dead heads of plants, sometimes on living leaves; occasionally at ground level and on walls. Calamistrum comprising a single row of bristles (reduced or absent in males).

    6. *Dictyna arundinacea* (Linnaeus) Female 2.5–3.5mm p. 83
    7. *Dictyna latens* (Fabricius) Male 2–2.5mm p. 85

0 5 10 15 20 mm

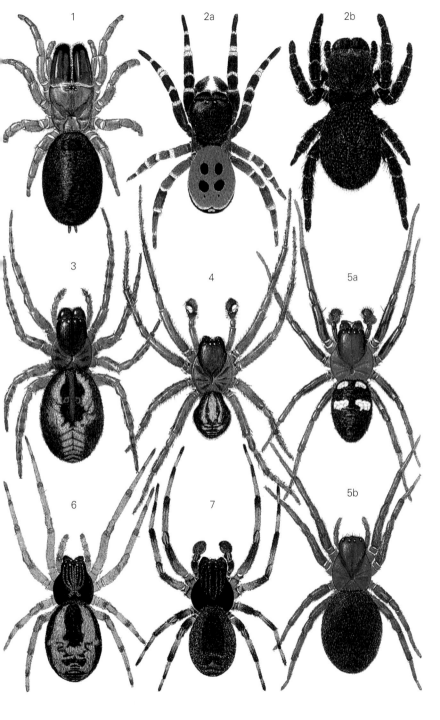

Plate 2

Uloboridae   p. 90
Spiders making either a horizontal orb web, with cribellate silk spirals and a broad band of silk running across the diameter (*Uloborus*) or a triangle web, the apex of which is held taut by the spider (*Hyptiotes*). Anterior lateral and posterior lateral eyes widely separated; metatarsus IV curved in profile, calamistrum comprising a single row of bristles.

Oecobiidae   p. 89
Spiders making a small, flat, circular web on flat surfaces indoors; web *c*.30mm diameter and often assuming a star shape. Eyes grouped closely together, posterior medians irregular in shape. Anal tubercle fringed with long, curved hairs. Calamistrum with a double row of bristles.

Haplogyne Spiders
Spiders which have only six eyes, simple male palpal organs and no epigyne in adult females.

Oonopidae   p. 91
Small, usually pinkish spiders, with six oval eyes set in a small group which is almost as wide as the head.

0   5   10   15   20 mm

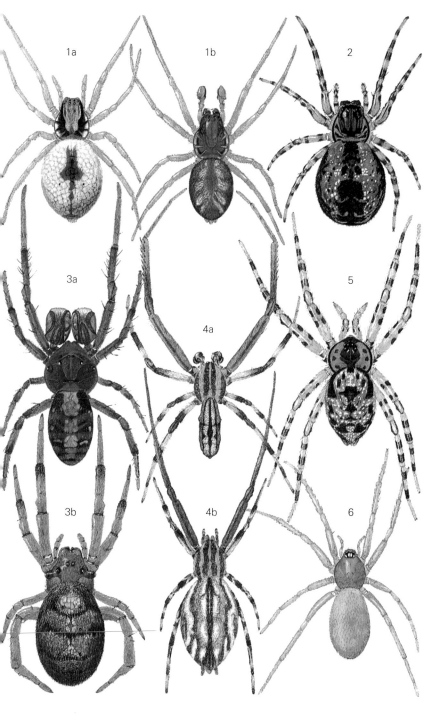

Plate 3

Haplogyne Spiders (continued)

Dysderidae p. 93

Spiders which hunt mainly at night. Six eyes arranged almost to form a circle.

   1. *Dysdera erythrina* (Walckenaer) Female 9–10mm p. 94
   2. *Harpactea hombergi* (Scopoli) Female 6–7mm p. 95

Segestriidae p. 96

Spiders living in a silk tube within holes in walls, bark etc. A series of strong threads radiates from the entrance. Six eyes arranged in three groups of two. First three pairs of legs directed forwards.

   3. *Segestria senoculata* (Linnaeus) Female 7–10mm p. 96
   4. *Segestria florentina* (Rossi) Female 13–22mm p. 97

Scytodidae p. 92

Spiders which hunt in houses, sticking prey down by squirting an oscillating spray of gum and poison from the fangs from a distance of 10mm or more. Carapace circular from above, very domed from the side, and of the same size as the abdomen. Six eyes arranged in three groups of two.

   5. *Scytodes thoracica* Latreille Male 3–5mm p. 93

Entelegyne Spiders

Spiders with eight eyes, more or less complex male palpal organs, and an epigyne in adult females. All spiders illustrated in the remaining colour plates belong to this group.

Pholcidae p. 98

Spiders spinning a web of loose, criss-cross threads; usually indoors, in corners of ceilings or in cellars. Very long, thin legs, the tarsi of which have false segments and are flexible. When disturbed, the spiders gyrate rapidly in the web as a defence mechanism.

   6. *Pholcus phalangioides* (Fuesslin) Female 8–10mm p. 98
   7. *Psilochorus simoni* (Berland) Female 2–2.5mm p. 99

Zodariidae p. 100

Fast-moving spiders which hunt at ground level and feed on ants. Anterior spinners very much larger than the rest, and arising from a large, pale, cylindrical projection (not visible from above). Anterior median eyes larger than the rest; posterior medians small and irregular. Upper surface of abdomen dark, under surface pale.

   8. *Zodarion italicum* (Canestrini) Female 2.5–3mm p. 100

Gnaphosidae p. 101

Mostly nocturnal hunting spiders, but *Micaria* hunts actively in sunshine. Most species have cylindrical spinners, the anterior pair of which are slightly longer than the rest and separated from each other by the diameter of one of them (spinners not typical in *Micaria*). In most species the posterior median eyes are oval, irregular or slit-like (but circular in *Scotophaeus* and some *Zelotes* which have very typical spinners).

   9. *Drassodes cupreus* (Blackwall) Female 9–18mm p. 104

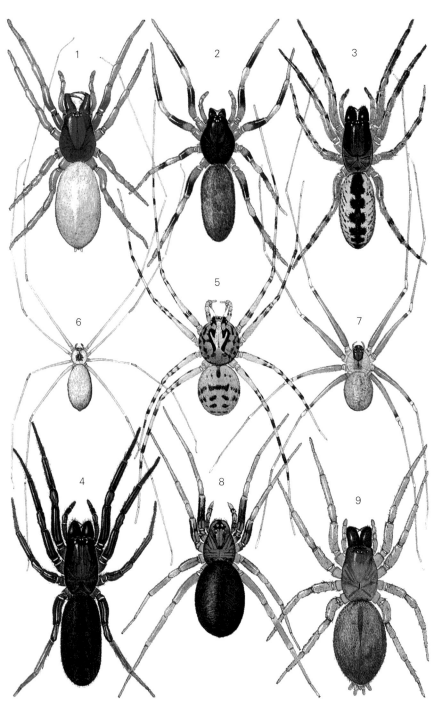

Plate 4

0   5   10   15   20 mm

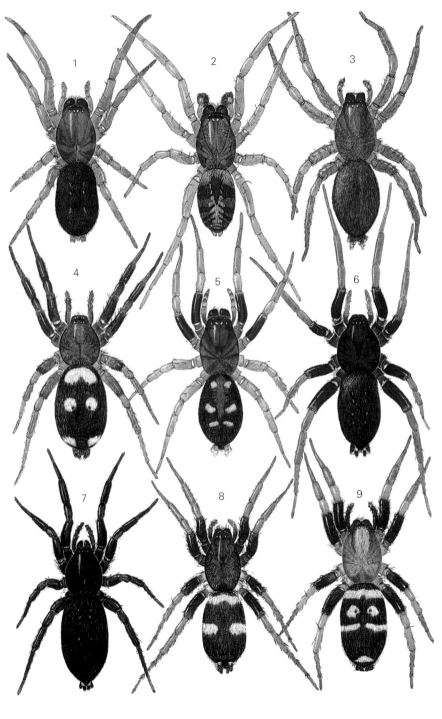

Plate 5

Spiders which hunt mainly at night, spending the daytime in a silken cell. The anterior spinners are more or less conical and close together. The labium is appreciably longer than broad. The posterior median eyes are circular; the eye region and front of the carapace are fairly broad. The genus *Clubiona* has the fourth pair of legs the longest; *Cheiracanthium* has the first pair longest and the chelicerae of males are enlarged.

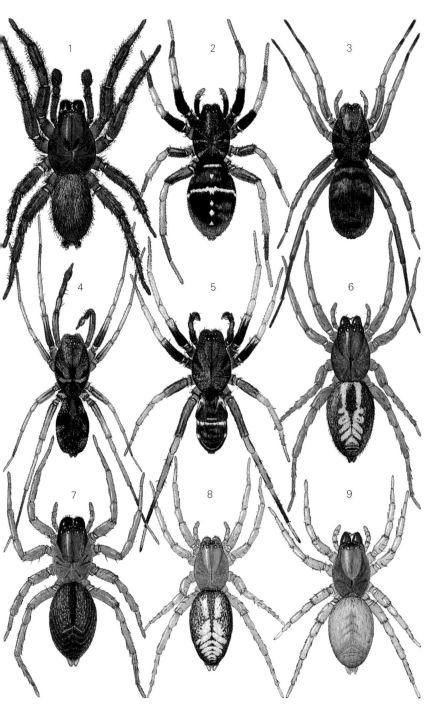

Plate 6

Liocranidae   p. 136

These spiders are mainly nocturnal hunters, but *Phrurolithus* species hunt during the day and are very active in sunshine. The eye group and front of the carapace are relatively narrow and the labium is roughly as broad as long.

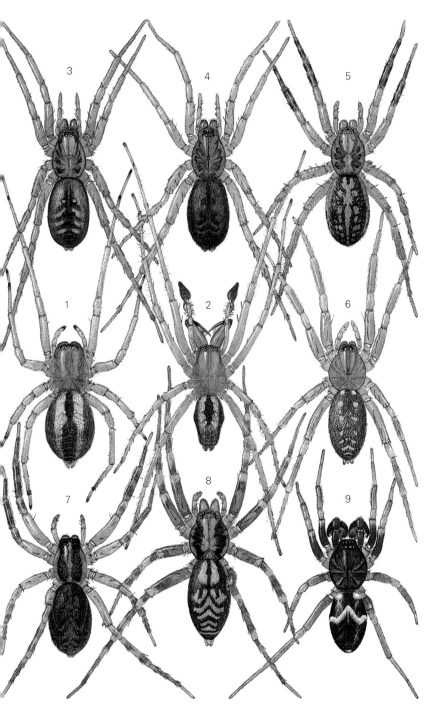

Plate 7

Zoridae
These spiders hunt on low vegetation and at ground level. The carapace is rather narrowed in front, with a row of four eyes on the front slope which are roughly the same size as those in the strongly recurved posterior row.

Anyphaenidae
These spiders hunt on the leaves of trees and bushes. The tracheal spiracles are easily visible midway between the spinners and the epigastric fold, on the underside of the abdomen.

Heteropodidae
These spiders catch prey in low vegetation, largely by waiting and grabbing rather than by active pursuit.

Thomisidae Misumeninae
These spiders lie in wait for prey and, although appearing conspicuous on the colour plates, are often well camouflaged in their natural surroundings. Legs I and II are noticeably stouter than III and IV and the spiders have a rather crab-like appearance. They mostly sit still, with the first two pairs of legs held apart, and seize prey which comes within grasp.

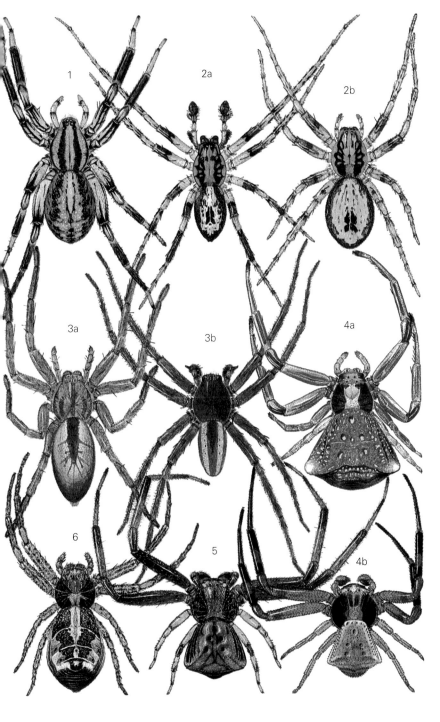

Plate 8

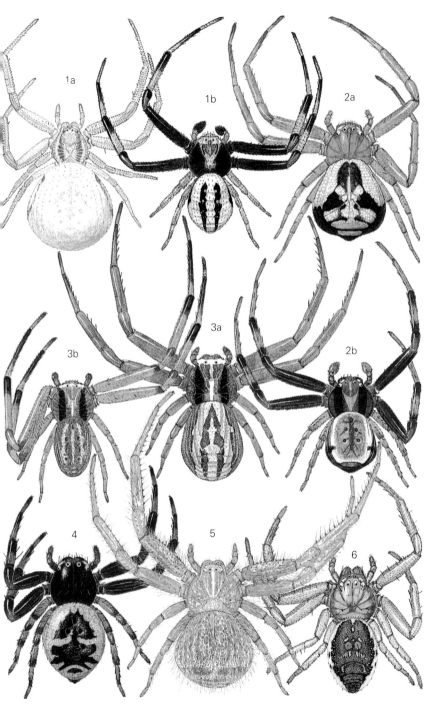

Plate 9

0   5   10   15   20 mm

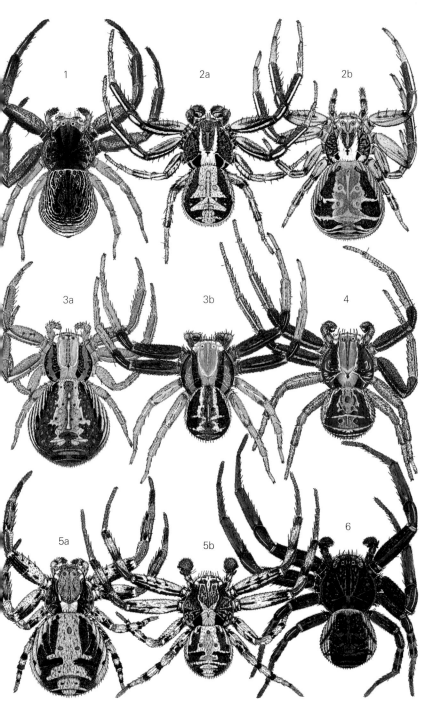

Plate 10

Thomisidae Philodrominae   p. 169
These spiders are less obviously crab-like than the Misumeninae, with legs I and II scarcely stouter than III and IV. Many species are extremely well camouflaged in their natural setting. In addition to waiting motionless and seizing insects which come within reach, they are also able to run very rapidly in pursuit of prey.

0   5   10   15   20 mm

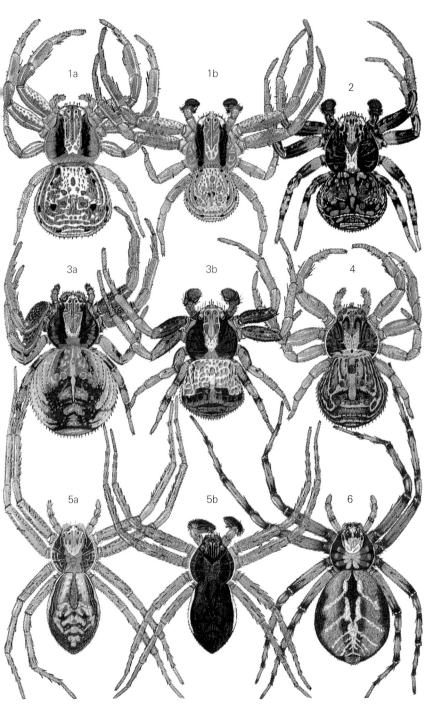

Plate 11

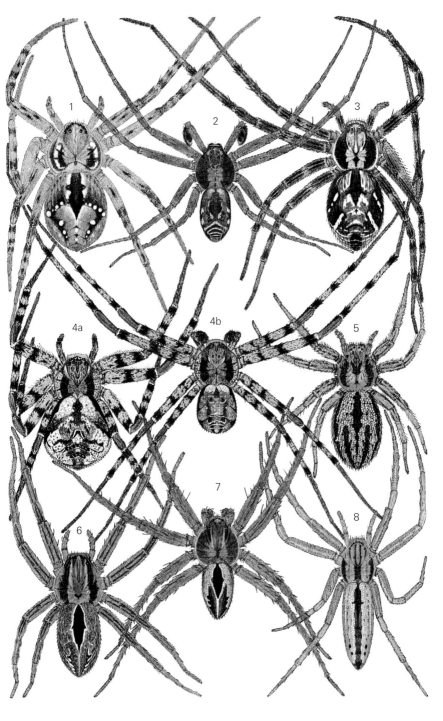

Plate 12

Salticidae   p. 179
These are hunting spiders with exceptionally good eyesight, stalking their prey and
finally leaping on it. They have a square-fronted carapace with four large, front-
facing eyes. Two very small eyes are situated a little further back, and a slightly
larger pair occur further back still.

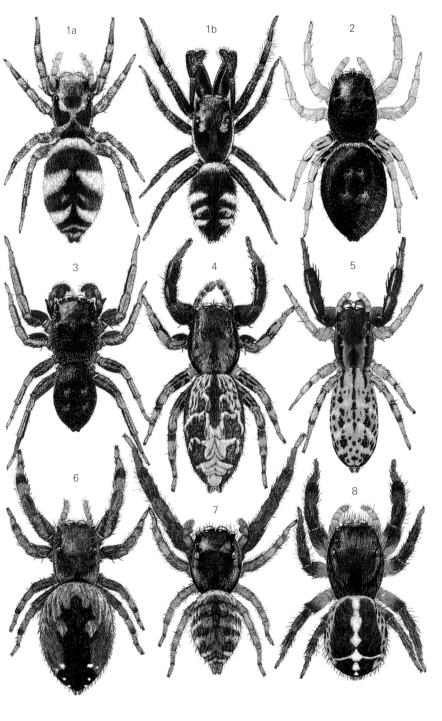

Plate 13

0   5   10   15   20 mm

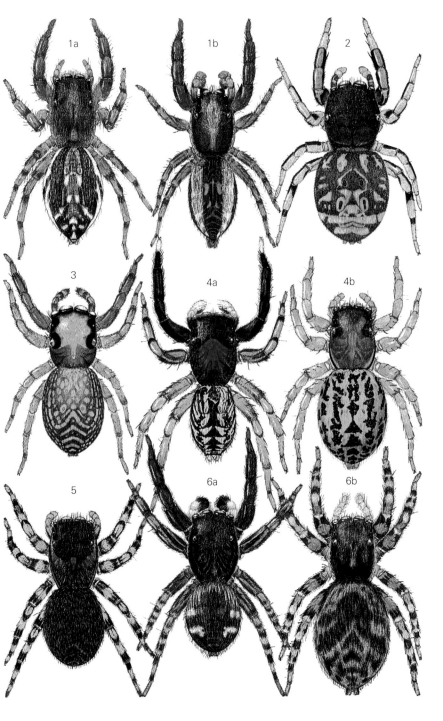

Plate 14

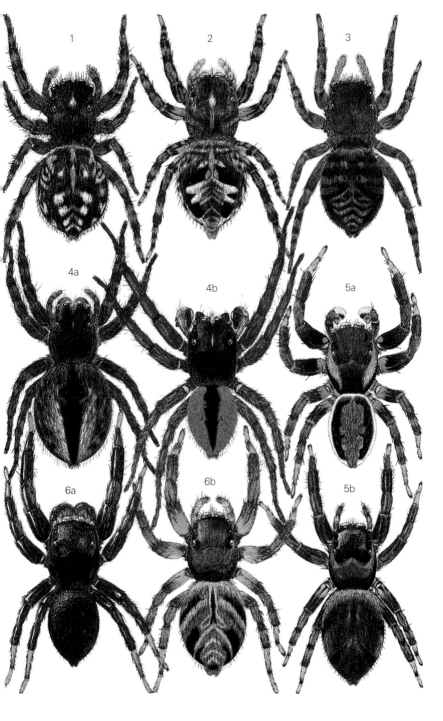

Plate 15

Oxyopidae   p. 206

These are long-legged, diurnal hunting spiders which run very rapidly on low vegetation in pursuit of prey. The eyes are arranged to form a hexagon and the leg spines are very long.

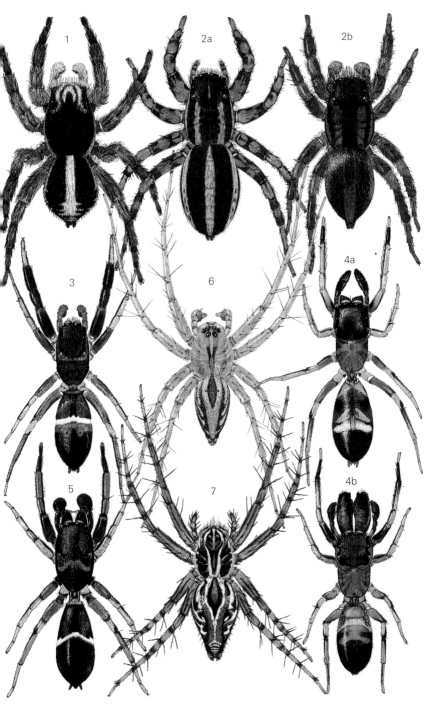

Plate 16

Lycosidae
These are hunting spiders, mainly at ground level. Females of most species carry their egg sacs attached to the spinners; the spiderlings clamber on to the abdomen and are carried around for the first week or so after emerging. The carapace has a row of small eyes on the front face, not easily seen from above; above and behind these a pair of larger eyes is visible and, further back still, another pair of equally large eyes.

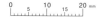

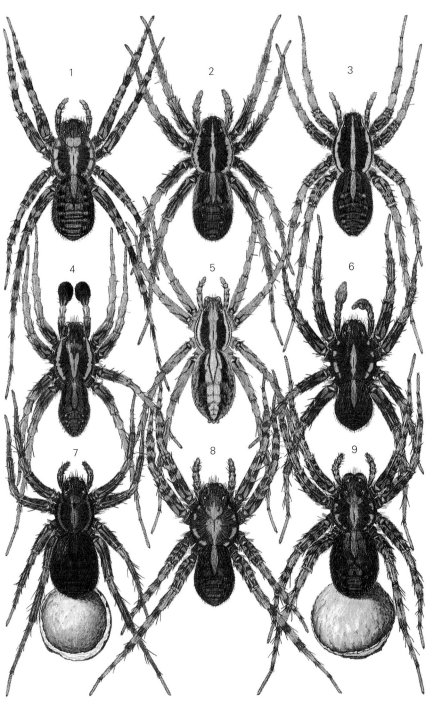

Plate 17

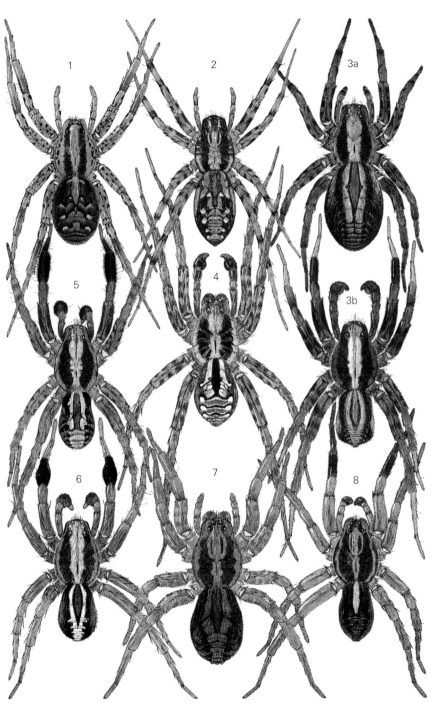

Plate 18

0   5   10   15   20 mm

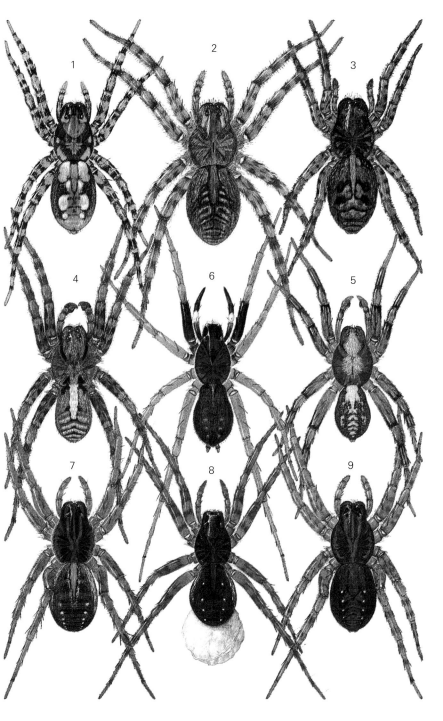

Plate 19

Pisauridae
These are hunting spiders, either on vegetation (*Pisaura*) or on the surface of water (*Dolomedes*). They have a row of four small eyes at the front of the carapace, which are easily seen from above. There is a pair of slightly larger eyes slightly behind these and another pair of similar size further back still.

Argyronetidae
This is the well-known 'water spider' and it lives an almost entirely submerged, aquatic existence. Legs III and IV are furnished with long, fine hairs in marked contrast to legs I and II.

Agelenidae
These spiders spin a tubular retreat from the opening of which extends either a sheet or a collar of silk. Those species which make a sheet run on its upper surface. The majority of species have the posterior spinners clearly longer than the anteriors, and of two segments. The tarsus of each leg has a series of trichobothria which increase in length towards the end of the segment.

0   5   10   15   20 mm

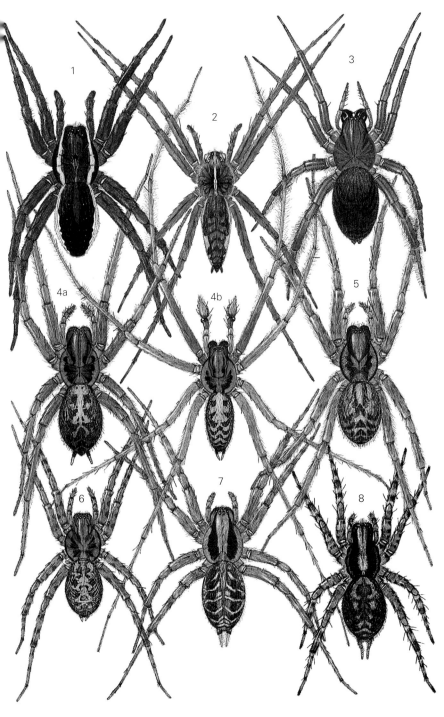

Plate 20

0　　5　　10　　15　　20 mm

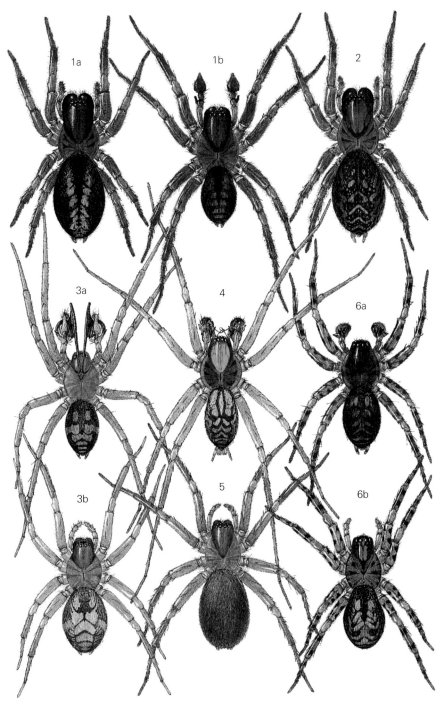

Plate 21

Hahniidae   p. 253

These spiders make small sheet webs at ground level. The spinners are arranged in
a transverse row and the tracheal spiracles are situated midway between the spinners
and the epigastric fold.

    1. *Antistea elegans* (Blackwall) Female 2.5–3mm   p. 253
    2. *Hahnia nava* (Blackwall) Male 1.5–2mm   p. 254
    3. *Hahnia montana* (Blackwall) Female 1.8–2mm   p. 254

Mimetidae   p. 257

These spiders invade the webs of other spiders and attack and eat the occupants. The
metatarsi and tarsi of the first two pairs of legs are furnished with a series of long
spines alternating with short ones. Metatarsi I and II appear curved when viewed
from the side. The abdomen bears two to four small tubercles, seen more easily in
profile in the commoner species.

    4. *Ero cambridgei* Kulczynski Female 2.5–3.25mm   p. 258
    5. *Ero furcata* (Villers) Male 2.5–2.75mm   p. 259
    6. *Ero tuberculata* (DeGeer) Female 3.5–4mm   p. 259

Theridiidae   p. 260

The commonest members of this large family spin a web of criss-cross threads in
vegetation; sticky droplets are present near the attachment of the threads which break
when insects encounter them. The latter are then either suspended helplessly, or
pulled further into the web as they struggle. Some species spin a reduced web, others have abandoned web spinning altogether. Many of the commoner species have a
rather globular abdomen with a pattern; in others the abdomen is shaped differently,
and a few species have no pattern. They all have a comb of serrated bristles on the
fourth tarsus, however it is difficult to see in small species and reduced in males. The
legs have very few spines.

    7. *Dipoena inornata* (O.P.-Cambridge) Female 1.8–2.25mm   p. 268
    8. *Dipoena melanogaster* C.L. Koch Female 2.5–3mm   p. 270
    9. *Episinus angulatus* (Blackwall) Female 3.75–4.5mm   p. 266

0   5   10   15   20 mm

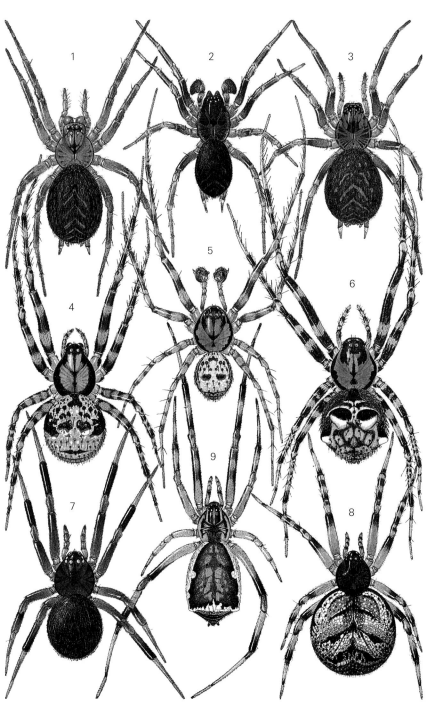

Plate 22

0   5   10   15   20 mm

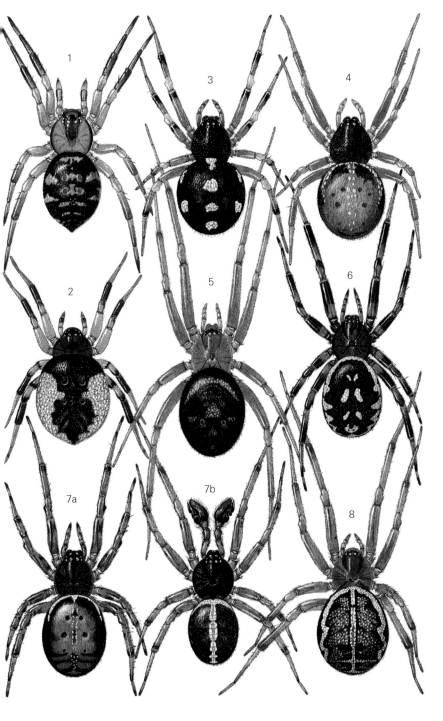

Plate 23

0   5   10   15   20 mm

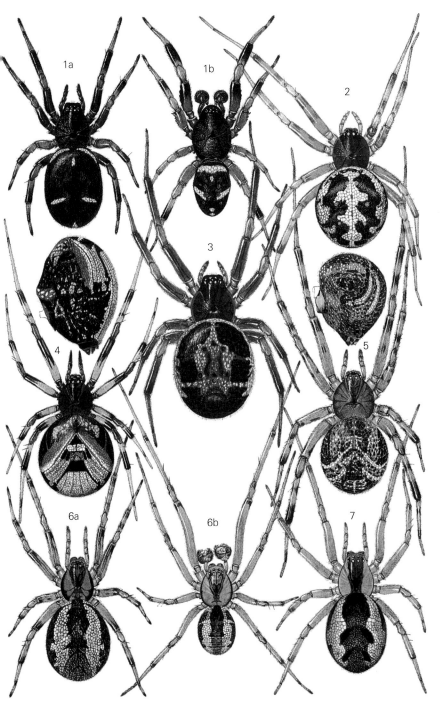

Plate 24

Theridiidae (continued)

0   5   10   15   20 mm

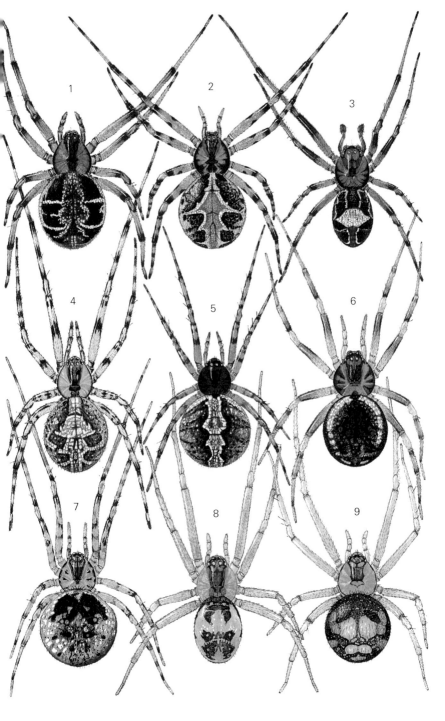

Plate 25

These spiders make a fine web of criss-cross threads in dark, damp habitats. The egg sac is carried attached to the spinners. Like the Theridiidae, they have a comb of serrated bristles on the fourth tarsus. They differ from the Theridiidae in having the front margin of the labium swollen.

These spiders spin a small orb web in which the radii are joined in groups of two or three before meeting at the centre. The spider sits at the centre, facing away from the web, holding a thread which runs to adjacent vegetation. The thread is pulled taut and the web assumes the shape of an umbrella turned inside-out. The thread is slackened when prey is snared, causing it to become more entangled. The abdomen is very globular and silvery and femur I is about twice as thick as femur IV when viewed from the side.

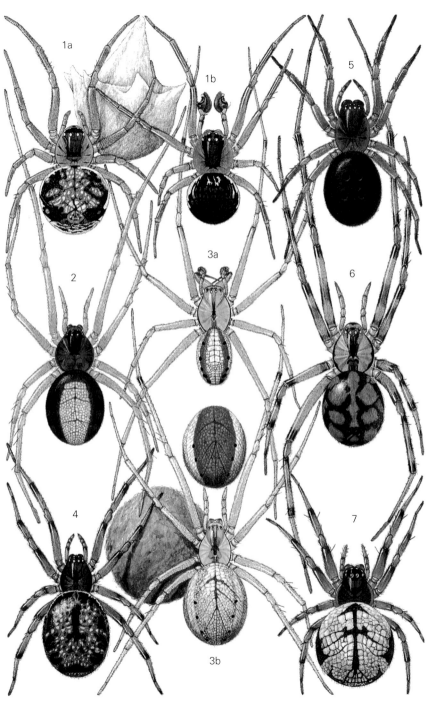

Plate 26

Tetragnathidae
The majority of species in this family spin an orb web which has a small hole at the hub and no signal line. *Pachygnatha* species are found near ground level and spin no web as adults. All species have the maxillae much longer than broad. *Tetragnatha* species are elongate spiders with long legs, bearing many spines, and large, divergent chelicerae. *Pachygnatha* have thick chelicerae but more normal body proportions and few leg spines. *Meta* species are also more normally proportioned, the chelicerae are not enlarged, and the legs bear many spines. Species of *Tetragnatha* often stretch their legs out along stems when alarmed; some species of *Meta* also do this, especially males.

0   5   10   15   20 mm

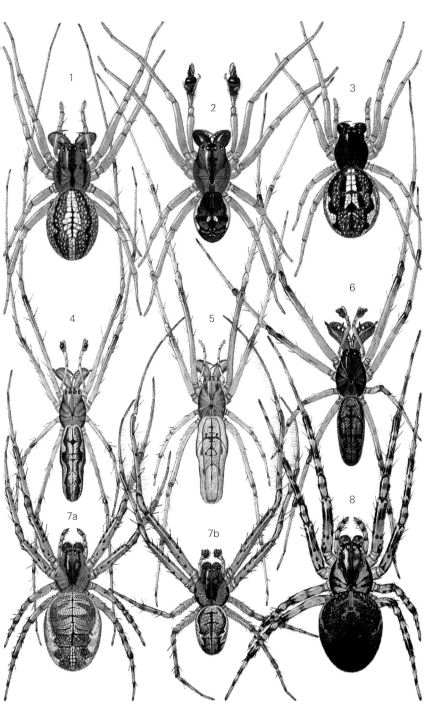

Plate 27

These spiders spin orb webs in which the centre, or hub, has a lattice of threads and no hole. There is a signal line leading away from the hub to a retreat. *Cercidia* spins a web with an open hub and no signal line; the web of *Zilla* has a closed hub, but no signal line. *Zygiella* spins an orb web with a sector missing; some *Araniella* webs may hardly resemble an orb. Species of *Cyclosa* and *Argiope* decorate their webs with bands of silk across the diameter. The distance between the anterior median eye and the front margin of the carapace (clypeus height) is generally less than twice the diameter of an anterior eye (exception: *Cercidia*). The chelicerae usually have a lateral condyle and in most species the legs are furnished with many spines.

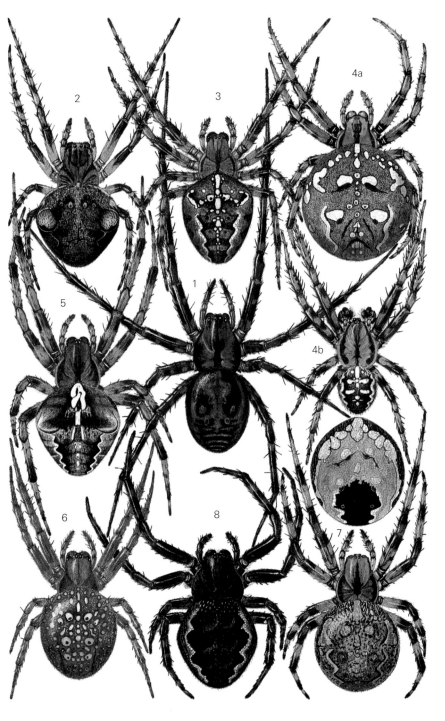

Plate 28

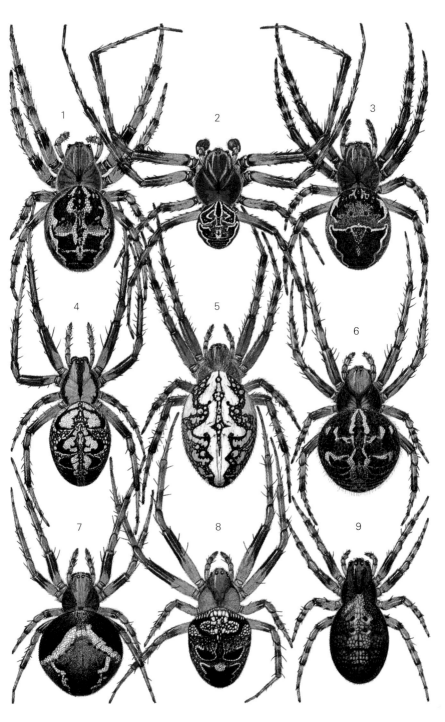

Plate 29

0   5   10   15   20 mm

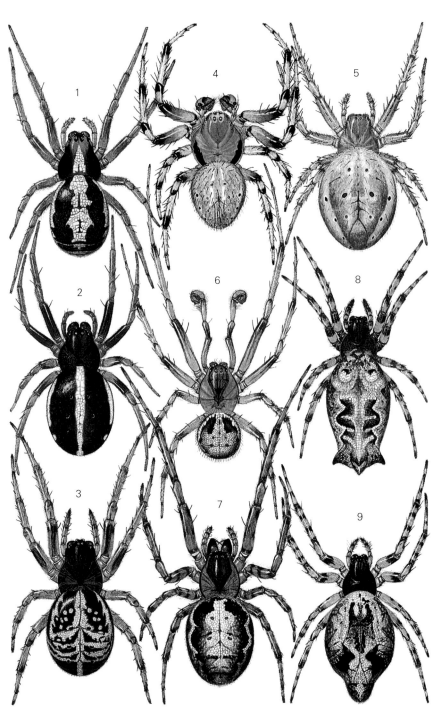

Plate 30

This is a large family with well over four hundred species in the region. Over three hundred of these have a grey or black abdomen with no pattern and are popularly called 'money spiders'. Males of some species have the head raised to form lobes or turrets. They cannot be described in detail in this guide, but a general account is given on pages 345–9. Just one species is illustrated in colour:
  3. *Dismodicus bifrons* (Blackwall) Female 2–2.5mm

Those members of the Linyphiidae which do have an abdominal pattern are illustrated in colour and described fully in the text. Most species spin sheet webs which often have a superstructure of vertical and criss-cross threads. The spiders run upside down on the underside of the web; insects landing on the sheet are seized from below. Some species may be found at ground level, others on vegetation or around houses. Some spin quite large sheets, occasionally domed; others make very small webs, or none. *Drapetisca* makes an incredibly fine web on the bark of trees. By far the commonest species is *Linyphia triangularis*. The height of the clypeus is generally greater than twice the diameter of an anterior eye (exceptions: *Tapinopa* and *Poeciloneta*).

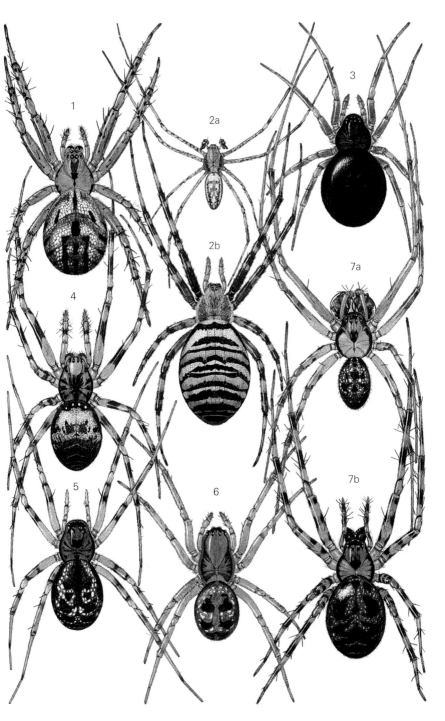

Plate 31

0   5   10   15   20 mm

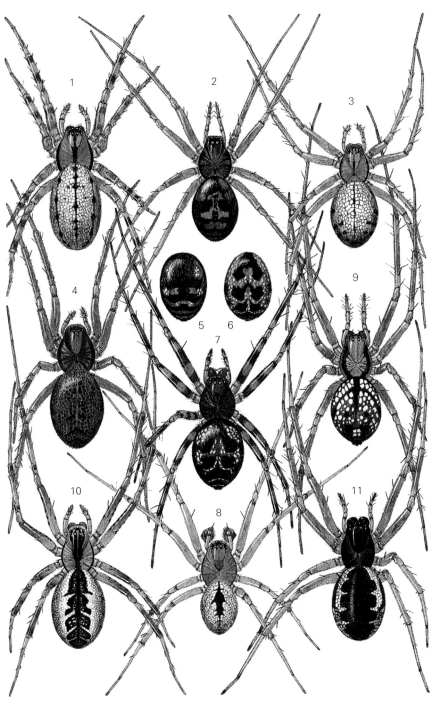

Plate 32

0   5   10   15   20 mm

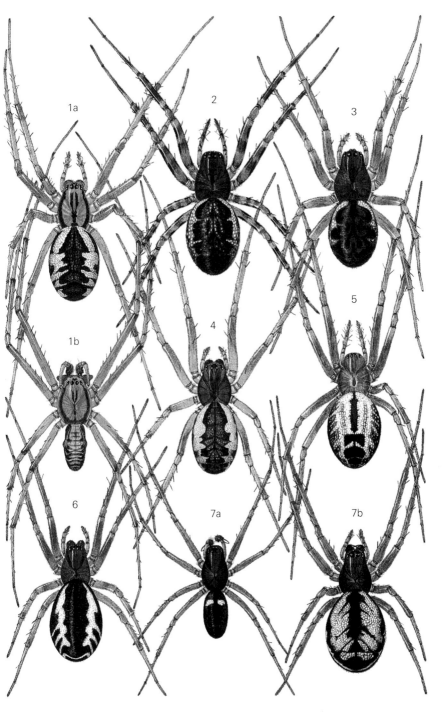

must be viewed from a strictly comparable position. Size affords the simplest way of separating males of this species from those of *H. helveola* and *H. pusilla*, since they are smaller than the former and larger than the latter (I have never come across any size overlap in males).

Habitat Generally away from woodland; amongst low vegetation in grassland and heathland and amongst stones or in crevices and depressions in open ground.

Maturity Summer, females to late autumn.

Distribution Not quite as common as *H. montana*, but equally widespread throughout Britain and northern Europe.

Hahnia helveola Simon 1875

Description /, 2.5–3mm; ?, 2.25–2.5mm. The carapace in this species is yellowish-brown with darker markings similar to those of *H. montana*, and the abdomen is yellowish with several broad, dark chevrons. The epigyne is very distinctive. Males are most easily distinguished from *H. nava* and *H. pusilla* by size (see *H. nava* above).

Habitat Amongst leaf-litter, detritus, moss and other low vegetation, usually in woods. **Maturity** Possibly all year; certainly late spring to winter.

Distribution Widely distributed throughout Britain and northern Europe; not as frequent as the previous species but may be locally abundant.

Hahnia pusilla C.L. Koch 1841

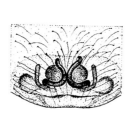
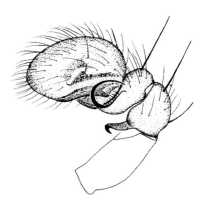

Description /?, 1.3–1.5mm. This is a rather pale species with a yellow-brown carapace and a yellowish-grey abdomen which generally has very few markings in the female. Males may have a darker abdomen with markings like that of *H. montana*. The epigyne is highly distinctive. Males are most easily distinguished from *H. nava* and *H. helveola* by size.

Habitat Amongst low vegetation and under stones, usually in damp situations.

Maturity Early summer to late autumn.

Distribution Widespread throughout Britain and northern Europe. Generally very uncommon and locally distributed, but then a number of specimens may be found together.

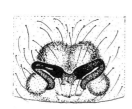

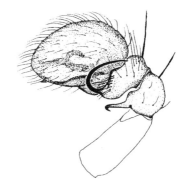

Hahnia candida Simon 1875

Description ♀ ♂, 1.3–1.4mm. This species has a very pale yellowish carapace and abdomen with no markings. The height of the clypeus is much wider than the diameter of an anterior lateral eye (a feature shared with *H. montana*, but not with the other species described, where it is narrower or only marginally wider). The species is smaller and much paler than *H. montana* and the epigyne and male palp are distinctive, the latter lacking a patellar apophysis.

Habitat Under stones on coastal cliffs and shingle and amongst heather inland; also from woodland sites in Europe. **Maturity** Possibly all year.

Distribution Very rare in Britain and recorded from only four sites in Dorset. Rare in Europe, but recorded from France, Belgium, Germany and further south and east in Europe.

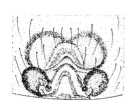

FAMILY MIMETIDAE

Genus *Ero*

Ero is the only genus of the family Mimetidae found in northern Europe, and all four species are described here. They are attractive little spiders with a globular abdomen which bears one or two pairs of small tubercles. The legs are usually clearly annulated and the metatarsi and tarsi of the first pairs are armed with a series of long spines alternating with short ones (see Family Key, p. 49). In Britain and the U.S.A. they are commonly called 'pirate spiders' but the German name 'Spinnenfresser'

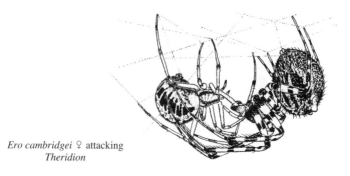

Ero cambridgei ♀ attacking
Theridion

(spider eaters) is perhaps more directly to the point! They seek out the webs of other spiders and, moving slowly and surreptitiously, pluck at the threads to attract attention. The occupant, sensing prey or perhaps a mate, is then attacked, quickly paralysed, and then sucked dry through a small hole in the legs. Spiders of this species spin no web of their own but do occasionally spin a few threads for moulting and mating. The latter takes place very quickly, although the initial approach by the male is slow and almost tentative. A nomadic lifestyle obviously requires some special provision for the eggs. Whilst the wandering wolf spiders (Lycosidae) carry their egg sacs around with them, *Ero* females suspend theirs on stalks, surround the sacs with wiry silk, and then abandon them (see Egg Sacs, p. 58). In the later part of the summer, these egg sacs are seen far more often than the spiders themselves, and each female probably makes two or three of them. The genus is readily identifiable with a lens, and the species can similarly be narrowed down to two groups of two on the basis of the number of abdominal tubercles; one of these groups is separable on size. Beyond this, higher magnification is needed in order to see details of the epigynes and male palps and identify the species.

Ero cambridgei Kulczynski 1911   Plate 21
Description ♀, 2.5–3.25mm; ♂, 2.5–2.75mm. The male is very similar to that illustrated for *E. furcata*. The abdomen has only one pair of small tubercles, which are more easily seen in profile (see illustration of *Ero* attacking *Theridion*) and this character is shared by *E. furcata*. The epigyne is distinguished from that of *E. furcata* by the shape of the central area and in lacking the dark spherical bodies posteriorly on

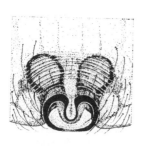

each side. The male palpal organs are distinctive, as are the structures arising from the upper part of the cymbium. The part of this structure nearest to the tibia is not notched as in *E. furcata*.

Habitat Found on low vegetation, bushes, and trees in various habitats, as they wander in search of the webs of comparably sized spiders to invade.

Maturity Summer and autumn.

Distribution Widespread in Britain and northern Europe and fairly common.

Ero furcata (Villers 1789)   Plate 21

Description ♀, 2.5–3.25mm; ♂, 2.5–2.75mm. The female is very similar to that of *E. cambridgei* and the abdomen has only one pair of tubercles. The epigyne is distinguished from that species by the spherical dark bodies on each side, near the posterior border. The male palpal organs are distinctive and the cymbial projection nearest to the tibia is notched, appearing as two pale lobes.

Habitat, Maturity and Distribution Similar to *E. cambridgei* and the two species may be found together.

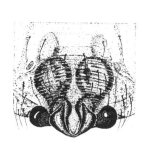 

Ero tuberculata (DeGeer 1778)   Plate 21

Description ♀, 3.5–4mm; ♂, 3mm. Male similar to the female illustrated but has a smaller abdomen. There are two pairs of tubercles on the abdomen, the rear pair being more widely separated. The colour of the abdomen varies from pale orange to almost black, but the areas behind the tubercles are always contrastingly pale. The

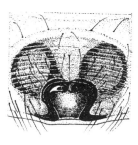 

epigyne is distinguished from that of *E. aphana* by the shape of the opening, which also lacks a dividing structure in the midline. The male palpal organs are easily distinguished by a whole range of differences.

Habitat Mainly found wandering on tall heather, but also on bushes and other vegetation. **Maturity** Summer and autumn.

Distribution Uncommon in Britain and very locally distributed in the more southern counties of England. Absent from Scandinavia but widespread throughout the rest of northern Europe.

Ero aphana (Walckenaer 1802)

Description ♀, 2.5–3.3mm; ♂, 2.4–2.6mm. This species is similar to *E. tuberculata* in having two pairs of tubercles on the abdomen, but the rear pair are not usually further apart than the front pair. The spider is smaller than *E. tuberculata*, has the epigyne opening divided, and has very distinctive male palpal organs.

Habitat Dry mature heathland; on heather and other low vegetation and bushes. **Maturity** Summer and autumn.

Distribution Rare in Britain and recorded only from five heathland sites in Dorset. Absent from Scandinavia; widespread in the rest of northern Europe, but commoner in the south of the region.

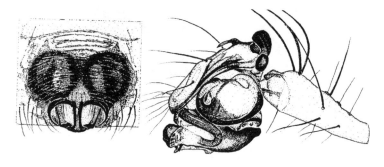

FAMILY THERIDIIDAE

This family is represented in northern Europe by seventy-six species in twelve genera. Fifty-seven of the most widespread species are described here. There have been recent arguments for further splitting of two of these genera; whilst not accepted here, the suggested changes are indicated within the text in order to facilitate reference to other publications. The various common names used for members of this family present the usual potential for confusion. In Britain, they are commonly referred to as 'comb-footed spiders'; unfortunately, in males and small species, the tarsal comb of serrated bristles is reduced, or absent. Really high magnification also reveals serrated bristles in many Araneidae. In the U.S.A., theridiids are called 'cobweb weavers' and the irregular, three-dimensional web made by many members of the family is called a 'cobweb'. (The origin of the word 'cob' seems uncertain but it is also used for a roundish piece of coal, bread bun or cattle cake, and for the heads of maize.) In Britain this term is used for the sheet webs made by domestic species of *Tegenaria* (Agelenidae) (p. 243). The common names of 'Kugelspinnen' (Germany) and 'kugleedderkopper' (Denmark) translate as 'ball-' or 'globe-spiders' which could refer to the globular abdomen of some species or reflect the three-dimensional nature of some webs, which may form a dense ball in the centre. However, genera such as *Episinus* have an elongate, angular abdomen and a very reduced web.

Members of the family Theridiidae exhibit great variety in shape and coloration; the majority have an abdominal pattern, but some are uniformly greyish or black and resemble those small members of the Linyphiidae known as 'money spiders'. The comb of serrated bristles is not visible with a lens, and sometimes not even with a microscope. The legs have very few spines, and this is a useful character, visible in the field, for separating theridiids with an abdominal pattern from the families Tetragnathidae, Araneidae and Linyphiidae (see Family Key, ♀ p. 54). The male palps of theridiids are always distinguishable from those of the Nesticidae, Tetragnathidae, Araneidae and Linyphiidae, with a microscope, by the absence of a conspicuous paracymbium. The latter is a structure projecting from, or close to, the cymbium near its joint with the tibia. In the Nesticidae it is very conspicuous (p. 297); in the Tetragnathidae it is long and in two parts, one or both of which may be hairy (p. 303); in the Araneidae it usually takes the form of a small knob (p. 318); in the Linyphiidae it is a separate U- or J-shaped structure, of varying complexity, situated between the tibia and the cymbium and attached to the latter by a transparent membrane (p. 355). Theridiids do have a paracymbium, but it is an inconspicuous, marginal hook near the tip of the palp.

Episinus angulatus ♀ on web

The individual catching threads of the Theridiidae consist of a strand of silk loosely attached, under tension, to the substrate (which may be the ground, a leaf surface, bark etc.). The loosely attached end has a number of sticky droplets along it. Insects sticking to the droplets struggle, break the attachment of the thread, and find themselves hanging helplessly in the air. The rare *Dipoena torva* attaches a few threads like this on the bark of pine trees specifically to catch wood ants as they make their way up and down the trunks. The hanging remains of ants are easier to find than the spider. Much closer to ground level, species of *Episinus* make a very simple H-shaped web and the two gummy threads attached to the ground are held by the legs (see illustration). *Achaearanea riparia* attaches many more of these threads to the ground and mainly catches ants. These types of web capture crawling insects. Many other theridiid species spin a three-dimensional criss-cross tangle of these threads, higher up on vegetation, which can develop into quite a dense structure and have sticky droplets near the ends (see Webs, p. 67). Flying insects find themselves gradually drawn further into the web as more and more threads break free. In all cases, the prey attracts the attention of the web owner and is further enmeshed in threads as the spider throws over more sticky threads using the tarsal comb. Some theridiids such as *Euryopis* have abandoned web building altogether and throw silk over their ant victims when they encounter them. Once immobilized by silk threads, the insect is bitten. Theridiids generally have quite weak-looking chelicerae which lack teeth; they do however have quite powerful, rapidly acting poison. Prey is sucked dry to leave a presentable husk and not chewed up into a pellet as happens with the Araneidae. Prey remnants are frequently taken apart and attached to the outside of the retreat.

In general, the two sexes are similar in overall appearance with males having a smaller abdomen. The chelicerae are enlarged in the males of a few species (e.g. *Enoplognatha ovata,* Plate 25) and some *Theridion* males have the epigastric region swollen. Some species have stridulatory apparatus of file and scraper type; the file is located on the rear of the carapace and is opposed by teeth on the overhanging abdomen. This is particularly well developed in species of *Steatoda*. I first heard this in use as a medical student. Quietly studying the anatomy of the brachial plexus, I became aware of a slight sound from a guitar standing in the corner. My initial thought was that one of the well-worn strings was very slightly creaking as if about to snap and I clearly remember tensing myself for this not uncommon event. It turned out to be a pair of *Steatoda bipunctata* mating inside! Whilst some male theridiids indulge in a good deal of stridulation, or vibrate the female's web with legs or palps, others exhibit little in the way of courtship preliminaries. Females sometimes place their egg sacs in a retreat and remain there until the eggs hatch. Females of *Theridion sisyphium* guard their greenish-blue egg sac in the retreat and later feed the young spiderlings by regurgitation. Later still, the young share large prey caught by the female. The blue egg sacs of *Enoplognatha ovata* are guarded by the female on the under surface of leaves, and *Theridion pallens* makes small white sacs which have several pointed projections (Plate 25). *Theridion instabile* and *T. bellicosum* (Plate 24) carry their eggs sacs attached to the spinners, as also does *T. bimaculatum* (Plate 25); those of *T. instabile* are pinkish-brown, whereas *T. bellicosum* and *T. bimaculatum* have such relatively large white sacs that they obscure all but the spider's legs when seen from behind.

Some of the species are identifiable with a lens on the basis of general appearance alone, but most will require examination of the epigyne and male palp. For example, *Theridion sisyphium* (Plate 24) is a very common spider with a distinctive appearance, but *T. impressum* is also fairly common, looks the same, and is reliably distinguished only by the epigyne and male palp.

The Key to the Genera is straightforward with a microscope, the family being split into three groups on the basis of the colulus. This is not usually visible with a lens, but the key works in an alternative form if you follow the symbol ❦, and should allow all but a few small, black-bodied spiders to be assigned to the correct genus. You may, of course, find it simpler just to look through Plates 21–25, comparing the specimen with the illustrations. If identifying preserved specimens, remember that any red coloration may quickly wash out in alcohol.

Key to the Genera

View the anterior spinners from below and look for a projecting structure called the colulus, or a pair of bristles, in the midline just anterior to them.

1. Colulus and paired bristles absent   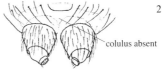   2

colulus absent

   Colulus relatively small (less than one-
      third the length of bristles) or absent
      and represented only by a pair of
      bristles   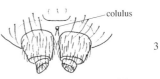   3

colulus

   Colulus larger (at least half the length of
      its bristles)   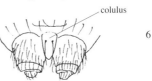   6

colulus

   ⁑ The colulus is not usually visible with a lens, although it is just discernible in some species of *Steatoda* and *Enoplognatha*. Therefore, follow the key from 2, then 3 and finally from 6. Some genera (e.g. *Euryopis*, *Achaearanea*) will key out positively on general appearance. Others, such as *Theridion*, will remain as possible suspects and are then separated at the end of the key.

2. Abdomen oval, but distinctly pointed posteriorly when
      viewed directly from above; it is also rather shiny   *Euryopis* p. 271

   Abdomen higher than long when viewed
      from the side   *Achaearanea* p. 277

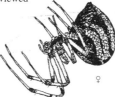

♀

   Abdomen globular or ovoid, and with a pattern or markings
      of some sort   *Theridion* p. 281

3. Abdomen broadened and truncated posteriorly, to form an
      angle on each side with the spinners projecting beyond.
      Leg III only about half the length of leg IV (or even less)   *Episinus* p. 266

   Abdomen globular or ovoid; leg III over half the length of leg IV   4

4.   Abdomen with a broad dark band in the
        midline (often darker at the front)
        flanked by light bands and
        sometimes with dark sides   *Anelosimus* p. 280

     Abdomen brownish-grey to
        black with no pattern, or
        with an entirely different pattern   5

5.   Size of adult spider 1.25–1.5mm. Anterior median eyes very
        small; the rest large and arranged in two groups of three.
        Abdomen of female black and very globular; abdomen of
        male with a brown scutum both above and below. Legs
        with weak spines   *Pholcomma* p. 295

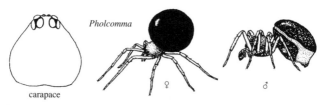

Pholcomma

carapace   ♀   ♂

     Size of adult spider 1.5–4mm. Eyes more evenly spaced.
        Carapace raised anteriorly (especially in males). Legs with
        no tibial spines. Abdomen globular and black; usually
        without markings (but see *Dipoena melanogaster* (Plate 21)
        which has tibial spines and an abdominal pattern)   *Dipoena* p. 268

6.   Size of adult less than 2.5mm. Carapace,
        sternum and chelicerae covered with
        distinct warty granulations. Carapace
        uniformly dark brown to black.
        Abdomen with a distinctive
        pattern (Plate 22) in the only
        two species   *Crustulina* p. 272

     Size of adult possibly less than
        2.5mm (but if so, lacking
        abdominal pattern), but possibly
        much larger. Carapace, sternum
        and chelicerae, although perhaps pitted or rugose, without
        distinct granulations. Abdomen possibly with a pattern,
        carapace possibly uniformly dark, but if so, size of adult
        greater than 2.5mm   7

7.   Abdomen grey to black with no pattern or light spots, but
        usually with two or three pairs of reddish impressed spots
        (sigilla) dorsally   8

     Abdomen with a pattern and /or markings of light, perhaps
        reticulated, spots; the latter may take the form of a thin line
        around the front of the abdomen, or cover the whole surface   10

8. Size of adult 1–1.25mm. Tarsi longer than metatarsi. All tibiae
        spineless   *Theonoe* p. 295

    Size of adult 1.7–4.5mm. Metatarsi longer than tarsi. All tibiae
        with one or two fine dorsal spines   9

9. All tibiae with only one fine dorsal spine not far
        from the patella. Chelicerae fairly robust
        but similar in both sexes. Legs
        progressively darker towards the
        extremities with tarsi much darker
        than femora   *Robertus* p. 293

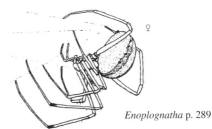

    All tibiae with two fine dorsal spines,
        one near each end of the segment.
        Chelicerae of males larger and more
        divergent than females and with large teeth. Legs
        more equal in colour throughout their length   *Enoplognatha thoracica* p. 290

10. Dorsal abdominal pattern light
        in colour; may be greenish-
        white, with or without red
        bands or a broad red band,
        and usually small paired,
        black spots. Some rare
        species have scattered light
        spots, a folium with dark
        lateral margins and a dark
        mark in the midline   *Enoplognatha* p. 289

    Dorsal abdominal pattern darker; reddish- or
        purplish-brown to black. Light spots
        present, but forming a white line
        around the front of the abdomen,
        sometimes a light band or series of
        spots or triangles in the midline,
        and sometimes light transverse
        bars at the sides   *Steatoda* p. 273

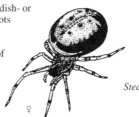

    ☝ Having worked through 2, 3, and 6 of the key, separately, you will now
    either have positively identified the genus, or have one or two suspects which
    may be separated as follows:

A. **Spider with an abdominal pattern or markings**: *Euryopis* and
        Achaearanea should have been positively identified, leaving
        Theridion. *Episinus* and *Anelosimus* should have been
        positively identified. *Crustulina* should have been positively
        identified by size and abdominal markings, leaving
        Enoplognatha and *Steatoda*.

1. Sternum pale yellow with narrow, black median line and
   black border; legs pale yellow with the extreme end
   of tibia I darkened. Two common species   *Enoplognatha* p. 289

2. Carapace with a well-defined darker mark in the midline,
   and possibly darker margins and radiating marks. (But
   see *T. mystaceum* (Plate 24) and *T. bimaculatum*
   (Plate 25).   *Theridion* p. 281

3. Carapace fairly uniformly brown or black; abdomen with
   a white line around the front end and usually white
   marks or a light band in the midline   *Steatoda* p. 273

4. Carapace brownish, sometimes with darker marks;
   abdomen with a dark mark in the midline and a folium
   with irregular dark margins. Four rare species   *Enoplognatha* p. 291

B. **Spider with a grey or black abdomen and no pattern**: As indicated in the
    Family Key, the specimen may be a 'money spider' (Linyphiidae p. 345) and
    in many cases it will be impossible to be certain without a microscope. The
    male of *Pholcomma gibbum*, with brown abdominal scuta, is identifiable with a
    lens; the globular abdomen of the female is not reliable on its own, and higher
    magnification is required to see the eyes. The genus *Robertus* (Plate 25) is
    fairly reliably identifiable by the legs, which are progressively darker towards
    the extremities with the tarsi darker than the femora. Most species have fairly
    obvious paired, impressed, reddish spots on the abdomen and the epigyne of
    the commonest species is discernible with a lens. *Theonoe* is not identifiable
    with a lens. *Dipoena* may be suspected if there are no spines on the tibiae
    (which may be darkened), but it is more likely that you will have obtained a
    microscope before you find one, since they are generally rather rare.

Genus *Episinus*

Three species of *Episinus* occur in northern Europe and all are of the same general
appearance, with the abdomen truncated and very short third legs. They make very
simple webs in the form of an H or inverted Y. The sticky ends of the threads are
attached to the substrate and are held by the spider (illustration p. 261). The commoner species occur at ground level, amongst grass and at the base of heather and
other low vegetation. The rare *E. maculipes* occurs on shrubs and trees, and the web
is made between leaves or branches. The sexes are similar in general appearance, but
males have a slimmer abdomen and the truncation is slightly less obvious. Courtship
is minimal and mating, which takes place in the summer, is brief. The egg sac is
white, roughly spherical and has coarse loops of silk on the exterior; it is generally
suspended under cover of vegetation. The species are best distinguished by the epigynes and male palps. Although these are fairly large, they are very similar in the three
species and not separable with a lens.

Episinus angulatus (Blackwall 1836)   Plate 21
Description ♀, 3.75–4.5mm; ♂, 3.5–4mm. Male similar to the female illustrated
but with a slimmer abdomen. The sternum is uniformly brown in colour. The epigyne is distinctive, although a little variable. The male palpal organs are distinguished by the arrangement of the ducts and by the structures near the tip.
Habitat Amongst low vegetation near ground level. **Maturity** Summer.

Distribution Widespread throughout Britain, but not generally very common. Widespread throughout northern Europe.

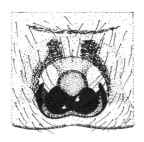
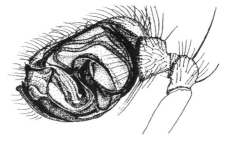

Episinus truncatus Latreille 1809
Description ♀, 3.5–4mm; ♂, 3.25–4mm. Similar to *E. angulatus* in general appearance and with a uniformly brown sternum. The femur, patella and tibia of leg I are entirely dark as are the tibiae of legs II and IV. The epigyne is distinctive and the male palpal organs distinguished by shape of the ducts and the structures near the tip of the palp.
Habitat and Maturity Similar to *E. angulatus*.
Distribution Most records are from heathland in southern England, where it may be locally frequent; also recorded from Ireland. Widespread in northern Europe.

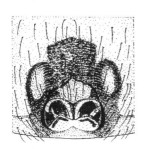
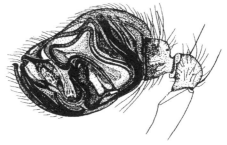

Episinus maculipes Cavanna 1876
Description ♀, 4.7–5.7mm; ♂, 4.25mm. Similar to *E. angulatus*, but generally slightly larger. Sternum brown, with a lighter median band (this perhaps not entirely reliable but present in all specimens seen). The epigyne is distinctive and the male palpal organs are distinguished by the shape of the ducts and the structures near the tip.
Habitat On the foliage of shrubs and trees. **Maturity** Summer.
Distribution Rare and recorded only from the Isle of Wight and Devon. Was found once in Essex in 1929, but not rediscovered. Recorded from France and southern and eastern Europe.

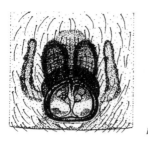
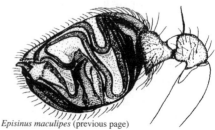

Episinus maculipes (previous page)

Genus *Dipoena*

Nine species of *Dipoena* occur in Europe, of which six are described here. One of the species is sometimes assigned to the genus *Lasaeola* and this is indicated, but not followed here. The head region of the carapace is elevated, especially in males. Most species have a uniformly black or greyish abdomen and the legs are spineless or have only a small patellar spine. *D. melanogaster* is unique in having an abdominal pattern and more leg spines. The species seem to feed almost exclusively on ants and occur at ground level, in low vegetation, bushes and trees, and on the bark of trees. Throughout the world, species of *Dipoena* seem to be generally rare. It is difficult to know whether this rarity is related to the time and methods of collecting in relation to the maturity and biology of the species. However, on balance it seems that rarity is almost a feature of the genus and that under-recording plays a relatively small part.

Apart from *D. melanogaster* and the male of *D. torva*, which are identifiable with a lens, a microscope is necessary in order to examine the epigynes and male palps. The leg markings and the relative lengths of metatarsus and tarsus I are also of some help, as are the shape of the carapace and the abdominal hairs.

Dipoena inornata (O.P.-Cambridge 1861)   Plate 21
Description ♀, 1.8–2.25mm, ♂, 1.5–1.7mm. The abdomen is covered with fairly long hairs which give the species a rather sleek appearance. Tibiae I and II are totally black; III and IV with black markings as illustrated. Metatarsus I about 1½ times as long as tarsus I. Epigyne and male palpal organs very distinctive.
Habitat On heather and other low vegetation and occasionally at ground level under stones. **Maturity** Summer.
Distribution Generally rare, but the commonest British species. Probably widespread but most records are from the south of England. Widespread but uncommon in northern Europe.

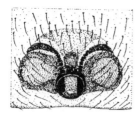
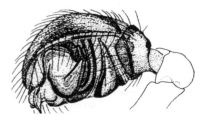

Dipoena prona (Menge 1868)
Description ♀, 2.5mm; ♂, 2mm. Generally slightly larger than *D. inornata*, with a more oval dark grey abdomen which is furnished with only very short hairs. The carapace protrudes in front of the eyes by about the same distance as that from the rear of a posterior median eye to the front of an anterior median eye. Legs yellowish-brown suffused with black. Metatarsus I about 1½ times the length of tarsus I. Epigyne rather variable but distinct from the other species. Male palpal organs very distinctive.
Habitat On heather, and low vegetation, but frequently at ground level under stones.
Maturity Summer.
Distribution Generally rare, with records from Norfolk, Suffolk and the southern counties of England. Widespread but generally rare in northern Europe.

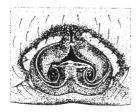 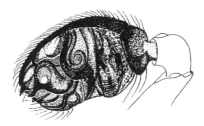

Dipoena tristis (Hahn 1833) (= *Lasaeola t.* (Hahn))
Description ♀, 3mm; ♂, 2.5mm. Slightly larger than the two species above. The abdomen is black, glossy (rather than sleek), with relatively sparse long hairs. The carapace does not protrude greatly in front of the eyes. Legs black, tarsi sometimes paler, with the first part of femur III and IV orange-brown. Metatarsus I about twice as long as tarsus I. Epigyne and male palpal organs very distinctive.
Habitat On heather, gorse and other low vegetation. **Maturity** Summer.
Distribution Rare and recorded mainly from sites in the south of England. Widespread and slightly more frequent in the rest of northern Europe.

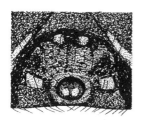 

Dipoena erythropus (Simon 1881)
Description ♀, 2.5mm; ♂, 2–2.5mm. This species has the carapace projecting ahead of the eyes as in *D. prona* (above). The abdomen is grey-brown with short, fine hairs. Legs uniformly yellow-brown with metatarsus I about 1½ times the length of tarsus I. The epigyne and male palpal organs are very distinctive.

Habitat On gorse bushes on heathland. **Maturity** Summer.
Distribution Very rare in Britain and recorded from a very few sites in southern England. Probably widespread in northern Europe, but generally rare.

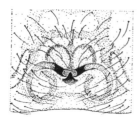
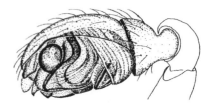

Dipoena melanogaster (C.L. Koch 1837)　　　　　　　　　　　　　　Plate 21
Description ♀, 2.5–3mm; ♂, 2.5mm. Females have a very distinctive appearance. The male has a smaller abdomen which is much darker and often only has a pair of light bands anteriorly. Metatarsus I is about twice as long as tarsus I and numerous spines are present on the legs. The epigyne and male palpal organs are distinctive.
Habitat On gorse and other bushes and on lower branches of pines. **Maturity** Summer.
Distribution Extremely rare in Britain. Recorded from a very few sites in southern England and from Ireland. Absent from Scandinavia and very rare in the rest of northern Europe.

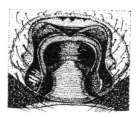
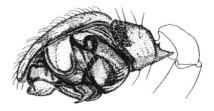

Dipoena torva (Thorell 1875)
Description ♀, 2.8–4mm; ♂, 2.5–3mm. This species is overall very dark, and the shiny, black abdomen has a bluish iridescence in good sunlight. The carapace of the female projects in front of the eyes, but not quite as much as in *D. prona*. The male carapace is remarkably elevated in a cylindrical fashion and has a horseshoe-shaped depression on the top. Metatarsus I is about twice the length of tarsus I. The epigyne and male palp are very distinctive.

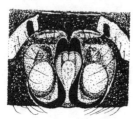
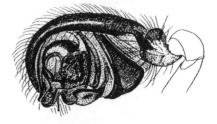

Habitat On the deeply fissured trunks of old Scots pine where the species catches wood ants travelling up and down the tree. Old pines in more open woodland appear to be necessary, as are the wood ant nests. **Maturity** Mid-summer, females to autumn. **Distribution** Restricted to Caledonian pine forests in Scotland. Recorded from Germany, Finland and in more southern and eastern areas of Europe.

Genus *Euryopis*

Four species of *Euryopis* occur in northern Europe and all have a rather shiny abdomen which is slightly pointed posteriorly. They appear to feed mainly on ants at ground level. I have never seen any web but have watched *E. flavomaculata* in wet moss, circling around its ant victim and immobilizing it with silk threads before biting a leg. Males are very similar to females in general appearance, but sometimes slightly darker. Although small, these spiders have a distinctive appearance and can be identified with a lens in the field; examination of the epigyne and male palpal organs requires a microscope.

Euryopis flavomaculata (C.L. Koch 1836)   Plate 22
Description ♀; 3.5–4mm; ♂, 3mm. The colour of the light spots on the abdomen varies a little, and they may be smaller or larger than illustrated. The epigyne varies in the degree of sclerotization and in some specimens may be almost totally black. The male palpal organs are highly distinctive.
Habitat Amongst moss in damp or boggy habitats; occasionally found higher up on vegetation in wet weather and possibly climbs higher at night.
Maturity Summer, females to autumn.
Distribution Widespread in Britain but generally very uncommon; frequent in some heathland sites in southern England. Widespread in northern Europe.

 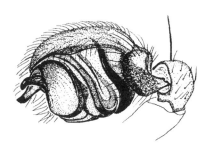

△ *Euryopis laeta* (Westring 1862)   Plate 22
Description ♀, 2.5–3mm; ♂, 2–2.5mm. Males are very similar to the female illustrated. The light spots on the sides of the abdomen sometimes appear distinctly silvery and metallic. The epigyne and male palp are highly distinctive.
Habitat In dry, often sandy habitats; amongst detritus, leaf-litter and low vegetation.
Maturity Summer.
Distribution Absent from Britain. Recorded from France, Germany and Scandinavia and possibly widespread in northern Europe. (Note: another species, *E. quinqueguttata* Thorell 1875, is of similar general appearance and size, but has a dark abdomen with five light spots – a pair near the front of the abdomen, a pair at

the midpoint, and a single midline spot above the spinners. It does not occur in Britain.)

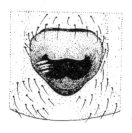
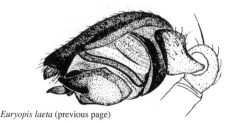

Euryopis laeta (previous page)

Genus *Crustulina*

The two northern European species in this genus have tiny warty granulations on the carapace and sternum. Whilst these cannot be seen with a lens, an impression of the rough texture is given by the reflection of sunlight. The two species differ greatly in general appearance and both are distinctive and identifiable with a lens in the field. They make rather insignificant webs in low vegetation. The egg sacs are white and spherical and seem frequently to be accompanied by the female in detritus, or deep within grass tussocks.

Crustulina guttata (Wider 1834)   Plate 22

Description ♀ ♂, 1.5–2mm. The male closely resembles the female in general appearance; the light spots may be a little larger or smaller than illustrated in either sex. The epigyne is a little variable, but distinctive, and the male palpal organs are easily distinguished from those of *C. sticta* with a microscope.

Habitat Amongst low vegetation, grass tussocks and detritus, usually on dry, sandy soil. Sometimes also occurs in dry leaf-litter (pine needles and broadleaf) and, perhaps because of the relative ease of sampling, may sometimes be found in large numbers. **Maturity** Summer.

Distribution Widespread in England, but few records for Scotland and Wales. Rather locally distributed, but may then be abundant. Widespread throughout northern Europe.

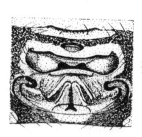
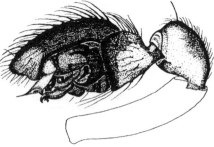

Crustulina sticta (O.P.-Cambridge 1861)   Plate 22
Description ♀ ♂, 2.5mm. Males are similar to the female illustrated but usually have clearer markings and the reddish impressed spots are larger. Darker females some-times resemble *Steatoda bipunctata* (Plate 22), but are only half the size of that species. The epigyne and male palpal organs are distinctive.
Habitat In damp habitats such as fens and bogs; amongst low vegetation.
Maturity Summer.
Distribution Locally distributed and uncommon with records from central, eastern and southern England. Recorded from France and Finland, but apparently rare or absent from much of northern Europe.

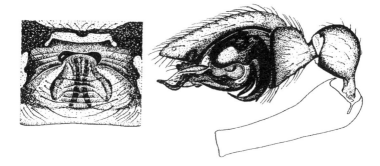

Genus *Steatoda*

Eight species of this genus occur in northern Europe and are described here. They gen-erally have a fairly robust appearance and, although markings vary greatly between different species, there is always a narrow white (or light) band around the front of the abdomen. The sexes are similar in general appearance, but males have a smaller abdomen which is usually more clearly marked. Some of the species occur almost exclusively in association with man, and adult females of some species are known to live for a number of years, surviving for long periods without water. Females of this genus have a particularly well-developed comb of serrated bristles on the fourth tar-sus and in large species, such as *Steatoda nobilis*, this comb is visible with a lens. Males have well-developed stridulatory apparatus, in the form of a series of ridges on the rear of the carapace which are opposed by teeth under the front end of the abdomen. Rapid vibratory movement of the abdomen produces a sound which is just about audible; louder if on a box or other sound-board. This is used in courtship, along with plucking and tapping movements by the legs and palps on the strands of the web. The webs are generally of typical theridiid design, with criss-cross threads which may become quite dense in the centre if undisturbed. *Steatoda phalerata* lives at ground level, is a more active hunter, and spins little or no web for prey capture.

The species are readily identifiable with a lens by their general appearance, and in most cases the epigynes and male palps are clearly discernible.

Steatoda grossa (C.L. Koch 1838)   Plate 22
Description ♀, 6.5–10mm; ♂, 4–6mm. The abdomen of the female is usually pur-plish-brown, but may be lighter or darker than illustrated with the markings more or

less defined. Males have a smaller abdomen with a much clearer white crescent on the front of the abdomen and white triangles and bars further back. The epigyne and male palpal organs are distinctive, but similar to those of *S. nobilis*.

Habitat Usually in houses, but occasionally in sheltered spots outside and away from habitations. **Maturity** Males late summer and autumn, females all year.

Distribution Recorded from the southern half of Britain, Wales and Ireland; commonest in coastal areas of south-west England but may well increase its range northwards. Widespread in northern Europe.

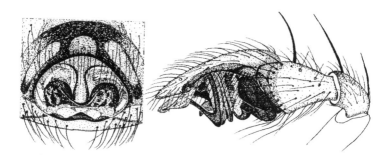

Steatoda albomaculata (DeGeer 1778)   Plate 22

Description ♀, 3.5–6mm; ♂, 4–5mm. Females sometimes lack the paired white spots on the abdomen and the latter is then entirely black apart from a narrow white band around the front. Males have a smaller abdomen with very clear markings (but see also *S. paykulliana*). The epigyne and male palpal organs are very distinctive and much larger than those of *S. paykulliana*.

Habitat Under stones and amongst detritus, or in a web low down on vegetation, on dry, sandy heathland; frequent on recently burnt heathland.

Maturity Males in spring and autumn, females all year.

Distribution Rare and locally distributed in south and south-east England. Widespread in Europe, as far north as Finland, but commoner in the south of the region.

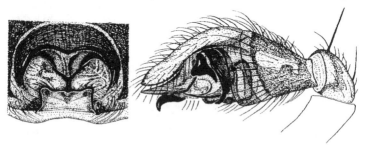

Steatoda bipunctata (Linnaeus 1758)   Plate 22

Description ♀, 4.5–7mm; ♂, 4–5mm. Both sexes are illustrated and have a very distinctive appearance despite some variation in the depth of colour. The epigyne and

male palp are distinctive, the latter being relatively large.
Habitat Mainly in and around houses; sometimes away from houses, on tree trunks. Quite frequent in domestic rubbish which has been dumped illegally, well away from houses. **Maturity** Summer and autumn, females all year.
Distribution Widespread and common throughout Britain and northern Europe.

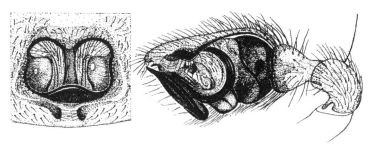

△ *Steatoda castanea* (Clerck 1757) (= *S. c.* (Olivier 1789))   Plate 22
Description ♀, 6–7mm; ♂, 5–6.25mm. The male is very similar to the female illustrated. The scattered white spots on the abdomen are characteristic, the light midline mark is more distinct than in females of *S. bipunctata* and the anterior white line continues around the sides. The epigyne and male palp are distinctive, the latter having a long tibia as in *S. triangulosa*, but they are much smaller than in *S. bipunctata*.
Habitat Mainly in and around houses; occasionally further afield.
Maturity Summer, females all year.
Distribution Absent from Britain. Widespread throughout northern Europe.

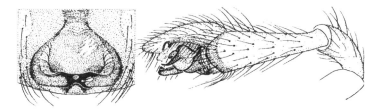

Steatoda phalerata (Panzer 1801)   Plate 23
Description ♀, 3.5–5mm; ♂, 4–4.5mm. The general appearance of this species is highly distinctive despite some variation in the size of the light marks. Males have a series of teeth on the underside of femora I and II. The species appears ant-like in the field – particularly males. The epigyne and male palpal organs are distinctive.
Habitat At ground level or low down in vegetation, in dry grassland or heathland. Usually found in the presence of ants and sometimes within ant nests. In the field and in captivity it feeds (perhaps almost exclusively) on ants, which are attacked with little or no prior immobilization with silk threads.
Maturity Summer to autumn, females all year.
Distribution Widespread throughout Britain and northern Europe. Generally uncommon and rather locally distributed.

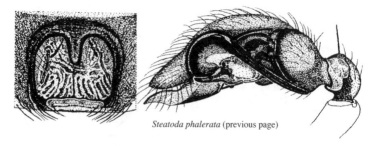

Steatoda phalerata (previous page)

Steatoda triangulosa (Walckenaer 1802)　　　　　　　　Plate 23

Description ♀, 4–5.2mm; ♂, 3.5–4mm. The male is very similar to the female illustrated and both are easily recognizable. The epigyne and male palp are rather small, the latter having a long tibia like that of *S. castanea*.

Habitat Mainly in and around houses; occasionally further afield. The web catches mainly crawling insects, particularly ants.

Maturity Summer and autumn, females possibly all year.

Distribution Recent record from a derelict housing site in England. Widespread in the rest of northern Europe with the possible exception of Scandinavia.

Steatoda nobilis (Thorell 1875)　　　　　　　　Plate 23

Description ♀, 8.5–14mm; ♂, 7–10mm. The male often has a clearer pattern than the female illustrated. Adults of both sexes are much larger than *S. bipunctata* and usually larger than *S. grossa*. The epigyne is rather variable and similar to that of *S. grossa*; the shape of the anterior margin and the relative width of the structure in the midline of the opening are reliable. The male palpal organs, although similar to those of *S. grossa*, are easily distinguished.

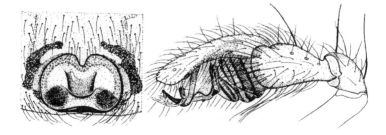

Habitat In and around houses and other buildings, but also established outdoors near the south coast of England. It is quite a large, introduced species and there have been instances of it biting people. **Maturity** Summer and autumn, females probably all year. **Distribution** Well established near the south coast of England. For well over a century, the species has been repeatedly introduced, from the Canary Islands and Madeira, with bananas. Its distribution in northern Europe is unclear at present, but in all probability it will have been introduced to some areas. The size of the spider makes it unlikely to remain overlooked for very long.

△ *Steatoda paykulliana* (Walckenaer 1806)
Description ♀, 8–13mm; ♂, 4.5–6mm. This species is not unlike *S. albomaculata*, but is generally larger. The female has a black abdomen with a pale yellow, orange or red line around the front; There may also be white chevrons or oblique lines along the length of the midline. Males have a white line around the front of the abdomen and a white median band which is extended laterally to form a series of two or three light triangles. The epigyne and male palp are surprisingly small for the size of spider, so much so that it is easily possible to overlook the slim palps of adult males when they are viewed from above. However, they are very distinctive.
Habitat Introduced to northern Europe with fruit from the Mediterranean. In central France it sometimes occurs under stones and in cracks in the ground.
Maturity Summer; females possibly all year.
Distribution Not, so far, established in Britain, but I have had a number of specimens from greengrocers and wholesale markets and there have been a number of other instances reported. The species is apparently established in parts of France and Germany but is mainly confined to southern Europe.

Genus *Achaearanea*

Six species of *Achaearanea* occur in northern Europe, of which five are described here. One of these, *A. simulans*, is sometimes listed as a subspecies of *A. tepidariorum* since it differs only in size. Whilst I still feel that this is correct, and more useful taxonomically, the general consensus is otherwise and I bow to this for the time being. The genus is easily recognizable in the field by the abdomen which, when viewed from the side, is much higher than long, with the spinners placed ventrally. Males are similar to females but have a smaller abdomen. The egg sacs are generally of brownish, papery silk; some species guard the sacs in a retreat, others hang them up in the web. The abdominal markings are extremely variable within each species and cannot be relied on for identification. The habitat sometimes offers a clue to the identity of females but examination of the epigynes and male palpal organs is necessary for certain identification.

Achaearanea lunata (Clerck 1757)   Plate 23

Description ♀, 2.5–3mm; ♂, 2.5mm. Male similar to the female illustrated, but has a smaller abdomen. The colour and markings are extremely variable, some specimens being quite pale, others almost black. The epigyne and male palpal organs are distinctive.

Habitat On the lower branches of trees and on bushes, usually in darker, shaded situations. The web is a usually a substantial tangle of threads, well above ground level, which mainly catches flying insects; it also tends to collect fragments of vegetation and dead, curled-up leaves. Leaves in the upper part of the web are used by females as a retreat, where they also guard the egg sacs. **Maturity** Summer.

Distribution Fairly uncommon. Recorded from Ireland and Wales, but most records are from southern England, tailing off north of the Midlands. Widespread throughout northern Europe.

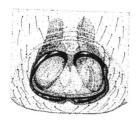
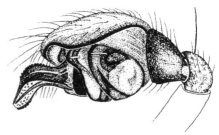

Achaearanea riparia (Blackwall 1834)

Description ♀, 3–3.5mm; ♂, 3–3.25mm. Similar in general appearance to *A. lunata* and equally variable, but abdomen usually more brownish with black and white markings. Usually slightly larger than *A. lunata*. The epigyne and male palpal organs are highly distinctive.

Habitat Web near ground level; upper part attached to low vegetation or overhanging banks, with sticky threads attached to the ground. It mainly catches crawling insects, with ants forming a principal part of the diet. The retreat, suspended near the top of the web, is a long, vertical silk tube which is disguised with debris and bits of vegetation and comes almost to resemble a tepee. **Maturity** Summer.

Distribution Rather rare in Britain but, with the exception of Scotland, widely distributed. Widespread in northern Europe.

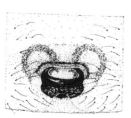
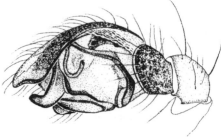

Achaearanea tepidariorum (C.L. Koch 1841)   Plate 23
Description ♀, 5–7mm; ♂, 3–4mm. Colour and markings extremely variable and may be much lighter or darker than illustrated. Epigyne and male palpal organs indistinguishable from those of *A. simulans* (below), but easily distinguished from the other species.
Habitat A cosmopolitan species, introduced from warmer countries. In northern Europe it occurs in heated greenhouses and sometimes in houses. It is occasionally found outside, particularly in the south of the region. The spider hangs its brownish, pear-shaped egg sacs up in the web.
Maturity All year.
Distribution Widespread throughout Britain and northern Europe, but has suffered considerably from the use of pesticides.

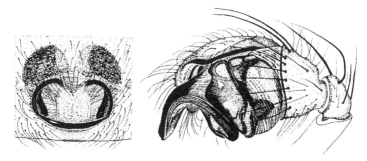

Achaearanea simulans (Thorell 1875) (= *A. tepidariorum simulans* (Thorell))
Description ♀, 3–5mm; ♂, 2–3mm. Indistinguishable from *A. tepidariorum* in general appearance, and equally variable in colour and markings. The epigyne and male palp are indistinguishable from those of *A. tepidariorum*; in both species (or races) there is slight variation in shape and the depth of sclerotization, and the actual size of the structures grades from one to the other. Differs from *A. tepidariorum* only in size. Whilst examples from either end of the spectrum look different, occasional specimens may be difficult to assign (and I would be pleased to see them).
Habitat On bushes and the lower branches of trees.
Maturity Summer, females to autumn.
Distribution Rare in Britain and recorded from a few localities in southern England. Widespread in northern Europe.

Achaearanea veruculata (Urquhart 1885)
Description ♀, 3.7–5.2mm; ♂, 2.5–3.5mm. Not unlike *A. tepidariorum*, but the abdomen usually has a clear, dark midline mark which is outlined with white. The sides are brownish with dark streaks. The epigyne and male palpal organs are distinctive.
Habitat On trees and bushes.
Maturity Summer, females to autumn.
Distribution Established in the Isles of Scilly following introduction from New Zealand or Australia at the start of the century. No records from the rest of northern Europe.

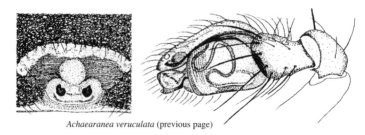

Achaearanea veruculata (previous page)

Genus *Anelosimus*

Three species of *Anelosimus* occur in northern Europe and are described here. In the field, they may be distinguished from other theridiids by the dark median band on the abdomen; this is usually darker at the front end. The species spin a web of criss-cross threads on bushes, the lower branches of trees and in the heads of plants. Males of *A. aulicus* are identifiable in the field with a lens, but the rest will require examination of the epigyne and male palpal organs at higher magnification.

Anelosimus vittatus (C.L. Koch 1836)   Plate 23
Description ♀, 3–3.5mm; ♂, 2.5–3.5mm. Abdominal markings slightly variable; may be lighter or darker and sometimes suffused with red. Occasional dark specimens may be confused, at first glance, with *Dictyna arundinacea* (Plate 1), especially when spun up in the dead flower heads of plants. The epigyne and male palpal organs are distinctive.
Habitat On bushes, trees, and in the heads of tall plants.
Maturity Spring and summer.
Distribution Widely distributed in Britain; rare in Wales and Scotland but fairly common elsewhere. Widespread and common throughout northern Europe.

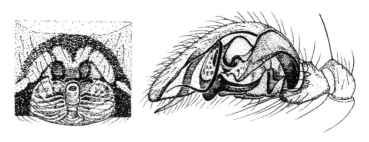

△ *Anelosimus pulchellus* (Walckenaer 1802)
Description ♀, 3–3.5mm; ♂, 2.5–3.5mm. Indistinguishable in general appearance from *A. vittatus* but with distinctive epigyne and male palpal organs.
Habitat and Maturity Similar to *A. vittatus*.
Distribution Absent from Britain. Widespread throughout northern Europe, but generally uncommon.

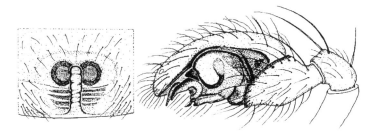

Anelosimus aulicus (C.L. Koch 1838)   Plate 23
Description ♀, 3–3.5mm; ♂, 2.5–3mm. Both sexes are illustrated; there is some variation in the depth of colour and the clarity of markings. The epigyne is distinctive and the peculiar male palps are easily discernible with a lens in the field.
Habitat On low plants and bushes, particularly gorse. **Maturity** Summer.
Distribution Rather rare in Britain and recorded from south and south-east England. Recorded from Germany and commoner in southern Europe.

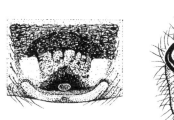
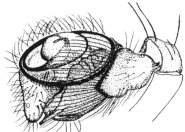

Genus *Theridion*

Twenty-two species of *Theridion* are known to occur in northern Europe and seventeen of these are described here. Some species have been assigned to separate genera by some authors. The reasons for this are clear to see, but if these criteria were applied consistently throughout the genus the result would be a large number of very small genera and this is less helpful taxonomically. Although not adopted here, the suggested changes are indicated within the text.

The species spin webs of criss-cross strands which may be on bushes and trees, in low vegetation, on bark and window frames and in cavities under boulders. The majority of species guard the egg sac, either in a silk retreat covered with vegetation and prey remains, or under cover of a leaf. Some carry the egg sac around, lycosid-style, attached to the spinners.

Males are broadly similar to females in general appearance, but have a smaller abdomen and a more concentrated pattern. In the males of some species, the epigastric region (on the underside of the abdomen) is swollen, and this is most easily seen in profile. A few of the species can be identified by their general appearance, but most will require examination of the epigyne and male palpal organs – at higher magnification than a ×10 lens.

Theridion sisyphium (Clerck 1757)   Plate 24
Description ♀, 3–4mm; ♂, 2.5–3mm. Male similar to the female illustrated, but with a smaller abdomen. Very similar in general appearance to *T. impressum* but differs in the epigyne, which has a more or less circular opening, and in the structure of the male palpal organs.
Habitat Web on bushes (especially gorse) and low vegetation. Retreat, near the top of the web, is covered with bits of vegetation and prey remains. The greenish-blue egg sac is guarded by the female, who later feeds the young by regurgitation and shares large prey items with them. **Maturity** Summer, females to autumn.
Distribution The commonest species of the genus, widespread throughout Britain and northern Europe.

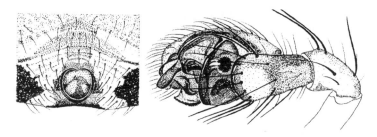

Theridion impressum L. Koch 1881
Description ♀, 4–4.5mm; ♂, 2.5–3.5mm. Very similar to *T. sisyphium* in general appearance but distinguished by the epigyne (which is broader than long and has paired, funnel-like openings, with a lightly sclerotized lip around them) and by the structure of the male palpal organs (especially near the tip).
Habitat Similar to *T. sisyphium*, but occurs more often on lower vegetation as well as on bushes. Retreat, egg sac, maternal feeding and maturity similar to *T. sisyphium*.
Distribution Widespread throughout Britain and northern Europe, but more locally distributed and generally less common than *T. sisyphium*.

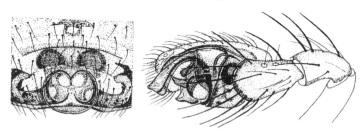

Theridion pictum (Walckenaer 1802)   Plate 24
Description ♀, 3.5–4.8mm; ♂, 2.25–3.5mm. The midline band is sometimes less obviously red, occasionally white, and the colour fades rapidly on preservation. Males similar to females in colour and markings, but with a smaller abdomen and the epigastric region greatly swollen. The epigyne varies somewhat in shape and in

most females, the opening is sealed (after mating) with a smooth plug (the epigyne on the right of the two illustrations). The male palpal organs are distinctive.

Habitat On bushes and low plants in damp habitats. The young feed communally on prey caught by the female as with *T. sisyphium*. **Maturity** Summer.

Distribution Widespread throughout Britain and northern Europe, but rather locally distributed.

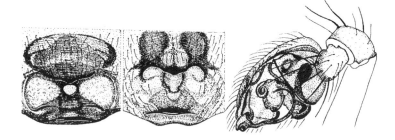

Theridion hemerobius Simon 1914

Description ♀, 3–4.5mm; ♂, 3–3.5mm. Most specimens resemble *T. varians* (Plate 24) in general appearance, but some are like *T. blackwalli* or *T. pictum* (but less reddish). Males have the epigastric region swollen. The epigyne resembles that of *T. pictum*, but is smaller, has a different posterior margin, and lacks the sclerotized lip anterior to the opening. The palpal organs differ from those of *T. pictum* in several respects, as do the number of spines on the palpal tibia and patella, those on the latter being relatively long.

Habitat On vegetation (and other structures) near water.

Maturity Summer to autumn.

Distribution Uncertain in Britain; recorded from Sussex. Although previously confused with *T. pictum* it seems unlikely that it has been overlooked in Britain to any great extent. Widespread throughout the rest of northern Europe.

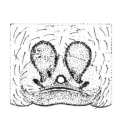

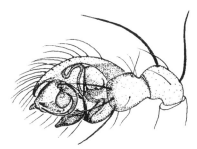

Theridion varians Hahn 1833   Plate 24

Description ♀, 2.5–3.5mm; ♂, 2.25–2.75mm. Male similar to the female illustrated, but with a smaller abdomen and a swollen epigastric region. Specimens of either sex are occasionally almost completely black. The epigyne is distinctive, but

in most females the opening is filled with a hard, smooth plug (epigyne on the right of the two illustrated). The male palpal organs are distinctive. (Note: Another northern European species which closely resembles *T. varians* is *T. petraeum* L. Koch 1872 (♀, 4mm; ♂, 3.5mm.) which has a different epigyne and male palp)
Habitat On low vegetation, bushes, trees and other structures.
Maturity Summer to autumn.
Distribution Widespread throughout Britain and northern Europe.

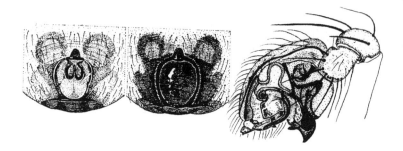

Theridion pinastri L. Koch 1872
Description ♀, 2.5–3.5mm; ♂, 2.25–2.75mm. This species resembles *T. mystaceum* in general appearance but has a paler brown carapace and the median band on the abdomen is reddish-brown. Males similar to females but with a smaller abdomen and swollen epigastric region. The epigyne is usually plugged (right-hand epigyne illustration) and it is unusual to find a female before the male does. The male palpal organs are distinctive.
Habitat In pine woods and on heathland, on bushes, heather and other low vegetation. **Maturity** Summer to autumn.
Distribution First discovered in Britain in 1977 and since then further specimens have been found in the south of England. Widespread in northern Europe, but perhaps largely absent from the north of the region.

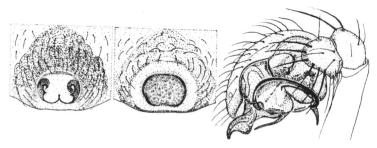

Theridion simile C.L. Koch 1836   Plate 24
Description ♀ ♂, 2–2.5mm. Female similar to the male illustrated but with a larger abdomen. The single conspicuous light triangle or diamond shape on the abdomen

is distinctive in both sexes, but some specimens of *T. familiare* can look similar. The epigyne is a little similar to that of *T. familiare* (below) but has relatively smaller spermathecae which do not extend far ahead of the opening. The male palpal organs are distinctive.

Habitat On gorse bushes, heather and other vegetation. **Maturity** Summer.

Distribution Commoner in southern England on heathland, less frequent in the Midlands and progressively rarer further north, although has been recorded in north-east Scotland.

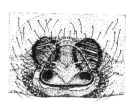 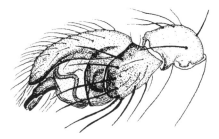

Theridion familiare O.P.-Cambridge 1871

Description ♀, 1.5–2mm; ♂, 1.5mm. Similar to *T. melanurum* (Plate 24) but with a paler carapace and a more reddish-brown abdomen with the first part of the midline band widened to form a rectangle. The epigyne has relatively larger spermathecae than that of *T. simile*, and these are situated further ahead of the opening, and the looped ducts are usually visible. The male palpal organs are distinctive.

Habitat In or near houses. **Maturity** Summer and autumn.

Distribution Rare; more frequent in southern England and probably restricted to the southern half of England.

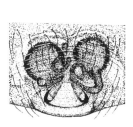 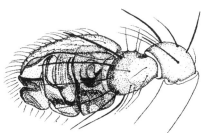

Theridion melanurum Hahn 1831

Description ♀, 2.5–3.75mm; ♂, 2.25–3.75mm. Very similar to *T. mystaceum* (Plate 24) in all aspects of its general appearance, but usually larger, and both sexes may be much darker or lighter in colour. Males very similar to females, but have the epigastric region swollen. The epigyne is distinguished from that of *T. mystaceum* by the differently shaped opening and the absence of visible ducts. The male palp is very

similar to that of *T. mystaceum* but the tibia is longer relative to other palpal structures; the latter also differ in shape and relative proportions.
Habitat Usually on or around buildings (e.g. window frames), but occasionally on vegetation away from houses. **Maturity** Summer, females to autumn.
Distribution Widespread in England and fairly common as far north as Yorkshire; recorded from Wales but apparently rare in northern England and Scotland.

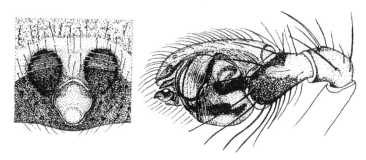

Theridion mystaceum L. Koch 1870   Plate 24
Description ♀ ♂, 1.5–2.5mm. Male similar to the female illustrated but has the epigastric region swollen. Both sexes may be much darker or lighter than illustrated. The epigyne has a more circular opening than that of *T. melanurum* and parts of the coiled ducts are visible both within, and on each side of the opening. The male palp has a relatively shorter tibia than in *T. melanurum* (usually with fewer long spines) and the shape and proportions of other parts of the palpal organs also differ.
Habitat Usually on tree trunks and bushes away from houses. **Maturity** Summer, females to autumn.
Distribution Widespread throughout Britain and northern Europe.

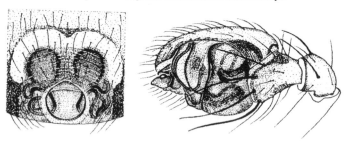

Theridion blackwalli O.P.-Cambridge 1871   Plate 24
Description ♀, 2.5–3mm; ♂, 2–2.5mm. Males similar to the female illustrated; the abdominal pattern varies in both sexes and some specimens may have little or no trace of the light marks. The epigyne and male palpal organs are highly distinctive.
Habitat Amongst grass and other low plants, on tree trunks and in or near houses.
Maturity Summer, females to autumn.

Distribution Rare in Britain, but widespread in England and recorded from Ireland. Widespread in the rest of northern Europe, but rare.

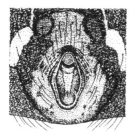 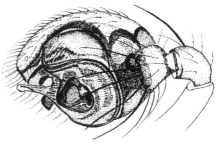

Theridion tinctum (Walckenaer 1802)   Plate 24
Description ♀, 2.5–3.5mm; ♂, 2.5mm. Males are similar to females but have a smaller abdomen. The colour and markings of the abdomen vary considerably in both sexes; the dark areas may be more or less extensive (occasionally entirely black in males) and may be suffused with reddish-brown. The epigyne and male palpal organs are distinctive.
Habitat On the lower branches of trees (especially yew), bushes and low vegetation.
Maturity Summer, females to autumn.
Distribution Fairly frequent in England, as far north as Yorkshire, but commoner in the south. Recorded from Wales and Ireland and widespread throughout the rest of northern Europe.

 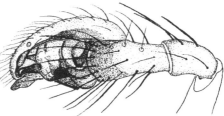

Theridion instabile O.P.-Cambridge 1871
(= *Rugathodes instabilis* O.P.- Cambridge)   Plate 24
Description ♀, 2–2.5mm; ♂, 1.75–2.25mm. Males similar to the female illustrated but have enlarged chelicerae, each with two teeth (one large and one small). Females may have a slightly more globular abdomen than illustrated. In either sex the dark abdominal markings may form a pair of longitudinal bars or, in males, a solid black area. The epigyne is similar to that of *T. bellicosum*, but differs in having relatively small spermathecae compared to the size of the opening, and differently shaped ducts. The male palpal organs differ particularly in the structures near the tip.
Habitat On low vegetation in marshy areas; the female carries the brownish egg sac

attached to the spinners. **Maturity** Summer to autumn, females through winter.
Distribution Uncommon and very locally distributed throughout England; more frequent in the south. Recorded from southern Ireland. Uncommon in the rest of northern Europe; recorded from France and Belgium, but apparently rare or absent elsewhere.

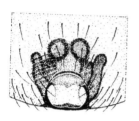 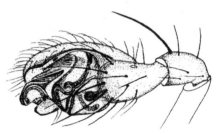

Theridion bellicosum Simon 1873 (= *Rugathodes bellicosus* (Simon))   Plate 24
Description ♀, 1.5–2mm; ♂, 1.75mm. Males similar to females but have enlarged chelicerae, each with two or three small teeth. The epigyne is similar to that of *T. instabile* but has relatively large spermathecae compared to the size of the opening, and shorter, angled ducts. The male palpal organs are easily distinguished by the structures near the tip.
Habitat Under stones on high ground; typically in large, dark cavities within boulder- or block-scree where it spins flimsy criss-cross threads. The female carries the relatively huge white egg sac attached to the spinners.
Maturity Summer to autumn, females possibly until later.
Distribution Northern Scotland, northern England and North Wales. Very locally distributed but may be abundant in the appropriate habitat.

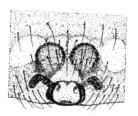 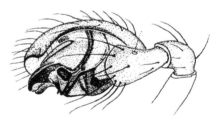

Theridion pallens Blackwall 1834 (= *Paidiscura p.* (Blackwall))   Plate 25
Description ♀, 1.7–1.75mm; ♂, 1.25–1.5mm. Both sexes are illustrated and, although somewhat variable in colour and markings, have a distinctive appearance. The epigyne and male palpal organs are also distinctive.
Habitat On low vegetation, bushes and the lower branches of trees. The female makes white egg sacs which carry several pointed projections (Plate 25) and are guarded amongst a few threads under the shelter of a leaf.
Maturity Summer; females throughout winter.
Distribution Common and widespread throughout Britain and northern Europe.

 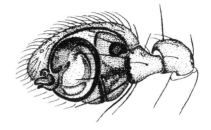

Theridion bimaculatum (Linnaeus 1767)   Plate 25
(= *Neottiura bimaculata* (Linnaeus))
Description ♀, 2.5–3.25mm; ♂, 2.5–3mm. Males are similar to females in general appearance, but have the eye region raised, a pair of long hairs between the anterior eyes, a tubercle in the middle of the sternum and a spur at the base of femur IV. The light median band may be whiter or yellower than illustrated, broader or narrower, and in males it is frequently absent. The epigyne is small, but distinctive. The male palpal organs are relatively large and the overall structure is discernible with a lens.
Habitat On low vegetation, bushes and the lower branches of trees. The female carries her large white egg sac attached to the spinners.
Maturity Summer; females to autumn.
Distribution Widespread throughout Britain and northern Europe. Very locally distributed, but then often present in very large numbers.

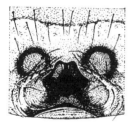 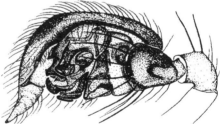

Genus *Enoplognatha*

Eight species of *Enoplognatha* are recorded from northern Europe, seven of which are described here. There has been confusion over the identity of a few rare species and the names used for some have changed several times in the last decade. In addition, one common *Enoplognatha* was found to comprise two species and first recognized in Britain as late as 1983. In view of this, the distribution of some species is uncertain. The genus contains species which differ considerably from one another. One of the commonest, *E. ovata*, is pale and long-legged, sometimes with red markings, whilst another is black and superficially resembles a money spider (Linyphiidae). Males of all species have elongate chelicerae which bear two or three teeth. The commonest species live on vegetation, others at ground level. The epigynes are relatively small and the male palpal organs of similar structure, but the commonest species are separable with a field microscope.

Enoplognatha ovata (Clerck 1757)   Plate 25

Description ♀, 4–6mm; ♂, 3–5mm. Both sexes and three colour forms are illustrated. The paired black spots are always present but, *in either sex*, the abdomen may be entirely pale yellow-green, or marked with a pair of red stripes, or have a single broad red band. The sternum is pale yellow with a narrow black median line and black margins. The male chelicerae are enlarged and divergent. The epigyne is similar to that of *E. latimana* (below), but differs in the shape of the posterior margin and lacks the sclerotized ridges on each side. The male palpal organs are most easily distinguished by the form of the hooked conductor (near the tip of the palp) which has the tip directed downwards.

Habitat On low vegetation and bushes. The female makes a bluish egg sac (Plate 25) which is guarded under cover of a leaf; the latter is often slightly rolled, with silk threads spanning across the edges. **Maturity** Summer.

Distribution Very common and widespread throughout Britain and northern Europe.

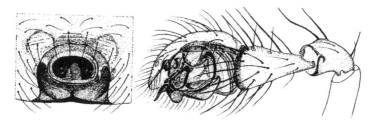

Enoplognatha latimana Hippa & Oksala 1982

Description ♀, 4–6mm; ♂, 3–5mm. Very similar to *E. ovata* in general appearance, but usually without red markings and with fewer, or no black spots. The epigyne is distinguished from that of *E. ovata* by the shape of the posterior margin, which also extends on each side to form sclerotized ridges. The male palpal organs are most easily distinguished by the hooked conductor (near the tip of the palp) which has the tip directed upwards.

Habitat and Maturity Similar to *E. ovata*.

Distribution Less common than *E. ovata* and perhaps more frequent in the south of England and Wales. Widespread throughout northern Europe.

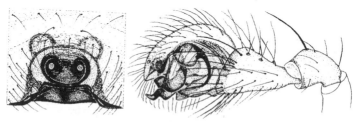

Enoplognatha thoracica (Hahn 1833)

Description ♀, 3.5–4mm; ♂, 2.5–3mm. This species is dark, sometimes almost completely black, and not unlike the illustration of *Robertus lividus* (Plate 25); but the tibiae have two dorsal spines and the difference in colour between the femora and tarsi is generally less obvious. Males have enlarged chelicerae and an abdominal scutum (the latter not easily seen). The epigyne and male palp are distinctive, although the former can be very dark and the structures difficult to make out.

Habitat Under stones and detritus in a variety of habitats, including woodland and heathland. Females usually found with whitish egg sacs in late summer and autumn,

Maturity Summer to autumn.

Distribution Fairly common and widespread throughout Britain and northern Europe.

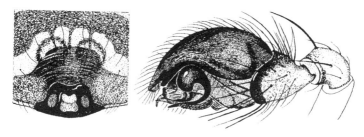

Enoplognatha mordax (Thorell 1875) (= *E. crucifera* (Thorell) and *E. schaufussi* (L. Koch))

Description ♀, 3.5–4.5mm; ♂, 3–3.5mm. The carapace is yellow to brown with few markings. The abdomen has a clear leaf-like pattern with dark edges; it is not unlike that of *Zygiella x-notata* (Plate 29) except that the edges have sharper black points and, in the midline, there is a dark line flanked by white spots. The underside of the abdomen is black, with a pair of longitudinal white lines. Males have enlarged chelicerae. The epigyne is distinctive, as are the male palpal organs.

Habitat At ground level in sandy areas and saltmarshes on the coast.

Maturity Summer.

Distribution Rare in Britain but recorded from coastal sites in southern England, East Anglia, south Wales and south-west Scotland. Rare, but probably widespread in northern Europe.

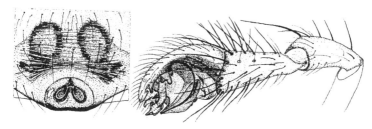

Enoplognatha tecta (Keyserling 1884)

Description ♀, 4.5–6mm; ♂, 4–4.5mm. Similar to *E. mordax* (above) and *E. oelandica* (Plate 25) but markings less clear and greyish-brown. There is a dark midline mark on the abdomen, dorsally, which is flanked by white spots; additionally, there is a pair of dark patches anteriorly and a single dark patch in the posterior mid-line. Ventrally, the abdomen has scattered white spots, but no paired longitudinal white lines (cf. *E. mordax*) or large white square (cf. *E. oelandica*). Males have enlarged chelicerae. The epigyne and male palpal organs are distinctive.

Habitat At ground level in marshy habitats. **Maturity** Summer.

Distribution Extremely rare in Britain and recorded from one locality in southern England. Rare in northern Europe but recorded from France and Germany.

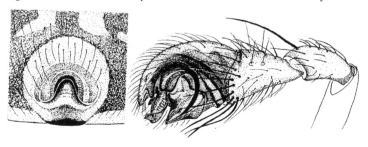

Enoplognatha oelandica (Thorell 1875)   Plate 25

(Note: this species used to be known as *E. mandibularis* in Britain. The latter is not a synonym, but a different species, described below. In previous work, my illustration of the male palp of *E. oelandica* is in fact of *E. mandibularis*. There were no British males available at the time, and the French specimen turns out to have been *E. mandibularis*. Since then a British male has been found and is illustrated here. I thank J. Murphy for bringing this to my attention and R.D. Jones for the loan of the single British specimen.)

Description ♀, 3–5mm; ♂, 2.5–3mm. Male similar to the female illustrated but with clearer markings. The white spots on the ventral side of the abdomen form a large square in the midline. Males have enlarged chelicerae. The epigyne and male palpal organs are distinctive.

Habitat On sand dunes and dry, sandy heathland; under stones or amongst vegetation. **Maturity** Summer to autumn.

Distribution Very rare in Britain, with a few records from the south and south-east of England. Possibly widespread in northern Europe, but previous identification problems make records uncertain.

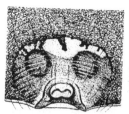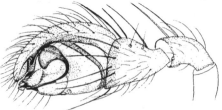

△ *Enoplognatha mandibularis* (Lucas 1846)
Description ♀, 4–6mm; ♂, 3–4mm. Similar to *E. oelandica*, but the ventral side of the abdomen lacks a well-defined white square (at least in all specimens seen). Males have enlarged chelicerae. The epigyne and male palpal organs are distinctive (but the latter were illustrated as *E. oelandica* in my previous work).
Habitat and Maturity Possibly similar to *E. oelandica*.
Distribution Absent from Britain. Possibly widespread but rare in the more southerly parts of northern Europe, but records probably unreliable.

Genus *Robertus*

Nine species of *Robertus* are known to occur in northern Europe, of which four of the most widespread are described here. They all have a greyish, unicolorous abdomen which usually bears two or three pairs of reddish impressed spots; the latter are also conspicuous in some 'money spiders' (Linyphiidae). Although superficially having the appearance of a 'money spider', species of *Robertus* can usually be distinguished in the field by the tarsi, which are appreciably darker than the femora. The difference is subtle (compare *R. lividus* (Plate 25) with *Dismodicus bifrons* (Plate 30) but seems surprisingly reliable. However, examination of the epigyne and male palpal organs is necessary to confirm the identity of both genus and species. The chelicerae are relatively robust in both sexes, but those of males are not enlarged. The species live at ground level, under stones and detritus and amongst leaf-litter and moss.

Robertus lividus (Blackwall 1836)   Plate 25
Description ♀♂, 2.5–4mm. Male similar to the female illustrated, but with a smaller abdomen. Some specimens have the abdomen a paler greenish-grey with the reddish spots more conspicuous. The epigyne of this species is usually discernible with a lens; the male palpal organs are fairly large and can also often be identified in the same way. With higher magnification there should be no problem with this or the other species.

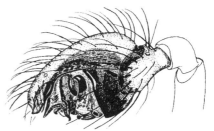

Habitat Under stones and detritus, amongst grass and moss and in leaf-litter; in a variety of habitats, including woodland and high, open moorland. **Maturity** All year. **Distribution** By far the commonest species; widespread throughout Britain and northern Europe.

Robertus arundineti (O.P.-Cambridge 1871)
Description ♀, 2.25–2.5mm; ♂, 2–2.25mm. Similar to *R. lividus* in general appearance, but smaller. Epigyne and male palpal organs distinctive.
Habitat Under stones and detritus, amongst grass, leaf-litter and moss; sometimes in marshy habitats. **Maturity** Possibly all year.
Distribution Widespread throughout Britain and northern Europe but generally rather uncommon.

 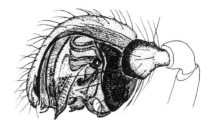

Robertus neglectus (O.P.-Cambridge 1871)
Description ♀, 2–2.25mm; ♂, 1.75–2mm. Similar to *R. lividus* in general appearance, but smaller than that species, and *R. arundineti*. The epigyne and male palpal organs are distinctive.
Habitat and Maturity Similar to *R. lividus*.
Distribution Widespread throughout Britain and northern Europe but generally uncommon.

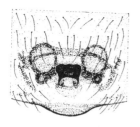 

Robertus scoticus Jackson 1914
Description ♀, 2mm; ♂, 1.75–2mm. Similar to the foregoing species in general appearance, but smaller still. The epigyne and male palpal organs are distinctive.
Habitat Amongst moss, grass, pine needles and detritus in damp habitats.
Maturity Summer to late autumn, possibly all year.

Distribution Rare in Britain and recorded from two adjacent areas of Caledonian pine forest in Scotland. Widespread in northern Europe, but generally rare.

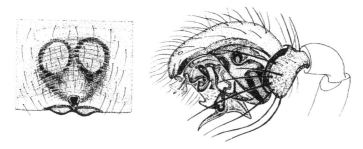

Genus *Pholcomma*

There is only one species of *Pholcomma* in northern Europe. The female has a very globular, black abdomen but can only be distinguished with certainty from the 'money spiders' (Linyphiidae) by examination of the eyes and epigyne. The male is easily recognised by the abdominal scuta. The species is found mainly at ground level and little is known of the biology.

Pholcomma gibbum (Westring 1851)
Description ♀ ♂, 1.25–1.5mm. Both sexes, and the arrangement of the eyes, are illustrated in the Key to the Genera (p. 264). Despite its small size, the male can be identified in the field with a lens. Higher magnification is required for examination of the eyes, epigyne and male palpal organs which are very distinctive.
Habitat Usually found at ground level amongst moss, grass and detritus in a wide variety of habitats. I have seen both sexes high up on the heads of grasses at night.
Maturity Late summer to spring, females perhaps all year.
Distribution Common and widespread throughout Britain and northern Europe.

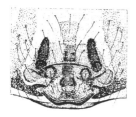

Genus *Theonoe*

A single species of *Theonoe* occurs in northern Europe. It has the appearance of a very small 'money spider' (Linyphiidae) and higher magnification is necessary for identification even to family level. Little is known of the biology.

Theonoe minutissima (O.P.-Cambridge 1879)

Description ♀♂, 1–1.25mm. This small species has a yellowish-brown to deep orange-brown carapace and legs. The abdomen is greyish, with no pattern, and there are two pairs of reddish impressed spots – fairly large in males but often absent in females. The epigyne and male palpal organs are distinctive.

Habitat At ground level, under stones, amongst detritus, grass and moss in a variety of habitats including woodland, heathland, on high ground and in sphagnum bogs. **Maturity** Summer to autumn.

Distribution Uncommon, but perhaps frequently overlooked. Widespread throughout Britain and northern Europe.

 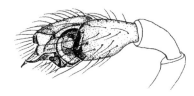

FAMILY NESTICIDAE

This family is represented in northern Europe by the single genus *Nesticus*. The genus *Eidmanella* is not part of the European fauna, but one species *Eidmanella pallida* is occasionally imported with plants from the Western Hemisphere (Mexico, southern U.S.A. and the West Indies) and specimens have been found in hothouses. There seems to be no evidence that the species has become properly established either in Britain or in the rest of northern Europe.

Genus *Nesticus*

Two species of *Nesticus* are known to occur in Europe and only one, *Nesticus cellulanus*, in northern Europe. The species resembles members of the Theridiidae and has a comb of serrated bristles on tarsus IV, but has the front margin of the labium rather swollen and sausage-like (see Family Key, p. 54). Although these characters are not easily seen with a lens, the general appearance of the spider, combined with the habitat, allow relatively easy recognition of the species. The male palpal organs have a large curved structure called the paracymbium arising near the joint with the tibia and projecting upwards and forwards. This is easily seen with a ×10 lens and the epigyne of females is also clearly discernible if not too deeply sclerotized.

    The species makes a fine web of criss-cross threads in dark, damp situations. The threads have gummy droplets near their point of attachment as in the Theridiidae,

Nesticus cellulanus ♀ with egg sac

and prey seems to consist mainly of crawling insects. The two sexes are similar in general appearance, the male having a slimmer abdomen. Courtship and mating appear to be very brief. Females carry their egg sac attached to the spinners and probably produce several sacs. Sometimes these are very large, their diameter exceeding the length of the spider, but later in the year females may be found with sacs scarcely bigger than the abdomen. The general appearance of the spider, the dark, damp habitat and the method of carrying the egg sac could, rarely, lead to confusion with *Theridion bellicosum* (Plate 24, p. 288), but the latter species is half the size and lacks markings on the legs.

Nesticus cellulanus (Clerck 1757)   Plate 25
Description ♀, 3.5–6mm; ♂, 3–5mm. The abdominal pattern is generally as illustrated, but some specimens may have the markings broken up or even absent. The carapace markings are fairly constant and the legs are usually clearly annulated, but sometimes more, sometimes less than illustrated. The epigyne and male palpal organs are highly distinctive.
Habitat In damp, dark habitats, indoors and outside – cellars, caves, drains, sewers, trenches with overhanging vegetation, cavities under boulders and in suitable dark, damp spots in woodland. They also seem to like living under dumped sheets of corrugated iron. **Maturity** Summer to autumn, females probably all year.
Distribution Locally distributed, but then often abundant. Widespread throughout Britain and northern Europe.

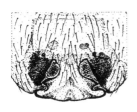
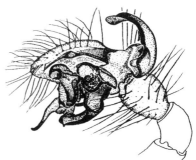

FAMILY THERIDIOSOMATIDAE
Genus *Theridiosoma*
There is one European member of the Theridiosomatidae, in the genus *Theridiosoma*, and it has the general appearance of a small theridiid. *Theridiosoma gemmosum* is a rare species with a globular, silvery abdomen and femur I about twice as thick as femur IV when viewed from the side. A single spine is present on femur I. It is further distinguished from members of the Araneidae and Theridiidae by the absence of a claw on the female palp. The small orb web has the radii joined in groups of two or three before meeting at the centre. The spider sits at the centre, facing away from the web, holding a thread which runs to adjacent vegetation. This thread is pulled taut and the web assumes the shape of an umbrella turned inside-out

(see Webs, p. 68). When an insect is snared, the supporting thread is slackened and the prey becomes more entangled. The sexes are similar in general appearance and the male palps are relatively large. The stalked egg sacs are suspended from vegetation, usually higher up than the web (see Egg Sacs, p. 59).

Theridiosoma gemmosum (L. Koch 1877)　　　　　　　　　　　Plate 25
Description ♀, 2–3mm; ♂, 1.5–2mm. The globular, silvery abdomen is distinctive in both sexes, although the dark markings and reticulations are somewhat variable. The epigyne is distinctive, but may sometimes be covered by a transparent membrane. The male palpal organs are easily recognizable.
Habitat Amongst low vegetation in damp habitats. **Maturity** Summer.
Distribution Rare and recorded from localities in south and south-east England, south Wales and the south of Ireland. Rare in northern Europe and recorded from France, Holland and Germany.

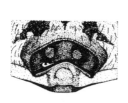
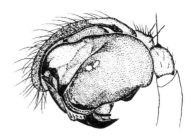

FAMILY TETRAGNATHIDAE

This family is represented in Europe by sixteen species in three genera; fifteen species are described here. The genus *Meta* has in recent years been split into *Meta* and *Metellina* by some authors and assigned to a separate family – Metidae. In my view, this move is incorrect; it may well be reversed in the future, and is not followed here. The species of *Meta* and *Metellina* are far more closely related than many species in other genera and their correct placement in the Tetragnathidae carries little doubt when one considers the structure of the epigynes, male palpal organs and webs. The abdominal patterns of the commoner species of *Meta* are very similar to *Tetragnatha* (but less elongate) and males even adopt the same pose along the stems of vegetation, with the long legs stretched out. The genus *Zygiella* has also recently been assigned to the Tetragnathidae but further study has led me to the view that it sits uneasily anywhere other than in the Araneidae.

Most species spin orb webs with a small hole in the hub (see Webs, p. 69), but older spiderlings and adults of *Pachygnatha* abandon web spinning and hunt at ground level. Species of *Tetragnatha* are elongate spiders with long chelicerae and legs; *Pachygnatha* species are of more 'normal' proportions but have large chelicerae which are elongate in males; *Meta* species are also more normally proportioned without enlarged chelicerae, but the males of some species are long-legged. All have relatively simple epigynes and male palpal organs which are very similar in design and function. The maxillae are longer than broad in all species (see Family Key, p. 55). The genera are easily separated, using a lens and the following key.

Key to the Genera

1. Abdomen and legs very long and thin. Chelicerae long and
   divergent with many teeth   *Tetragnatha* p. 301

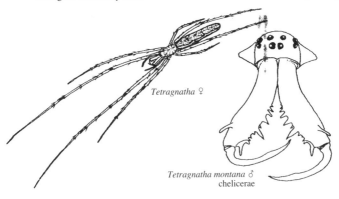

Tetragnatha ♀

Tetragnatha montana ♂
chelicerae

   Abdomen not elongate. Legs sometimes long. Chelicerae
   sometimes elongate   2

2. Legs with no spines, or just one
   on each patella. Chelicerae
   robust, sometimes elongate   *Pachygnatha* p. 300

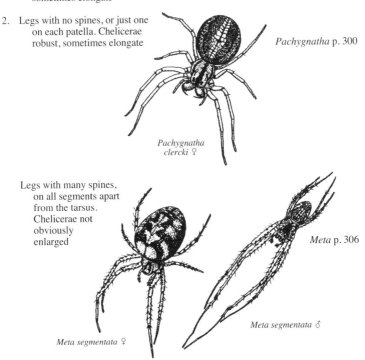

*Pachygnatha
clercki* ♀

   Legs with many spines,
   on all segments apart
   from the tarsus.
   Chelicerae not
   obviously
   enlarged   *Meta* p. 306

Meta segmentata ♂

Meta segmentata ♀

Genus *Pachygnatha*

All three European species of *Pachygnatha* are described here. They are found at ground level during the daytime, and although young spiderlings have been shown to make small orb webs near the ground, adults seem not to make webs at all. However, adults of all three species may be found quite high up on vegetation at night, often trailing large numbers of silk threads. Males have elongate, divergent chelicerae which hold those of the female during mating. The species are identifiable with a lens in the field on the basis of general appearance and size. Confirmation of identity is afforded by examination of the epigyne and male palpal organs.

Pachygnatha clercki Sundevall 1823   Plate 26
Description ♀, 6–7mm; ♂, 5–6mm. The male has a slimmer abdomen than the female illustrated, with a much clearer light midline stripe surrounded by a darker folium. The chelicerae are enlarged in the male and the fang has a shallow tooth-like projection which curves out from the inner edge. The epigyne is a lightly sclerotized transverse slit and the male palpal organs are distinctive.
Habitat Amongst low vegetation, moss, and leaf-litter in damp habitats. Higher up on vegetation at night. **Maturity** All year.
Distribution Fairly common; widespread throughout Britain and northern Europe.

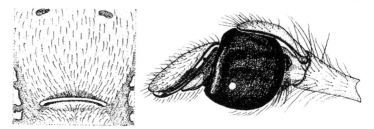

Pachygnatha listeri Sundevall 1830   Plate 26
Description ♀, 3.5–5mm; ♂, 3–4.5mm. Female similar to *P. clercki* but smaller and with a browner folium and less distinct light midline marks. The male sometimes has an even darker abdomen than illustrated, lacks the clear, light midline stripe present in *P. clercki* and is smaller than this species. The cheliceral fang lacks the projection on the inner edge which is obvious in males of *P. clercki*. The epigyne is a sclerotized tongue, visible with a lens. The male palpal organs are distinctive.
Habitat Almost always in leaf-litter in woods. Higher up on vegetation at night.

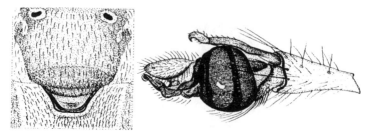

Maturity All year.
Distribution Less common than *P. clercki*; more locally distributed, but then often abundant. Widespread throughout Britain and northern Europe.

Pachygnatha degeeri Sundevall 1830   Plate 26
Description ♀, 3–3.75mm; ♂, 2.5–3mm. The carapace is darker in this species and the legs contrastingly lighter. The abdominal markings are distinctive and similar in both sexes, but may be more greenish or reddish than illustrated. The species is also smaller than the other two. The epigyne is a lightly sclerotized transverse slit but the male palpal organs are distinctive.
Habitat Usually amongst grass and low vegetation in a very wide variety of habitats (the largest number I have encountered in one spot were in brick rubble on a derelict industrial site!) **Maturity** All year.
Distribution The commonest species of the genus; widespread throughout Britain and northern Europe.

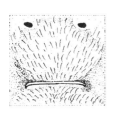 

Genus *Tetragnatha*

Seven of the eight European species of *Tetragnatha* are described here. Their extremely elongate appearance, long legs and enlarged chelicerae make them easily recognizable in the field. All species spin delicate-looking orb webs with relatively few radii, widely spaced spirals and a hole at the hub (see Webs, p. 68). The commoner species are usually found on vegetation near water or at least on boggy ground. There is no signal line leading from the centre of the web and no retreat. The spiders are often found sitting in the centre of the web, particularly at night. When alarmed, they leave the web and stretch themselves out along blades of grass or stems, thus becoming very inconspicuous. The name *Tetragnatha* means 'four-jawed' – in addition to having a pair of long divergent chelicerae, the maxillae are also almost as long and divergent, giving the appearance of four jaws. The chelicerae of males are often even longer than in females; they are used in mating, when the sexes meet head on, with little apparent courtship, and lock the chelicerae together using the fangs and various projections. The egg sacs are fastened to a leaf or stem and frequently look like a fragment of mould or bird-dropping (see Egg Sacs, p. 59).

The epigynes take the form of a broad, hairy tongue, projecting posteriorly from the epigastric fold. The shape of this projection, the overall size of adult females and their general appearance is usually sufficient to enable identification. Unfortunately it is sometimes difficult, especially for the beginner, to know for sure whether females are fully adult, since subadults also have a (smaller) projecting structure. In case of difficulty, the epigyne of preserved specimens should be removed and the spermathecae examined from behind (or cleared by immersion in clove oil).

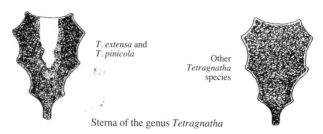

T. extensa and
T. pinicola

Other
Tetragnatha
species

Sterna of the genus *Tetragnatha*

Illustrations of these structures are given below each epigyne. The male palpal organs are mostly very similar to one another but are distinguished by the structures leading up to and including the tip (view from exactly the same angle as the illustrations) and by the shape and proportions of the other structures. All of this will require higher magnification than a lens.

The species are conveniently split into two groups on the basis of markings on the sternum (illustrated): in *T. extensa* and *T. pinicola* there is a distinct light mark in the midline; the rest of the species lack a light mark. **The commonest two species are *T. extensa* and *T. montana* and many specimens of these are likely to be encountered before any of the others.**

Tetragnatha extensa (Linnaeus 1758)   Plate 26

Description ♀, 6.5–11mm; ♂, 6–9mm. Both sexes have a light midline mark on the sternum. Males are similar to the female illustrated, but have a slimmer abdomen and slightly larger chelicerae. The colour of the abdomen varies somewhat and some specimens may be more yellowish or greenish. The shape of the epigyne is usually distinctive, as is the tip of the male palpal organs.

Habitat On grasses and other low vegetation close to water or in boggy habitats.

Maturity Summer.

Distribution Common and widespread throughout Britain and northern Europe.

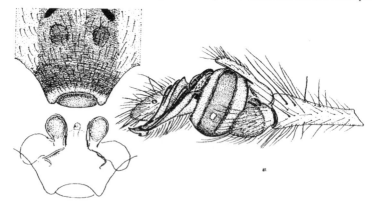

Tetragnatha pinicola L. Koch 1870
Description ♀, 5–6mm; ♂, 4.5–5mm. This species, like *T. extensa*, has a light midline mark on the sternum, but is smaller. The problem lies in distinguishing females from juveniles and subadults of *T. extensa*. However, the dorsum of the abdomen in *T. pinicola* is very silvery – not just spots of silver but a uniform sheet with very fine reticulations – and the spider has thinner legs. If the specimen fits this size and description it can be reliably distinguished from adult and immature females of *T. extensa* by measuring the relative width of femur I and length of femur III (with a microscope eyepiece scale), when the ratio femur I width/femur III length is less than 0.176 in *T. pinicola* (more than 0.205 in *T. extensa*). The spermathecae are clearly different in *T. pinicola* and males are distinguished by size (adulthood being obvious) and the tip of the palpal organs.
Habitat Usually on trees, occasionally on low vegetation, and often away from water. **Maturity** Summer.
Distribution Most records are from southern England, but has been recorded from Cumbria. Possibly widely distributed, but rare, and many old records are uncertain. Widespread in northern Europe but generally uncommon or rare.

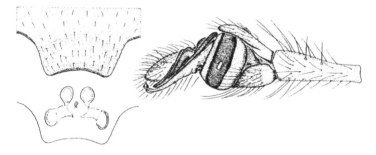

Tetragnatha montana Simon 1874   Plate 26
Description ♀, 6.5–11mm; ♂, 6–9mm. Females similar to the male illustrated, but with slightly smaller chelicerae and abdomen. The sternum is uniformly brownish with

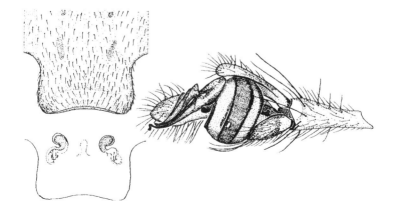

no light median mark. The species is generally larger than *T. obtusa* and does not have the head region of the carapace darkened; it is lighter than *T. nigrita* but very similar to *T. dearmata*. The epigyne is generally distinctive as are the male palpal organs. **Habitat** On low vegetation, bushes and trees; sometimes near water, but also occurs further away from water than *T. extensa*. **Maturity** Summer.

Distribution Common and widespread throughout Britain and northern Europe.

Tetragnatha obtusa C.L. Koch 1837

Description ♀, 5–7mm; ♂, 3.5–5.5mm. This species has the head region of the carapace distinctly darker, forming a dark triangular region which comes to a point near the fovea. This is distinctive in the field but fades somewhat in preserved specimens. The abdominal pattern usually has clear dark margins and is constricted near the midpoint. The epigyne is not always easily distinguished, but the spermathecae are quite different from the other species. The male palpal organs are distinctive.

Habitat On trees in damp woodland; also on pines near heathland. **Maturity** Summer.

Distribution Widespread, but very locally distributed in England, Wales and southern Ireland; generally rare or absent in large parts of Scotland and Northern Ireland. Widespread in the rest of northern Europe.

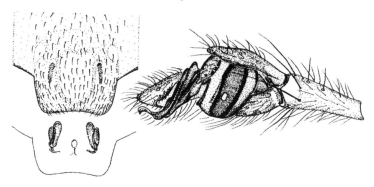

Tetragnatha nigrita Lendl 1886   Plate 26

Description ♀, 7–10mm; ♂, 5–8mm. Females are similar to the male illustrated but have slightly smaller chelicerae and sometimes have more distinct white markings at the edge of the folium. The species is overall much darker than the others and the

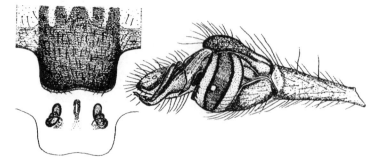

epigyne, spermathecae and male palpal organs are distinctive.
Habitat Generally on trees. **Maturity** Summer.
Distribution Generally rare and recorded from the southern half of England and Ireland. Uncommon but widespread in northern Europe.

△ *Tetragnatha dearmata* Thorell 1873
Description ♀, 8–10mm; ♂, 6–8mm. Similar in general appearance to *T. montana*. The epigyne is generally distinctly different from that of *T. montana*, as are the male palpal organs.
Habitat Generally on trees, especially pines. **Maturity** Summer.
Distribution Absent from Britain. Widespread in northern Europe.

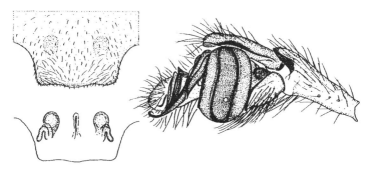

Tetragnatha striata L. Koch 1862
Description ♀, 8.5–12mm; ♂, 8–10mm. The female is illustrated between the epigyne and male palp and shows the camouflage position sometimes adopted by all

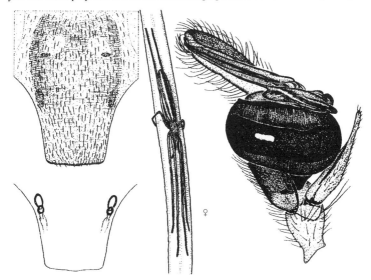

species of *Tetragnatha* (and males of *Meta*). The epigyne and male palpal organs are very distinctive in this species.

Habitat On reeds and other vegetation in or very close to water. **Maturity** Summer. **Distribution** Rare and very locally distributed, with records from relatively few localities scattered throughout England, Wales and Ireland. Widespread but uncommon throughout the rest of northern Europe.

Genus *Meta*

This genus contains five European species, all of which are described here. The genus has sometimes been assigned to a separate family, Metidae, and the three commonest species (*M. segmentata, M. mengei, M. merianae*) to a separate genus, *Metellina*.

Meta segmentata and *M. mengei* are probably the most common and abundant orb-weaving spiders in northern Europe. The web has a small hole at the hub, has more radii, and spirals more closely set, than in *Tetragnatha*, and is relatively small compared to the size of spider (see Webs, p. 69). There is no signal thread leading

Meta menardi ♀ with egg sac

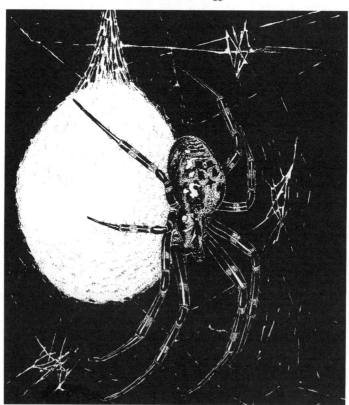

away from the hub and no retreat. *M. merianae* is also common, but only in shaded, damp situations, and spins a much finer, larger web similar to that of *Tetragnatha* species. *Meta menardi* and *M. bourneti* are larger, brownish spiders which live in completely dark habitats.

Males of *M. segmentata* and *M. mengei* are very commonly seen (at the appropriate season) close by the edge of the females' webs. The first two pairs of legs are rather long; when disturbed they stretch themselves out along vegetation like species of *Tetragnatha*. Females will also do this, but less readily, and the more rotund abdomen reduces the camouflage effect. Males of *Tetragnatha* and *Pachygnatha* hold the chelicerae of the female with their own whilst mating. In *Meta* courtship and mating are triggered by the female catching prey and the male approaches her only when she and her chelicerae are busily engaged in feeding on the wrapped insect. Egg sacs are roughly spherical and attached, near the web, to vegetation or bark. The egg sacs of the two cave-dwelling species are relatively large and suspended on silk threads; sometimes large numbers are seen in caves, and when on the ceiling, appear like miniature light bulbs.

The genus is easily recognizable with a lens and the species are also identifiable in this way – although higher magnification is required to see details of the epigynes and male palpal organs. Males resemble females but have a smaller abdomen and the first two pairs of legs are much longer.

Meta segmentata (Clerck 1757) (= *Metellina s.* (Clerck))
Description ♀, 4–8mm; ♂, 4–6mm. Very similar to *M. mengei* in general appearance, and equally variable in colour and markings. Generally, the anterior part of the abdominal pattern is a little darker and more angular, enclosing more clearly defined lighter triangles, but this is not reliable and may also occur in *M. mengei*. The illustration of *M. segmentata* catching a fly shows the underside of the female spider,

Meta segmentata ♀

which has a dark median band flanked by a pair of light bands. In females of *M. segmentata*, the dark midline band does not extend forwards beyond the epigyne. The latter is distinguished by the dark line curving from below each spermatheca and out along the line of the epigastric fold. There are no dark markings anterior to the epigyne. Males are distinguished with a lens by the absence of long ventral hairs on metatarsus and tarsus I, and, at higher magnification, by the form of the palpal organs. The season of maturity also gives a guide (not infallible) to identity.

Habitat On vegetation or anything else which will support the orb web, from near ground level up to about 2m above. **Maturity** Late summer to late autumn.

Distribution Abundant throughout Britain and northern Europe.

♂ metatarsus and tarsus I

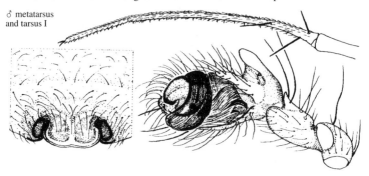

Meta mengei (Blackwall 1869) (= *Metellina m.* (Blackwall))   Plate 26

Description ♀, 3.5–6mm; ♂, 3.5–5mm. Both sexes are illustrated but are just as variable in colour and markings as *M. segmentata*. In females, the dark midline band on the underside of the abdomen extends forwards beyond the epigyne (cf. *M. segmentata*). This is seen on the illustration of the epigyne. The latter is distinguished by the dark mark projecting from below each spermatheca, which does not curve around to join the epigastric fold. Males are easily distinguished with a lens in the field by the long ventral hairs on metatarsus I and II and, at higher magnification, by the form of the palpal organs. The season of maturity gives a guide to possible identity and 'm' before 's' makes this easily remembered.

Habitat Similar to *M. segmentata*. **Maturity** Most numerous in spring to early summer, but may be found at all times of the year.

♂ metatarsus and tarsus I

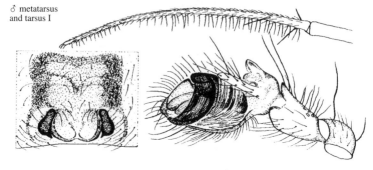

Distribution Abundant throughout Britain and northern Europe.
Meta merianae (Scopoli 1763) (= *Metellina m.* (Scopoli))   Plate 26
Description ♀, 5.5–9mm; ♂, 4.5–7.5mm. Males similar to the female illustrated, but having a smaller abdomen and longer front legs. The markings are generally as illustrated, and those on the carapace and legs are particularly constant. The abdomen occasionally has a broad, cream-coloured longitudinal band in the midline which can be very striking (present to a variable degree in less than 0.5% of specimens examined). The spider is distinctive enough to be identifiable on general appearance. The paracymbium on the male palp is visible with a lens, but higher magnification is required to see details of the epigyne and male palpal organs.
Habitat Always in damp, shaded sites – overhanging vegetation by streams and ditches, under bridges, at the threshold zone of caves and other holes, and in darker parts of damp woodland. The web is relatively fine, more like those of *Tetragnatha*.
Maturity Spring and summer, females to autumn.

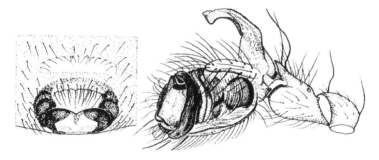

Distribution Common and widespread throughout Britain and northern Europe.
Meta menardi (Latreille 1804)   Plate 27
Description ♀, 12–15mm; ♂, 10–11mm. Males similar to the female illustrated but with a slimmer abdomen and longer legs. Female and egg sac also illustrated on p. 306. The epigyne and male palpal organs are similar to those of *M. bourneti* but can usually be distinguished with a lens (easily with higher magnification).
Habitat Usually in situations of total darkness – the deep interior of caves, culverts, ice-houses, Nissen huts, sewers, and in the middle portion of long railway tunnels.
Maturity All year.
Distribution Widespread throughout Britain and northern Europe. Common in

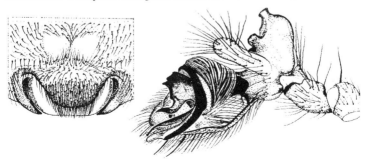

Meta bourneti Simon 1922
Description ♀, 13–16mm; ♂, 10–13mm. Very similar to *M. menardi* in general appearance, although the legs are not usually annulated. Distinguishable only by the epigyne and male palpal organs – usually with a lens, but easily with higher magnification.
Habitat and Maturity Similar to *M. menardi*.
Distribution Supposedly rare, with relatively few records from England and Wales. However, I rather suspect that the species is sometimes overlooked and is under-recorded – I know that some experienced arachnologists never bother to examine specimens fully and just assume them to be *M. menardi*. This applies equally to the rest of northern Europe.

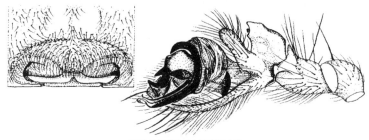

FAMILY ARANEIDAE

This family is represented in northern Europe by seventeen genera; of the fifty known species, forty of the most widely distributed are described. The genus *Zygiella* has sometimes been assigned to the family *Tetragnathidae* but this is not accepted here; despite certain anomalies, the genus sits uneasily anywhere other than in the Araneidae. The two species in the genus *Atea* should, I believe, be assigned to *Araneus* but are here considered separately to avoid undue confusion with other literature.

The small height of the clypeus, the lateral condyle on the chelicerae and the auxiliary foot claws are illustrated in the Family Key (pp. 51–6). The species spin orb webs with a closed hub, the hole having been filled with a lattice of silk threads (see Webs, p. 70). A strong signal thread leads from the hub to a retreat amongst nearby vegetation or other structures, the spider waiting there and rushing down into the web in response to vibrations from ensnared prey. *Cercidia* is an exception in spinning a web with an open hub and no retreat, *Zilla* has a closed hub and no retreat, and the webs of some *Araniella* often scarcely resemble an orb web when made within the confines of a curled leaf. Araneids generally have a number of strong teeth on the chelicerae and prey is chewed and mashed with digestive juices. The end result is an unrecognizable pellet of insect remains, as opposed to the near-perfect, sucked-out husks left by theridiids and thomisids.

Males resemble females in patterns and markings, but have a much smaller abdomen; the carapace is sometimes rather narrower at the front, and the front legs may be furnished with stout spines. Courtship involves the male plucking and jerking the web of the female, which usually results in her adopting the mating position with little delay. After mating, the male usually manages to escape and subsequently mate again. Eventually, males become less adept with age and are sometimes eaten by females. In *Argiope*, the female usually starts to eat the diminutive male during mating, and this occurs as normal practice in some other araneids not found in the region.

The following key should allow relatively easy identification of the genus with adult specimens; reference to Plates 27–30 will provide clarification and may allow identification of immatures to genus level.

Key to the Genera

1. Posterior row of eyes distinctly procurved when viewed directly from above. Abdomen of female distinctively marked with transverse black stripes and alternate white and yellow stripes between. Female quite large (11–15mm, or more if well fed and full of eggs); male much smaller (4–4.5mm) with an elongate, brownish abdomen   *Argiope* p. 338

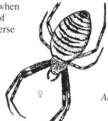

   Posterior row of eyes straight or recurved. Spider with different abdominal markings. Less disparity in size between the sexes   2

2. Abdomen with black markings which in the midline are shaped rather like a cricket bat   *Mangora* p. 337

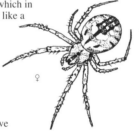

   Abdominal markings not as above   3

3. Abdomen oval, longer than wide, and distinctly pointed at the front end   4

   Abdomen possibly oval, but not distinctly pointed at the front end. May possibly be pointed at the rear end   5

4. Size of adult spider 3–5mm. Abdomen reddish-brown with lighter reticulated areas and dark bars. Three or four short, dark spines present on each side of the pointed front end   *Cercidia* p. 326

   Size of adult spider 7–14mm. Abdomen with clear lobed pattern of white in the midline, surrounded by dark marbling on a pale yellowish background   Δ *Aculepeira* p. 324

5.   Abdomen oval, bright green or yellow-green,
         with paired black spots in the rear half,
         which are often surrounded by white.
         Often with a red spot just above the
         spinners. (Only very rarely with a
         clear pattern and this usually reddish,
         yellow-green and white). Adult size
         3.5–10mm   ♀   *Araniella* p. 327

     Abdomen not *bright* green; if green at all
         then duller, lacking paired black spots, possibly not oval,
         usually with a distinct pattern, and possibly larger than 10mm   6

6.   Abdomen with one to four conical projections at the rear
         end. (The single tubercle in the male of *C. conica* is   ♀
         often small. This spider has a black carapace
         which is narrow and projecting at the front.
         Femora I and II are pale yellow with the distal
         half black. There is an abdominal pattern and
         the spider is less than 4.5mm long.)   *Cyclosa* p. 336

     Abdomen without projections at the rear end,
         although there may be paired tubercles nearer
         the front   7

7.   Abdomen glossy and oval (or slightly broader at the rear).
         Usually marked with a pair of broad, dark, longitudinal
         bands which are separated and bordered by light areas
         (may be entirely black in male)   8

     Abdomen not particularly glossy. Usually round or slightly
         triangular in shape and, if anything, slightly broader near
         the front end. Markings not as above   9

8.   Posterior median eyes the largest;
         quadrangle formed by the median eyes
         wider behind than in front, or
         rectangular   *Hypsosinga* p. 330

                                            ♀

     Anterior median eyes the largest; quadrangle
         formed by the median eyes wider in front
         than behind.   *Singa* p. 332

                                            ♀

9. Posterior median eyes considerably closer to one another than to laterals   10

Posterior row of eyes more or less equidistant. Spinners of orb webs which almost always have a sector missing   *Zygiella* p. 333

♀

10. Adult size 2–4mm. Distinctive abdominal pattern in both sexes; abdomen greatly overhanging carapace, particularly in female. Male palp with only one patellar spine and no tibial spines. Epigyne with straight, narrow scape (tongue-like process) originating from the anterior part and projecting only slightly beyond the posterior border   *Zilla* p. 326

♀

Generally larger spiders with a different appearance. Male palp with two patellar spines and, possibly, tibial spines. Epigyne with scape arising anteriorly, centrally or from posterior border, but either S-shaped, or not projecting beyond the posterior border, or projecting considerably beyond the posterior border   11

11. Epigyne with a long scape, often wrinkled, originating anteriorly and about twice the length of the rest of the underlying structure. Male palpal organs, viewed from the side, with a distinct hook (terminal apophysis) near the tip   *Araneus* p. 316

♀

Epigyne with a shorter, S-shaped, or less wrinkled scape. Male palpal organs without a distinctly hooked terminal apophysis near the tip   12

12. Epigyne with a short scape (about half the length of the underlying structure) originating anteriorly (never centrally or from the posterior part; it is sometimes torn off during mating). Male palpal organs, viewed from the side, with a bifid structure (median apophysis) projecting below the midpoint

♀

Larinioides p. 321

Epigyne with an S-shaped scape. Male palpal
    organs, viewed from the side, with a structure
    below the midpoint (median apophysis)
    which is trifid at one end and curves to a
    point at the other end.   *Atea* p. 322

Structures not exactly as above   13

13. Spider very dark and with a very flattened
        appearance. Abdominal pattern
        comprising a wide, blackish folium
        edged with white (this border
        sometimes being broken up into
        white spots)   *Nuctenea* p. 319

Spider not like this   14

14. Abdomen with a pair of well-defined
        dorsal tubercles – one on each side
        towards the front end   *Gibbaranea* p. 315

Abdomen lacking tubercles   15

15. Abdomen almost as broad as long; sometimes
        circular from above, sometimes roundly
        triangular. Epigyne broader than long.
        Male palp with a long tibial spine as
        well as patellar spines   *Agalenatea* p. 325

Abdomen longer than wide. Epigyne longer
    than wide. Male palp with no spine on
    the tibia   *Neoscona* p. 323

Genus *Gibbaranea*

Four species of *Gibbaranea* occur in northern Europe, three of which are described here. In both sexes of all species, the abdomen has a pair of conspicuous dorsal tubercles, situated one on each side of the front half. *Araneus angulatus* has similar tubercles and very small tubercles are sometimes apparent in *A. diadematus* but both of these species have very different epigynes and male palpal organs.

Gibbaranea gibbosa (Walckenaer 1802)   Plate 27
Description ♀, 5–7mm; ♂, 4–5mm. Males similar to the female illustrated, but with a smaller abdomen and the median eyes projecting forwards slightly. The epigyne and male palpal organs are distinctive.
Habitat On trees and bushes. **Maturity** Summer.
Distribution Widespread in England and southern Ireland; recorded from Wales and Scotland but much commoner in the southern counties of England. Widespread throughout northern Europe but generally uncommon.

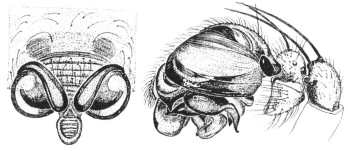

△ *Gibbaranea bituberculata* (Walckenaer 1802)
Description ♀, 5–6mm; ♂, 5mm. This species has a brownish abdomen – not greenish as in *G. gibbosa*. The female resembles *Araneus angulatus* (Plate 27) but has larger abdominal tubercles and is only about half the size. Males are similar, but have a smaller abdomen. The epigyne is similar to that of *G. omoeda* but is easily distinguished by the way in which the central structure curves around to join the anterior margin. Females do not have the median eyes projecting forwards as in *G. omoeda*. The structure of the male palpal organs is distinctive.
Habitat Webs on low vegetation near the ground and in hedgerows. **Maturity** Summer.

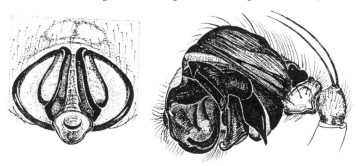

Distribution Was once frequent at one site in Britain – Burnham Beeches, Buckinghamshire. The bushes and other plants supporting this species were cut to the ground in 1954, despite the site having been notified as an SSSI three years earlier. The species is now almost certainly extinct in Britain. Widespread in northern Europe, but generally uncommon.

△ *Gibbaranea omoeda* (Thorell 1870)
Description ♀, 9–10mm; ♂, 7–8mm. The female is illustrated next to the epigyne and male palp, and males are similar, but with a smaller abdomen. The female has the median eyes projecting forwards on a prominent square tubercle. Whilst this is normal in males of all species, it is not a feature of the other *Gibbaranea* females described and seems to be a reliable guide even in immature specimens. The epigyne is distinguished most easily by the way in which the central structure curves around to join the anterior margin. The male palpal organs are distinctive.
Habitat On pine trees, usually high up. **Maturity** Summer.
Distribution Absent from Britain. Widespread throughout northern Europe.

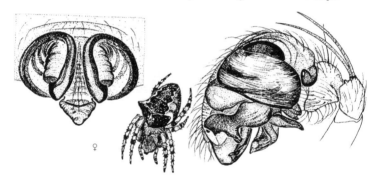

♀

Genus *Araneus*

Nine species of *Araneus* occur in northern Europe and six of the most widespread species are described here. The two species in the genus *Atea* (p. 322) should probably be considered as belonging to *Araneus*.

Araneus diadematus is without doubt the commonest and best known of this genus of orb weavers, and has a distinctive white cross on the abdomen. The species is sometimes known as the 'garden spider', although it is by no means the commonest spider in gardens and is generally commoner on gorse bushes away from human influence. The abdominal markings have given rise to the names of 'diadem spider' and 'cross spider'; the latter seems to have unduly vexatious implications. In Denmark the species is known as the 'korsedderkop' and in Germany the all-embracing name 'Gartenkreuzspinne' is used. Whatever you want to call it, it is a good species in which to observe web-building, prey capture and mating. The female places her spherical egg sac in a sheltered spot, remaining with it until she dies in late autumn. The spiderlings emerge the following May and, initially, cluster together in a fuzzy ball which 'explodes' on the slightest disturbance (see Egg Sacs, p. 60).

Araneus angulatus Clerck 1757   Plate 27

Description ♀, 12–19mm; ♂, 10–12mm. Males are similar to the female illustrated but have a smaller abdomen and are usually darker. The epigyne and male palpal organs are distinctive.

Habitat In woodland, on bushes and trees. **Maturity** Summer to autumn.

Distribution Rare in Britain and restricted to counties bordering the south coast of England. Widespread in northern Europe, but relatively uncommon.

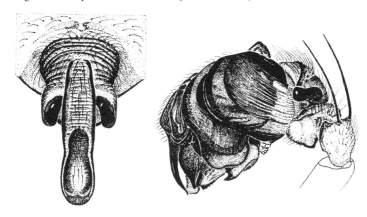

△ *Araneus nordmanni* (Thorell 1870)

Description ♀, 9–13mm; ♂, 5–6mm. The female is illustrated alongside the epigyne and male palp; the broad white borders to the folium are distinctive. Males are very similar but have a smaller abdomen. The epigyne and male palpal organs are distinctive.

Habitat In mountainous areas. **Maturity** Summer and autumn.

Distribution Absent from Britain. Uncommon in Scandinavia and Germany.

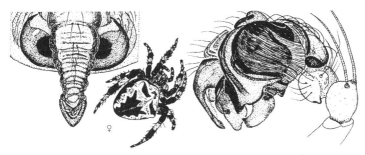

Araneus diadematus Clerck 1757   Plate 27

Description ♀, 10–18mm; ♂, 4–8mm. Males similar to the female illustrated but with a smaller abdomen. There is great variation in the depth of colour, some

specimens being pale yellowish, others almost black, but the markings are usually visible to some extent. The epigyne and male palpal organs are distinctive.
Habitat On bushes and other vegetation on heathland, in woodland and also in gardens. **Maturity** Summer to autumn.
Distribution Common and widespread throughout Britain and northern Europe.

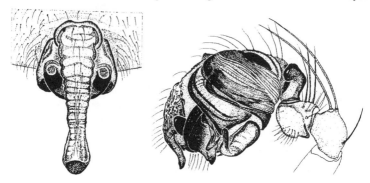

Araneus quadratus Clerck 1757   Plate 27
Description ♀, 9–20mm; ♂, 6–8mm. Both sexes are illustrated. The colour, in both sexes, is extremely variable and ranges from pale yellow, to green, orange, red and dark reddish-brown. The white patches are more conspicuous on dark specimens. The female illustrated is full of eggs; other specimens may have a smaller abdomen. The epigyne and male palpal organs are distinctive.
Habitat On tall grasses, heather and bushes such as gorse. Females construct a substantial retreat of tough, papery silk. **Maturity** Summer to autumn.
Distribution Common and widespread throughout Britain and northern Europe.

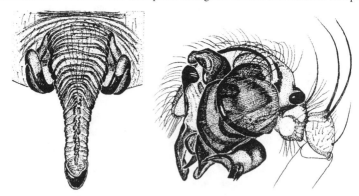

Araneus marmoreus Clerck 1757   Plate 27
Description ♀, 5–14mm; ♂, 5–7mm. Two distinct colour forms are illustrated; the form with the dark brown abdominal mark is generally much commoner. Intermedi-

ate specimens are not infrequent and there is considerable variation in colour. The epigyne and male palpal organs are distinctive.

Habitat Tall grasses, gorse bushes and the lower branches of trees.

Maturity Summer to autumn.

Distribution Fairly widespread in Britain but rather locally distributed and uncommon. Widespread in the rest of northern Europe.

 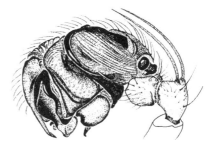

Araneus alsine (Walckenaer 1802)   Plate 27

Description ♀, 7–13mm; ♂, 5–6mm. This spider has an unmistakable appearance; the colour of the abdomen varies from pale orange to quite a deep purplish-red. Males similar to the female illustrated, but have a smaller abdomen and are generally darker. The epigyne and male palpal organs are distinctive.

Habitat In damp woodland clearings. The web is spun on fairly low vegetation and the retreat seems always to consist of one or two dried leaves, either naturally curled or held with silk to form an inverted cone. Although appearing very conspicuous on Plate 27, the spider is easily overlooked in its habitat. **Maturity** Summer to autumn.

Distribution Rare in Britain and very locally distributed. Most records are from the Midlands and southern England, but has been recorded from Wales and Scotland. Widespread in northern Europe.

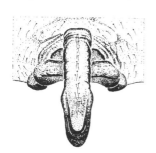 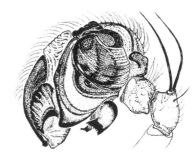

Genus *Nuctenea*

Only two species of *Nuctenea* are known from northern Europe and they are very similar in general appearance, being very dark in colour and having a rather flattened appearance. The flattening of the body relates to the species living under bark, or within other narrow crevices, during the daytime, emerging only at dusk to spin a web. The genus is easily identifiable with a lens and adults are usually identifiable to species level on the basis of size.

Nuctenea umbratica (Clerck 1757)   Plate 27
Description ♀, 11–14mm; ♂, 8–9mm. Males are similar to the female illustrated. Both sexes may be slightly lighter in colour, or be so dark that the light margins of the folium are reduced to a series of paired light spots. The epigyne and male palpal organs are distinctive.
Habitat Concealed under the bark of trees, particularly of dead wood, during the daytime. Also on fence-posts, gates and road signs. Often there is an orb web (or its tattered remains) from the previous night. The spider emerges just as it is getting dark to spin a new web, and catches moths and other night-flying insects.
Maturity Males in summer, females all year.
Distribution Common and widespread throughout Britain and northern Europe.

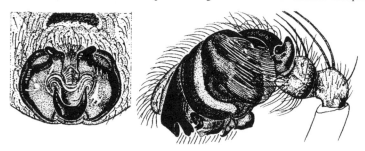

△ *Nuctenea silvicultrix* (C.L. Koch 1844)
Description ♀, 6–9mm; ♂, 5–8mm. Indistinguishable from *N. umbratica* in general appearance, but smaller. The epigyne and male palpal organs are distinctive.
Habitat Usually on pine trees and always in boggy habitats.
Maturity Possibly all year.
Distribution Absent from Britain. Probably confined largely to Scandinavia and the eastern part of northern Europe. It is possible that the species has been overlooked in Britain, since *N. umbratica* is a very distinctive species and many experienced arachnologists possibly do not bother collecting and examining specimens – especially smaller specimens which might be dismissed as subadults.

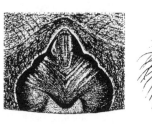 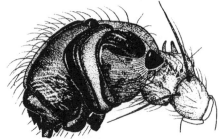

Genus *Larinioides*

There are five species of *Larinioides* known to occur in Europe and the three most widespread are described here. They were at one time included in the genus *Araneus*, but differ considerably in the structure of the epigynes and male palpal organs. All of the species spin orb webs, often close to water. Males are similar to females, but have a smaller abdomen with a clearer pattern and longer legs. They are identifiable in the field with a lens; both the epigyne and the distinctive, bifid median apophysis projecting below the male palpal organs are easily discernible, but higher magnification is required to see more details of the structures.

Larinioides cornutus (Clerck 1757)   Plate 28
Description ♀, 6–9mm; ♂, 5–8mm. Males similar to the female illustrated but with a smaller abdomen and clearer pattern. The colour varies considerably in both sexes and may be a much paler greyish-yellow, or very much darker with more contrasting edges to the folium. The epigyne is distinctive, but the narrow scape, arising from the anterior margin, is frequently torn off during mating. The projecting, bifid median apophysis of the male palpal organs is distinctive.
Habitat On grasses, reeds and other vegetation usually near water (including the sea). Females make a retreat of tough, papery silk.
Maturity Summer to late autumn; possibly all year.
Distribution Common and widespread throughout Britain and northern Europe.

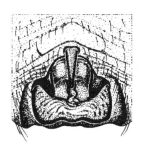 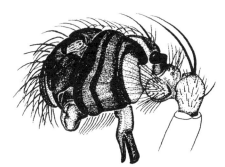

Larinioides sclopetarius (Clerck 1757)   Plate 28
Description ♀, 10–14mm; ♂, 8–9mm. This species is larger than the other two and has a distinctly velvety appearance. In both sexes, the head region of the carapace is clearly outlined with white hairs, as are the dark markings on the abdomen. The female is illustrated alongside the epigyne and male palp. The epigyne and male palpal organs are distinctive, the latter having a broader median apophysis than *L. cornutus*.
Habitat On buildings, bridges and fences near water – seldom on vegetation apart from wandering males. **Maturity** Summer to late autumn, possibly all year.
Distribution Very locally distributed throughout England and Wales and generally rather uncommon. Widespread throughout northern Europe but apparently not recorded from Finland.

♀

Larinioides sclopetarius (previous page)

Larinioides patagiatus (Clerck 1757) Plate 28

Description ♀, 5–7mm; ♂, 5–6mm. Males are similar to the female illustrated, but have a smaller abdomen with a darker pattern. In both sexes, the dark part of the folium at the front of the abdomen may be missing. The epigyne and male palpal organs are distinctive.

Habitat On bushes and trees, sometimes with the retreat under bark. Not as markedly associated with water as the other two species.

Maturity Summer to late autumn, possibly all year.

Distribution Widespread throughout Britain, but very locally distributed and generally rather rare. Widespread in northern Europe, but locally distributed and uncommon.

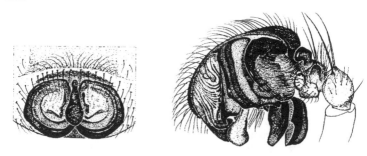

Genus *Atea*

The two species in this genus resemble one another closely in general appearance. As mentioned earlier, they should probably be included in the genus *Araneus*. The epigynes have an S-shaped scape and both the genus and species are identifiable with a lens, although higher magnification is required to see details of the structures. The male palpal organs have a distinctive median apophysis which is trifid at one end and pointed at the other. Higher magnification is required to see this properly.

Atea sturmi (Hahn 1831) (= *Araneus s*. (Hahn)) Plate 28
Description ♀, 3–5mm; ♂, 3–4mm. Males are similar to the female illustrated but are generally darker and have a smaller abdomen. The markings and colour are rather variable in both sexes but are usually as illustrated. The epigyne and the male palpal organs are distinctive.
Habitat On evergreen trees and bushes. **Maturity** Spring, females to late summer.
Distribution Widespread throughout Britain but generally uncommon. Very locally distributed but may then be found in some numbers. Similar distribution throughout the rest of northern Europe.

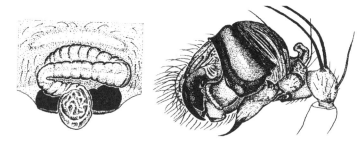

Atea triguttata (Fabricius 1775) (= *Araneus triguttatus* (Fabricius))
Description ♀, 4.5–6mm; ♂, 3–4.5mm. Very similar to *A. sturmi* but usually slightly larger. Females have a more distinctly triangular abdomen with less well-defined markings. The epigyne and male palpal organs are distinctive.
Habitat On deciduous trees and bushes. **Maturity** Spring, females to late summer.
Distribution Much rarer than *A. sturmi* and most records are from southern England. Records in England are from as far north as Lincolnshire and it has also been recorded from Scotland. Absent from Scandinavia; widespread throughout the rest of northern Europe.

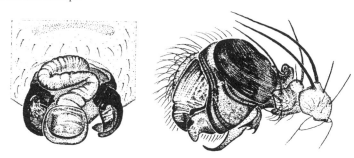

Genus *Neoscona*

The single European species of *Neoscona* has very clear and distinctive markings. The web is spun on low vegetation and usually has a damaged appearance. The spider waits for prey on a platform of fine silk. The general appearance of this species allows identification in the field and the epigyne is discernible with a lens.

Neoscona adianta (Walckenaer 1802)   Plate 28

Description ♀, 5–7mm; ♂, 4–5mm. Males are similar to the female illustrated but with a slimmer abdomen. Although there is some variation in colour, the markings are constant and very distinctive. The epigyne and male palpal organs are also distinctive.

Habitat On low vegetation such as heather, grass and gorse.

Maturity Summer to autumn.

Distribution Generally uncommon, apart from in the south and south-east of England where it may be locally frequent. Recorded from as far north as Yorkshire and also from Wales and southern Ireland. Widespread, but locally distributed throughout most of northern Europe.

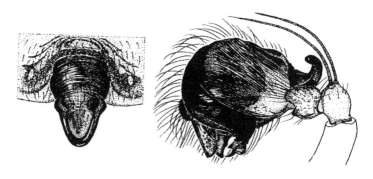

△ Genus *Aculepeira*

Of the two European species of *Aculepeira*, only one occurs in the north. At one time the species were included in the genus *Araneus*, but differ considerably in general appearance and in the epigynes and male palpal organs. The abdomen is pointed at both ends and this, together with the striking abdominal pattern, makes it an easily identifiable species. The orb web is spun on bushes and has the hub furnished with a dense lattice of threads. The spider waits for prey on a platform of fine silk.

△ *Aculepeira ceropegia* (Walckenaer 1802)   Plate 28

Description ♀, 12–14mm; ♂, 7–8mm. The female has a very distinctive appearance; ventrally, the abdomen has a light median stripe, extending from the epigyne three-quarters of the way back to the spinners. The latter are not terminal, but are considerably overhung by the pointed abdomen. The male is illustrated alongside the epigynes and male palp; it has a decidedly spiny appearance and a group of stout spines are present on tibia II. The epigyne varies considerably in appearance, since the scape may sometimes have been torn off, and two examples are illustrated. The male palpal organs are distinctive.

Habitat In bushes and low vegetation. **Maturity** Summer.

Distribution Absent from Britain, although several specimens were once found in Chepstow in 1853. Widespread in northern Europe, but rare in the north of the region.

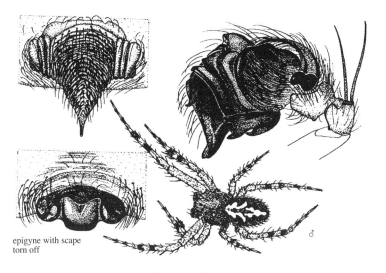

epigyne with scape
torn off

Genus *Agalenatea*

The single European member of this genus has a reddish-brown abdomen which is almost as broad as long and in many females appears circular when viewed from above. The spider spins an orb web which has a dense lattice of silk at the hub; it waits for prey on a platform of fine silk spun at the edge of the web.

Agalenatea redii (Scopoli 1763)   Plate 28

Description ♀, 5.5–7mm; ♂, 3.5–4.5mm. The abdomen may be even broader or more circular than illustrated, or may be slightly more triangular. The markings vary a little; the light inverted V at the front end of the abdomen may be enlarged to form a pair of white lobes; other specimens may have the posterior part of the pattern in the form of a solid brown triangular area, similar to that in the common form of *Araneus marmoreus* (Plate 27). Males have a more triangular abdomen and a dark cardiac mark outlined with white. The epigyne is a broad lip, which varies a little in the angle of protrusion; it is easily discernible with a lens. The male palp has a long spine on the tibia, as well as a pair on the patella, and the palpal organs are distinctive.

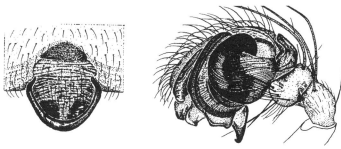

Habitat On heather, gorse bushes and other low vegetation.
Maturity Spring and summer.
Distribution Widespread in England, Wales and the south of Ireland. Very locally distributed and much more frequent on heathland in southern England. Apparently absent from Scotland and Finland. Widespread throughout the rest of northern Europe.

Genus *Zilla*

The single European member of this genus has distinctive markings on the abdomen. The latter sometimes overhangs and completely obscures the carapace when the spider is hanging in the web. The web has a large latticed area of threads at the hub and there is no signal-line or retreat. The spider waits for prey at the centre of the web.

Zilla diodia (Walckenaer 1802)   Plate 28
Description ♀, 3–4mm; ♂, 2–2.5mm. Males similar to the female illustrated, but having a smaller abdomen. The colour and markings are fairly constant. The epigyne is sometimes just discernible with a lens, as is the single spine on the patella of the male palp; higher magnification reveals the distinctive appearance of both structures.
Habitat On heather, bushes and the lower branches of trees, often in rather dark, shaded situations. **Maturity** Summer.
Distribution Restricted to the more southern counties of England. Absent from Scandinavia but widespread throughout the rest of northern Europe.

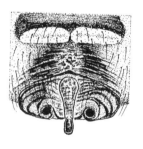 

Genus *Cercidia*

The single European species in this genus has an oval abdomen which is pointed at the front end. On each side of the front margin there are three or four short, black spines – more easily seen from an angle or from the side. There is a dorsal scutum over the front part of the abdomen which is usually visible in males, but not easily seen in females. The spider spins an easily overlooked orb web near ground level amongst vegetation. The web usually has a hole at the hub and there is no signal-line or retreat. The spider waits at the hub for prey, but the slightest disturbance causes it to drop to the ground, and most specimens will probably be collected by sieving litter or grubbing about.

Cercidia prominens (Westring 1851)   Plate 28
Description ♀, 3.5–5mm; ♂, 3–4mm. The colour may be paler and more orange-red than illustrated, or darker. Males have a slightly darker scutum over the front part of the abdomen and stout spines on tibia II. The spider is identifiable with a lens by its general appearance; higher magnification is required to see details of the epigyne and male palpal organs.
Habitat At the base of vegetation, often at the edge of banks, footpaths and other clearings. **Maturity** Spring to autumn, females possibly all year.
Distribution Widespread throughout England and Wales but rather uncommon. Rare or absent in most of Scotland and Ireland. Widespread in the rest of northern Europe but generally uncommon.

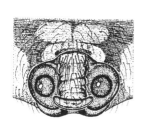
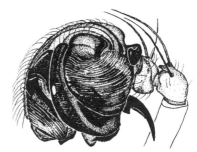

Genus *Araniella*

Six species of *Araniella* are found in Europe and the five most widespread are described here. They are easily recognized in the field by the bright green abdomen, which has a series of small, paired, black spots. Usually there is a small red spot just above the spinners. One rare species often has an orange-red folium on the abdomen, but the paired black spots are still present. These spiders all spin small orb webs on low vegetation, bushes and trees. Frequently the webs hardly resemble an orb at all, being very eccentric with many of the threads arranged in a rather haphazard fashion. This is particularly evident in smaller webs spun within the confines of the underside of a single leaf. Males have a smaller abdomen and a relatively large, reddish, well-marked carapace; the front pairs of legs are also well marked. Females cover their egg sacs with a relatively large volume of woolly, straw-coloured silk and remain with them for a short time, usually under cover of leaves. The females die fairly soon after egg laying in the autumn and, later, the leaves and egg sacs fall to the ground. I have seen spiderlings of the commoner species emerge at ground level in the spring.

Whilst the genus is readily identifiable in the field, identification of the species requires a microscope. Epigynes are sometimes identifiable with a field microscope, but some specimens will prove difficult without higher magnification. The distinguishing features of the male palpal organs are best seen from below and this is difficult with a field microscope, unless the specimen is particularly obliging. Very rarely, specimens may appear rather intermediate, possibly due to hybridization. Failure to identify correctly may have led to considerable under-recording of some species.

Araniella cucurbitina (Clerck 1757)   Plate 29
Description ♀, 4–6mm; ♂, 3.5–4mm. Males are similar to the illustration of *A. opisthographa* (Plate 29). In both sexes there is a red spot just above the spinners, not visible in dorsal view. Immature specimens frequently have more extensive red markings. The epigyne is similar to that of *A. opisthographa* but is relatively shorter and broader. The male palpal organs, viewed from below, are distinguished by the relative size and shape of the component structures.
Habitat On low vegetation, bushes and trees, in a wide variety of situations.
Maturity Summer to autumn.
Distribution Common and widespread throughout Britain and northern Europe.

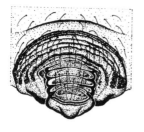
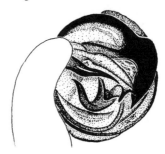

Araniella opisthographa (Kulczynski 1905)   Plate 29
(= *A. opistographa* (Kulczynski))
Description Indistinguishable in size and appearance from *A. cucurbitina*. The epigyne has a relatively longer, narrower scape and the male palpal organs, viewed from below, are distinctly different in structure.
Habitat and Maturity Probably similar to *A. cucurbitina*.
Distribution Common and widespread throughout Britain and northern Europe. Failure to identify the species has no doubt led to considerable under-recording and the relative distribution is uncertain.

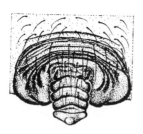
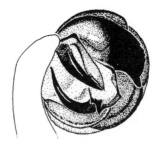

Araniella inconspicua (Simon 1874)
Description ♀, 5–5.5mm; ♂, 4–4.5mm. Similar to *A. cucurbitina* and *A. opisthographa* in general appearance and with epigyne and male palpal organs

similar to *A. alpica*. The epigyne is distinguished from that of *A. alpica* by having the scape broader at its tip and by lacking the bulges on each side near the posterior border when viewed ventrally (NB bulges may be seen if viewed slightly from behind). The male palpal organs are distinctive when viewed from below.
Habitat Mostly on trees, mainly oaks and pines. **Maturity** Spring to late summer.
Distribution Apparently rare and confined to south and south-east England. Apparently rare in northern Europe but possibly under-recorded.

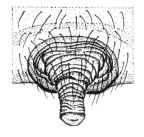 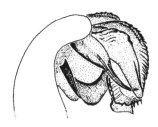

Araniella alpica (L. Koch 1869)
Description ♀, 5–6mm; ♂, 4–5mm. Similar to *A. cucurbitina* and *A. opisthographa* in general appearance and with epigyne and male palpal organs similar to those of *A. inconspicua*. The epigyne has a narrow tip to the scape and a pair of bulges is conspicuous on each side, near the posterior border, when viewed ventrally.
Habitat On trees and shrubs – yew, beech, dogwood. **Maturity** Summer.
Distribution Rare in Britain and recorded from only six localities in the south of England. Widespread throughout the rest of northern Europe, but generally uncommon.

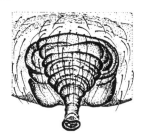 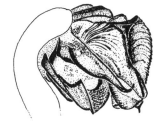

Araniella displicata (Hentz 1847)
Description ♀, 5–11mm; ♂, 4–5mm. This species has a reddish-brown or orange folium on the abdomen with light marks in the midline and narrow white bands around the sides, which include the lines of paired black spots. The epigyne and male palpal organs are distinctive.
Habitat On trees, particularly pines. **Maturity** Late spring to early autumn.
Distribution Rare in Britain and recorded from a few localities in the south of England. Widespread but generally rare in the rest of northern Europe.

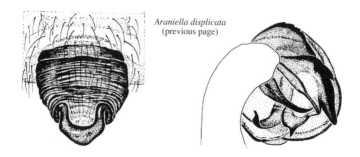

Araniella displicata
(previous page)

Genus *Hypsosinga*

All four European species of *Hypsosinga* are described here. They have a shiny, oval abdomen marked with broad, dark brown or black bands. The males may be entirely black. They spin orb webs very close to the ground amongst low vegetation, often near water. The male palpal organs have a transparent scale-like structure attached to the embolus which breaks off and lodges in the epigyne during mating. The scale is visible at the tip of the palp illustrated for *H. sanguinea* and a fragment is illustrated in the epigyne of *H. albovittata*. Sometimes the epigyne is completely obscured by transparent scales. One species is identifiable by its general appearance. The others require examination of the epigyne and male palpal organs with a microscope.

Hypsosinga albovittata (Westring 1851)   Plate 29
Description ♀, 2.5–3.5mm; ♂, 2.25–3mm. The white median mark on the carapace is very distinctive, as is the abdominal pattern. Males have a narrower white mark on the carapace and the white midline markings on the abdomen are sometimes confined to the front half. Both sexes, and immatures, are identifiable with a lens. The epigyne and male palpal organs are distinctive.
Habitat Web close to ground level amongst vegetation, usually on heathland.
Maturity Summer.
Distribution Widely distributed throughout Britain, but rather uncommon. Widespread throughout the rest of northern Europe.

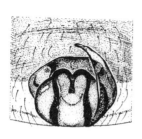

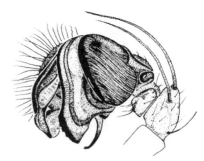

Hypsosinga pygmaea (Sundevall 1832)
Description ♀, 3.5–4.5mm; ♂, 2.5–3mm. Females resemble *H. sanguinea* in general appearance, but the carapace is often darker with lighter margins. The abdominal bands are often black, and the median stripe more yellowish. Some females and most males have an entirely black abdomen. The leg markings differ from those of *H. sanguinea* in that the females have unmarked yellow-orange legs and the males have the end of femur I darkened. The epigyne and male palpal organs are distinctive.
Habitat Low vegetation, sometimes in damp habitats, often on chalk grassland.
Maturity Spring and summer.
Distribution Widely distributed throughout Britain and the rest of northern Europe, but rather uncommon.

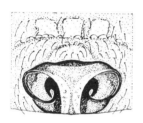 

Hypsosinga sanguinea (C.L. Koch 1844)   Plate 29
Description ♀, 3–4mm; ♂, 2.5–3mm. The carapace may be a little paler than illustrated in both sexes, and the broad abdominal bands may be darker. The midline band is usually almost white, as illustrated. The legs usually have similar markings in both sexes. The epigyne and male palpal organs are distinctive.
Habitat Amongst heather and other low vegetation often in damp habitats.
Maturity Spring and summer.
Distribution Rather rare and locally distributed; mainly in southern England but recorded from the Midlands and also the west of Ireland. Widespread throughout northern Europe but generally uncommon.

Hypsosinga heri (Hahn 1831)
Description ♀, 3.5–4.5mm; ♂, 2–2.5mm. The abdominal markings are similar to those of *H. sanguinea* (Plate 29); sometimes the bands are reddish-brown with paired darker marks along their length. Females have an orange carapace, with dark marks in the midline and along the junction between the head and thoracic parts; occasionally the whole head region is dark. Males have an orange carapace with a dark brown head. The epigyne and male palpal organs are distinctive.
Habitat On low plants, near water. **Maturity** Summer.
Distribution Recorded many years ago from two sites in England (in Berkshire and Cambridgeshire); not rediscovered and may be extinct in Britain. Absent from Scandinavia and generally rare in the more southerly parts of northern Europe.

 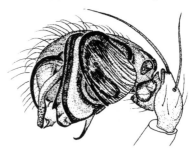

Genus *Singa*

Only two species of *Singa* occur in northern Europe, both of which are described here. They differ from *Hypsosinga* in having the quadrangle formed by the median eyes wider in front than behind. They spin orb webs, generally low down on vegetation in damp habitats, sometimes on the banks of streams.

Singa hamata (Clerck 1757)   Plate 29
Description ♀, 5–6mm; ♂, 3–4mm. Males are similar to the female illustrated, but with a smaller abdomen. The markings are somewhat variable; the dark parts of the pattern may be darker than illustrated and the light areas more yellowish. The epigyne is similar to that of *S. nitidula* but differs in the structures on either side of the scape and in the pointed processes on each side. The male palpal organs are distinguished particularly by the structures near the tip.

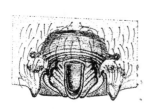 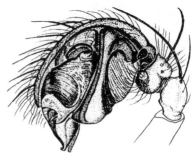

Habitat Web on low vegetation in damp habitats, with pinkish retreat for egg sacs on vegetation near the web. **Maturity** Spring and summer.
Distribution Rare, but probably fairly widespread in Britain. Uncommon, but widespread throughout the rest of northern Europe.

△ *Singa nitidula* C.L. Koch 1844
Description ♀, 5–6mm; ♂, 3–4mm. The female is illustrated alongside the epigyne and male palp. The abdomen is rather narrower and more cylindrical than in *S. hamata* and the lighter parts of the pattern form much thinner lines. Males are similar but with an even slimmer abdomen. The epigyne differs from that of *S. hamata* in the structures on each side of the scape, and the processes on either side are rather more rounded. The male palpal organs are distinguished mainly by the structures near the tip.
Habitat On vegetation by the side of rivers and streams.
Maturity Spring and summer.
Distribution Absent from Britain and much of Scandinavia. Recorded from Finland and widespread throughout the rest of northern Europe, but locally distributed.

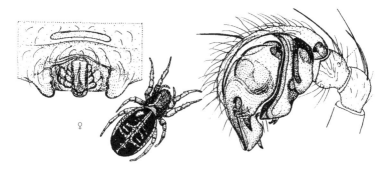

Genus *Zygiella*

Five species of *Zygiella* occur in northern Europe and four of the most widespread are described here. As discussed earlier, some recent authors have assigned this genus to the family Metidae. I do not regard the latter as being a valid family or consider that *Zygiella* belongs anywhere other than in the Araneidae. Aside from my personal view, it does seem likely that this position will eventually prevail; sticking to it now may avoid undue confusion when consulting other literature in the future.

The orb webs of *Zygiella* species are recognizable in the field, since a small sector in the upper part of the web is left open and free of spirals. When making the web, the spider changes direction each time it reaches this point (see Webs, p. 71). Within and just behind this vacant sector is a single strong strand of silk, the signal line, which leads to the retreat. The spider waits for prey in the retreat with the tip of the first legs on the signal line. One obvious possible reason for this arrangement lies in the habitat. Window frames, walls, and the surface of bark and rocks offer scarcely more than a two-dimensional space. In many situations it would be difficult to angle the signal thread far enough back for the spider to avoid catching the spirals in its rush to catch prey. *Zygiella atrica* spins a typical web with a vacant sector on vegetation, but later in the year, when egg sacs and the retreat are placed further back in the vegetation, part of the vacant sector may be filled in. A similar thing may happen with *Z. x-notata* which occurs around houses, typically on window frames. On older sliding-sash windows, the depth in the bottom half is considerably more than at the top. In the autumn, females with egg sacs in the bottom half frequently add strands to the vacant sector, but I have seldom seen this in the top half.

Apart from the characteristic webs, all the species have a similar and distinctive general appearance. The species are usually identifiable in the field with a lens; a field microscope makes it easier still.

Zygiella x-notata (Clerck 1757)   Plate 29

Description ♀, 6–7mm; ♂, 3.5–5mm. Males very similar to the female illustrated but with a smaller abdomen and longer legs. The epigyne is a broad, dark, sclerotized lip with openings on each side. The male palpal organs are distinctive and the palpal tibia and patella are not elongated as they are in the other common species, *Z. atrica*.

Habitat Almost always close to human habitations; on window-frames, under guttering, on fences etc. If the web is disturbed, the spider remains in its retreat.

Maturity Mid-summer to autumn, females all year.

Distribution Widespread and abundant throughout Britain. Widespread in northern Europe apart from Finland; perhaps commoner in the west and often occurring away from houses further south.

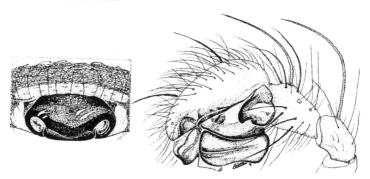

Zygiella atrica (C.L.Koch 1845)   Plate 29

Description ♀, 6–6.5mm; ♂, 3.5–5mm. Females are similar in colour to the male illustrated, but with a larger abdomen as illustrated for *Z. x-notata*. The reddish marks on the front of the abdomen are distinctive in this species and the light part of the folium is particularly silvery. The epigyne is overall a little more square than in *Z. x-notata* and is lighter in the central part. The male palp has an extremely long patella and tibia and this is visible even to the naked eye.

Habitat On heather, gorse bushes and a wide variety of other vegetation, usually away from houses but quite frequent in gardens. Also on rocks and breakwaters by the sea. If the web is disturbed, the spider drops from its retreat like a stone, trailing a dragline. **Maturity** Summer, females to late autumn.

Distribution Widespread throughout Britain and northern Europe.

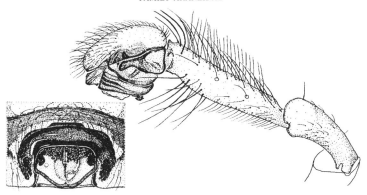

△ *Zygiella montana* (C.L.Koch 1839)

Description ♀, 6–7mm; ♂, 4–5mm. Similar in general appearance to *Z. x-notata*, but the sternum is uniformly very dark brown, whereas in the other species it is brown with a paler midline mark. The epigyne and male palpal organs are distinctive.

Habitat In mountainous regions, up to the tree line; on huts, fences, tree trunks and rocks.

Maturity Summer to autumn, females all year.

Distribution Absent from Britain and large parts of northern Europe. Recorded from mountainous areas in Germany.

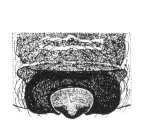
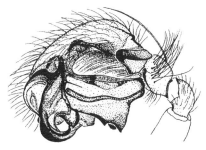

Zygiella stroemi (Thorell 1870)

Description ♀, 4–4.5mm; ♂, 3–3.5mm. Similar in general appearance to *Z. atrica* but smaller. The folium usually has a broader dark outline than *Z. atrica*, and the light area between is brownish with yellow or white patches, rather than silvery. The epigyne forms a long, dark tongue and the male palpal organs are very distinctive.

Habitat Usually found on pine trunks where it spins a delicate web with a retreat in fissured bark; has also been found in a hut.

Maturity Summer to autumn, females all year.

Distribution Generally rare in Britain and recorded from localities in Scotland and southern England; sometimes abundant locally. Widespread in northern Europe, but commoner in the north and east of the region.

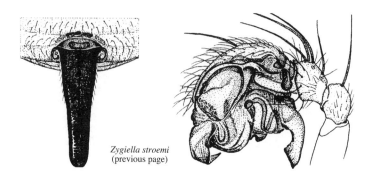

Zygiella stroemi
(previous page)

Genus *Cyclosa*

Two species of *Cyclosa* occur in northern Europe and are described here. The posterior end of the abdomen has a single tubercle in *C. conica* and four in *C. oculata*; the latter has an additional pair of tubercles nearer the front end. The colour illustrations (Plate 29) show the legs stretched out, but when occupying their webs the spiders draw the legs up to cover the carapace – see illustration of *C. conica* alongside the epigyne and male palp. The web usually has an irregular band of silk across it, sometimes called a 'stabilimentum'. This acts as a form of camouflage, when the spider occupies the centre of the web in line with it, and adds little or nothing to the 'stability' of the web (see Webs, p. 72). The species are easily identified by their general appearance and also by the epigynes and male palps.

Cyclosa conica (Pallas 1772)   Plate 29

Description ♀, 4.5–7mm; ♂, 3–4.5mm. The colour and markings are extremely variable. The single abdominal tubercle is distinctive in females but varies a little in size. Males have a more rudimentary tubercle, and the dark brown or black carapace projects narrowly in front, where it carries the median eyes. Femora I and II are pale yellow in the male with the distal half black. The epigyne and male palpal organs are distinctive. The illustration of the female alongside shows the typical stance on the web.

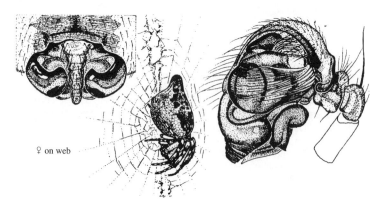

♀ on web

Habitat On bushes, often evergreens, in dark, moist woodland.
Maturity Spring and summer.
Distribution Widespread throughout Britain and northern Europe, but locally distributed because of the habitat.

△ *Cyclosa oculata* (Walckenaer 1802)   Plate 29
Description ♀, 5–6mm; ♂, 3.5–4mm. The abdomen has a pair of tubercles near the front end, two in the midline posteriorly and one on each side. Males are very similar to the female illustrated. The epigyne is distinctive, the tip of the scape projecting at right angles (illustrated in outline). The male palpal organs vary a little, but the structures near the tip are distinctive.
Habitat On bushes and low vegetation in sunny, open areas. **Maturity** Summer.
Distribution Absent from Britain and the north of the region. Records from France, Belgium, and Germany, but uncommon. More frequent in southern Europe.

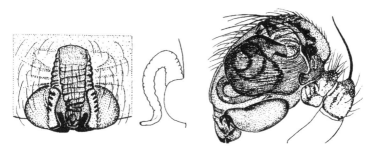

Genus *Mangora*

The single northern European species of *Mangora* has an unmistakable appearance. The spider spins an orb web on bushes and low vegetation and sits in wait for prey at the centre of the hub.

Mangora acalypha (Walckenaer 1802)   Plate 30
Description ♀, 3.5–4mm; ♂, 2.5–3mm. The pear-shaped carapace is rather convex in the thoracic region. Males are similar to the female illustrated but the carapace is slightly narrower at the front end. The three longitudinal bars in the rear half are often

joined to form a dark rectangle. The epigyne and male palp are distinctive, but not discernible with a lens.

Habitat On low vegetation, heather, gorse and other bushes.

Maturity Summer.

Distribution Fairly common, sometimes abundant, in southern England. Much rarer in the north of England, recorded from Wales and southern Ireland, but not from Scotland. Widespread and common throughout northern Europe, but rarer in the north and not recorded from Finland.

Genus *Argiope*

One species of *Argiope* occurs in northern Europe; a second, *Argiope lobata* (Pallas), is found to the south of the region and females of this species have three or four large lobes along the side of the abdomen. Females of *Argiope bruennichi* have a quite unmistakable appearance and make large orb webs, near ground level, which have a zig-zag ribbon of silk running from side to side (see Webs, p. 73). Immatures seem to add more silk decoration to the webs than do adults. Whilst the females are large and striking spiders, males are very much smaller and of an overall pale brown colour. They are frequently eaten by the females, and this sometimes starts whilst mating is in progress. Females make a large brown flask-shaped egg sac (see Egg Sacs, p. 59) Identification of this species should present few problems.

Argiope bruennichi (Scopoli 1772)   Plate 30

Description ♀, 11–15mm; ♂, 4–4.5mm. Both sexes are illustrated, but not to the same scale; the male is relatively even smaller than depicted! The epigyne and male palp are distinctive.

Habitat Web near ground level amongst long grass; often at the edge of fields, clearings and wasteland.

Maturity Summer, females to autumn.

Distribution Well established in localities near the south coast of England but absent from the rest of Britain. Locally distributed in France, Belgium, Holland and Germany, and commoner to the south and west of the region.

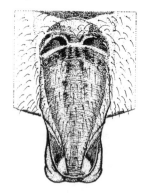 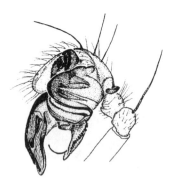

FAMILY LINYPHIIDAE

This is the largest family of northern European spiders and contains well over four hundred species in over one hundred and twenty genera. Most species make sheet webs, with no retreat, and run upside-down on the underside of the sheet. The majority are known in Britain as 'money spiders'. This is undoubtedly the best known and most frequently used common name for a group of spiders in this country. The name applies to fairly small, grey or black-bodied spiders, with no pattern. They travel through the air on strands of silk and have a tendency to land on one's clothing – supposedly heralding good luck and fortune. The name does not apply to all members of the Linyphiidae; those with patterns and markings are definitely excluded. Nor does it apply to all spiders which are entirely black, since both size and shape have to be right. In support of this argument, try offering someone a *Zelotes latreillei* (8mm, Plate 4), a *Dismodicus bifrons* (2.5mm, Plate 30) and *Linyphia triangularis* (6mm, Plate 32) and asking them to identify which one is the 'money spider'. In the majority of cases a shrewd taxonomic judgement is reached in seconds. This experiment also works if juveniles of *Zelotes* and *Linyphia* are offered as choices. Naturally, if *Robertus lividus* (4mm, Plate 25) were offered there might be some difficulty, and there would be more confusion with other theridiids such as *Pholcomma* and *Theonoe*, but these are very few in number and in any case have evolved specifically to outwit those beginning the study of spiders! More seriously, these few theridiids would not normally be encountered as 'money spiders' because they do not seem to be particularly dispersive. In the U.S.A., 'money spiders' are called 'dwarf spiders', in Germany 'Zwergspinnen' and in Denmark 'dværgedderkopper'. Although this fascinating group of spiders is discussed briefly (p. 345), it is not possible to include detailed descriptions and illustrations here; they would double the size of the book and the vast majority are in any case not identifiable in the field. Experience shows that most beginners ignore the 'money spiders', in the (mistaken) belief that they are too difficult. With a microscope, preserved specimens and the literature, identification is actually quite easy.

Some members of the Linyphiidae have distinctive markings and abdominal patterns and are readily identifiable in the field. They are sometimes called 'linen weavers', are sometimes larger than the 'money spiders', and make more conspicuous sheet webs (see Webs, p. 74). In the U.S.A. they are called 'sheetweb weavers', in Germany 'Baldachinspinnen', and in Denmark 'baldakinspindere'. Flying insects, hitting the superstructure of threads, fall on to the sheet below and are seized by the spider hanging upside-down below the web. The males of some species have ridges on the outer surface of the chelicerae and an opposing tooth on the inner side of the palpal femur. This is used in stridulation during courtship. Some females and juveniles have similar apparatus which is perhaps used for more general communication. Relatively little is known of the biology of most of these species and there is great scope for research.

The family Linyphiidae has sometimes been considered in two subfamilies, the Linyphiinae and the Erigoniinae. The latter group was once elevated to family status, the Micryphantidae, by some continental workers. (Incidentally, this division does not coincide with the common names of 'money spider' and 'linen weaver'.) It is now generally accepted that there is no phylogenetic basis for such a division and the sub-families are no longer recognized.

The following key is designed specifically for use in the field and utilizes easily visible characters. It is entirely artificial and relates only to the species described in this guide. For example, *Lepthyphantes ericaeus* has a grey abdomen with no pattern and will key out under 'money spiders', but *L. minutus*, with clear markings, will key out to *Lepthyphantes* and is fully described and illustrated. Two species of *Gonatium* have no pattern, but are easily distinguished by colour. By far the commonest species, in sheet webs on bushes, is *Linyphia triangularis* (Plate 32, p. 365, Webs, p. 74) and it may save some time if you fully acquaint yourself with this species first.

Key to the Genera

1. Abdomen distinctly red- or orange-brown in colour, with no
    clear pattern   2

    Abdomen not particularly red or orange; if any reddish areas
    are present, then forming part of a pattern   3

2. Spider entirely orange-red in colour   *Gonatium* p. 349

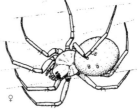

    ♀

    Abdomen reddish with spinners and tip of abdomen
    black. Carapace and legs brownish   *Ostearius* p. 350

    ♀

3. Abdomen pale grey to black with no clear pattern or
    markings. There may be very vague paler spots, ill-defined
    pale chevrons, or a slightly paler median band and most
    species have two pairs of small reddish spots on the
    dorsum of the abdomen. Males of some species have lobes,
    turrets or other projections on the head. (NB a small
    number of Theridiidae (p. 266, B.) have a similar appearance;
    also, if the abdomen is very thin and cylindrical, check 5,
    below.)   Money spiders p. 345

    Abdomen with a pattern or at least white spots or dark bars   4

4. Abdomen brown with two or
    three thin black chevrons
    posteriorly and some black
    marks on the side. Epigyne of
    female very conspicuous as a
    large projecting tongue

    ♀   *Helophora* p. 363

Abdomen possibly with chevrons, but these forming part of
an overall pattern, and abdomen not otherwise uniformly
brown

5

5. Abdomen narrow, cylindrical and black
with a pair of clear white patches
anteriorly. No trace of pattern on
the rest of the abdomen (white
patches sometimes small or
absent, but the tubular
abdomen is distinctive)

Microlinyphia
(males only) p. 369

and, sometimes   *Linyphia hortensis* males p. 365

Abdomen possibly narrow and cylindrical. Possibly with a
pair of white patches, but also with a discernible pattern
on the rest of the abdomen

6

6. Abdomen, viewed from the
side, globular and higher
than long (less obvious in
males, but these have a
very bulbous, hairy head).
Carapace with broad dark
bands on each side near
the margin

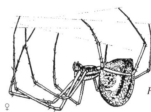

Floronia p. 363

Abdomen not like this. Possibly fairly high, but if so the
carapace lacks broad dark bands

7

7. Abdomen, viewed from the side, rather higher at the
posterior end.

Δ *Frontinellina* p. 369

Abdomen not like this

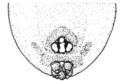

8

8. Abdomen, viewed from below, with a
group of three or four white spots
immediately in front of the spinners

9

Abdomen possibly with white spots ventrally, but not with a
small group just in front of the spinners

10

9. White spots very striking. Legs yellow, paler than abdomen and annulated with black. Male with enormous palpal organs. Sheet web typically at the base of trees and shady overhanging banks

Labulla p. 352

White spots less striking, sometimes small and coalescing. Legs not particularly paler than the abdomen and any annulations less contrasting. Carapace with a dark median mark like a tuning fork. Sheet web in and around houses, or in domestic rubbish away from houses

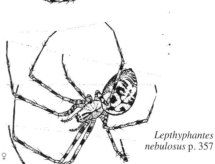

Lepthyphantes nebulosus p. 357

10. Height of clypeus less than the diameter of the anterior median eyes, which are larger than the rest. Epigyne of female projects conspicuously and is identifiable in the field. The web, near ground level or on low vegetation, is a glistening sheet which often appears as though a slug has travelled over it. Size of adult spider 2.5–4.5mm

Tapinopa p. 352

Height of clypeus only 1–1½ times the diameter of the anterior median eyes which are smaller than the rest. Epigyne of female a pinkish, broad, projecting plate. Found under stones, in moss and occasionally on vegetation. Size of adult 1.75–2.6mm

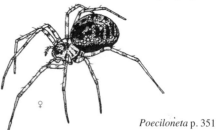

Poeciloneta p. 351

Clypeus higher than this. Epigyne may or may not project conspicuously   11

11. Abdomen mainly whitish dorsally, with a slightly reticulated appearance. Possibly with a fine, dark, median line, but no dark, dentate cardiac mark, no folium, no broad dark bars and no broad chevrons. Paired dark spots are present and these may join to form thin lines at the sides and in the midline. Carapace with dark margins and dark median line   12

Abdomen mainly whitish dorsally but with a contrastingly dark, dentate cardiac mark in the anterior half of the midline. Dark bars, chevrons or triangles may be present in the posterior half   15

Abdomen possibly with reticulated white areas dorsally, but without a dark cardiac mark in the anterior midline. May have a dark folium, broad dark bars or chevrons   13

12. Abdomen slightly elongate with three longitudinal rows of black spots (one row midline, two lateral). Legs faintly annulated. Size of adults 4–6.5mm. Male palp, from the side, looks like a horse's head   ♀   *Stemonyphantes* p. 353

Abdomen less elongate with paired black spots in the posterior half which sometimes extend to form narrow, broken chevrons. Legs not annulated. Male palp with a conspicuously thick patellar spine. Male head projecting conically in eye region. Size of adults 3–4.5mm   ♀   *Bolyphantes* p. 355

13. Carapace yellow-brown with black margins and three or four pairs of black triangles (opposite each leg, pointing inwards). Legs pale with black annulations. Female palp with conspicuously long, strong spines. Epigyne of female a conspicuous projecting tongue. Abdominal pattern generally as shown; occasionally entirely black. Adult size 3.2–4mm. Found on bark of trees or in adjacent leaf-litter   ♀   *Drapetisca* p. 350

Carapace, although possibly with radiating striae, not as above. Different abdominal pattern   14

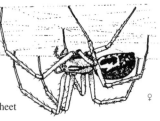

14.   Carapace with a conspicuous tuning fork mark in the midline, the 'prongs' of which are clearly separated and narrow. Femora without dark spots. Abdomen of female with a purplish-brown folium and light and dark streaks on the sides. Epigyne of female not projecting. Male with long, divergent chelicerae. Ubiquitous; sheet web on bushes, trees or any other vegetation with stiff foliage

Linyphia triangularis p. 365

Carapace with a tuning fork mark in the midline, the prongs of which are broad and scarcely separated. Femora clearly spotted with black, especially ventrally. Abdomen with a purplish-brown folium in both sexes; small white spots on the sides but no clear dark streaks. Epigyne of female projecting like a spoon. Male chelicerae not enlarged. Sheet web on conifers

Pityohyphantes p. 364

Carapace without a tuning fork mark in the midline   16

15.   Cardiac mark followed by only very narrow chevrons in the posterior half of the abdomen, and these may be absent or reduced to spots

Lepthyphantes expunctus p. 362

Cardiac mark followed by three almost rectangular black patches in the posterior half

Δ *Neriene emphana* p. 368

Cardiac mark followed by a white area which is bordered by three or four black triangles (apices pointing laterally)

Microlinyphia impigra p. 370

Cardiac mark broad and dentate, sometimes with fine lines extending from it. Followed by (and continuous with) a series of overlapping dark triangles. The dark midline mark is sometimes narrow, occasionally wider and invading light areas

Microlinyphia pusilla p. 369

16. Abdomen with broad, continuous, dark brown or purplish
    folium which is bordered by white   17

    Abdomen with pattern of dark chevrons or paired dark bars
    on a greyish background which often contains small white
    spots   18

17. Folium with fairly rounded lobes;
    usually uniformly dark with few
    markings and no light spots   *Linyphia hortensis* p. 365

                                                                        ♀

    Folium usually with more angled
    lobes, distinctly darker margins,
    and containing a few darker
    marks and small light spots   *Neriene* p. 366

                                                                        ♀

18. Metatarsi with no spines   *Bathyphantes* p. 354

                                                                        ♀

    Metatarsi with at least one spine, and
    sometimes several   *Lepthyphantes* p. 357

                                                                        ♀

Money Spiders

As discussed earlier, the popular name 'money spider' does not have a precise scientific meaning but refers to those members of the Linyphiidae which have a grey
or black abdomen and no pattern or markings. Just one example, *Dismodicus bifrons*,
is illustrated in colour (Plate 30). It is a convenient group to exclude from this guide,
since they are mostly not identifiable in the field. Their exclusion allows fuller coverage of the other species. A small number of species in the family Theridiidae have
a 'money spider' appearance (p. 266, B.) and are fully described. Some members of
the genera *Bathyphantes* and *Lepthyphantes* have no abdominal markings and are
excluded, whilst others with distinctive patterns are fully described. I do concede that
some dark, but patterned species such as *Lepthyphantes* might be seen as 'money
spiders', but the semantics need not conflict with the stated scope of this guide. In
the U.S.A. they are called 'dwarf spiders' ('Zwergspinnen' in Germany, 'dværgedderkopper' in Denmark). In France the 'araignée (rouge) porte-bonheur' presumably
applies to the well-known red spider mite, which is not a spider at all (p. 10).

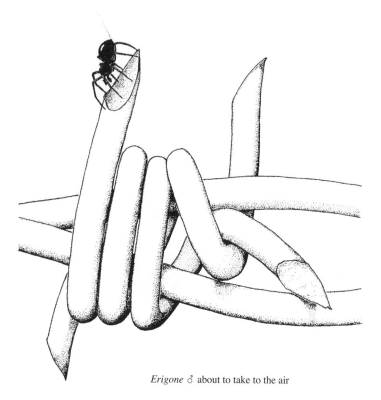

Erigone ♂ about to take to the air

There are over three hundred species in the region, ranging in adult size from less than 1mm to 5.5mm, with most species being around 2mm. Little is known of their biology, but most of the species spin tiny sheet webs in a variety of situations. They constitute a much larger proportion of spider species in more northerly latitudes and are less numerous in warmer regions of the world, although even here they find suitable conditions on mountain ranges. Adults of various species are found throughout the year, but they form an even greater proportion of spiders which are adult and active in late autumn and through the winter. They are often present in large numbers and, on damp mornings, most people will have noticed hundreds of tiny sheet webs on lawns and across depressions in bare ground. Whilst spiderlings of most species will disperse by air, this 'ballooning' is most noticeable in the money spiders. Vast populations of these spiders (perhaps in meadows, sewage filter beds or dung heaps) may at times disperse *en masse*, filling the air with strands of silk and covering large areas with a dense mantle of shimmering threads. Although the airborne threads are extremely fine, they catch the sunlight intermittently as they drift along. In Britain, masses of these floating threads are known as gossamer. In France the term 'fil de la Vierge' is used, and in Germany 'Sommerfläden'; in Denmark 'flyvende sommer' ('flying summer') seems particularly apposite. The phenomenon occurs mostly in late summer and autumn, when a warm sunny day follows a cold spell. The ground is warmed by the sun, air currents are rising, and the spiders develop the urge to take to the air. Climbing to the highest point, on vegetation or fences, the spider stands on tiptoe, pointing the spinners skywards. One or more strands of silk are let out and sometimes they have tiny 'kites' of fluffy silk attached to them. These are pulled upwards by the air currents and, once there is sufficient drag, the spider lets go with the foot claws and becomes airborne. It is difficult to know what effect these spiders have on populations of small insects, but it seems certain that the use of pesticides will in the long term favour the insects. The spiders

Hypomma fulvum ♂ (2.5mm)

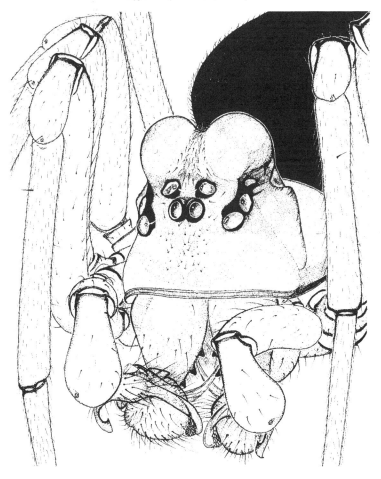

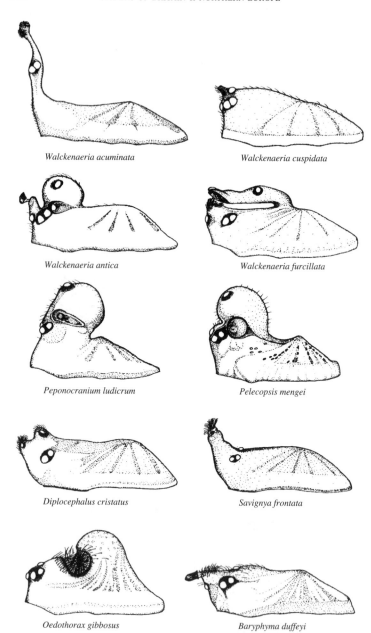

Walckenaeria acuminata

Walckenaeria cuspidata

Walckenaeria antica

Walckenaeria furcillata

Peponocranium ludicrum

Pelecopsis mengei

Diplocephalus cristatus

Savignya frontata

Oedothorax gibbosus

Baryphyma duffeyi

Carapaces of male 'money spiders' (Linyphiidae)

mostly take longer to mature and lay fewer eggs, whereas the insects will bounce back quickly and be subject to less predation.

The males of some species have the head region modified to form lobes, turrets and other projections and these may carry one or more pairs of eyes. Some of these lobes have a small pit or groove on each side and, in some species, it is known that these are gripped by the female's chelicerae during mating. In some species, such as *Walckenaeria acuminata*, *W. furcillata* and *Oedothorax gibbosus*, males can be identified solely on the basis of the carapace. Many others have broadly similar lobes on the head (or none) and identification is ultimately based on the structure of the palpal organs. They are actually quite easy to identify, but a microscope with up to ¥90 magnification is necessary. Most specimens will require examination in alcohol, and you will need the appropriate literature (p. 375). The keys utilize the tibial spines and metatarsal trichobothria, narrowing specimens down to a handful of species which are then separable by size, epigynes and male palpal organs.

Genus *Gonatium*

Four species of *Gonatium* occur in northern Europe and the two most widespread species have an overall reddish-orange appearance.

Gonatium rubens (Blackwall 1833)
Description ♀, 2.6–3.2mm; ♂, 2.5–2.6mm. The carapace and legs are reddish-orange; abdomen similar in life, but fades to brownish-grey on preservation. Males have the head region narrowed and raised into a conical projection. Tibia I is swollen and hairy on the under surface of the distal third of its length. The epigyne is distinctive, but sometimes dark and difficult to discern with a lens. The male palp has a swollen femur which is furnished with a number of short, thick spines and has a pointed dorsal apophysis. This is discernible with a lens, as is the relatively small patella.
Habitat On low vegetation, bushes and sometimes at ground level; usually in more open habitats than *G. rubellum*, but the two species often occur together.
Maturity All year.
Distribution Common and widespread throughout Britain and northern Europe.

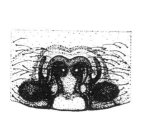 

Gonatium rubellum (Blackwall 1841)
Description ♀, 2.8–3.4mm; ♂, 2.5–2.8mm. Very similar to *G. rubens* in general appearance. Males have the head region less obviously raised and tibia I much less

obviously swollen. The epigyne is often discernible with a lens and the patella of the male palp is obviously broader than the femur.
Habitat On low vegetation, bushes and sometimes at ground level; usually in wooded areas, but may occur together with *G. rubens*. **Maturity** All year.
Distribution Common and widespread throughout Britain and northern Europe.

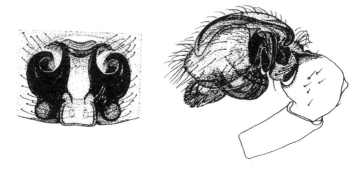

Genus *Ostearius*

The single European species in this genus has unique coloration and markings and is found all over the world in a wide variety of habitats.

Ostearius melanopygius (O.P.-Cambridge 1879)

Description ♀ ♂, 2–2.6mm. The abdomen is reddish with the spinners and the tip of the abdomen black. The carapace is brown with darker markings. Males have a small conical tooth-like projection on the front of each chelicera, which is visible with a lens. Epigyne and male palpal organs distinctive, but not discernible with a lens.
Habitat Found in a very wide variety of situations, sometimes in association with man. **Maturity** Spring to late autumn, females possibly all year.
Distribution A cosmopolitan species; widespread throughout Britain and Europe.

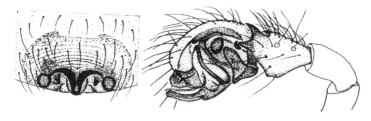

Genus *Drapetisca*

The single European species of *Drapetisca* has a distinctive general appearance and occurs on or near trees. Although free-running on bark and amongst leaf-litter, it also spins an incredibly fine web on the bark of trees. It is sometimes possible to see a few threads of this web if the sun catches it at just the right angle, but usually its presence is only detectable by the fact that the spider's legs are not quite touching the bark.

Drapetisca socialis (Sundevall 1833)   Plate 30
Description ♀ ♂, 3.2–4mm. The carapace markings are a little variable, but generally quite distinctive. The abdominal pattern shows rather more variation and,
although usually as illustrated, some specimens may be much darker, even black, on
very dark bark. The female palps are furnished with long, stout spines. The epigyne
is discernible with a lens, as also is the blunt projection above the base of the cymbium of the male palp.
Habitat On the bark of trees, especially beech, and amongst adjacent leaf-litter.
Maturity Summer to late autumn.
Distribution Widespread throughout Britain and northern Europe.

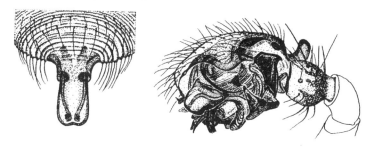

Genus *Poeciloneta*
The single northern European species of *Poeciloneta* is a small spider with a distinctive general appearance.

Poeciloneta variegata (Blackwall 1841) (= *P. globosa* (Wider))   Plate 30
Description ♀, 1.8–2.6mm; ♂, 1.75–2.4mm. Males are similar to the female illustrated but have a smaller abdomen. The abdominal pattern varies a little and
may have more or fewer shining white patches than illustrated. The epigyne is
a broad, projecting tongue, pinkish in colour, and discernible with a lens. The
male palpal organs are distinctive but higher magnification is required to see
details of the structure.
Habitat Under stones on open ground, and amongst moss, grass and leaf-litter.
Maturity Spring to late autumn.
Distribution Widespread thoughout Britain and northern Europe; fairly common,
but locally distributed.

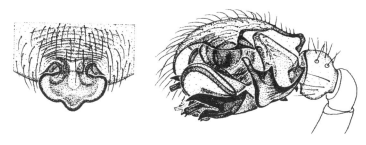

Genus *Tapinopa*

The single European species in this genus has a distinctive appearance which is similar in both sexes. The head region of the carapace is relatively long and broad and overhangs the chelicerae. The anterior median eyes are larger than the rest and the height of the clypeus is much narrower than their diameter. The chelicerae are furnished with five or six long teeth. The spider spins a sheet web which often has glistening bands of silk on it, giving the appearance, in sunlight, of a mucous trail left by a slug or snail. The web is usually situated near ground level amongst low vegetation, on banks or at the base of trees; occasionally it may be situated higher up in vegetation.

Tapinopa longidens (Wider 1834)   Plate 30

Description ♀, 2.5–4.5mm; ♂, 2.5–4.3mm. Males are similar to the female illustrated, but have a smaller abdomen and the head region of the carapace is furnished with a group of stout hairs. The epigyne is discernible with a lens as also is the projection above the male palpal tarsus. Higher magnification is required to see details of other structures.

Habitat In a variety of situations but perhaps commonest in woodland.

Maturity Summer to autumn, females through the winter and occasionally in spring.

Distribution Common and widespread throughout Britain and northern Europe.

 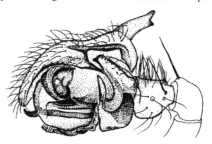

Genus *Labulla*

The single European species of *Labulla* has a very distinctive appearance. The group of white spots on the underside of the abdomen, just in front of the spinners, is very noticeable in the field. The spider spins a sheet web near ground level, either between exposed roots of trees, or across clefts near the base of the trunk, or amongst low vegetation in shady, overhanging banks.

Labulla thoracica (Wider 1834)   Plate 30

Description ♀, 3.4–6.4mm; ♂, 4.5–5.5mm. Both sexes are illustrated. The epigyne is discernible with a lens and the male palpal organs so large that the species is readily identified with the naked eye alone.

Habitat Web near ground level, usually in shaded areas of woodland.

Maturity Late summer to winter.

Distribution Common and widespread throughout Britain and northern Europe.

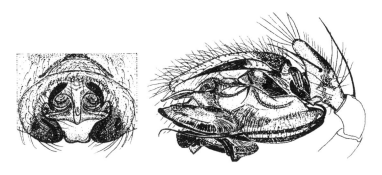

Genus *Stemonyphantes*

The single northern European species of *Stemonyphantes* has a whitish abdomen marked with longitudinal lines of dark spots. It is usually found at or near ground level under stones and detritus and, whilst it sometimes spins an insignificant sheet web, usually only a few threads are apparent. Occasionally it is found higher on vegetation, particularly during the night. Another closely related species, *S. conspersus* (L. Koch), occurs in Czechoslovakia and further to the east.

Stemonyphantes lineatus (Linnaeus 1758)   Plate 31

Description ♀, 4–6.8mm; ♂, 4–5.4mm. The white abdomen may be tinged with pink, yellow or green, and the dark longitudinal lines may be broken to form a series of spots. Males are similar to the female illustrated, but the abdomen is smaller and metatarsus I is slightly swollen and curved on its lower surface. The epigyne is discernible with a lens as also are the male palpal organs, which appear rather like a horse's head.

Habitat Under stones and detritus, and amongst low vegetation, in a variety of situations, including gardens, heathland and the seashore. Occasionally higher on vegetation, especially at night.

Maturity Summer and autumn, females sometimes in winter.

Distribution Widespread throughout Britain and northern Europe. Locally distributed, but may then be abundant.

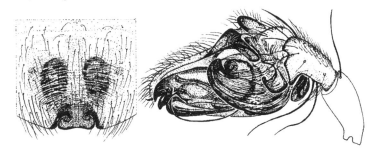

Genus *Bathyphantes*

Seven species of *Bathyphantes* occur in northern Europe, and several more species, now assigned to the genera *Kaestneria* and *Diplostyla*, are also recorded from the region. They have rather variable abdominal markings, generally of black bars or chevrons on a grey background, but sometimes are uniformly grey to black. They are similar in general appearance to species of *Lepthyphantes* but may be distinguished by the lack of spines on the metatarsi. Only four species are described here; the epigynes and male palpal organs cannot be discerned with a lens.

Bathyphantes approximatus (O.P.-Cambridge 1871)   Plate 31
Description ♀, 2.2–3.2mm; ♂, 2.5–3mm. Males similar to the female illustrated but having a smaller abdomen. The pattern is variable; may approach that of *Lepthyphantes zimmermanni*, or may be absent. The epigyne and male palpal organs are distinctive.
Habitat Amongst moss and low vegetation, usually in damp habitats.
Maturity Summer, autumn and spring.
Distribution Widespread throughout Britain and northern Europe but rather locally distributed.

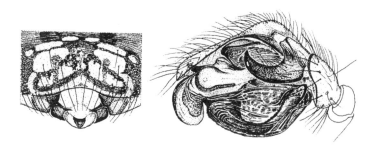

Bathyphantes nigrinus (Westring 1851)
Description ♀, 2.2–3.1mm ♂, 2.3–2.9mm. Similar in general appearance to *B. approximatus* and equally variable in the abdominal pattern. The epigyne and male palpal organs are distinctive.
Habitat In moss, undergrowth and grass. **Maturity** Spring to autumn.
Distribution Common and widespread throughout Britain and northern Europe.

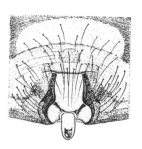
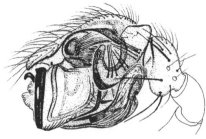

Bathyphantes gracilis (Blackwall 1841)
Description ♀, 1.5–2.4mm; ♂, 1.4–2mm. Similar in general appearance to *B. approximatus* and equally variable in the abdominal pattern. The epigyne is similar to that of *B. parvulus* (below). The male palpal organs are most easily distinguished from those of *B. parvulus* by the hairs projecting from the lower part of the J-shaped paracymbium.
Habitat, Maturity and Distribution Similar to *B. nigrinus*.

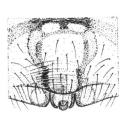 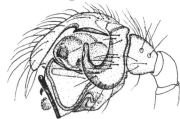

Bathyphantes parvulus (Westring 1851)
Description ♀, 1.8–2.6mm; ♂, 1.7–2.2mm. Similar to *B. approximatus* in general appearance and equally variable in the abdominal pattern. The epigyne differs from that of *B. gracilis* in the shape of the anterior border and in the broader crescent-shaped structure just posterior to it. The J-shaped paracymbium of the male palpal organs has no hairs projecting from its lower part, and there are other differences in the palpal organs.
Habitat, Maturity and Distribution Similar to *B. nigrinus*.

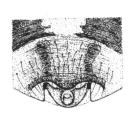 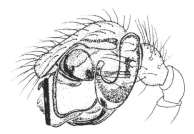

Genus *Bolyphantes*

Four species of *Bolyphantes* occur in northern Europe, and the two most widespread are described here. They are often found on low vegetation and bushes, where they spin a typical linyphiid sheet web, but may also be found at ground level, under stones and amongst detritus and moss.

Bolyphantes luteolus (Blackwall 1833)   Plate 31
Description ♀, 2.7–4.3mm; ♂, 2.8–3.5mm. Males similar to the female illustrated, but having a smaller abdomen and the head region of the carapace elevated (as illustrated). This does not protrude conically between the median eyes, as in *B. alticeps*, and males can be identified on this basis with a lens. The epigyne has the central tongue

wider than the U-shaped scape projecting from the posterior border. The male palpal patella has a stout spine in which the jagged end appears like a snapped broom-stick.
Habitat On bushes, grasses and other low vegetation and amongst moss, leaf-litter and detritus at ground level. **Maturity** Summer to late autumn.
Distribution Widespread throughout Britain and Ireland, but commoner in the north. Widespread throughout northern Europe, but rarer in the south.

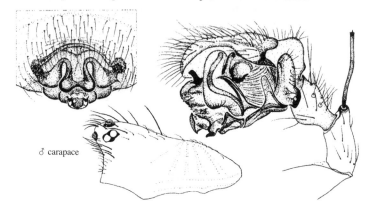

♂ carapace

Bolyphantes alticeps (Sundevall 1833)
Description ♀, 3.5–4.5mm; ♂, 3–4mm. Very similar to *B. luteolus* in general appearance. Males are distinguishable, with a lens, by the carapace, which is elevated and protrudes conically between the median eyes. The epigyne has the central tongue of the same width or narrower than the U-shaped scape projecting from the posterior border. The male palpal patella has a stout spine which is tapered and serrated.
Habitat and Maturity Similar to *B. luteolus*.
Distribution Widespread in the most northern parts of England and Wales, and in Scotland. Absent or very rare in Ireland and most of England and Wales. Widespread in northern parts of Europe; generally absent or rare in the south of the region.

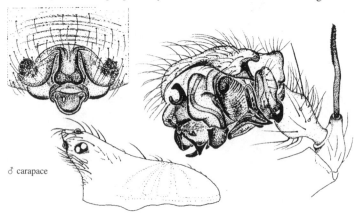

♂ carapace

Genus *Lepthyphantes*

This is a large genus, with over fifty species in northern Europe and twenty-one species in Britain. Some of these spiders are extremely common and twelve of the most wide-spread species are described here. Those included all have an abdominal pattern, made up of dark bars or chevrons on a lighter yellowish-grey background which often contains lighter spots. The abdomen tends to be rather pointed posteriorly. All species have at least one metatarsal spine on each leg, which distinguishes them from species of *Bathyphantes*. Common species with a uniformly grey or black abdomen are not included here and will have keyed out simply as 'money spiders'. All *Lepthyphantes* spin sheet webs typical of the family, but the size of web depends on the species and the situation; they can become quite large in sheltered or undisturbed spots.

The species *L. nebulosus* and *L. expunctus* should have keyed out separately. The species described here can also be separated into two groups on the basis of the spines on metatarsus I:

Metatarsus I with more than one spine: *L. nebulosus, L. leprosus, L. minutus, L. alacris.*

Metatarsus I with only one spine: *L. obscurus, L. tenuis, L. zimmermanni, L. cristatus, L. mengei, L. flavipes, L. tenebricola, L. expunctus.*

The species are easily identifiable by their epigynes and male palpal organs, but a microscope is necessary in most cases. The male palpal organs have a large, roughly U-shaped paracymbium which is useful in identification, but many other aspects of palpal structure also show differences between species.

Lepthyphantes nebulosus (Sundevall 1830)
Description ♀, 3.4–4.6mm; ♂, 3.4–4.2mm. The female is illustrated in the Key to the Genera (p. 342) In both sexes, the abdomen has a small light spot ventrally, just anterior to the spinners and the carapace has a distinct, dark, tuning fork mark in the midline. The epigyne is easily discernible with a lens. The male palp may also some-times be discernible with a lens and the patella is furnished with two or three spines (only one in other species).
Habitat In and around houses; occasionally in domestic rubbish dumped away from houses. **Maturity** All year.
Distribution Much commoner in the more southerly parts of Britain, becoming increasingly rare in northern England and absent from most of Scotland. Widespread throughout the rest of northern Europe.

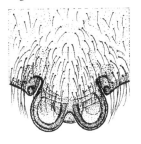 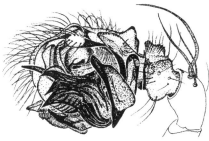

Lepthyphantes leprosus (Ohlert 1865)

Description ♀, 2.5–4mm; 2.5–3.5mm. The female is illustrated alongside the epigyne and male palp. The spider is generally smaller than *L. nebulosus*, and lacks the bifurcate tuning fork mark on the midline of the carapace and the light spot in front of the spinners. The epigyne and male palpal organs are not fully discernible with a lens but are very distinctive at higher magnification.

Habitat and Maturity Similar to *L. nebulosus*.

Distribution Widespread throughout Britain and northern Europe.

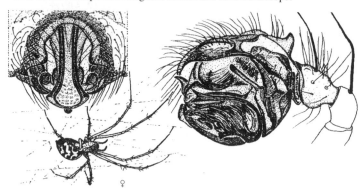

♀

Lepthyphantes minutus (Blackwall 1833)   Plate 31

Description ♀, 3.5–4mm; ♂, 3–4mm. Despite its name, this is one of the **larger** species of *Lepthyphantes* (see The Names and Classification of Spiders, p. 36). This species has a distinctive appearance, clearly annulated legs, and is larger than the rest of the species described below. The male is distinguishable with a lens in the field by the spine on the palpal patella which is conspicuously thicker than the leg spines. Higher magnification is necessary to see details of the palpal organs and epigyne, although the latter is readily identifiable with a field microscope.

Habitat Almost always in a sheet web at the base of trees.

Maturity Summer to late autumn, females possibly later.

Distribution Widespread throughout Britain and northern Europe.

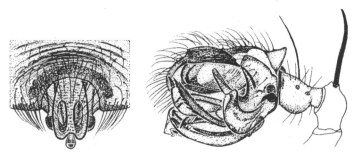

Lepthyphantes alacris (Blackwall 1853)
Description ♀, 2.6–3.3mm; ♂, 2.4–2.7mm. The abdomen in this species usually has a dark midline mark in the anterior half from which two pairs of dark lines curve out to the sides. Following this are two fairly narrow chevrons, and the greyish background has a few yellowish spots. Sometimes the pattern is more like that of *L. zimmermanni* (Plate 31). The legs are not annulated. The epigyne and male palpal organs are not discernible with a lens, although the spine on the male palpal patella is usually conspicuously long. With higher magnification, this can be seen to be serrated or feathery towards the tip and the palpal organs and epigyne appear distinctive.
Habitat In moss, low vegetation, undergrowth, and leaf-litter in a variety of situations but usually in woods. **Maturity** Possibly all year.
Distribution Widespread throughout Britain and northern Europe.

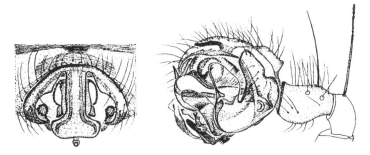

Lepthyphantes obscurus (Blackwall 1841)
Description ♀, 1.9–2.4mm; ♂, 1.8–2.3mm. The abdominal pattern is similar to that of *L. zimmermanni* (Plate 31), a broad dark median band in the front half being followed by three or four dark, curved bars. The legs are not annulated. The projecting epigyne is sometimes discernible with a lens, as is the conspicuous projection on the upper part of the cymbium in the male palp. Higher magnification is required to see details of the structures, which are then very distinctive.
Habitat In moss, grass, low vegetation and bushes and in leaf-litter, in a wide variety of situations. **Maturity** Spring to autumn.
Distribution Widespread and fairly common throughout Britain and northern Europe.

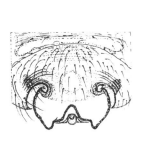

Lepthyphantes tenuis (Blackwall 1852)   Plate 31

Description ♀, 2.1–3.2mm; ♂, 2–2.6mm. The abdomen usually has fairly distinctive markings which allow the species to be distinguished from *L. zimmermanni* in the field. The legs are not annulated. The epigyne is discernible only with higher magnification, as are the male palpal organs. The latter have a U-shaped paracymbium which bears two small teeth.

Habitat In low vegetation, moss and leaf-litter in a wide variety of habitats.

Maturity All year.

Distribution Very common and widespread throughout Britain and northern Europe.

Lepthyphantes zimmermanni Bertkau 1890   Plate 31

Description ♀, 2.1–3.2mm; ♂, 2–2.6mm. The abdominal pattern is generally as illustrated and the legs are not annulated. The epigyne and male palpal organs can be distinguished only with higher magnification, but are distinctive. The U-shaped paracymbium of the palpal organs has a single small tooth on the margin near the tibia.

Habitat In low vegetation, moss and leaf-litter in a wide variety of habitats.

Maturity All year.

Distribution Very common and widespread throughout Britain and northern Europe.

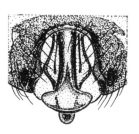 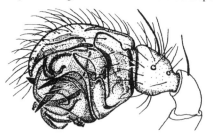

Lepthyphantes cristatus (Menge 1866)

Description ♀, 2–2.8mm; ♂, 2–2.5mm. The abdominal pattern may resemble that of *L. tenuis* and *L. zimmermanni* and the legs are not annulated. The epigyne and male palpal organs are distinctive at higher magnification. The male palpal cymbium has a small pointed projection dorsally, the tibia has several long spines, and the U-shaped paracymbium has a small tooth on the posterior margin and a blunt tooth opposite.

Habitat In moss, grass, undergrowth and leaf-litter. **Maturity** All year.

Distribution Fairly common; widespread throughout Britain and northern Europe.

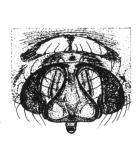 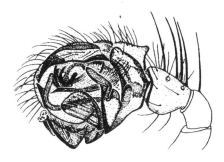

Lepthyphantes mengei Kulczynski 1887

Description ♀, 1.6–2.2mm; ♂, 1.5–2mm. The abdominal pattern is a little like that of *L. zimmermanni* but the spider is smaller. The legs are not annulated. The epigyne is similar to that of *L. flavipes* but is easily distinguished by the circular notches on each side of the central tongue. The paracymbium of the male palpal organs has a shallow tooth near the posterior margin.

Habitat, Maturity and Distribution Similar to *L. cristatus*.

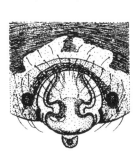 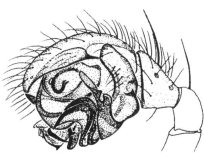

Lepthyphantes flavipes (Blackwall 1854)

Description ♀, 1.9–2.5mm; ♂, 1.8–2mm. The abdominal pattern usually resembles that of *L. zimmermanni* but sometimes is uniformly dark; the legs are not annulated. The epigyne has an almost circular central tongue. The male palpal paracymbium

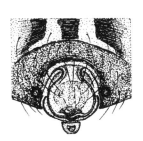 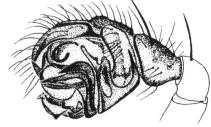

has a single long tooth near the posterior margin.
Habitat, Maturity and Distribution Similar to *L. cristatus*.

Lepthyphantes tenebricola (Wider 1834)
Description ♀ ♂, 2.4–3mm. The abdominal pattern is similar to that of *L. zimmer-manni* and the legs are not annulated. The epigyne is distinctive and the paracymbium of the male palpal organs has two teeth which are usually joined by a ridge.
Habitat Usually in woodland leaf-litter.
Maturity All year.
Distribution Locally distributed, but then often abundant. Widely distributed in Britain, but slightly commoner in the north. Widespread in northern Europe.

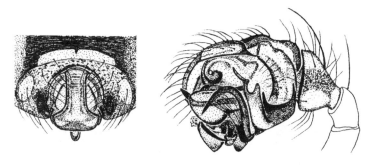

Lepthyphantes expunctus (O.P.-Cambridge 1875)   Plate 31
Description ♀ ♂, 1.8–2.5mm. The whitish abdomen, with a dark cardiac mark followed by thin bars or chevrons, is similar in both sexes and allows identification in the field. The species bears a resemblance to *Bolyphantes* but is smaller and the latter species never have such a broad cardiac mark. The epigyne and male palpal organs are distinctive.
Habitat On the lower branches of pines and amongst adjacent vegetation. Almost always on the edge of woodland or plantations, alongside paths or clearings.
Maturity Summer and autumn.
Distribution Locally abundant in parts of Scotland, with a few records from northern England; absent from the rest of Britain. Widespread in the rest of northern Europe.

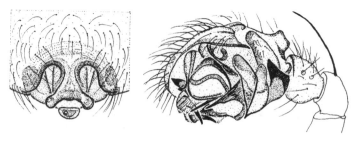

Genus *Helophora*

The single northern European species of *Helophora* almost always occurs on low vegetation in woodland and is generally identifiable with a lens.

Helophora insignis (Blackwall 1841)   Plate 31

Description ♀, 3.5–4mm; ♂, 3–3.8mm. Males are similar to the female illustrated but have a smaller abdomen. The depth of colour of the abdomen varies a little but the thin black chevrons are generally evident and there are a few black streaks on the sides. The epigyne is a large tongue, easily discernible with a lens; it may project from the abdomen at a considerable angle or lie more or less flat. Subadult females have a projection in the epigyne area, but this is pale and lacks the definition of the adult structure. Although higher magnification is required to see the male palpal organs, the shape of the structures near the tip is usually discernible with a lens.
Habitat On low vegetation in damp woodland. **Maturity** Autumn and winter.
Distribution Widespread throughout Britain, but locally distributed because of the habitat. Commoner in the north than the south and may be abundant in some situations. Widespread in northern Europe.

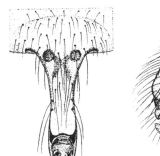 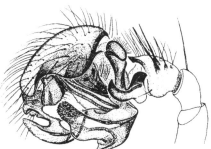

Genus *Floronia*

The single northern European species has a distinctive appearance and is identifiable with a lens. The spider spins a sheet web on bushes and low vegetation. The abdomen is distinctly higher than long in females; the white spots on the abdomen usually contract if the spider is disturbed and drops off the web.

Floronia bucculenta (Clerck 1757)   Plate 31

Description ♀ ♂, 4–5mm. The female is also illustrated alongside the epigyne and male palp. Males are similar, but the abdomen is not as globular; the male carapace is bulbous in the head region and furnished with long hairs. The broad, dark bands on the carapace are distinctive in both sexes. The epigyne is discernible with a lens and some details of the male palpal organs can sometimes be seen. Higher magnification allows easy confirmation of identity.
Habitat On low vegetation and bushes in a variety of habitats.
Maturity Summer and autumn.
Distribution Very locally distributed and generally uncommon; very few records from Scotland and Ireland; slightly more frequent towards the south of England. Widespread in the rest of northern Europe.

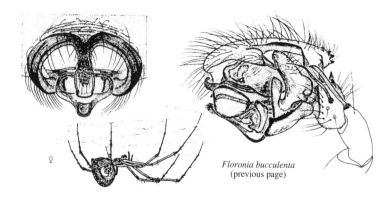

♀

Floronia bucculenta
(previous page)

Genus *Pityohyphantes*

The single northern European species is easily identifiable in the field.

Pityohyphantes phrygianus (C.L. Koch 1836)   Plate 31

Description ♀, 4–6mm; ♂, 4–5mm. Males are similar in general appearance to the female illustrated, but have a smaller abdomen. The abdominal pattern is similar to that of *Linyphia triangularis*, but the sides lack dark markings. The femora are usually clearly spotted with black. The epigyne is discernible with a lens as also are the male palpal organs and the blunt apophysis on the palpal patella.

Habitat On the lower branches of trees in conifer plantations.

Maturity Spring to autumn.

Distribution Appears to be restricted mainly to Scotland and northern England, but may have been overlooked in plantations elsewhere. Widespread in the rest of northern Europe.

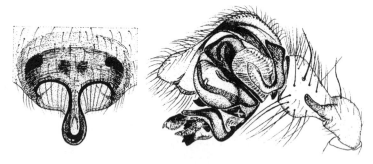

Genus *Linyphia*

Four species of *Linyphia* are known to occur in northern Europe and the two most widespread are described here. Several more species were once considered in this genus, but have for some years been assigned to the genera *Neriene*, *Frontinellina* and *Microlinyphia*. The species *L. triangularis* is extremely common and in the summer and autumn it will be found hanging under its sheet web on most bushes and any other vegetation with reasonably stiff foliage (see Webs, p. 74).

Linyphia hortensis Sundevall 1830 — Plate 31

Description ♀, 4–5mm; ♂, 3–5mm. Males are generally similar to the female illustrated, but with a narrower abdomen and the white borders of the folium reduced to a pair of white patches near the front end. The folium itself is usually visible, but occasional specimens are very dark with only the two white patches visible and these will have keyed out along with *Microlinyphia* males. The epigyne and male palpal organs are not easily discernible with a lens, but the latter can be separated from those of *Microlinyphia* by the absence of a hooped embolus. At higher magnification, the structures are very distinctive.

Habitat On low vegetation in woods. **Maturity** Summer.

Distribution Fairly common and widespread in Britain, but rather locally distributed. Widespread throughout the rest of northern Europe.

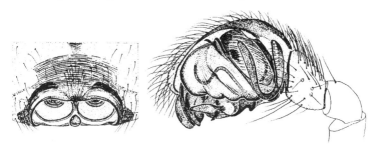

Linyphia triangularis (Clerck 1757) — Plate 32

Description ♀, 5–6.6mm; ♂, 4.6–6mm. Both sexes are illustrated and have a very distinctive appearance. The midline abdominal pattern of females may sometimes be very similar to that of *Pityohyphantes phrygianus* (Plate 31) but is always distinguishable by the dark streaks on the sides. The tuning fork mark in the midline of the carapace is a little variable in the depth of colour but is easily visible with a lens. Males have long, divergent chelicerae. The epigyne is discernible with a lens but the detailed structure of this and the male palpal organs is only visible with higher magnification.

Habitat On any bush or plant with stiff foliage and on trees, sometimes fairly high up. **Maturity** Mid-summer to late autumn.

Distribution Ubiquitous. Widespread throughout Britain and northern Europe.

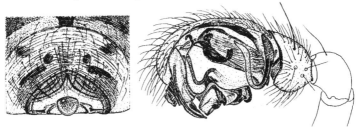

Genus *Neriene*

Seven species of *Neriene* occur in northern Europe, six of which are described here. They were formerly included in the genus *Linyphia*, and *Neriene* is sometimes regarded as a subgenus of *Linyphia*. Most of the species spin sheet webs which, in the case of *N. montana*, may be quite large and strong-looking. *N. radiata* spins a remarkable domed web with a superstructure of fine threads (see Webs, p. 74) and in the U.S.A. is known as the 'filmy dome spider'.

Neriene montana (Clerck 1757)   Plate 32

Description ♀, 4.4–7.4mm; ♂, 4–7mm. Males are similar to the female illustrated but have a slimmer abdomen. The legs are clearly annulated in both sexes. The epigyne is similar to those of *N. clathrata* and *N. furtiva*, but differs in the relative size of the opening and in the shape of the posterior border. *N. montana* is also generally much larger and the other species lack clear leg annulations. The male palpal organs are distinctive.

Habitat On bushes and low vegetation and on tree trunks, logs and a variety of other structures in a range of habitats. **Maturity** Spring to late summer.

Distribution Common and widespread throughout Britain, but rather locally distributed. Widespread throughout the rest of northern Europe.

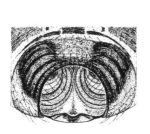
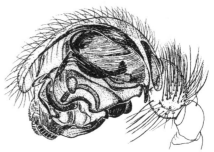

Neriene clathrata (Sundevall 1830)   Plate 32

Description ♀, 3.7–5mm; ♂, 3.4–4.8mm. Males are similar to the female illustrated but have a slimmer abdomen and the folium is usually darker. The darker W-shaped markings on the folium are generally distinctive and the legs are not annulated. The epigyne has a relatively smaller opening than in *N. montana* and *N. furtiva* and the male palpal organs are distinctive.

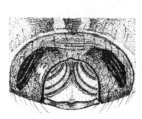
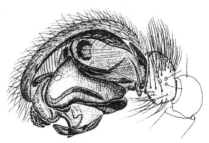

Habitat On low vegetation and bushes, in a variety of habitats.
Maturity Spring to late autumn.
Distribution Common and widespread throughout Britain and northern Europe.

Neriene peltata (Wider 1834)   Plate 32
Description ♀, 2.8–3.7mm; ♂, 2.2–3.5mm. Males are similar to the female illustrated but have a slimmer abdomen and a relatively broader folium. The legs are not annulated. The epigyne and male palpal organs are distinctive.
Habitat On low vegetation, bushes and the lower branches of trees.
Maturity Spring to autumn.
Distribution Common and widespread throughout Britain and northern Europe.

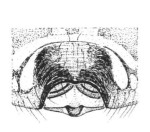
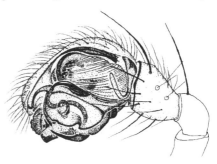

Neriene furtiva (O.P.-Cambridge 1871)
Description ♀, 3–4.5mm; ♂, 3.5–4.5mm. Similar in general appearance to *N. clathrata*, but the markings within the folium are less clear and take the form of dark bars rather than being W-shaped. The legs are not annulated. The epigyne has a relatively thin posterior lip and the male palpal organs are distinctive.
Habitat On low vegetation, heather, bushes and the lower branches of trees in fairly dry situations. **Maturity** Summer.
Distribution Generally rare in Britain; recorded from the Midlands, South Wales, East Anglia but most frequent on heathland in southern England. Widespread throughout the rest of northern Europe.

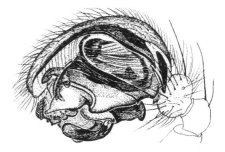

Neriene radiata (Walckenaer 1841) (= *N. marginata* (C.L. Koch))

Description ♀, 3.5–6.5mm; ♂, 3.5–5.5mm. The abdominal pattern is a little like that of *N. peltata* (Plate 32) but is dark brown to black on a pale background. The dark patch in the anterior midline contains four to six pairs of white spots, and behind this are two broad, dark, transverse bands. The carapace is brownish with paler, thickened edges and often a number of light patches just inside the margin; the head region is sometimes darker. The legs are not annulated and there are no spines on the femora. The epigyne and male palpal organs are distinctive.

Habitat On low vegetation and bushes, the domed web being very distinctive (p. 74).

Maturity Summer.

Distribution Rare in Britain and recorded only from a few localities in Scotland. Widespread in the rest of northern Europe.

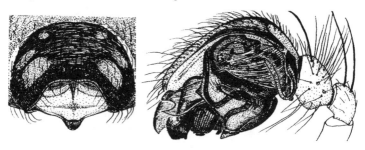

△ *Neriene emphana* (Walckenaer 1841)   Plate 32

Description ♀, 4–6mm, ♂, 3.7–5.6mm. Males are similar in general appearance to the female illustrated but have a slimmer abdomen and the epigastric region (on the underside) is conspicuously swollen. The epigyne and male palpal organs are distinctive.

Habitat In woodland, coniferous and deciduous, on bushes and the lower branches of trees. The web is sometimes very slightly domed, but never to the extent found in *N. radiata*, and may be more or less flat.

Maturity Summer.

Distribution Absent from Britain. Widespread in the rest of northern Europe, but its northern limits are Denmark and southern Finland.

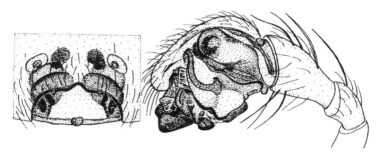

△ Genus *Frontinellina*

Only one species of *Frontinellina* occurs in northern Europe. The abdomen, viewed from the side, is rather higher at the posterior end. The spider builds a saucer- or bowl-shaped web on bushes and trees with a looser, flat web 10–20mm below. The spider hangs upside down from the upper web. In the U.S.A., a related species spins a very similar web and is commonly called the 'bowl and doily spider'.

△ *Frontinellina frutetorum* (C.L. Koch 1834)   Plate 32

Description ♀, 3.5–5.6mm; ♂, 3.5–5mm. An additional illustration of the female, in profile, appears alongside the epigyne and male palp. The male is similar, but the abdomen slimmer. There are no spines on femur I. The epigyne and male palpal organs are very distinctive.

Habitat On bushes and the lower branches of trees in a 'bowl and doily' web.

Maturity Late spring to autumn.

Distribution Absent from Britain. Recorded from as far north as southern Finland (but not Denmark), from France, Belgium, Germany and to the south and east of the region. Not common, but sometimes locally abundant.

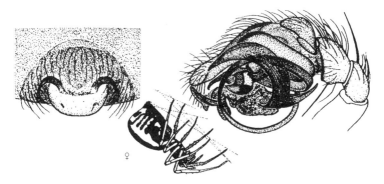

♀

Genus *Microlinyphia*

Two species of *Microlinyphia* occur in northern Europe and are described here. They make horizontal sheet webs which are typical of the family. Males of both species have a tubular, dark brown or black abdomen which usually has a pair of white patches at the front end; they bear very little resemblance to the females. Males of *Linyphia hortensis* (p. 365) are occasionally similar. Females are distinguishable in the field by their general appearance, and the male palpal organs are distinguishable with a lens in the field by the relative size of the hooped embolus.

Microlinyphia pusilla (Sundevall 1830)   Plate 32

Description ♀, 3–5mm; ♂, 3–4mm. Both sexes are illustrated. Males vary very little in general appearance, although some older specimens may have a rather shrunken abdomen. Females may sometimes have a broader median band on the abdomen with the light margins rather narrower. The epigyne is fairly dark, with a small scape protruding from beneath an angular arch. The male palpal organs have a much larger hooped embolus than in *M. impigra*.

Habitat On grass and other low vegetation in a wide variety of both wet and dry habitats.
Maturity Summer.
Distribution Common and widespread throughout Britain and northern Europe.

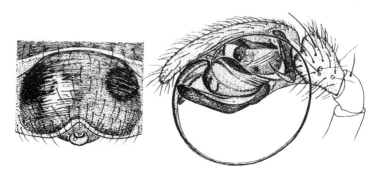

Microlinyphia impigra (O.P.-Cambridge 1871)
Description ♀, 3.6–5.4mm; ♂, 3.5–4mm. The abdomen of the female is illustrated in the Key to the Genera (p. 344) and is whitish with a dark cardiac mark followed by a series of dark triangles (apices pointing outwards). The male is similar to that of *M. pusilla* but the white patches are frequently absent. The epigyne has a small scape-like protrusion which is continuous at its base with the arches anterior to the openings. The hooped embolus in the male palpal organs is much smaller than in *M. pusilla*.
Habitat Amongst low vegetation in marshy habitats.
Maturity Summer to autumn.
Distribution Much less common than *M. pusilla*; probably fairly widespread but locally distributed in Britain. Widespread throughout the rest of northern Europe.

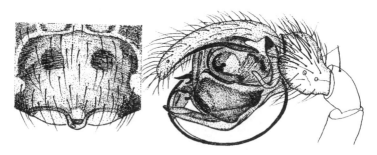

Glossary

Abdomen The posterior (rear) of the two major divisions of the body of a spider.

Accessory claws Serrated, thickened hairs near the true claws in some spiders.

Anal tubercle A small projection, dorsal to the spinners, carrying the anal opening.

Annulations Rings of pigmentation around leg segments.

Anterior Nearer the front or head end.

Ballooning Aeronautical dispersal by means of air currents acting on strands of silk.

Book lung An air-filled cavity, containing stacks of blood-filled leaves, opening on the underside of the abdomen.

Branchial operculum A sclerotized, hairless plate overlying the book lung.

Calamistrum A comb-like series of hairs on metatarsus IV of cribellate spiders.

Carapace The exoskeletal covering, or shell, over the dorsal (upper) surface of the cephalothorax.

Cardiac mark An elongate midline mark on the anterior, dorsal surface of the abdomen which overlies the heart.

Catalepsy The action of feigning death; induced by disturbance.

Cephalothorax The anterior (front) of the two major divisions of the body of a spider.

Chelicerae The jaws, each one comprising a large basal part and a fang.

Chitin A linear homopolysaccharide found as the characteristic molecule in the cuticle of arthropods. The molecules are layered in chains and cross-linked to form the strong, lightweight basis of the cuticle.

Claw tuft A bunch of hairs at the tip of the leg tarsus in spiders with only two claws.

Clypeus The area between the anterior row of eyes and the anterior edge of the carapace.

Colulus A small midline appendage or tubercle arising just in front of the anterior spinners in some spiders.

Conductor A semi-membranous structure in the male palp which supports and guides the embolus in insemination.

Condyle A smooth, rounded protuberance sometimes present on the outer side of the chelicera, near its base.

Coxa The segment of leg nearest the body; modified in the palp to form the maxilla.

Cribellum A spinning organ just in front of the spinners which appears as a transverse plate. Only present in cribellate spiders, which also have a calamistrum.

Cymbium The broadened, hollowed-out tarsus of the male palp within which the palpal organs are attached.

Distal Pertaining to the outer end, furthest away from the body or point of attachment.

Dorsal Pertaining to the upper surface.

Dorsum The upper surface.

Ecdysis Moulting; the periodic casting off of the cuticle.

Embolus The structure, in the male palp, containing the terminal part of the ejaculatory duct and its opening. It may be very small, or long, whip-like or coiled and is sometimes divided into several structures.

Entelegyne The group of spiders in which the females have an epigyne.

Epigastric fold A fold and groove separating the anterior part of the ventral abdomen (with epigyne and book lungs) from the posterior part.

Epigyne A more or less sclerotized and modified external structure associated with the reproductive openings of adult females of most spider species.

Exoskeleton The hard, external, supportive covering found in all arthropods.

Exuviae The parts of cuticle cast off during moulting.

Fang The claw-like part of each chelicera; the poison duct opens near its tip.

Femur (pl. **femora;** adj. **femoral**) The third segment of the leg, counting from the body.

Folium Any pattern of pigment on the dorsum of the abdomen which is fairly broad and leaf-shaped.

Fovea A short median groove on the thoracic part of the carapace which marks the internal attachment of the gastric muscles.

Gossamer A light film of silk threads, or groups of these floating through the air.

Haematodocha A balloon of elastic connective tissue between groups of sclerites in the male palp which distends with blood during insemination causing the sclerites to separate and rotate.

Haplogyne The group of spiders in which the females have no epigyne.

Head The part of the carapace carrying the eyes which is separated from the thorax by a shallow groove.

Labium The lip, under the mouth opening and between the maxillae, attached to the front of the sternum.

Lateral Pertaining to the side.

Lanceolate Tapering to a point.

Lyriform organ A sensory organ near the distal end of limb segments formed of a group of parallel slit organs.

Maxilla The mouthparts on each side of the labium which are the modified coxae of the palps.

Median In the midline or middle.

Median apophysis A sclerite arising from the middle division of the male palpal organs.

Metatarsus (pl. **metatarsi**; adj. **metatarsal**) The sixth segment of the leg, counting from the body.

Orb web A two-dimensional web, roughly circular in design (and, strictly speaking, a misnomer). Silk threads radiate like spokes from a central hub. These are then overlaid with a spiral of silk, running from the periphery almost to the hub.

Palp Short for pedipalp. The appendage arising just in front of the legs, the coxa of which also forms the maxilla. It has no metatarsal segment and in adult males is greatly modified for the transfer of semen.

Palpal organs The more or less complex structures found in the terminal part of the adult male palp. They comprise groups of sclerites separated from each other and the cymbium by up to three haematodochae and contain the semen reservoir which opens via ducts through the tip of the embolus.

Paracymbium A structure in the male palp branching from, or loosely attached to, the cymbium.

Patella (pl. **patellae**; adj. **patellar**) The fourth segment of the leg or palp, counting from the body.

Pedicel The narrow stalk connecting the cephalothorax and the abdomen.

Pheromone A chemical secreted by an animal in minute amounts which brings about a behavioural response in another, often of the opposite sex.

Phylogenetic Pertaining to evolutionary relationships between and within groups.

Posterior Near the rear end.

Process A projection from the main structure.

Procurved Curved as an arc having its ends ahead of its centre.

Prolateral Projecting from, or on, the side facing forwards.

Proximal Pertaining to the inner end; closest to the body or point of attachment.

Punctate Covered with tiny depressions.

Recurved Curved as an arc having its ends behind its centre.

Reticulated Like network.

Retrolateral Projecting from, or on, the side facing backwards.

Rugose Rough, wrinkled.

Scape A finger-, tongue-, or lip-like projection from the midline of the female epigyne.

Sclerite Any separate sclerotized structure connected to other structures by membranes.

Sclerotized Hardened or horny; not flexible or membranous.

Scopula (pl. **scopulae**) A brush of hairs on the underside of the tarsus and metatarsus in some spiders.

Scutum A hard, often shiny, sclerotized plate on the abdomen of some spiders.

Septum A partition separating two cavities or parts.

Serrated Saw-toothed.

Sigillum (pl. **sigilla**) An impressed, sclerotized spot, often reddish-brown. Often present on the dorsal surface of the abdomen and marking points of internal muscle attachments.

Slit organ A stress receptor in the exoskeleton.

Spermathecae The sacs or cavities in female spiders which receive and store semen.

Spiderling The nymphal or immature spider, generally resembling the adult, but smaller; fully mobile and no longer dependent on yolk.

Spine A thick, stiff hair or bristle.

Spinners Paired appendages at the rear end of the abdomen, below the anal tubercle, from the spigots of which silk strands are extruded.

Spiracle The opening of the tracheae on the underside of the abdomen.

Sternum The heart-shaped or oval exoskeletal shield covering the under surface of the cephalothorax

Stridulating organ A file-and-scraper for sound production; may be variously located on chelicerae, palps, legs, abdomen and carapace.

Subadult Almost adult; the last instar before maturity.

Synonym Each of two or more scientific names of the same rank used to denote the same taxon. The senior synonym is the name first established.

Tarsus (pl. **tarsi**; adj. **tarsal**) The most distal (or end) segment of a leg or palp.

Taxon Any taxonomic unit (eg. family, genus, species).

Taxonomy The theory and practice of classifying organisms; part of systematics, the study of the kinds and diversity of organisms.

Thorax That part of the cephalothorax behind the head region and separated from it by a shallow groove.

Tibia (pl. **tibiae**; adj. **tibial**) The fifth segment of the leg or palp counting from the body.

Tracheae Tubes through which air is carried around the body and which open at the spiracles.

Trichobothrium (pl. **trichobothria**) A long, fine hair rising almost vertically from a socket on the leg. Trichobothria detect air vibrations and currents.

Trochanter The second segment of the leg or palp, counting from the body.

Ventral Pertaining to the underside.

Associations, Societies and Journals

The British Arachnological Society

The British Arachnological Society exists to promote the study of arachnids in Britain and throughout the world. Membership is open to all persons interested in arachnology and currently consists of over 650 members and subscribers worldwide, both amateur and professional. Members participate in spider identification courses, ecological surveys, field meetings, lectures and conversaziones, as well as informal, local meetings arranged through the membership list. A postal library of around six thousand scientific papers, books and photographic slides is available to members resident in Britain. The Society publishes a **Bulletin** and **Newsletter** which are circulated together three times a year. Details are available from:

S.H. Hexter, BAS Membership Treasurer, 71 Havant Road, London E17 3JE.

The Spider Recording Scheme

This was established in 1987 by the British Arachnological Society in association with the Biological Records Centre. The eventual aim is to produce an up-to-date distribution atlas of British spiders based on records from each 10km square in the country. Obviously a certain degree of proficiency will have to be reached before participating in the scheme and this is most easily achieved by attending a field course. New or unusual records are always checked and help is given with any difficult specimens. Details are available from: D.R. Nellist, 198A Park Street Lane, Park Street, St. Albans, Herts, AL2 2AQ.

The American Arachnological Society

This society produces the **Journal of Arachnology** and a newsletter. Details are available from: Dr N.I. Platnick, American Museum of Natural History, Central Park West at 79th Street, New York, N.Y. 10024, U.S.A.

Société d'Arachnologie

This society produces the journal **Revue Arachnologique**, details of which are available from: J.C. Ledoux, 43 rue Paul-Bert, 30390 Aramon, France.

Arachnologische Mitteilungen

This journal began publication in 1991. Details are available from:
Franz Renner, Sonnentaustr. 3, D-88410, Bad Wurzach, Germany.

Beiträge zur Araneologie - Papers on Araneology; began publication in 1988. Details are available from: J. Wunderlich, Hindenburgstr. 94, D-75334 Straubenhardt, Germany

The Field Studies Council

This organization runs a wide variety of courses, including some on spiders, at its ten residential centres in England and Wales. Details from: Field Studies Council, Central Services, Preston Montfort, Shrewsbury, Shropshire, SY4 1HW.

The Scottish Field Studies Association

This organization runs a wide variety of courses, including some on spiders, at its single residential field centre. Details from: Scottish Field Studies Association, Pinewoods, 10 Stormont Place, Scone, Perth PH2 6SR, or Kindrogan Field Centre, Enochdhu, Blairgowrie, Perthshire, PH10 7PG.

Suppliers of Equipment and Books

Many equipment suppliers advertise in natural history magazines and journals; microscopes are sometimes available second-hand.

Suppliers of microscopes, lighting, field microscopes and lenses
Hampshire Micro, Oxford Road, Sutton Scotney, Hants, SO21 3JG.

Suppliers of Geoscope Microscope
The Natural History Museum Catalogue, Euroway Business Park, Swindon SN5 8SN.

Suppliers of specimen tubes and other equipment
Watkins & Doncaster, Four Throws, Hawkhurst, Kent.

Suppliers of books on natural history
E.W. Classey Ltd, PO Box 93, Faringdon, Oxon, SN7 7DR.
Natural History Book Service, 2 Wills Road, Totnes, Devon, TQ9 5XN.

Selected Bibliography

Only a very few books are listed here. Many of them contain further references.

Identification
These works allow the identification of the British and most north European spiders not covered by this field guide:
Heimer, S. & Nentwig, W. (Eds) 1991 *Spinnen Mitteleuropas: Ein Bestimmungsbuch* Paul Parey, Berlin & Hamburg.
Locket, G.H. & Millidge, A.F. 1951 *British Spiders*, Vol.I. Ray Society, London.
Locket, G.H. & Millidge, A.F. 1953 *British Spiders*, Vol.II. Ray Society, London.
Locket, G.H., Millidge, A.F. & Merrett, P. 1974 *British Spiders*, Vol.III. Ray Society, London.
Roberts, M.J. 1985 *The Spiders of Great Britain and Ireland* Vols 1 & 3. Harley Books, Colchester.
Roberts, M.J. 1987 *The Spiders of Great Britain and Ireland* Vol.2. Harley Books, Colchester.
Roberts, M.J. 1993 *The Spiders of Great Britain and Ireland* Compact Edition, Vols 1–3. Harley Books, Colchester.
The following photographic guide will also be found useful in the field (and will possibly be reprinted soon):
Jones, R.D. 1983 *The Country Life Guide to Spiders of Britain and Northern Europe* Hamlyn, London.

General Reading
Bristowe, W.S. 1939 *The Comity of Spiders* Vol. 1. Ray Society, London.
Bristowe, W.S. 1941 *The Comity of Spiders* Vol. 2. Ray Society, London.
Bristowe, W.S. 1958 *The World of Spiders* Collins New Naturalist Series, London.
Chinery, M. 1993 *Spiders* Whittet Books, London.
Foelix, R.F. 1982 *Biology of Spiders* Harvard University Press, London.
Hillyard, P. 1994 *The Book of the Spider* Hutchinson, London.
Hubert, M. 1979 *Les Araignées* Boubée, Paris.

Murphy, F. 1980 *Keeping Spiders, Insects and other Land Invertebrates in Captivity* Bartholomew, Edinburgh.

Nentwig, W. (Ed.) 1987 *Ecophysiology of Spiders* Springer-Verlag, Berlin & Heidelberg.

Preston-Mafham, R. 1991 *Spiders, an Illustrated Guide* Blandford, Poole.

Preston-Mafham, R. & K. 1984 *Spiders of the World* Blandford, Poole.

Sauer, F. & Wunderlich, J. 1984 *Die Schönsten Spinnen Europas* Karlsfeld.

Shear, W.A. (Ed.) 1986 *Spiders: Webs, Behavior, and Evolution* Stanford University Press, Stanford.

Witt, P.N. & Rovner, J.S. (Eds) *Spider Communication – Mechanisms and Ecological Significance* Princeton University Press, Princeton.

Index

Figures in bold type refer to colour plates